P9-EDW-323

THE GOSPEL ACCORDING TO JOHN

The Gospel According to John

VOLUME I

by

Oliver B. Greene

The Gospel Hour, Inc., Oliver B. Greene, Director
Box 2024, Greenville, South Carolina 29602

© Copyright 1966 by Oliver B. Greene

All rights reserved

Printed in the United States of America

First printing, July 1966 — 10,000 copies
Second printing, October 1968 — 15,000 copies

$6.00

226.5
G 8349
v.1

LIFE Pacific College
Alumni Library
1100 West Covina Blvd.
San Dimas, CA 91773

FOREWORD

I have long been aware of the need for a verse-by-verse commentary on The Gospel of John, and the Lord has laid it on my heart to attempt such an exposition.

John's Gospel is long and, in many places, quite detailed. Its presentation therefore will require more than one volume and will involve many months of study and dedicated work.

Since The Gospel According to John is known as "the salvation Gospel," it should be understood by and made familiar to all who are interested in soul winning. Its message should also be presented with such clarity and power as to make it effective in reaching the hearts of sinners who read it. This I have tried to do in this volume—and in those that will follow.

The key to John's Gospel is found in chapter 20, verses 30 and 31: "And many other signs truly did Jesus in the presence of His disciples, which are not written in this book: *but these are written, that ye might believe that Jesus is the Christ, the Son of God; and that believing ye might have life through His name.*"

John presents Christ as the Eternal Word incarnate, very God in flesh, revealing God in the terms of a human life. The details recorded in John's Gospel are sufficient evidence of his personal association with the people and the experiences of which he writes. In fact, he stresses the word "witness," using it frequently to set forth *the verified facts* of that personal experience.

John gives careful attention to time, place, and details such as only an eyewitness could give. For example, he tells us that Nathanael was standing *under a fig tree* when Jesus first saw him. He notes that there were *six* waterpots

52553

at the wedding in Cana. He speaks of the lad with *five* barley loaves and *two small* fishes. He recalls that *Mary* sat in the house when *Martha* went forth to meet the Lord as He returned to Bethany after the death of Lazarus. He mentions the details of Jesus' washing the disciples' feet, of Peter's sword striking an ear from the servant of the high priest; he even gives the servant's name. He records the coming of Nicodemus (with Joseph of Arimathea) to bury Jesus, and gives names and weights of the spices brought for the embalming of the Lord's body.

John was not drawing on his imagination when he wrote the Gospel that bears his name, for only an eyewitness could record such details; and while his main interest was to focus the minds of his readers on Jesus Christ—His work and His words—we cannot but be aware of the revealed spiritual growth of John himself until faith and love finally master his entire life.

May the truths set forth on the pages of this volume find responsive hearts among those who read it, that souls may be led into a personal knowledge of the Lord Jesus Christ to the glory of God.

The Author

CONTENTS

THE GOSPEL ACCORDING TO JOHN

INTRODUCTION

The four Gospels—Matthew, Mark, Luke, and John—each present the Saviour in a different aspect. Both Luke and John plainly state the *purpose* for which they wrote the Gospels that bear their names. In Luke 1:4—the key verse to that book—we read, *"That thou mightest know the certainty of those things, wherein thou hast been instructed."* We might say that the key to Luke's Gospel hangs by the front door, whereas the key to The Gospel of John is found at the back door: "And many other signs truly did Jesus in the presence of His disciples, which are not written in this book: *But these are written, that ye might believe that Jesus is the Christ, the Son of God; and that believing ye might have life through His name"* (John 20:30,31).

Matthew is the "kingdom" Gospel, presenting Emmanuel—God in the midst of the Jews. In relation to the Jews and earthly dispensations, Matthew traces Christ the Saviour from Abraham and David, and also shows the three things which take the place of Judaism: the Kingdom (ch. 13), the Church (yet future at that time—ch. 16), and the Kingdom in glory (ch. 24).

Mark presents Christ Jesus as the Servant-Prophet, and gives no genealogy.

Luke presents Him as the Son of man, more in relation to that which exists at present—that is, heavenly grace, God's unmerited, unearned favor to man. Luke also gives the genealogy of Jesus all the way to Adam.

Matthew, Mark, and Luke all three present Christ Jesus the Saviour in His patient, humble, long-suffering ways of grace in this world of sin. Those three Gospels always speak of the Christ as man, presented TO men in such a way that man may receive Him. They also point out that

He was rejected by the masses—even His own people—and that He was crucified, buried, raised, ascended, and is now living in the heavenlies with the Father.

The Gospel of John, however, presents the Lord in quite another manner. John presents the *Divine Person* who came from the bosom of the Father, taking a body of flesh and coming down to man, God manifested in flesh in this world. He declares the Incarnation to be a proven fact upon which all in man's history depends. In the Gospel of John there is no longer a question of genealogy; no longer a need for the messenger who goes before, declaring, "Prepare ye the way of the Lord, make His paths straight"; no longer Messiah coming according to prophecy; no longer Emmanuel— JESUS who will save His people from their sins. John's Gospel opens with the tremendous statement, *"In the beginning was the Word, and the Word was with God, and the Word was God."* In the very beginning of this glorious Gospel it is God Himself *AS God* who, in the Man Christ Jesus, shows Himself to men.

Let us look again at the key to the Gospel of John: *"But these are written, that ye might believe that Jesus is the Christ, the Son of God; and that believing ye might have life through His name"* (John 20:31). It is uniquely significant (and certainly not by accident) that this passage is at the close of the book. Here at its climax where the details are retrospective, John recalls to the mind of the reader the tremendous truths set forth, and the unfolding of the glories of the Person who is the center, soul, and heartbeat of the great subject, object, and scope of this beloved Gospel.

The key to the Gospel of John sets forth three things about Christ:
1. *His deity:* He is the Son of God.
2. *His humanity:* He is Jesus, Saviour.
3. *His messiahship:* He is Christ, He was God's Christ in the beginning, He became Jesus man's Saviour when He left the Father's bosom and was born of the virgin Mary.

Christ's deity, His humanity, and His messiahship are easily traceable throughout the Gospel of John.

Also, in this key verse John points out that which has been repeatedly pointed out with respect to human responsibility toward Christ Jesus the Saviour—*"that ye may believe"*—and the *effect* of believing: "that believing, *ye might have life through His name."*

The paramount *subject* of this Gospel is Christ's relationship with the Father as the only begotten OF the Father. John presents Him as follows:

1. Christ was in the beginning with the Father (ch. 1, v. 1).
2. He was manifested in the flesh (ch. 1, v. 14).
3. Christ Jesus, manifested as the Son of God, revealed the Father in word, in deed, and in public testimony (ch. 1, v. 15 through ch. 12, v. 50).
4. Christ Jesus the Saviour was privately manifested to His disciples as the Son of God (ch. 13, v. 1 through ch. 17).
5. Christ Jesus the Saviour was manifested as the Son of God in His betrayal by Judas Iscariot, in His mock trial, and in His horrible death (ch. 18, v. 1 through ch. 19, v. 42).
6. Christ Jesus our Saviour was vindicated as the Son of God and declared as the Son of God in His resurrection and in revealing Himself to His disciples, making known to them that He was Christ (ch. 20, v. 1 through ch. 21, v. 25).

It is impossible to rightly appreciate the words and deeds of Christ Jesus the Lord unless we know who He is, and one need not read many verses in the Gospel of John to know that the Christ of God, Jesus our Saviour, was in the beginning *with* God, that He was ONE with God, co-equal with Him in all things. When we realize that our Saviour was God in flesh, then we are in a position to appreciate His words, which are "spirit and life" (John 6:63). When we realize who He is (the Word made flesh to tabernacle among men), then we are in a position to appreciate His deeds and His miracles. Jesus was the Word, the Word was with God in the beginning, the Word *was* God; but in the fulness of time the Word was made flesh as foreordained of God before the world was (Gal. 4:4,5; I Pet. 1:20).

John the beloved disciple gave himself to Jesus with a passion of devotion never equaled by any other mortal; and having done so, his heart closed around its object and Jesus became all-in-all to him; he had no room for lesser love. John's fellowship with Christ was one long-sustained walk of love, joy, happiness, and peace. We read very little of what John himself said or did during the Lord's ministry, but he listened to Jesus and watched Him so closely that invisible glory possessed by the Saviour but hidden from others was seen by John. He heard words with a deeper meaning than did the others who followed Jesus. For instance, Simon Peter loved his Lord devotedly, but he never fully lost consciousness of himself. Peter spoke of the Master *and himself* while John, like Mary of Bethany, lost all sense of others, even of himself, in his devotion to his Lord. He saw in Jesus a ray of the glory of the only begotten of the Father, full of grace and truth.

After Jesus was arrested, while Peter sat with the enemies of the Lord, John the Beloved was in the inner chamber *with* Him. While many of the disciples were hiding, John stood at the foot of the cross with Mary the mother of Jesus, and it was to this beloved disciple that Jesus committed the care of His mother just before He died. No wonder God the Father dictated this salvation Gospel to John the Beloved.

In Matthew, Mark, and Luke, Christ is viewed in human relationship; but John shows that Jesus, who was born in a manger and died on a cross, had *higher* glories than those of a king. This Gospel shows that He who humbled Himself, took a servant's place, and died the death of the cross was *in the beginning* with God, *equal* with God. John points out that He who became the Son of man was none other than God Himself, and that He forever remains the only begotten of the Father.

The *theme* of the Gospel of John is *the deity of Christ.* In this Gospel as nowhere else in all the Bible the *Godhead* of Christ is presented and spelled out. *This* was "the great God and our Saviour Jesus Christ" (Tit. 2:13). In this Gospel we see the full unveiling of the divine glories of Christ Jesus our Saviour. We see God's Christ dwelling with God before time began (John 1:1,2). In John's Gospel we learn that "the only begotten of the Father" was full of grace and truth. *Grace* saves us, and *truth* sets us free!

It is in John's Gospel that John the Baptist announces Jesus as "the Son of God" (John 1:34). It was John who recorded the first miracle of Jesus (John 2:11). John penned down for us the powerful statement of Jesus, "Destroy this temple, and in three days I will raise it up" (John 2:19); and it is in John's Gospel that we learn, "The Father loveth the Son, and hath given all things into His hand" (John 3:35).

It is in the Gospel of John that Jesus declared, "For as the Father raiseth up the dead, and quickeneth them; even so the Son quickeneth whom He will. For the Father judgeth no man, but hath committed all judgment unto the Son: that all men should honour the Son, even as they honour the Father. He that honoureth not the Son honoureth not the Father which hath sent Him" (John 5:21—23).

It is in the Gospel of John that we read the words of Jesus: "Before Abraham was, I AM"—words that so upset the scribes, Pharisees, and elders that they wanted to destroy Him (John 8:58).

Only John records the conversation between Jesus and Philip when Philip said, "Show us the Father, and it sufficeth us." Jesus replied, "HE THAT HATH SEEN ME HATH SEEN THE FATHER!" (John 14:8,9).

In John 1:11—13 we read, "He came unto His own, and His own received Him not. But as many as received Him, to them gave He power to become the sons of God, even to them that believe on His name: which were born, not of blood, nor of the will of the flesh, nor of the will of man, but of God." There is nothing in any other of the Gospels that reads like this. It is only in the Gospel of John that the new birth is brought before us, showing that *by* the new birth we become members of the family of God, *born* of God. John also makes it clear that the family of God reaches beyond Israel and takes in ALL who believe. In the Gospel of Matthew, Jesus instructed the twelve to go to the lost sheep of the house of Israel, but such is not true in the Gospel of John. In chapter 1, verse 16, he declares, "And of His fulness have all we received, and grace for grace." Thus John declares that the Gospel is for all peoples, not only for the Jews. The Jewish nation *never* received of His fulness; this can be said of believers only. John reveals that *"whosoever will"* may eat of the bread of life, drink of the water of life, walk in the light, and through the blood of Jesus Christ, God's Son, be cleansed from all sin.

We do not read in Matthew, Mark, or Luke, "I am the Good Shepherd, and know my sheep, and am known of mine. As the Father knoweth me, even so know I the Father: and I lay down my life for the sheep. *And other sheep I have, which are not of this fold: them also I must bring, and they shall hear my voice; and there shall be one fold, and one Shepherd"* (John 10:14—16).

Without a doubt the sheep spoken of in verses 14 and 15 were the nation Israel, but who are the "other sheep"? Paul answers in Romans 4:16: "Therefore it is of faith, that it might be by grace; to the end the promise might be sure to all the seed; not to that only which is of the law, but to that also which is of the faith of Abraham; who is the father of us all." The *other sheep* are believers among the Gentiles. In the Church there is neither Jew nor Gentile, neither bond nor free—all are one in Christ. The Church is one body made up of ALL born again, blood-washed believers (I Cor. 12:12,13; Eph. 5:25—30). There is but one fold, one flock made up of all believers, whether Jew or

Gentile.

It was to John the Beloved that God gave *this* tremendous portion of His Holy Word: "And one of them, named Caiaphas, being the high priest that same year, said unto them, Ye know nothing at all, nor consider that it is expedient for us, that one man should die for the people, and that the whole nation perish not. And this spake he not of himself: but being high priest that year, he prophesied that Jesus should die for that nation; and not for that nation only, but that also He should *gather together in one* the children of God that were scattered abroad" (John 11: 49—52). Caiaphas was not speaking this great truth of himself, but God was speaking through him. What a tremendous prophecy! Caiaphas uttered words that day that he himself did not fully understand, but the message he gave declared the divine purpose in the death of Christ Jesus the Saviour and revealed the glorious fact that others outside of Israel would be brought into the fold. "Children of God that were scattered abroad" points unmistakably to the peoples of the nations who would believe and be saved.

Matthew, Mark, and Luke do not give words like those of John 14:1—3: "Let not your heart be troubled: ye believe in God, believe also in me. In my Father's house are many mansions: if it were not so, I would have told you. I go to prepare a place for you. And if I go and prepare a place for you, I will come again, and receive you unto myself; that where I am, there ye may be also."

It is also the Gospel of John that reveals the relationship between the Holy Spirit and the born again believer. Matthew, Mark, and Luke *speak* of the Spirit, but John the Beloved reveals that it is a divine imperative that we be BORN of the Spirit (John 3:5). However, the new birth is not the end of the Spirit's ministry in this Dispensation of Grace. He is our Comforter and He will abide forever (John 14:16).

There is no other chapter in the Bible like John 17! In

this, His intercessory prayer, we hear Jesus say, "Father,
the hour is come; glorify thy Son, that thy Son also may
glorify thee: As thou hast given Him power over all flesh,
that He should give eternal life to as many as thou hast
given Him" (vv. 1 and 2). "As many as thou hast given
Him" speaks of the whole family of God, the completed
New Testament Church.

In verse 20 of the same chapter we read, "Neither pray
I for these alone, but for them also which shall believe on
me through their word."   No doubt "these alone" refers
to those who were believers at that very moment, the disciples and other Jewish Christians; but "them also which
shall believe" points to Christians in this present day and
all who have believed since the day those words were spoken.

It was John the Beloved who gave us these seven tremendous statements from the lips of Jesus:

"I AM that bread of life" (John 6:48).

"I AM the light of the world" (John 8:12).

"I AM the door" (John 10:9).

"I AM the Good Shepherd" (John 10:11).

"I AM the resurrection and the life" (John 11:25).

"I AM the way, the truth, and the life" (John 14:6).

"I AM the true vine" (John 15:1).

These seven "I AM'S" look back to the time when God
appeared to Moses through the burning bush and bade him
go down to Egypt to Pharaoh and deliver His message concerning His people. Moses asked, "When I come unto the
children of Israel, and shall say unto them, The God of

your fathers hath sent me unto you; and they shall say to me, What is His name? what shall I say unto them?" God replied, "Thus shalt thou say unto the children of Israel, *I AM hath sent me unto you*" (Ex. 3:13,14). The Divine Person who is the center and soul of the Gospel of John is *the great "I AM"* who was in the beginning.

My heart's desire as I prepare this series of studies is that the Scriptures will be opened up so effectively that all who read these lines will be enlightened, encouraged, strengthened, edified, and built up in the faith. God *granting* this desire, I shall count my time well spent and rejoice in your blessing as you study these pages.

CHAPTER I

1. In the beginning was the Word, and the Word was with God, and the Word was God.

2. The same was in the beginning with God.

3. All things were made by him; and without him was not any thing made that was made.

4. In him was life; and the life was the light of men.

5. And the light shineth in darkness; and the darkness comprehended it not.

6. There was a man sent from God, whose name was John.

7. The same came for a witness, to bear witness of the Light, that all men through him might believe.

8. He was not that Light, but was sent to bear witness of that Light.

9. That was the true Light, which lighteth every man that cometh into the world.

10. He was in the world, and the world was made by him, and the world knew him not.

11. He came unto his own, and his own received him not.

12. But as many as received him, to them gave he power to become the sons of God, even to them that believe on his name:

13. Which were born, not of blood, nor of the will of the flesh, nor of the will of man, but of God.

14. And the Word was made flesh, and dwelt among us, (and we beheld his glory, the glory as of the only begotten of the Father,) full of grace and truth.

15. John bare witness of him, and cried, saying, This was he of whom I spake, He that cometh after me is preferred before me: for he was before me.

16. And of his fulness have all we received, and grace for grace.

17. For the law was given by Moses, but grace and truth came by Jesus Christ.

18. No man hath seen God at any time; the only begotten Son, which is in the bosom of the Father, he hath declared him.

19. And this is the record of John, when the Jews sent priests and Levites from Jerusalem to ask him, Who art thou?

20. And he confessed, and denied not; but confessed, I am not the

Christ.

21. And they asked him, What then? Art thou Elias? And he saith, I am not. Art thou that prophet? And he answered, No.

22. Then said they unto him, Who art thou? that we may give an answer to them that sent us. What sayest thou of thyself?

23. He said, I am the voice of one crying in the wilderness, Make straight the way of the Lord, as said the prophet Esaias.

24. And they which were sent were of the Pharisees.

25. And they asked him, and said unto him, Why baptizest thou then, if thou be not that Christ, nor Elias, neither that prophet?

26. John answered them, saying, I baptize with water: but there standeth one among you, whom ye know not;

27. He it is, who coming after me is preferred before me, whose shoe's latchet I am not worthy to unloose.

28. These things were done in Bethabara beyond Jordan, where John was baptizing.

29. The next day John seeth Jesus coming unto him, and saith, Behold the Lamb of God, which taketh away the sin of the world.

30. This is he of whom I said, After me cometh a man which is preferred before me: for he was before me.

31. And I knew him not: but that he should be made manifest to Israel, therefore am I come baptizing with water.

32. And John bare record, saying, I saw the Spirit descending from heaven like a dove, and it abode upon him.

33. And I knew him not: but he that sent me to baptize with water, the same said unto me, Upon whom thou shalt see the Spirit descending, and remaining on him, the same is he which baptizeth with the Holy Ghost.

34. And I saw, and bare record that this is the Son of God.

35. Again the next day after John stood, and two of his disciples;

36. And looking upon Jesus as he walked, he saith, Behold the Lamb of God!

37. And the two disciples heard him speak, and they followed Jesus.

38. Then Jesus turned, and saw them following, and saith unto them, What seek ye? They said unto him, Rabbi, (which is to say, being interpreted, Master,) where dwellest thou?

39. He saith unto them, Come and see. They came and saw where he dwelt, and abode with him that day: for it was about the tenth hour.

40. One of the two which heard John speak, and followed him, was Andrew, Simon Peter's brother.

41. He first findeth his own brother Simon, and saith unto him, We have found the Messias, which is, being interpreted, the Christ.

42. And he brought him to Jesus. And when Jesus beheld him, he said, Thou art Simon the son of Jona: thou shalt be called Cephas, which is by interpretation, A stone.

43. The day following Jesus would go forth into Galilee, and findeth Philip, and saith unto him, Follow me.

44. Now Philip was of Bethsaida, the city of Andrew and Peter.

45. Philip findeth Nathanael, and saith unto him, We have found him, of whom Moses in the law, and the prophets, did write, Jesus of Nazareth, the son of Joseph.

46. And Nathanael said unto him, Can there any good thing come out of Nazareth? Philip saith unto him, Come and see.

47. Jesus saw Nathanael coming to him, and saith of him, Behold an Israelite indeed, in whom is no guile!

48. Nathanael saith unto him, Whence knowest thou me? Jesus answered and said unto him, Before that Philip called thee, when thou wast under the fig tree, I saw thee.

49. Nathanael answered and saith unto him, Rabbi, thou art the Son of God; thou art the King of Israel.

50. Jesus answered and said unto him, Because I said unto thee, I saw thee under the fig tree, believest thou? thou shalt see greater things than these.

51. And he saith unto him, Verily, verily, I say unto you, Hereafter ye shall see heaven open, and the angels of God ascending upon the Son of man.

The Deity of Christ

Verses 1 and 2: *"In the beginning was the Word, and the Word was with God, and the Word was God. The same was in the beginning with God."*

The Word was *uncreated;* the Word is *eternal;* the Word *had* no beginning, for *the Word WAS* IN the beginning:

"The Word was with God, and the Word was God." The Word was personal; the Word was divine. Here in the very first of John's Gospel is presented the Person of Christ Jesus our Lord—what He is *in Himself.* He is not here presented in His relative characters—He is not presented as Christ the head of the Church nor as Christ the High

Priest, both of which deal with His relationship to men on earth. John's Gospel begins with the divine and eternal existence of the *Person* Christ Jesus, the eternal, only begotten Son of God.

In Genesis 1:1 we read, "In the beginning God created the heaven and the earth." The Old Testament reveals creation (including the creation of man) and records the responsibility of man toward God; but John declares *that which PRECEDED creation:* the WORD had no beginning, the WORD was not created, the WORD was *before anything was.* John does not say, "In the beginning God *created* the Word." He says, "In the beginning WAS the Word." Dearly beloved, ALL things are founded, exist, and remain because of and upon Him who was before any created thing; all is founded upon the *uncreated existence* of God who created all things. At the beginning of "things"—yea, before anything WAS—*He was.* He HAD no beginning.

"In the beginning was the Word"—but there is *more* to this remarkable passage. The Word was personally distinct:

"The Word was with God, and the Word was God." The Word had eternal existence and distinct personality— and God's personality is as eternal as His nature: "Lord, thou hast been our dwelling place in all generations. Before the mountains were brought forth, or ever thou hadst formed the earth and the world, *even from everlasting to everlasting, THOU ART GOD"* (Psalm 90:1,2).

"The same was in the beginning WITH God." Revealed here is the Saviour in His eternal existence—His nature, and His Person. He was God's Christ and was with God in the beginning, before *anything* was created. In these first two verses of John's Gospel is found the *basis of the doctrine* of the Gospel which is the power of God unto salvation, the Gospel which brings eternal life and eternal joy to those who believe.

Christ's Pre-Incarnation Work

Verses 3—5: *"All things were made by Him; and with-*

*out Him was not any thing made that was made. In Him
was life; and the life was the light of men. And the light
shineth in darkness; and the darkness comprehended it not."*

Verses 1 and 2 precede Genesis 1:1, and now we come
to the *beginning* of Genesis—that is, Christ *created* all
things, the world and all that is therein. Here we have
what He is in His attributes. Believers have to do with
Him in that which He IS, and we must never *forget* what
He is, no matter how great the things He has done or is
able to do. He IS the Creator. All that subsists subsists
by Him and because of Him:

"God, who at sundry times and in divers manners spake
in time past unto the fathers by the prophets, hath in these
last days spoken unto us by His Son, whom He hath appointed heir of all things, by whom also He made the
worlds. . . Thou, Lord, in the beginning hast laid the foundation of the earth; and the heavens are the works of thine
hands" (Heb. 1:1,2,10).

By His Word God has revealed Himself—His purpose,
His love, and His plan. The Word of God underlies all
available knowledge and understanding of God insofar as
man is concerned. Jesus left the Father's bosom for the
specific purpose of *declaring* God to man (John 1:18). In
the Old Testament era God spoke in various ways through
various instruments. He spoke by His prophets, and on
occasion by other methods such as the burning bush and
Balaam's donkey (Ex. 3:2; Num. 22:22—31); but at ALL
times His revelation has been through His Word. *Now,* in
these last days, God's last, full, and personal expression is
in the Man Christ Jesus. (Study Hebrews 1:1—3 and Colossians 1:15—19.)

Christ Jesus is the one full revelation of God to man.
No more is needed, no more will be given. The complete
Word, the complete plan for salvation and human guidance,
has been given in Jesus. ALL things—individually and col-
lectively—were created by Him:

"To us there is but one God, the Father, of whom are all things, and we in Him; and one Lord Jesus Christ, *by whom are all things, and we by Him*" (I Cor. 8:6). "For *by Him were all things created*, that are in heaven, and that are in earth, visible and invisible, whether they be thrones, or dominions, or principalities, or powers: *all things were created by Him, and for Him*" (Col. 1:16).

You will notice that verse 3 of this first chapter of John's Gospel tells us that "all things were made BY Him," but the WORD was not "made." *In the beginning, the Word WAS.* Also in this verse we pass from the sphere of the pure and eternal into the sphere of created things, things which now exist because they were created, made by Him who had no beginning but was IN the beginning before anything was.

The Word was Mediator of creation: God simply spoke and the words brought "things." Matter is not eternal, nor is it self-derived. *All things ARE* because God spoke; all things created were created by and through the Son. (Study Ephesians 1:10 and Colossians 1:17.) Without Him, apart from Him, was not anything made that is made or that now exists. Christ is the Creator and the Preserver of all things.

"In Him was life." "Life" is one of the outstanding words of John's Gospel; it is used thirty times. In fact, the Gospel of John was *written* that we who believe might have LIFE through Jesus' name.

The life spoken of here is the true spiritual life, eternal life, which consists in communion with God; and the only possible way to commune with God is in Christ Jesus— "Christ in you, the hope of glory" (Col. 1:27). "In Him was life" means that in the eternal ages behind us, the Godhead appointed Christ the source, origin, fountain, and cause of life: "For as the Father hath life in Himself; so hath He given to the Son to have life in Himself" (John 5:26). From Christ flows all life, and apart from Him all is darkness and death. Jesus said, "I am the resurrection and the life: he that believeth in me, though he were dead, yet shall he live: and whosoever liveth and believeth in me shall never die" (John 11:25,26 in part). "For with thee is the fountain of life: in thy light shall we see light" (Psalm 36:9). "And this is the record, that God hath given to us eternal life, and this life is in His Son" (I John 5:11).

"In Him was life" cannot be said of creatures. Creatures have life, but not in themselves. Christ becomes our life, *eternal* life, when we believe in His shed blood and trust His saving grace.

In Him was life—*"and the life was the light of men."* In the beginning was the Word, the Word was with God, the Word WAS God. *"God is light, and in Him is no darkness at all"* (I John 1:5). The Psalmist tells us that the entrance of the Word brings light, and that the Word is a lamp to our feet, a light to our pathway (Psalm 119:105, 130). John 3:19 tells us, "This is the condemnation, that light is come into the world, and men loved darkness rather than light, because their deeds were evil." Yet God delights in the sons of men (read Proverbs 8) and it is in man that He will make Himself to be seen and known:

"Without controversy great is the mystery of godliness: God was manifest in the flesh, justified in the Spirit, seen of angels, preached unto the Gentiles, believed on in the world, received up into glory" (I Tim. 3:16). God was manifest in the flesh and was seen of angels. Angels are the highest expression of God's power in creation, but it is in *man* that He pleases to show Himself—morally and in holiness and pure love. Believers at all times should be imitators of God—Christ is our life, in Him was light, and we are "light in the Lord" (Eph. 5:8). When we possess Christ in our hearts we should be shining lights. "If we walk in the light, as HE is in the light, we have fellowship one with another, and the blood of Jesus Christ His Son cleanseth us from all sin" (I John 1:7). Believers should walk even as HE walked, for according to the Scripture, "both He that sanctifieth and they who are sanctified are all of one" (Heb. 2:11).

In I Corinthians 1:30,31 we read, "But of Him are ye
in Christ Jesus, who of God is made unto us wisdom, and
righteousness, and sanctification, and redemption: That,
according as it is written, He that glorieth, let Him glory
in the Lord." Christ is made unto us *redemption*—and redemption develops and puts on display all the moral qualities of Jehovah God Himself, along with His nature and
His love and light. We in Christ and Christ in us is the
fruit and expression of *all that God IS* in the fulness and
revelation of Himself; we are partakers of divine nature
(II Pet. 1:4).

WHY has God made possible this wonderful redemption
and given us the privilege of becoming His children? Ephesians 2:7 answers: *"That in the ages to come He might
shew the exceeding riches of His grace in His kindness
toward us through Christ Jesus."*

*"The light shineth in darkness . . . the darkness com-
prehended it not."* Apart from God, the natural man is
not light. Without any part of the nature of God, the natural man is darkness; he has within him no power to receive the light. Jesus was God in flesh, Divine nature in
flesh; but the natural man "saw no beauty in Him" to desire Him. On the contrary, the world said, "Away with
Him! Crucify Him!" Apart from the miracle of the new
birth, man has within his nature no power or ability to
receive the light or to see its beauty. It is *the entrance of
the WORD* that brings light and life. Thus the light that
was brought down in Jesus *"shineth in darkness"* but unregenerated men and the forces of hell could not *comprehend*
that light.

Nowhere in the Word of God do we read that believers
are *love*. GOD is love; love is His nature. We are not
love, but in Christ we become LIGHT:

"For ye were sometimes darkness, *but now are ye light
in the Lord:* walk as children of light" (Eph. 5:8).

Having been made partakers of divine nature through the

miracle of the new birth, we walk in love because He who IS love is our life. We follow in His steps because we are led by the Spirit; therefore we walk in light. It is the duty of a believer—a *joyful* duty—to walk in perfect obedience to God's will, counting it a privilege to be a child of God through faith in the shed blood of His only begotten Son.

In the original language the word here rendered "comprehend" is actually *apprehend.* It has been suggested that the meaning here is, "the light shineth in darkness" but the darkness did not apprehend it (or take hold of it). It is true that those to whom Jesus came (His own people, Israel) did not understand, and they did not receive Him. Therefore, *"the darkness"* here would be the spiritual condition of the world when Jesus came into it, and the spiritual powers of darkness did not *apprehend* the light He brought.

Every man who is born into this world physically is lightened by his Creator (John 1:9), but the *unregenerated* man disregards the light, *repels* it, and is therefore plunged into darkness. The natural man refuses to live up to the light he has, he loves darkness rather than light because it is his nature to do evil (John 3:19). *Natural* darkness yields to light, but the spiritual darkness referred to here is so *hopelessly* dark that it neither apprehends or comprehends the light. Here is clearly pointed out the fearful, solemn condition of fallen man, and nothing short of a divine miracle of saving grace can bring the unbeliever out of darkness into God's marvelous light.

In the first three chapters of John's Gospel we find:

1. Divine provision of life through the coming of the Light (ch. 1, v. 9).
2. The means of life through *acceptance* of the Light by those who will hear the Gospel and come TO the Light (ch. 1, v. 12).
3. The necessity for life in that without the Light all men abide in darkness (ch. 3, vv. 15 through 19).

4. The evidence of spiritual life—those who believe from
   the heart come to the Light (ch. 3, vv. 20,21).

The Message

"This then is the message which we have heard of Him,
and declare unto you, that God is light, and in Him is
no darkness at all. If we say that we have fellowship with
Him, and walk in darkness, we lie, and do not the truth:
But if we walk in the light, as He is in the light, we have
fellowship one with another, and the blood of Jesus Christ
His Son cleanseth us from all sin" (I John 1:5—7).

The Ministry of John the Baptist

Verse 6:   *"There was a man sent from God, whose name
was John."*

Beginning with this verse, a complete change of subject
is introduced.   We change from "The Word" (which was
in the beginning with God and which was God) to the
forerunner of Christ, referred to here as "a man."   Then
by way of contrast we are shown that the One of whom
John bore witness was *more* than "a man"—He was the
God-Man.

John was *"sent from God."*   Every man who is a faithful witness of the Lord Jesus Christ is a God-sent man.
The name "John" signifies "the gift of God," and John
Baptist was sent from God—commissioned and equipped—
to declare the coming of the King.

Verse 7:   *"The same came for a witness, to bear witness
of the Light, that all men through Him might believe."*

John Baptist came to bear witness of THE LIGHT—and
that Light is none other than the Lord Jesus Christ, "the
Light of the world."

I previously pointed out that all unbelievers are blind
and in total darkness, spiritually speaking.   I now ask,

Who needs to be reminded that it is light, when night has departed and day has dawned? Who needs to be reminded that the sun is shining in its full strength? The answer is clear: *the blind,* the unsighted one, needs to be reminded. How tragic that Jesus needed a forerunner! He was THE Light of the world, yet He was born into a dark world into the midst of a blinded humanity who groped in darkness day by day. God sent John to bear witness of the Light because He would not allow His Son to come into the world unrecognized and unannounced. God sent angels and the heavenly hosts to announce the birth of His Son, and then just before His public ministry began, John the Baptist, sent of God, appeared on the scene preaching, "Repent! For the kingdom of heaven is at hand!" John did not point men to himself, but to the One who was preferred before him: the Lord Jesus Christ, Messiah, Saviour, King.

John Baptist came *"for a witness."* Thus the Holy Spirit defines the character of a minister's office. Every true minister is a witness, and a witness knows what he is talking about. He does not speculate, he does not simply give his "opinion." He speaks the truth; *Jesus* is truth (John 14:6), and every true minister of God is a *minister* of truth.

John Baptist came *"to bear witness of the Light"* — and it should be the singular purpose of every minister to do the same! According to I John 1:5 the message is, *"God is LIGHT,* and in Him is no darkness at all." The man of God is not to attract men to himself, he is not to talk about himself. It is his mission to preach Christ. Paul said, *"We preach Christ crucified,* unto the Jews a stumblingblock, and unto the Greeks foolishness; but unto them which are called, both Jews and Greeks, Christ the power of God, and the wisdom of God" (I Cor. 1:23,24).

"Christ crucified" is the only message the Holy Spirit will own or honor. Jesus said of the Spirit, "He shall glorify me: for He shall receive of mine, and shall shew it unto you" (John 16:14). To the Corinthians Paul said, "I determined not to know any thing among you, *save Jesus Christ,*

and Him crucified" (I Cor. 2:2).

John bore witness of the Light (in order that) *"all men through Him might believe."* This statement points to the *design* of the ministry. The only possible way for men to become believers is through hearing and receiving the testimony of God-called, God-sent preachers. They are God's witnesses.

Romans 10:13—17 sheds light on this verse:

"For whosoever shall call upon the name of the Lord shall be saved. How then shall they call on Him in whom they have not believed? and how shall they believe in Him of whom they have not heard? and how shall they hear without a preacher? and how shall they preach, except they be sent? As it is written, How beautiful are the feet of them that preach the Gospel of peace, and bring glad tidings of good things! But they have not all obeyed the Gospel. For Esaias saith, Lord, who hath believed our report? So then faith cometh by hearing, and hearing by the Word of God."

What clear, understandable truth is set forth here! *Whosoever* shall *call* shall be saved—but how shall they call before they *believe* and how shall they believe before they *hear*? How shall they hear without a preacher, and how shall they preach except they be *sent*? God calls the witness, the witness preaches the Word, declaring that God is love, God is light, God is life. The minister preaches the Gospel, the unbeliever *hears* the Gospel, the Word of God; the Word brings faith, and faith exercised in the finished work of Jesus brings salvation! "Faith cometh by hearing, and hearing by the Word of God."

It is the joy of God to save *"whosoever"* will come to Him by Jesus Christ. Not all will come, but all are *invited.* It is not God's will that any should perish, but that all should come to repentance. God sent not His Son into the world to condemn the world, but that the world through Him might be saved. Jesus is the propitiation for our sins, and for the sins of the whole world. He came unto His very own, but they received Him not.

Verse 8: *"He was not that Light, but was sent to bear witness of that Light."*

John Baptist was not *"that Light."* The "Light" here spoken of, like the "Life," is found only in God. God is the author of light and life, and apart from Him there IS no light, there is no life. Even the born again believer has no life in *himself*—the life we possess is the life of God, even divine nature.

Jesus said of John the Baptist, "He was a burning and a shining light" (John 5:35). In the Greek this would read, "He was the lamp that burneth and shineth." John was the *lamp,* but Jesus was the LIGHT. A lamp has no light of its own; the light must be supplied. There must be oil in the lamp, a wick to burn, and someone must *light* the lamp before it becomes "a burning and a shining light." A lamp will *burn out* over a period of time, but the LIGHT which John announced is eternal!

Christ the True Light

Verse 9: *"That was the true Light, which lighteth every man that cometh into the world."*

Men who have given their lives to the study of the Greek language tell us that this verse in the original reads thus: "He was not THE Light, but came that he might bear witness of THE Light. There was the true Light, even THE Light which lighteth every man, coming into the world." Since Christ did come into the world, Christ *"coming into the world"* has provided light for everyone, a light for "whosoever will."

There are many "lights," but there is only *one TRUE Light.* In II Corinthians 11:14 we read that Satan himself is "transformed into an angel of light." Christ came (the True Light) in contrast with all of the false lights that were (and are) in the world. Today, as then, there are many "lights"—but only ONE true Light. Christ the true Light is the only one who can bring light and life into the heart of an unbeliever.

The true Light is in contrast with the shadows and types of the Old Testament ritual. The true Light is UNDE-RIVED light—that is, Jesus did not come into the world to reflect light from another. He WAS the true Light. The moon borrows its light from the sun, but Christ *Himself* is light. Light is Christ's own essential and underived glory, and since the true Light has come into the world there is light for every man. Therefore if we walk in darkness we have no one to blame but ourselves.

There is a teaching that *all* men are *born* with a spark of divinity in them—born with an "inner light"; and that all we need do is *develop* that light and cause it to shine brightly. Such doctrine is definitely unscriptural. The Word of God teaches that we are born in sin and shapen in iniquity. Through the disobedience of one man, sin moved upon *all* men and thus all men are sinners by birth. Man is NOT born with an inner spark of divinity; he is *totally depraved!* The grace of God takes care of babies and innocent little children who die before they reach the age of the knowledge of good and evil; but when a person reaches the age of accountability to God, that person *must* be born again if he would enter the kingdom of God. We do not "cultivate" an inner light; *we receive THE Light* by receiving the Word, and the entrance of the Word *brings* light. The verse is simply saying, "The true Light has come, and this Light will light every man who comes into the world *IF that man will come TO the Light.*" Christ is the true Light—and He died for all mankind—both *before and after* the cross. He died for every man "which cometh into the world" (John 3:16; II Pet. 3:9). If millions of men and women love spiritual darkness rather than light, the blame must be laid on their own blind hearts and not on Christ. He came into the world "to seek and to save *that which was LOST!*"

Man is evil by nature. To be fit for heaven he must have a new heart, and that heart can come only through the new birth. "Therefore if any man be in Christ, he is a new creature: old things are passed away; behold, all things are become new" (II Cor. 5:17). The unregenerate heart is deceitful and desperately wicked, but when God saves us He puts a new heart within us and gives us a new spirit.

Verse 10: *"He was in the world, and the world was made by Him, and the world knew Him not."*

This verse speaks for itself. *All things* were created by the Son, and yet when He came into the world which He had made, that world did not know Him or receive Him.

Believers and Unbelievers

Verses 11—13: *"He came unto His own, and His own received Him not. But as many as received Him, to them gave He power to become the sons of God, even to them that believe on His name: which were born, not of blood, nor of the will of the flesh, nor of the will of man, but of God."*

He who spoke the world into existence came down from heaven to where men are. He came not as a judge, not as a dictator, but "made like unto His brethren"—harmless, holy, undefiled, meek as a lamb. He sought not to be ministered unto, but to minister. He healed the sick, fed the hungry, cleansed the leper, raised the dead. He came unto His very own (the people Israel) *but they received Him not!*

There might have been some excuse for the *world's* rejection of God's Son because the world was in ignorance and spiritual darkness; but *Israel* should have recognized Him. They searched the Scriptures, they knew the law, they had the books of Isaiah, Jeremiah, Zechariah, Psalms; but they were blinded by their unbelief—an unbelief for

which there was absolutely no excuse. Therefore when their
Messiah came, instead of opening their arms to welcome
Him they took up stones to stone Him. They drove Him
from their cities and attempted to banish Him from the
earth which was created by Him and for Him. They in-
sulted Him, accused Him, called Him an impostor and an
illegitimate.

What did Jesus do when His people rejected Him? Did
He turn His wrath upon them? Did He turn them over to
Satan to be forever damned in the lake of fire? Did He
say to the heavenly Father, "Destroy them! Send down
fire upon Israel"? No! Thank God for these words from
verse 12:

"As many as RECEIVED Him" (Jew, Gentile, rich, poor,
bond or free) *"to them gave He power to become the sons
of God."* If you are an unbeliever, then *"as many as received Him"* includes you, for it includes everyone and ex-
cludes no one. The Light came that ALL men, *every* man,
might see the light; and to those who receive the Light
He gives power to become the sons of God. Notice that
He GIVES the power. Man cannot produce the power to
become a child of God. It cannot be worked up, prayed
down, bought, or lived. GOD BESTOWS the power that
transforms us from dead sinners into living sons of God,
walking in His light.

". . . even to them that believe on His name." "ON"
signifies committal. Just as we drive our automobile onto
a ferryboat or a bridge, just as we get on an airplane, we
believe ON Jesus for salvation. When we believe on Him a
birth takes place—but man does not "born" *himself.* The
new birth does not come through the will of the flesh nor
the will of man: it is the direct result of the divine power
of Almighty God. *No man*—not even Adam with all that
he possessed in the Garden of Eden—has ever been willing
to let God tell him what to do and what not to do until
that man has had a miracle performed in his heart and
spirit. Therefore, God GIVES power to those who will

receive Jesus—power to become sons of God, born into the
family of heaven.   God does the "borning."   Man's part
is simply to receive the Lord Jesus Christ and believe on
His name.

*"Neither is there salvation in any other: for there is
none other name under heaven given among men, whereby
we must be saved"* (Acts 4:12).   The angel of the Lord instructed Joseph that when Mary brought forth a Son (that
which was conceived in her of the Holy Ghost) they should
call His name JESUS, "for He shall save His people from
their sins" (Matt. 1:21).   *Jesus* means "Saviour," and He
saves us when we believe on His name and receive Him
by faith.   God, through the power of the Gospel (the incorruptible Word) "borns" us into the family of heaven
(Rom. 1:16,17; 10:17; I Pet. 1:23; Eph. 2:8—10).

John clearly points out and stresses the fact that human
generation has nothing to do with divine and spiritual generation.   Notice: *"Which were born"* (or begotten) *"not
of blood"* (the element of physical life—Lev. 17:11), *"nor
of the will of the flesh"* (from the natural or human im-
pulse or design), *"nor of the will of man"* (the Greek word
used here for *man* signifies the male, suggesting human de-
termination) *"BUT OF GOD!"*   Human generation has nothing to do with regeneration.   *"Salvation is of the Lord"*
(Jonah 2:9).

The Incarnation

Verse 14:   *"And the Word was made flesh, and dwelt
among us, (and we beheld His glory, the glory as of the
only begotten of the Father,) full of grace and truth."*

Here we learn that Christ became something He had not
been before.   He was in the beginning with the Father, but
now He had become something different from what He had
been in all eternity.   Yet *even in flesh* Christ revealed the
life of God, He *continued to be* all that He *had been.*   To
become flesh was a voluntary act; it was not forced upon

Him.   He *willingly* became flesh—and please notice that
He came INTO flesh, not OUT OF flesh. Jesus was not
human nature that blossomed into a beautiful personality.
Christ took up HIS abode in flesh; flesh DID NOT become
the Word, but the WORD became *flesh.*

Christ was God and man linked in one Person. He was
the eternal God against whom man had sinned, and yet
He was the man who had offended the eternal God.   Christ
was the God-Man, and what the law, though holy and
good, could not do because of the weakness of the flesh,
Jesus *did* because He was God IN flesh. He came—not to
destroy the law, but to fulfill it—and He did fulfill every
jot and every tittle (Matt. 5:17,18).

The human nature of Christ Jesus is the *ark* of the New
Testament, uniting the eternal God and man forever.   The
all-important truth set forth in this verse is *the reality of
His Incarnation.*   "The Word was made flesh, and dwelt
among us."   Christ really became a man, a man like ourselves in all things, *sin apart.*   Like all men, He was born
of a woman—but His birth was miraculous.   There has
never been, nor will there ever be, another birth like that
of the Lord Jesus. Born of a virgin, He took His flesh from
Mary, but His blood was the blood of God (Acts 20:28).

Luke 2:52 tells us that "Jesus increased in wisdom and
stature, and in favour with God and man." Thus we know
that He grew as a baby, as a boy, and from boyhood to
manhood.   From the Scriptures we know that *in His humanity* He became thirsty, hungry, tired, as all men do.
He wept, He felt pain, He rejoiced, He marveled.   He was
moved with compassion—and on occasion He was moved
to anger: *"And when He had looked round about on them
with anger, being grieved for the hardness of their hearts,*
He saith unto the man, Stretch forth thine hand.   And he
stretched it out: and his hand was restored whole as the
other" (Mark 3:5).   See also Matthew 21:12,13 and John
2:13—16.   He studied the Scriptures as other men, He suffered, He was tempted.   But in all things, at all times,

under all circumstances, He submitted His human will to
the divine will of the eternal God and Father. At the appointed time, in the appointed hour, in that body of flesh
He shed His blood and died the death of the cross—the
most horrible death man could die in that day. Yet all
the time He was here on earth, in His ministry, in His
death, and even in His burial, He was very God as well
as very man—unimpeachable God, and unimpeachable man.

This union of flesh and Divinity, the union of two natures in Christ's Person, is without a doubt one of the
greatest mysteries of the Christian religion, as well as one
of the great truths of Christianity. In I Timothy 3:16 we
read, "Without controversy *great is the mystery of godliness:*
God was manifest in the flesh, justified in the Spirit, seen
of angels, preached unto the Gentiles, believed on in the
world, received up into glory."

I am not suggesting that I *understand* the two natures
of our Lord's person. He was man and He was God, yet
His two natures remained perfect and distinct. He was
God and man at the same time, yet His divine and human
natures were never confounded. His divinity was never
laid aside, it was only veiled by flesh; and His earthly life
was never for one moment unlike our own except that He
never sinned. Christ Jesus was God in all His perfection,
yet He was perfect man from the very moment He was born
of the Virgin Mary. That same God-Man is now in heaven
sitting at the right hand of the Father to intercede for us.
He is still man as well as God:

"For there is one God, and one Mediator between God
and men, the MAN Christ Jesus" (I Tim. 2:5).

"God, who at sundry times and in divers manners spake
in time past unto the fathers by the prophets, hath in these
last days spoken unto us by His Son, whom He hath appointed heir of all things, by whom also He made the
worlds; who being the brightness of His glory, and the express image of His person, and upholding all things by the
word of His power, *when He had by Himself purged our*

*sins, SAT DOWN ON THE RIGHT HAND OF THE MAJ-
ESTY ON HIGH"* (Heb. 1:1—3).

Though God became flesh in the fullest sense in the
person of Jesus, sin apart, He never ceased to be the great
Eternal Spirit, the Eternal Word, the true Eternal God.
Every moment of His earthly ministry He was truly and
entirely God, yet He was just as truly and entirely man.
To deny that He was God and yet man is liberalism, modernism, and pure heresy.

Jesus *as man* knows our infirmities—He tasted life as we
do, He was tempted in all points as we are tempted (though
He was without sin); He can feel our frailties and our infirmities, yet He is God who so loved us that He forgives
us in spite of our sins when we believe on His name and
receive His finished work. Our Mediator, the Man Christ
Jesus, now sits at the right hand of the Majesty on high;
but He can sympathize with us because He was one with
us here on earth; and yet He can deal with God on equal
terms for us because He is very God.   This union gives
infinite value to His righteousness.   Christ is made unto
US righteousness (I Cor. 1:30).   We become righteous by
believing on Him; His righteousness is imputed to us.   The
Word tells us that *Abraham* believed God and it was counted to him for righteousness.   God imputes righteousness
when we believe on Jesus, and apart from HIM we have
no righteousness.   Yet when His righteousness is imputed
to us, we then possess the righteousness of One who was
God as well as man.

The same is true concerning the *blood* of Jesus.   The
blood He shed for sinners was the blood of God even though
He died as a man.   God cannot die, but *God became flesh*
in order that He might taste death for every man (Heb.
2:9,14,15).   He died on the cross as man, He was raised
from the dead because death could not hold Him, and when
He rose from the dead He became the head of the body
of believers, the New Testament Church.   He arose—not
as man, but as GOD.

"The Word was made flesh and dwelt among us." The
Greek language here reads "tabernacled, or dwelt in a tent,"
but this does not mean that Jesus dwelt in His human body
as we might dwell in a tabernacle or house, and then when
He ascended to heaven *left* that body. Christ took human
nature, and throughout eternity He will continue to be a
Man. There is a Man in heaven (I Tim. 2:5) and He will
always be there. He continues now, and shall ever continue, as true man.

"We beheld His glory." Even though the Word was
made flesh, John and others witnessed the glory of God
and saw displayed in Jesus ample proof that He was not
just man, but that He was truly the only begotten Son of
God. In the first few verses of John's First Epistle, he
declares that he *saw* the Man Christ Jesus, he *heard* Him,
he *touched* Him, and he was very *sure* of his testimony.

The *"glory"* here no doubt applies to the Transfiguration. Peter, James, and John were invited to go to the
Mount with Jesus, where Moses and Elijah came down and
discussed the crucifixion that would be accomplished at
Jerusalem. There they saw Jesus "transfigured before them:
and His face did shine as the sun, and His raiment was
white as the light" (Matt. 17:2). John speaks of this as
"the glory as of the only begotten of the Father," meaning glory as became or was suitable to the One who is
the only begotten Son of Almighty God, glory such as none
other could display. This "glory" does not apply to the
miracles Jesus performed during His earthly ministry. John
is here giving testimony that they saw Christ's *glory*—such
glory as man had never beheld, glory that could be ascribed
only to the Son of God. Christ did not glisten in *worldly*
grandeur or *earthly* glory such as the Jews expected of their
Messiah. So far as Israel as a nation was concerned, "there
was no beauty that they should desire Him." But He was
dressed in and fully possessed the glory of grace, truth,
and holiness.

"Glory as of the only begotten of the Father." New

Testament Greek authorities tell us that the word "as" does not here belong to similarity or comparison, but rather to confirmation and unquestionable definition. John is saying that the disciples beheld glory such as was becoming and could be possessed only by the only begotten and true Son of the living God.

"Only begotten of the Father" describes Christ's eternal existence, His eternal generation, His eternal Sonship. Christ is the Person who alone was begotten of the Father from all eternity. Even though "in the fulness of time" He was born of the virgin, He has been God's beloved Son from all eternity. He was in the beginning with the Father.

God has always had a Son—this is declared in Proverbs 30:4: "Who hath ascended up into heaven, or descended? Who hath gathered the wind in His fists? Who hath bound the waters in a garment? Who hath established all the ends of the earth? What is His name, *and what is His Son's name,* if thou canst tell?"

The same truth is found in Psalm 2:7: "I will declare the decree: the Lord hath said unto me, *Thou art my Son; this day have I begotten thee."*

However, the Sonship declared in our present verse is not to be dated from any day. Sonship here is the *everlasting* Sonship of Jesus. God lives and operates in the eternal present; there was never a time when God was not, and the same is true of the Son. It is also true that He was promised in the Garden of Eden (Gen. 3:15) but did not come until the fulness of the time arrived (Gal. 4:4,5). This is one of the divine facts which we receive, believe, and reverence *by faith.* We must not attempt to define or understand it, but we know it is true. The Scriptures clearly teach the unity of the Godhead—three Persons, one substance: from everlasting to everlasting, Father, Son, and Holy Ghost.

The Scriptures clearly teach (with equal distinctiveness) that Sonship describes the everlasting union and relationship which has existed between the first and second Persons of the Godhead, and that Christ Jesus is the only begotten and eternal Son of God. The only begotten Son was before the foundation of the world, and the Father loved Him before the world was (John 17:24).

Our finite minds cannot comprehend the depth of this tremendous truth, but we can receive and accept it because it is God's Word and "the just shall live by *faith*," not by understanding. All born again Christians believe that the Trinity, made up of Father, Son, and Holy Ghost, is ONE. We believe the glory is equal and the majesty is co-eternal. We believe as the Father is, so is the Son; the Son is not inferior to the Father, but the Father is not the Son, neither is the Son the Father. I repeat: We do not attempt to explain it, we simply *believe it because GOD SAID IT.*

Christ is equal to God the Father as touching His Godhead, but the Son is inferior to the Father as touching His manhood. In His manhood He was God in flesh. He took the sinner's place, and in order to *take* the sinner's place it was necessary that He be made like unto His brethren in all things, sin apart. James 1:13 tells us that God cannot be tempted with evil, and if He were to provide salvation, it was necessary that the substitute be tempted in all points as we are, conquer temptation and be without sin. Jesus did just that. He was God in flesh, He was tempted in all points as we are, yet He did not sin. He alone could take the sinner's place.

"Full of grace and truth" does not point to the Father, but to Jesus the Son. He was born JESUS, *Saviour* (Matt. 1:21). We are saved by *grace* through faith (Eph. 2:8; Rom. 10:17). Jesus said, "Ye shall know the *truth*, and the truth shall make you free. . . If the *Son* therefore shall make you free, ye shall be free indeed" (John 8:32,36). I am not suggesting that God is not grace and truth—He IS; but it was the Word in flesh who was "full of grace" and full of truth. The Word IS *truth*, and the Word in flesh was *grace*—the grace of God brought down to man. He was the full truth

concerning the way of accepting the grace of God. He
was the grace of God on display, and He declared the truth
of God concerning the acceptance of God's grace for salvation.   It is God who saves, but He saves us *for Christ's
sake* (Eph. 4:32).   In Christ Jesus dwelt the fullness of the
Godhead bodily.   He opened the treasurehouse of Almighty
God and made known grace and truth in His own Person,
even though He was very man.

The WORD was "in the beginning"—there was never a
time when the WORD was not; but Jesus was something
new upon the earth: He was *the Word in FLESH* and He
tabernacled among men to declare God's love, God's grace,
and God's truth.   The WORD *will be* throughout all eternity.   In John 12:46—48 Jesus declared, "I am come a light
into the world, that whosoever believeth on me should not
abide in darkness.   And if any man hear my words, and
believe not, I judge him not: for I came not to judge the
world, but to save the world.   He that rejecteth me, and
receiveth not my words, hath one that judgeth him: *THE
WORD THAT I HAVE SPOKEN, the same shall judge
him in the last day."*   Notice He did not say, "the word
that *I will speak,"* but "the word that *I have spoken."*

The Witness of John Baptist

Verses 15—18:   *"John bare witness of Him, and cried,
saying, This was He of whom I spake, He that cometh
after me is preferred before me: for He was before me.
And of His fulness have all we received, and grace for
grace.   For the law was given by Moses, but grace and
truth came by Jesus Christ.   No man hath seen God at any
time; the only begotten Son, which is in the bosom of the
Father, He hath declared Him."*

These verses contain three tremendous declarations concerning our Lord and Saviour—three tremendous stones in
the foundation of Christianity:
1. *Christ is the only one who can supply all spiritual needs*

of all believers:

"Of His fulness have all we received, and grace for grace" (v. 16). "It pleased the Father that in Him should all fulness dwell . . . in whom are hid all the treasures of wisdom and knowledge" (Col. 1:19; 2:3). In Christ, the Christian finds every need supplied. Our sufficiency is in Him, in Him we are complete. In Jesus is laid up heaven's treasure, and in that treasure is stored anything and everything the believer needs. In Him the sinner finds salvation, in Him the believer finds grace to overcome, strength to bear the burdens. In Him is found the supply for every need, whether that need be physical, spiritual, mental, temporal, or eternal.

From Eden to Calvary the blood was a divine necessity if God were to pass over sin. *All* saved souls from Abel down to this present time have received salvation from Jesus Christ alone. From all eternity, even before the foundation of the world, *only Jesus* satisfied God concerning the atonement for sin, redemption of sinners, and grace to keep the believer and present him faultless in that great day.

2. *Christ is superior to Moses, the Gospel of grace is superior to the Mosaic Law:*

"The law was given by Moses, but grace and truth came by Jesus Christ" (v. 17). Moses was God's servant, ministering the moral and ceremonial law to Israel. He was a *faithful* servant (Heb. 3:5), but he was *only* a servant. Likewise, the law was holy and good and just—but the law could not justify the sinner: "Therefore by the deeds of the law there shall no flesh be justified in His sight: for by the law is the knowledge of sin" (Rom. 3:20). The law had no healing power, no forgiving power. The wound sin had dealt the human race could not be bound up by the law. On the contrary, ". . . the law worketh wrath: for where no law is, there is no transgression" (Rom. 4:15).

The law pronounced a curse, not a blessing; it was a "schoolmaster" pointing men to Christ: "Wherefore the law

was our schoolmaster to bring us unto Christ, that we might
be justified by faith. But after that faith is come, we are
no longer under a schoolmaster" (Gal. 3:24,25). The law
was *only* a schoolmaster; it could not make the individual
perfect as pertaining to conscience; it was "a figure for the
time then present, in which were offered both gifts and sacrifices, that could not make him that did the service perfect, as pertaining to the conscience" (Heb. 9:9).

The law was the ministration of death and condemnation: "If the ministration of death, written and engraven
in stones, was glorious, so that the children of Israel could
not stedfastly behold the face of Moses for the glory of his
countenance; which glory was to be done away: How shall
not the ministration of the Spirit be rather glorious? For
if the ministration of condemnation be glory, much more
doth the ministration of righteousness *exceed* in glory"
(II Cor. 3:7—9). The light presented to sinners by Moses
through the law was only as the twinkling of a star compared to the Sun of Righteousness (Mal. 4:2).

Moses was God's servant—but Christ was God's only
begotten Son, and He came with the authority, the ability,
and the key to unlock God's treasurehouse of grace and
truth: "Moses verily was faithful in all His house, as a
servant, for a testimony of those things which were to be
spoken after; *BUT CHRIST AS A SON OVER HIS OWN
HOUSE; whose house are we,* if we hold fast the confidence and the rejoicing of the hope firm unto the end"
(Heb. 3:5,6).

"Grace and truth came by Jesus Christ." God's only
begotten Son declared God's grace when He made known
to all men God's gracious, simple, understandable plan of
salvation by grace through faith in the shed blood of the
Lamb. With this message Jesus opened to all mankind the
fountain of living water and the fountain of God's mercy
to those who will hear and believe. *Truth* came by Christ
when He, in flesh, fulfilled every type and shadow of the
Old Testament, making known to all the world that He

was the true sacrifice, the true mercyseat, the true and everlasting High Priest of God.

Oh, yes, there was grace and truth under the law of Moses, but "the grace of God that brings salvation" appeared in the Man Christ Jesus. The truth about redemption through the shed blood came when Jesus appeared in flesh and declared the divine imperative that He be lifted up that sinners might be drawn to Him. God's *grace* in its fullness, and *truth* in its fullness weré made known when Jesus came into the world and announced that He had come, not to be ministered unto, but to minister, and to give His life a ransom for sinners.

3. *Christ Jesus alone has revealed God to man:*

"No man hath seen God at any time; the only begotten Son, which is in the bosom of the Father, He hath declared Him" (v. 18).

Mortal eye has never gazed upon the eternal God who was in the beginning. No man could look upon God and live. To Moses He said, "Thou canst not see my face: for there shall no man see me, and live. . . Behold, there is a place by me, and thou shalt stand upon a rock: and it shall come to pass, while my glory passeth by, that I will put thee in a clift of the rock, and will cover thee with my hand while I pass by: and I will take away mine hand, and thou shalt see my back parts: but my face shall not be seen" (Ex. 33:20—23). But in the Man Christ Jesus, man finds revealed all that he needs to know or is capable of knowing about the eternal God, Father of our Lord Jesus Christ. The fullness of God dwelt in Jesus, and God is revealed to us by His only begotten Son, who chose to take upon Himself our nature, and in the form of man *exhibit TO man* all that our finite minds can comprehend concerning God the Father. In our limitations we can never grasp the magnitude of God's existence from all eternity— His perfections and His power. So long as we tabernacle in a body of flesh, we can see and understand God only through His Son Jesus Christ.

In the death of Jesus is revealed God's perfect wisdom,
His almighty power, His unknowable love to sinners, His
holiness which is far beyond the comprehension of the mind
of man, and His hatred of sin—hatred such as mortal man
finds impossible to understand. Such divine truths could
not be presented to mankind in a clearer, more understandable way than in the spotless life and the horrible death
of Christ Jesus, the Lamb of God. In HIM, God was manifested in flesh, for Christ was the brightness of the Father's glory, the express image of His Person (Heb. 1:3).
Jesus said, "I and my Father are one. . . He that hath seen
me hath seen the Father" (John 10:30; 14:9).

There is much error concerning the Holy Trinity, and we
must carefully study and rightly divide the Word concerning the Godhead; but we need not fear giving all honor,
glory, and praise to God the Son. It is impossible to exalt Him too highly, for the only way we can please God
the Father is *through* the Son: "For the Father judgeth
no man, but hath committed all judgment unto the Son:
That all men should honour the Son, even as they honour
the Father. He that honoureth not the Son honoureth not
the Father which hath sent Him" (John 5:22,23).

"John bare witness of Him." Throughout the ministry
of John the Baptist he was careful to make it clear that
HE was to decrease while CHRIST was to *increase.* He
continually proclaimed Christ's greatness and his own inferiority.

John cried, *"He that cometh after me is preferred before me: for He WAS before me."* In the Greek language,,
"cried" suggests the cry of one making a proclamation, a
very *loud* cry. Thus it was that John proclaimed the Christ.
Even though John was born six months before Jesus was
born into this world, he declared, "He was *before* me."
In other words, "He existed before I was born." John,
the anointed of God, possessed great spiritual knowledge
and understanding, as proved in his understanding of the

pre-existence of Christ. Jesus WAS before John—in existence, in position, in dignity, and in power.

"Of His fulness have all we received." All who believe
on Jesus have received an abundant supply of grace,
strength, power, and whatever else is needed. *Whatever*
our need, it is met in Jesus, and He is the only one who
can supply our spiritual needs. Please notice that we do
not receive sparingly or partially, but *fully.* God does not
give salvation in different measures or portions. When we
receive the grace of God we receive even grace *upon* grace.
When one is redeemed, he is *fully* redeemed.

The expression *"grace for grace"* is singular, found nowhere else in all of the Word of God. Great men have dis-
agreed concerning the meaning of the phrase, but there is
no doubt in my mind that it means "grace in the place
of grace"—*constant* grace, fresh grace every day, abundant
supplies of new grace for every need, every moment of every day, so long as we remain in this tabernacle of flesh.
It means new grace to take the place of old grace—unfail-
ing, abundant grace, a continual filling up of the supply
of grace for our needs. *Paul* prayed for God to remove the
"thorn" from his flesh. God did not remove the thorn, but
He assured Paul, *"My grace is sufficient for thee!"* Whatever we are called upon to face, whatever our needs may
be, there is new grace every moment as we need it—even
unto the end.

I have heard Christians testify that they are concerned
about dying, sometimes fear grips their heart when they
think of dying; but let me assure you that it is not *dying*
grace we need so long as we are living: *we need grace
to live a victorious life!* When the time comes for us to
depart this life, God will give dying grace—He has a fresh
supply each time a saint leaves this life to be with Him.
Consider *Stephen:* he was stoned to death, but as the
stones pounded the life from his body, God rolled back the
firmament and Stephen saw Jesus standing at God's right
hand! When *we,* my fellow believer, need dying grace, we

may not be stoned to death, we may not be burned at the
stake for our testimony; but however and whenever we depart this life there will be a fresh supply of grace, *abundant* grace, in that hour.

"*The law was given by Moses.*" In this verse is shown
the inferiority of the law compared to the marvelous Gospel
of God's grace. In clear, strong contrast it shows the char-
acteristics of the old dispensation and those of the new—
the Dispensation of Law in contrast with the Dispensation
of Grace.

By Moses came the moral law, full of high and holy
demands and very stern threatenings against all disobedience. By Moses came also the ceremonial law, filled with
burdensome sacrifices offered again and again, many times
the same sacrifice offered over and over again; but ordinances, ceremonies, holy days, holidays, and feasts could
never take away the sins of the sinner nor heal the worshipper's conscience and give him a perfect conscience before God. At the very best, these were but *shadows* of
good things to come, and "*Christ is the END of the law
for righteousness to every one that believeth*" (Rom. 10:4).

"*Grace and truth came by Jesus Christ.*" Christ came
from the Father's bosom, full of grace and truth, and declared God's plan of salvation *by* grace *through* faith, salvation that offers complete and perfect pardon for every
poor, hell-deserving sinner who will believe on the Lord
Jesus Christ and trust in His shed blood.

Christ was *truth* on exhibition. He was the Truth be-
cause He was the true Sacrifice, the true Priest, the true
Atonement for sin. He was the truth that sets men free
(John 8:32,36).

The Law of Moses could not save the soul. The law
threatened, but it did not help men become righteous, with
a perfect conscience before God. The law *commanded,* but
it could not heal the sin-sick heart. The law showed men
the *exceeding sinfulness* of sin, but it could not take away
that sin. The law was a shadow of things to come, and

paved the way for the appearing of Him who kept every facet of the law—the Great Physician who brought grace, truth, and healing to poor, sin-sick souls. Jesus plainly said that He came to *fulfill* the law, not to destroy it; and He DID fulfill it. *Now,* all true believers are perfect law-keepers—but only IN CHRIST.

"The law" stands for the Old Testament dispensation in general, a dispensation of command and demand. The law *required*—the grace of God GIVES. The law exposed and condemned sin—the grace of God *takes AWAY* sin and pardons the sinner. The law *contained* truth, it showed a partial glimpse of truth—but Jesus IS truth, and grace and truth go much deeper, much further, than the law. Grace and truth were in the old economy in some measure, but the *fullness* of grace and truth could only be in Christ, "He that is holy, He that is true, He that hath the key of David" (Rev. 3:7). See also Isaiah 22:22.

In John's Gospel the name *"Jesus Christ"* appears only here. *"Jesus"* stands for grace, and He WAS God's grace wrapped up in flesh. *"Christ"* stands for truth: Christ was *God,* and God cannot lie (Heb. 6:18; Tit. 1:2).

"No man hath seen God at any time." Here Christ is seen in His infinite personal superiority to Moses, to the prophets, and to all men. No man has ever seen God the Father, the eternal Spirit (John 4:24). Abraham, Moses, Joshua, David, Isaiah, Daniel, Jeremiah—these were great, stalwart men of God, good men and holy, but they were incapable of beholding Almighty God face to face. What they knew about God the Father and what they wrote about Him *they knew by revelation* as the Holy Ghost dictated to them. They were servants of the most high God, they were prophets anointed and appointed by Him, and He gave them revelation in sundry ways; but they did not see Him face to face.

Christ was more than a servant: He was the only be-gotten SON of God, He was in the beginning WITH God. He is the One who is (and has always been) most intimately

united with God the Father, equal to Him in all things.
While Jesus tabernacled here on earth, God in flesh, He
revealed to man all that mortal can understand and bear
to know concerning Almighty God the eternal Spirit. He
revealed God's holiness, compassion, and power. He revealed God's hatred of sin and His love for sinners. He
brought to light the great mystery of how God can still
be God and yet be just, holy, and righteous while He justifies the ungodly:

"But now the righteousness of God without the law is
manifested, being witnessed by the law and the prophets;
even the righteousness of God which is by faith of Jesus
Christ unto all and upon all them that believe: for there
is no difference: for all have sinned, and come short of
the glory of God; being justified freely by His grace through
the redemption that is in Christ Jesus: whom God hath
set forth to be a propitiation through faith in His blood,
to declare His righteousness for the remission of sins that
are past, through the forbearance of God; *TO DECLARE,
I SAY, AT THIS TIME HIS RIGHTEOUSNESS: THAT
HE MIGHT BE JUST, AND THE JUSTIFIER OF HIM
WHICH BELIEVETH IN JESUS.* Where is boasting then?
It is excluded. By what law? of works? Nay: but by the
law of faith. Therefore we conclude that a man is justified by faith without the deeds of the law" (Rom. 3:21—28).

God's appearances to mortal man as mentioned in the
Old Testament were *not* appearances of Almighty God, eternal Spirit and Father of our Lord Jesus Christ. He whom
Abraham, Daniel, Moses, Jacob, Joshua, and Isaiah saw
(usually appearing as the "Angel of the Lord") was not
God the eternal Spirit, first Person of the Trinity, but *the
Son,* second Person of the Trinity. God the eternal Spirit
is inaccessible to sense perception. Mortal man cannot have
visible fellowship with the eternal God. (Study I John
4:12,20.) The eternal God is "Infinite Spirit" and Infinite
Spirit cannot be the object of human vision. The divine
glory of God was veiled in flesh. God is pure, righteous,

holy, absolute in every detail, incomprehensible by human reason. (Study Isaiah 40:18—28.)

In Job 11:7 we read, *"Canst thou by searching find out God? Canst thou find out the Almighty unto perfection?"* God is not found by searching, He is not understood through human wisdom. Mortal man's unaided powers cannot discover God, cannot love and worship Him as man ought to do. Such knowledge and understanding as will cause man to trust, love, and hope in God, and be obedient TO God, has never been the *discovery* of man; it comes only through the revelation of God Himself.

In Old Testament days, God spoke by the prophets— men who were chosen by Him and qualified for the ministry. These men revealed all that was possible for *them* to reveal, but in these "last days" God has spoken through His only begotten Son; therefore He has spoken in fullness, for Christ was the fullness of the Godhead bodily.

"In the bosom of the Father" denotes the intimate fellowship, love, trust, understanding and union that existed from all eternity between the Father and the Son. Such eternal communion as existed between God the Father and God the Son is closer and deeper than man's mind can begin to conceive. Here, John not only expresses the timeless, enduring relation between Father and Son; he also points out where Christ is *now,* where He *has been* and *will be* throughout eternity—His own natural and eternal place "in the bosom of the Father." The fact that Jesus took a body of flesh made no difference. The fact that He (as a Man) now sits at the right hand of the Father still makes no difference.

"The Father" and "The Son" are key words of the Gospel of John. The expressions "the Father" and "my Father" occur almost one hundred times in this Gospel, and the revelation of God the Father through Jesus the Son is the fundamental truth set forth. God the Father is in the Son, the Son is in the Father. Father and Son are one, yet God the Father is the *first* Person of the Trinity, Jesus

the Son is the *second* Person of the Trinity. All things
belonging to God the Father also belong to Jesus the Son—
"all mine are thine, and thine are mine" (John 17:10).

But Jesus *left* the bosom of the Father and came into the
world to declare God to man, and *"He HATH declared
Him."* Every word the Saviour spoke, every miracle He
performed, every step He took was for a singular purpose—
to make known the love of God, the mercy of God, the tenderness of God, and to declare the salvation that had been
brought down to man. Jesus the Son is God's Expositor
or Interpreter; He hath "expounded" God the Father. We
do not find the truth about God in philosophy or science,
in mathematics or in the test tube. When we look for the
truth about God the eternal Spirit we must look to a life
once lived right here in this world—the life of the Lord
Jesus Christ; for He and *He alone* has declared God.

In the closing statement of this verse we see the manner
in which *the invisible God* was made visible: IN CHRIST
JESUS. Here is declared the way in which grace and truth
came to man. Christ is the Gospel, the Gospel is Christ.
Christ is Christianity, Christianity is Christ. To receive
Christ is to receive eternal life. To be saved is to be in
Christ, to be in Christ is to be in the fellowship of the Father, *one* with the Father and the Son forever, hid with
Christ in God (Col. 3:3). Christ is perfect love, perfect
wisdom, absolute truth, and pure righteousness. To have
Christ is to have the Father and the Son. He who does
not possess the Son does not possess the Father, and any
preacher or teacher who declares any other doctrine is to
be ignored and refused fellowship. Born again people are
to reject anyone who does not preach the doctrine of Jesus
Christ. (Please study carefully the second epistle of John.)

The Record of John Baptist Concerning Himself

Verses 19—28: *"And this is the record of John, when
the Jews sent priests and Levites from Jerusalem to ask*

him, Who art thou? And he confessed, and denied not;
but confessed, I am not the Christ. And they asked him,
What then? Art thou Elias? And he saith, I am not. Art
thou that prophet? And he answered, No.

"Then said they unto him, Who art thou? that we may
give an answer to them that sent us. What sayest thou of
thyself? He said, I am the voice of one crying in the wilderness, Make straight the way of the Lord, as said the
prophet Esaias.

"And they which were sent were of the Pharisees. And
they asked him, and said unto him, Why baptizest thou
then, if thou be not that Christ, nor Elias, neither that
prophet? John answered them, saying, I baptize with water: but there standeth one among you, whom ye know not;
He it is, who coming after me is preferred before me, whose
shoe's latchet I am not worthy to unloose.

"These things were done in Bethabara beyond Jordan,
where John was baptizing."

In the previous verses we studied the deep, weighty,
but clear statements concerning Christ's incarnation and His
divine nature. Now we come to the account of the days
of His earthly ministry, His works and His words among
men.

In these verses we see John Baptist as an example of
true humility. He was an eminent saint of Almighty God.
Few names stand higher in all of the Bible than does that
of John the Baptist. Jesus declared, "Among them that
are born of women there hath not risen a greater than John
the Baptist . . ." (Matt. 11:11). But in spite of his greatness and his unusual knowledge of Christ, he was humble
and self-abased; there was no sinful pride in him. He
could have been highly honored by the Jews but he de-
clined their honors and turned a deaf ear to their flattery,
declaring that he was simply "the voice of one crying in
the wilderness." To exalt Christ and bring glory and honor
to HIM was the singular desire of John's heart and the

primary mission of his ministry.   He was truly "clothed
with humility." (Study I Peter 5:5.)

We find another example in these verses—a *sad* example
of the blindness of unbelievers.   The Jews who came to
question John professed to be learned men, students of the
Scriptures.   They boasted that they were children of Abraham, possessors of the covenants.   They were sticklers for
the law, they professed to know God's will, they prided
themselves in believing God's promises and they were looking for their promised Messiah; but they were self-appointed
leaders of the blind, because they themselves sat in total
darkness. (Study Romans 2:17—20.)   At that very moment,
John said, there was One standing among them whom they
knew not, even their Messiah.

"This is the record of John" (the Greek word here translated *record* is rendered *witness* in verse 7, and means that
this is the testimony John gave) *"when the Jews sent priests
and Levites from Jerusalem"* to question him.   When did
John give this testimony?   When did this incident occur?
Most Bible scholars agree that it was after the baptism of
Jesus, at the end of the forty days of fasting and the temptation in the wilderness.   (Read the record in Matthew
4:1—11.)   Notice in verse 29 of our present chapter we read,
"The NEXT day John seeth Jesus coming unto him."   It
is extremely important that we pay close attention to the
"days" that are so carefully pointed out in this first chapter of John's Gospel.

When John speaks of *"the Jews"* he is generally speaking of the enemies of Jesus.   This is an expression peculiar
to the Gospel of John, and many outstanding Bible students
believe this indicates that this Gospel was not written in
Palestine or in Jerusalem.   It would also indicate that John's
Gospel was written especially for the Gentile Christians
scattered throughout the world, and that it was written
much later than the other Gospels.

The priests and Levites who were sent to question John
the Baptist were an authoritative committee appointed and

sent from the Sanhedrin—the ecclesiastical council of the Jews. They were sent to question him concerning his authority for baptizing and carrying out his ministry. They wanted to know who he was and *by what authority* he did what he was doing.

It is worthy of note that the chief priests, scribes, and elders gave more honor to John the Baptist than to Christ Jesus. They esteemed John because of his lineage—they *knew* who *his* father was; but when *Jesus* appeared on the scene they referred to HIM as "the carpenter's son." They knew John was the son of Zacharias, a priest, and therefore John was himself a Levite. Their question, then, pertained to his office and his ministry, not to his ancestry. They were interested in what John claimed to be. Did he think he was the Messiah? Did he claim to be some great prophet? With what authority had he gone into the ministry, and by whose authority did he baptize?

John was a sensational person. He attracted tremendous crowds, and Mark 1:5 tells us that "there went out unto him all the land of Judaea, and they of Jerusalem, and were baptized of him in the river of Jordan, confessing their sins." Therefore the Sanhedrin in Jerusalem decided it was time to find out more about this new preacher, and time to do something about the great crowds that were following him. His extraordinary personality and his exceedingly successful ministry suggested to the Jews that John the Baptist might be the expected Redeemer, and so they sent a committee to inquire of him, *"Who ART thou?"*

John confessed, *"I am NOT the Christ."* The strong language and the form of speech used here sets forth the idea that John shrank back with holy indignation that these men could be so ignorant as to think that *he* might be the Christ! They should *know* that such an one as he could not be the Redeemer, the Christ, the King of the Jews, and he declared the Christ to be far superior to himself.

We must bear in mind the fact that Christ had not been openly manifested at this time. It was JOHN who was before the public eye, and multitudes were flocking to him, being baptized of him, becoming his disciples. Surely Satan must have whispered in John's ear, *"Why not* announce that you are the Messiah? These people will believe you and accept you." But if such temptation came to the forerunner of our Lord, he instantly said in his heart, "Get thee behind me, Satan," for without hesitation he confessed, *"I am not the Christ!"*

They next asked him, *"What then?   Art thou Elias?"* Coming from the Jews this was not an unnatural question; it was based on the prophecy of Malachi 4:5: "Behold, I will send you Elijah the prophet before the coming of the great and dreadful day of the Lord." John's mode of dress— leather girdle and camel's hair—together with his food of locusts and wild honey, his preaching, and his appearance in the wilderness certainly constituted a great similarity between himself and the prophet Elijah. The Jews therefore thought that if he were not the Christ, he might very well be Elijah. But again John gave emphatic denial. He said, "I am not Elijah."

A question might arise here concerning the seeming contradiction between this verse and Matthew 17:11 where Jesus said, "Elias truly shall first come, and restore all things." And now John the Baptist declares, "I am NOT Elias." How can we reconcile these two statements? We must remember to compare Scripture with Scripture, spiritual things with spiritual, and rightly divide the Word:

After Elijah was taken up in a chariot of fire, the Word of God records two future comings. The first coming is in spirit only, and John the Baptist *was the SPIRIT of Elijah.* The second coming of that prophet will be his literal appearance on this earth, an appearance of the same man whom Elisha saw taken up to heaven. This second coming of Elijah will be fulfilled by one of the two witnesses in Revelation 11. He will come as a prophet to Israel during the time of the Great Tribulation. John the Baptist is speaking of the literal second coming of Elijah,

and what he said to the Jews, in essence, was: "I am
NOT Elijah as you speak of him. I am not he who was
taken up to heaven in a chariot of fire. I am not the forerunner of Christ when He comes to reign in glory; I am His
forerunner when He comes as a Lamb for the slaughter,
when He comes in humiliation to offer His blood for the
remission of sins. I am not the Elijah who will come to
prepare the way for the conquering King of kings and Lord
of lords; I am the *spirit* of Elijah, and I have come to prepare the way for the meek and lowly Lamb of God, Saviour of sinners. I am NOT the Elijah you are thinking
about."

There is no contradiction here. What John said is truth,
what Jesus said is truth; and in Matthew 17:12, continuing
from verse 11, Jesus said, "I say unto you, That *Elias is
come ALREADY.*" In other words, "Elias *shall* come,
Elias IS come." *In spirit* Elijah came when John the Baptist came, but the *man* Elijah will come in the end time.
There are two comings of Jesus: first as the Lamb, second
as the Lion of the Tribe of Judah; first in humility, second
in power and great glory. What John the Baptist was to
the first coming of Christ, Elijah will be to His second
coming.

The Jews then asked, *"Art thou that Prophet?"* and John
answered, *"No."* In Deuteronomy 18:15 Moses prophesied
concerning "that Prophet": "The Lord thy God will raise
up unto thee a Prophet from the midst of thee, of thy brethren, like unto me; unto Him ye shall hearken." John the
Baptist was a prophet; he would not deny that fact—but
he was not "that Prophet" spoken of by Moses. It seems
that the Jews who questioned John did not understand that
the Prophet of whom Moses spoke and *the Messiah* were
one and the same Person. Their questioning here would
indicate that they looked for *Christ* as one Person and "that
Prophet" as another. They were looking for two different
people.

When John answered, "No, I am not that Prophet," they

then asked him, *"WHO ART THOU? that we may give
an answer to them that sent us. What sayest thou of thyself?"* Here we find *proof* that these men were not just
idle inquirers. They were sent by the Sanhedrin at Jerusalem and they were to report back to that body on what
they discovered concerning this remarkable man with such
remarkable ministry.

In answer to that question John replied, *"I am the voice
of one crying in the wilderness, Make straight the way of
the Lord!"* John's statement here concerning himself refers
to Scripture found in Isaiah 40:3: "The voice of him that
crieth in the wilderness, Prepare ye the way of the Lord,
make straight in the desert a highway for our God!" The
priests and Levites should have *known* who he was, and
he reminds them that there is no excuse for their *not* knowing. They had the books of Isaiah, Jeremiah, Ezekiel, Zechariah; they had the Psalms. Had they known the Scriptures
as they professed to know them they would have recognized "the voice of one crying in the wilderness." In other
words, John told them, "That prophecy given to Isaiah is
this very day fulfilled before your eyes. *I am that voice,*
I am that person whom Isaiah saw and heard in the vision
and of whom he wrote in his prophecy. I am NOT the
Christ, the Messiah; I am only a voice going before Him.
I have not come to work miracles nor to draw men to myself. I have come to prepare the way of the Lord, to announce the coming of Messiah, and, through the message
of the Gospel, to make ready the barren hearts of the Jewish nation—a people dwelling in a wilderness of darkness,
sin, and unbelief. My mission is to cry aloud, to warn,
to invite men to prepare for the coming of the Messiah."

Why was John *"crying in the wilderness"* instead of in
the temple? Why did he make his proclamation in the wilderness of Judaea instead of in the temple in Jerusalem?
The answer is that Judaism was in the wilderness of unbelief. Israel had become a nation of legalists. "The wilderness" symbolized the spiritual barrenness of Israel, and

God sent John to the wilderness to make the announcement of the coming of Messiah. God refused to recognize the self-righteous formalism of the religion of the Jews, and thus the one sent of Him to announce the Christ made the announcement outside the religious system of that day.

"They which were sent were of the Pharisees," and the Pharisees were noted for their strict adherence to ceremonies, ordinances, forms, and rituals. Naturally, they were not satisfied with the ministry of John the Baptist; they did not consider him qualified to baptize and carry out a ministry. In the words of Jesus, they "rejected the counsel of God against themselves, being not baptized of him" (Luke 7:30).

The testimony in Luke would indicate that they who asked these questions of John asked them in a thoroughly hateful and unfriendly spirit. They really had no desire to learn God's truth, they were not trying to learn if John was the true Messiah; they simply questioned him because he had not come to them for credentials to minister in their area. (There are religionists *today* who act as though they were "lords over God's heritage." They do not want anyone preaching in their territory unless he is invited and sanctioned by their committee.)

The Pharisees then asked John, *"Why baptizest thou then, if thou be not that Christ, nor Elias, neither that Prophet?"* This tells us that the committee who questioned John expected the Messiah and His forerunner to baptize whenever and wherever they appeared; therefore it was not the ordinance *as such* that they questioned, but John's authority to *administer* baptism. The same is true today. A minister who does not bow to the religious rulers of this day is not allowed to baptize members into the leading denominations.

Verses 26 and 27 give John's answer to this threatening question from the Pharisees. What he said was, in essence, "I baptize with water; He who will come after me will baptize hearts. I am not baptizing by my own authority,

but because I am commissioned by One far superior to me,
One who was preferred before me because He WAS before
me.   I am not making disciples for myself, but for Him
who is far greater than I.   I am not trying to start a new
religion, I do not ask any man to follow *me*.   Those whom
I baptize are instructed to believe on Him who will come
after me, whose shoes I am not worthy to unloose.   Even
now He stands among you, but you are so blinded by the
religion and tradition of your fathers that you cannot see
Him.   It is He in whose name I baptize, it is He whose
coming I proclaim."

"Whom ye know not" implies much more than simply
not knowing Jesus by *sight*.   They not only did not recognize Him with the human eye, they were in ignorance even
concerning His *coming*.   They were looking for one who
would conquer their oppressors, lift the Roman yoke, and
set up a mighty kingdom.   They were not looking for the
suffering Messiah, the Lamb of God—wounded for their
transgressions, bruised for their iniquities, nailed to a cross
bearing the sin of us all.

The meaning of verse 27 is the same as that of verse 15.
Even though from the standpoint of time Jesus began His
public ministry after John, from the standpoint of dignity
He was *above* John and He was *before* him in all eternity,
"in the beginning" with the Father.   John's uppermost desire was to exalt Christ and abase himself, to point men
to Jesus and away from his own person.   In those days it
was the duty of a servant to remove the shoes and bathe
the feet of visitors, especially a visitor of such standing as
a governor or king.   So what John was saying in verse 27
was that he was not worthy even to perform the most humble duties of a household servant so far as Christ's superiority was concerned.

*"These things were done in Bethabara beyond Jordan,
where John was baptizing."*   This name should hold a dear
and warm place in the hearts of all believers.   It was here
that the first disciples of Jesus were called and baptized.

It was here that the foundation of the Church was laid. It was here *"the next day"* that Jesus was publicly proclaimed "the Lamb of God which taketh away the sin of the world." It was from here, on "the day after," that Andrew, the patron saint of all soul-winners, and "another disciple" followed Jesus to see where He lived. Interesting and important events occurred at "Bethabara beyond Jordan."

John was preaching there because multitudes went out to hear him and to be baptized, and it was necessary that he be near a supply of water. Palestine is a very dry country, and the multitudes who came to hear John preach also needed water. We know from Judges 7:24 that Bethabara was near much water. It was therefore a logical place for John to conduct his ministry.

John's ministry was short, but it was of extreme importance. From the great ecclesiastical council of the Sanhedrin to the humble shepherds and lowliest people, his message aroused attention, drawing out vast multitudes to hear him— and leaving the Jews without excuse for not accepting their Messiah. When they later refused to believe on Him, they could not accuse Him of coming to them unannounced or taking them by surprise. If the Old Testament Scriptures were not sufficient identification and warning, John the Baptist had clearly and confidently proclaimed the coming of the King of the Jews. There was no doubt in the mind of John as to who he was and what his mission on earth was to be (study Luke 1:17—80); but what counted with him was the One whom he had come to announce and for whom he was ordained to prepare the way.

The Lamb Announced

Verses 29—34: *"The next day John seeth Jesus coming unto him, and saith, Behold the Lamb of God, which taketh away the sin of the world. This is He of whom I said, After me cometh a Man which is preferred before me: for*

*He was before me.   And I knew Him not: but that He
should be made manifest to Israel, therefore am I come
baptizing with water.   And John bare record, saying, I saw
the Spirit descending from heaven like a dove, and it abode
upon Him.   And I knew Him not: but He that sent me
to baptize with water, the same said unto me, Upon whom
thou shalt see the Spirit descending, and remaining on Him,
the same is He which baptizeth with the Holy Ghost.   And
I saw, and bare record that this is the Son of God."*

Here is one of the greatest texts in all of the Word of
God.   *All* Scripture is inspired and is profitable to us, but
some texts are richer than others and this is one of the
richest.

When Jesus came the first time—Lamb of God, Jesus,
Saviour—He came quietly, without display, without glory.
The Jews did not know of His coming, the rulers did not
know of it.   As John announced in verse 26, *He stood
among them* and yet they were not aware of His presence.
And here John the Baptist publicly announces the appearing, the visible revelation, of *"the Lamb of God, which
taketh away the sin of the world!"*

The name here given to Jesus goes much deeper than
merely signifying that He was meek, gentle, and humble
as a lamb: it means that He was *the Great Sacrifice for
sin* promised in the Garden of Eden and all through the
Old Testament.   The blood of the lambs that were slain
from Eden to Calvary pointed to *this* Lamb whom John
announced that day—the true Lamb which Abraham, on
Mount Moriah, told Isaac God would provide (Gen. 22:8).

Christ was the true Lamb to which every daily morning
and evening sacrifice in the temple had pointed, and if
Jesus had not come, those offerings would have been in
vain.   He was the Lamb concerning whom Isaiah prophesied.   (Study the entire 53rd chapter of Isaiah.)   He was
the Lamb typified by the Passover lamb in Egypt.   Here
was the Promised One, the Great Propitiation for sin, He

whom God the Father had covenanted from all eternity to
send into the world to make atonement for sin. John announced that day God's true and perfect Lamb.

Not only did John announce WHO the Lamb of God was,
he also announced WHY He had come: *to TAKE AWAY
the sin of the world.* How incomprehensible to the Jews!
They were expecting their Messiah—a mighty Ruler who
would put down the Romans; but John announced that
the Lamb of God had come to take away the sin of the
WORLD! John announced a *Saviour;* they were expecting
a King! They were expecting one who would *destroy* their
enemies, but John made it clear that the Lamb of God had
come to *save* His enemies. He came to do for sinners what
sinners could never do for themselves. He came to purchase with His life's blood what money could never purchase. He came to make known that which learning and
wisdom of men could never find out or obtain—the love
of God, the mercy of God, and God's salvation. Jesus is
the Prince of Peace. He came the first time that there
might be peace in the human heart; when He comes the
second time there will be *peace on earth* and good will
among men.

I would emphasize that Jesus came to take away the
sin of the *world*—not the sin of a few or of a select, elect
group. Jews, Gentiles, rich, poor, bond or free, learned or
unlearned, it makes no difference; He came to take away
the sin of *whosoever* will believe on His name and trust
in His precious blood shed on Calvary—and notice the word
"taketh." It does not say He TOOK away sin, nor that
He WILL take away sin, but that He *"TAKETH away"*
the sin of the world.

On the cross He did take away the sin that damns, He
purchased redemption; and the moment we believe in His
shed blood and trust in His finished work we are redeemed
just as fully as we will *ever be* redeemed; but Jesus ever
lives to make intercession for us, and when we become
born again believers He takes away the sin committed by

believers *daily,* cleansing, washing the spirit, the soul of
His child.   He daily grants fresh supplies of mercy and
grace.   On the cross He *died for sinners.* He ever *lives*
to intercede for believers.   In heaven now as our great
High Priest, He presents His sacrifice continually before
God the Father.

The same truth is stated in I John 1:7: "If we walk
in the light, as He is in the light, we have fellowship one
with another, and the blood of Jesus Christ His Son *cleanseth* us from all sin."

Not only was Jesus "the Lamb of God," not only had
He come to take away the "sin of the world," He also
would *baptize "with the Holy Ghost"* (v. 33).   John baptized with water, but the baptism of the Holy Ghost could
be administered only by Christ Jesus, the Lamb of God.

The baptism administered by John the Baptist did not
and could not save any person, any more than baptism can
save people today.   Water baptism has nothing to do with
redemption.   We *should be baptized in water* in the name
of the Father, and of the Son, and of the Holy Ghost—
not to BE redeemed, but *because we ARE redeemed.* Water
baptism signifies to a gainsaying world that we have *died*
to the world, we are buried with Christ and have been
raised to walk in newness of life.

But the baptism of the Holy Ghost occurs the split second we believe unto salvation, the very moment of the new
birth.   We are *born* of the Spirit (John 3:5); and *except* a
man be born of the Spirit, except a man *possess* the Spirit
(Rom. 8:9), except a man be *led by* the Spirit (Rom. 8:14),
except a man be *baptized* in the Spirit (I Cor. 12:12,13),
except a man be *sealed* by the Spirit (Eph. 4:30), *that person is NOT a child of God!*

The thief on the cross was never baptized in water.   He
called on Jesus, he asked to be remembered, and Jesus said,
"Today shalt thou be with me in Paradise!"   On the other
hand, Ananias and Sapphira were baptized in water, they
were received into the early church by the apostles in charge

—but they were NOT baptized by the Holy Spirit because they *lied* to the Spirit. (Read Acts 5:1—10.)

"The next day John seeth Jesus coming unto him." This proves that Jesus was not present with John when the priests and Levites came to question him concerning who he was and with what authority he baptized. Immediately after Jesus was baptized, He was led of the Spirit into the wilderness to be tempted of the devil (Mark 1:12,13; Matt. 4:1—11). Immediately after the forty days of fasting and the temptation, He came back to John the Baptist in the wilderness of Judaea. It was then that John saw Him coming and announced the approaching of the Lamb of God.

Notice what the Lamb of God came to take away: "the SIN"—s-i-n (singular), not S-I-N-S (plural). If Jesus came nineteen hundred years ago to take away the SINS of the world, then *He failed.* We have more species of sin on earth today than when Jesus was here. Satan and his cohorts work night and day to manufacture new types of sin. We know that there are only three avenues through which Satan tempts men: the lust of the flesh, the lust of the eyes, and the pride of life (I John 2:15—17; Matt. 4:1 ff); but *the TREE of sin* bears many kinds of fruit. Drunkenness, murder, lying, stealing, blasphemy, adultery—these sins are *fruits* of THE SIN that damns the soul. Jesus came to take away the SIN of the world, and that is *the sin of UNBELIEF:*

"He that believeth on Him is not condemned: but he that believeth not is condemned already, because he hath not believed in the name of the only begotten Son of God" (John 3:18).

Jesus said to His disciples, "Nevertheless I tell you the truth: It is expedient for you that I go away: for if I go not away, the Comforter will not come unto you; but if I depart, I will send Him unto you. *And when He is come, He will reprove the world of sin,* and of righteousness, and of judgment: *Of sin, because they believe not on me;* of righteousness, because I go to my Father, and ye see me no more; of judgment, because the prince of this world is judged" (John 16:7−11).

Notice in this passage Jesus declared that the Holy Spirit would convict men of SIN (singular), not SINS (plural). Unbelief is the sin that has damned every soul that burns in hell today, and unbelief is the sin that will damn every soul that is consigned to hell from this day forward!

In the passage previously quoted from Romans 10:13−17 we learned that "whosoever shall call upon the name of the Lord shall be saved," but it is impossible for any person to call on God for salvation in the name of Jesus until that person has first heard the Word of God and believed on Jesus as the SON of God, Saviour of sinners. *Unbelief* is the damning sin of man. But Jesus, God in flesh, took away THE SIN THAT DAMNS when He died on the cross. He lives today to take away our sins day by day. He came to declare God's love, God's mercy, and God's salvation to all−"whosoever believeth" in the name of the Son whom God sent to take away the sin of the world.

As Christians, we are invited to confess our sins, and He is faithful and just to forgive us our sins (plural). God's little children should not sin, but as long as we are in this world we will dwell in a body of flesh, and the flesh is weak. Therefore, if any little child does sin, we have an Advocate, One who is our Mediator and the propitiation for our sins:

"If we confess our sins, He is faithful and just to forgive us our sins, and to cleanse us from all unrighteousness. . . My little children, these things write I unto you, that ye sin not. And if any man sin, we have an Advocate with the Father, Jesus Christ the righteous: And He is the propitiation for our *sins:* and not **for** our's only, but also for the *sins* of the whole world" (I John 1:9; 2:1,2).

"For there is one God, and one Mediator between God and men, the Man Christ Jesus" (I Tim. 2:5).

Jesus *did* take away the SIN of the world, and that simply means that He died for every sinner who has ever

been born or ever will be born. His shed blood is sufficient to cover every sin that ever has been or ever will be
committed. We dare not limit the atonement purchased
through His shed blood. I believe in the sovereignty and
the foreknowledge of God, I believe in Bible election and
Bible predestination; but I do NOT believe that Jesus died
for only a few "elect." Certainly there will be those who
will spend eternity in hell, but they will do so because
they "deny the Lord that bought them and *bring upon
themselves* swift destruction" (II Pet. 2:1). Jesus said to
His own people, *"Ye will not* come to me, that ye might
have life" (John 5:40). He wept over Jerusalem: "O Jerusalem, Jerusalem, thou that killest the prophets, and stonest
them which are sent unto thee, *how often would I have
gathered thy children together, even as a hen gathereth
her chickens under her wings, AND YE WOULD NOT!"*
(Matt. 23:37). Peter makes it plain that God is "not willing that any should perish, but that all should come to
repentance" (II Pet. 3:9). Paul tells us that "God was in
Christ, reconciling the WORLD unto Himself" (II Cor.
5:19).

God pity any minister who preaches limited atonement!
The blood of Jesus Christ was shed for "whosoever." The
Scripture teaches no such thing as "universal salvation,"
but neither is "limited atonement" taught. Both of these
doctrines are dangerous heresy and absolutely contrary to
the Word of God. The tragedy of any person ending up
in hell is that Jesus *paid* the sin-debt, He bore the sins of
everyone, and all He asks anyone to do is receive His finished work, believe on His name, and confess Him before
men. Salvation is simple and plain. ALL can be saved
who *want* to be saved, but there is only ONE way—God's
way: *We must enter at the door.* "Verily, verily, I say
unto you, He that entereth not by the door into the sheep-
fold, but climbeth up some other way, the same is a thief
and a robber" (John 10:1). The Lamb of God, through His
shed blood, made atonement sufficient for each and every

person who has ever been born or ever will be born—but
His blood is efficient to believers only.

John's reference to Jesus as "the Lamb" who came to
make the one supreme sacrifice for sin again points out
the deep spiritual truths revealed to him. We do not find
such a statement made by any other disciple before the
Day of Pentecost. Others referred to Jesus as "Lord . . .
Christ . . . the Son of God . . . Messiah . . . King of Israel . . . the Son of David"; but only John the Baptist announced Him as the Lamb who had come to make the one
supreme sacrifice for sin that would satisfy God so thoroughly and so perfectly that it could be said of Him that
He came to take away THE SIN of the entire world. *Before* Calvary John saw the horrible death the Saviour would
die in making the vicarious sacrifice; and *today* many so-
called ministers cannot see that sacrifice, even on *this* side
of Calvary. A sermon without the blood is an empty sermon, and Satan does not care how long nor how loud a
minister preaches so long as he denies the vicarious sacrifice Jesus made when He died for the sin of the world.

Notice in verse 30 that John calls Jesus *"a Man."* He
had just declared Him as "the Lamb of God," but the
Lamb of God was also a Man. Then in the same sentence
John attempts to drive home to the hearts of his listeners
the fact that Jesus was eternal, that He had existed from
all eternity: *"After me cometh a Man which is preferred
before me: for HE WAS BEFORE ME."*

"I knew Him not!" (John did not know Christ's true
identity until God revealed it to him when Jesus came to
him to be baptized in Jordan.) In verse 33 the statement
"I knew Him not" is the same Greek used in verse 31.
John is simply saying, "I knew Him not perfectly, I did
not know Him distinctly and surely, though I did have an
impression when I first saw Him coming to be baptized,
an impression that He was One far greater than myself."

In Matthew's account of the baptism of Jesus we read,
"Then cometh Jesus from Galilee to Jordan unto John, to

be baptized of him. But John forbad Him, saying, I have need to be baptized of thee, and comest thou to me?" (Matt. 3:13,14). And after John baptized Jesus he understood clearly that he had baptized the Messiah. Thus we see that Matthew and John do not contradict each other. There is no doubt that the paths of John and Jesus had crossed before the Lord entered His public ministry, but at that time John did not know Him. Perhaps he thought, "This could be the Messiah," undoubtedly he knew that Jesus was a very unusual and extraordinary person; but at that time he did not know our Lord by sight. He knew Him *perfectly* after he witnessed the Holy Ghost descending and remaining upon Him.

"But that He should be made manifest to Israel, therefore am I come baptizing with water." Here John stresses the fact that he had come to make known to Israel *the Messiah*, the Lamb of God, the Saviour who was to take away their sin, He who was now approaching and whom he was pointing out to them in person. John did not enter the ministry of his own accord—he brought God's message. He did not even seek a following for himself—he sought to point men to the Lamb of God.

"And John bare record . . . ." John publicly testified that our Lord had been visibly and audibly acknowledged and sanctioned by God the Father, and that He was truly the Messiah. *"I saw . . . ."* John plainly *saw* what he is giving here in testimony, and what he saw was divine proof to him that Jesus was truly the Messiah, the Lamb of God.

John saw *"the Spirit descending from heaven like a dove, and it abode upon Him."* The Spirit settled upon Jesus and remained upon Him. "Like a dove" does not necessarily mean that the Spirit was in the shape of a dove. Matthew says the Spirit descended "like a dove," Luke says, "in a bodily shape like a dove"—but the shape of the body is not important. The important note here is the coming of the Spirit upon Jesus and remaining upon Him.

We are not to suppose that the Saviour did not possess the Spirit before His baptism—the Holy Ghost dwelt in Him "without measure" from the time of His incarnation; but the Spirit descending in bodily shape at the baptism of Jesus shows us the Trinity beyond any shadow of doubt: Jesus the Son standing in the water, God the Father speaking from heaven, the Holy Ghost in bodily form settling upon Jesus and remaining upon Him.

Also, we must remember that John the Baptist was a Levite and was quite familiar with the ceremonies through which the Jewish high priests and kings were solemnly inducted into their high offices. Therefore, as testimony to John the Baptist God sent visible recognition from heaven, thus announcing Jesus the Messiah, the anointed Priest, King, and Prophet. John had no doubt that he was in the presence of the Messiah.

"He that sent me to baptize with water, the same said unto me, Upon whom thou shalt see the Spirit descending, and remaining on Him, the same is He which baptizeth with the Holy Ghost." This would certainly indicate that John the Baptist was taught and trained by none other than Almighty God, just as He instructed the prophets in the Old Testament era. No doubt God revealed many things to John which are not recorded, but it is plain here that He revealed the fact that the One upon whom the Holy Ghost descended and remained was the One who would *baptize* with the Holy Ghost. It is Christ alone who will baptize the hearts of believers, and by that baptism unite them to the body, the New Testament Church of which He is the head and the foundation. To be baptized with the Holy Ghost is to be regenerated in heart, united to the body of Christ, possessing Him in the Person of the Holy Spirit, becoming bone of His bone and flesh of His flesh (Eph. 5:30).

None but Christ can baptize with the Spirit; He reserves this privilege and power for Himself. He does not communicate this divine power to earthly ministers. Ephesians

4:5 speaks of "one Lord, one faith, one baptism," and this does not mean *water* baptism.   It means the baptism by which all believers are baptized into the body of Christ: "For as the body is one, and hath many members, and all the members of that one body, being many, are one body: so also is Christ.   For by one Spirit are we all baptized into one body, whether we be Jews or Gentiles, whether we be bond or free; and have been all made to drink into one Spirit" (I Cor. 12:12,13).

Water baptism is of no avail unless the baptism of the Spirit has preceded it.   We are united to the *visible* church by water baptism, but if we have not been united to the *invisible* Church (the body of Christ) by the baptism of the Holy Spirit, then water baptism is but an empty ritual and will do us no good.

It is error to suppose that the Holy Ghost was not known until the Day of Pentecost.   The Holy Ghost was *in the beginning* with the Father just as truly as the Son was there.   Father, Son, and Holy Ghost were in the beginning; the Holy Ghost has manifested Himself in the hearts of believers in every age, and there has never been life eternal *apart* from the Holy Ghost.   However, in this dispensation He operates in the hearts of believers as never before.   In the Old Testament era He came upon men for specific purposes, in specific ministries, and departed; but since the Day of Pentecost He has been here continually, He abides in the heart of every born again believer, and apart from Him no one can be saved and made fit for the kingdom of heaven.

"I saw, and bare record, that THIS IS THE SON OF GOD."   After he baptized Jesus, John had no shadow of doubt in his mind as to who the Messiah was.   He understood perfectly that Jesus was the Messiah, "that Prophet that should come," the only begotten of the Father; and he unhesitatingly testified that this was the Christ, the Son of the living God, whom he had come to announce.   This was the purpose and the aim of John's ministry.

The Next Day

Verses 35—42: *"Again the next day after John stood, and two of his disciples; and looking upon Jesus as He walked, he saith, Behold the Lamb of God! And the two disciples heard him speak, and they followed Jesus.*

"Then Jesus turned, and saw them following, and saith unto them, What seek ye?   They said unto Him, Rabbi, (which is to say, being interpreted, Master,) where dwellest thou?   He saith unto them, Come and see.   They came and saw where He dwelt, and abode with Him that day: for it was about the tenth hour.

"One of the two which heard John speak, and followed Him, was Andrew, Simon Peter's brother.   He first findeth his own brother Simon, and saith unto him, We have found the Messias, which is, being interpreted, the Christ.   And he brought him to Jesus.   And when Jesus beheld him, He said, Thou art Simon the son of Jona: thou shalt be called Cephas, which is by interpretation, A stone."

The first time John the Baptist cried out, "Behold the Lamb of God," there were no visible results—no one was saved insofar as we know; but *"the next day"* John preached the same sermon again: *"Behold the Lamb of God!"* and two of his disciples who heard him *followed Jesus.*   It has been suggested that this was the beginning of the Church; but be that as it may, these two disciples of John heard the testimony of his preaching and followed the Christ to whom he directed them.   It is not the length of a sermon that counts, but what that sermon contains.   John's sermons were short and to the point—"Behold the Lamb of God"—but his testimony bore much fruit.

We know that one of these men who followed Jesus was Andrew, Peter's brother.   The name of the other is not given.   *Andrew* immediately became a soul-winner: *"He first findeth his own brother Simon, and saith unto him, We have found the Messiah . . . the Christ!"*   Like Andrew, when WE find Jesus He becomes precious to us.   We will

seek others, we will go after our unsaved loved ones and
those who have no loved ones to win them. We should
begin at home, but we should also give the Gospel to all
with whom we come in contact.

It is interesting to note that Simon Peter, one of the
greatest Christians who ever lived, was not converted in an
evangelistic campaign under the sound of singing and
preaching. Peter found the Lord through the quiet testimony of his brother Andrew. When Andrew met Jesus and
was convinced that he had found the Messiah, it so thrilled
his heart that he wanted Simon to know Him, too. The
Scriptures do not say a great deal about *Andrew,* but Simon
Peter, brought to Jesus as the result of private, quiet testimony by a relative, became a spiritual giant. He saw no
outstanding miracles, he was not under the influence of a
great "campaign"; he was led to Jesus through the testimony of one who had found the Messiah and wanted everyone else to know it. What a wonderful thing it would
be if all who find Jesus would go home and tell their friends
and family what great things the Lord has done for them!
(Read Mark 5:19.)

Some Bible scholars believe it was John the Beloved who,
along with Andrew, went home with Jesus that day. If
this be true, it is no wonder John emphasizes the *"days"*
of the ministry of Jesus. In John 1:29 he says, "The *next*
day John seeth Jesus"; in John 1:35, "Again the *next* day";
and in John 1:43, "the day *following.*" If John joined Andrew in following Jesus that day, it was indeed a great
day for him.

"John stood, and two of his disciples." Evidently there
was a spot near Bethabara where John the Baptist always
stood to preach. It could be that he had a crude rostrum
or pulpit from which he spoke and where he stood to receive those who came to be baptized.

"And looking upon Jesus as He walked . . . ." I can
picture Jesus as He walked among the crowds, those who
had gathered to hear John deliver another message. At

that time Jesus had not been recognized as the Messiah; the multitudes did not know who He was. It seems reasonable that He moved quietly among the people, in silent meditation.   He was God, but He was also as WE are from the human standpoint, and no doubt as He moved through the crowds He listened to their comments about John and about "that Prophet" who should come. John saw Him walking there, and cried out, *"Behold the Lamb of God!"*

This was the same statement he had made the day before—and nothing happened so far as we know; but the second day he cried again, "Behold the Lamb of God!" and something did happen: two of his disciples *heard* him, *and they "followed Jesus."*

It is scriptural to preach the same sermon more than once, because sometimes the Gospel falls on deaf ears the *first* time, but will be heeded the second time it is proclaimed.   It is good to preach again and again the great truths of salvation.

Here in the very beginning of the Gospel of John we see that "faith cometh by hearing, and hearing by the Word of God" (Rom. 10:17).   There was no miracle, no outstanding visible event.   John the Baptist simply said, "Behold the Lamb of God."   The two disciples *heard* him, they *believed* that the Person to whom he pointed them WAS the Lamb of God, and having that faith, *they followed Him.*   Dear sinner friend, when YOU believe what you hear from the Word of God concerning Jesus, you, too, will become His follower.   When you believe what the Bible declares about Him, you will be saved.   The only way to be saved is to hear the Word of God and believe the record He has given of His Son, the record clearly given in the Word:

"He that believeth on the Son of God hath the witness in himself: he that believeth not God hath made Him a liar; because he believeth not the record that God gave of His Son.   And this is the record, that God hath given to

us eternal life, and this life is in His Son. He that hath
the Son hath life; and he that hath not the Son of God hath
not life. These things have I written unto you that believe
on the name of the Son of God; that ye may know that ye
have eternal life, and that ye may believe on the name of
the Son of God" (I John 5:10—13).

Yes, John's message that day was short, but it was powerful. The Gospel (whether a few words or many) is the
power of God unto salvation; but *many* words of *man's
wisdom* may not accomplish *anything* to the glory of God.
No matter how long a minister preaches, if he preaches
not the Word of God then his time and effort are wasted.
It is the Gospel of God which is "the power of God unto
salvation to every one that believeth" (Rom. 1:16).

Paul defined the Gospel in I Corinthians 15:1—4:

"Moreover, brethren, I declare unto you the Gospel which
I preached unto you, which also ye have received, and
wherein ye stand; by which also ye are saved, if ye keep
in memory what I preached unto you, unless ye have believed in vain. For I delivered unto you first of all that
which I also received, how that *Christ died for our sins*
according to the Scriptures." The heart of Paul's preaching was always the cross, and apart from the message of
the cross there is no salvation. To the Galatians he said,
"God forbid that I should glory, save in the cross of our
Lord Jesus Christ, by whom the world is crucified unto
me, and I unto the world" (Gal. 6:14).

Jesus turned and said to the two disciples, *"What seek
ye?"* Jesus was a man, but He was also God. He was
the Man Christ Jesus here on earth, but at the same time,
He was God in heaven; therefore He knew the hearts and
intent of these two men. As was characteristic of Him,
He did not wait for them to open the conversation. He
wanted them to know that He was ready and willing to do
for them whatever they needed. *"What seek ye*—what can
I do for you? What is your motive in following me? Do
you truly believe that I am the Lamb of God, the Messiah?

What is it that you seek?"

They replied, *"Rabbi,* (which is to say, being interpreted, Master,) *where dwellest thou?"* The parenthetical statement here points out that John was writing primarily to Gentiles. Jewish readers would not have needed the interpretation of "Rabbi" for they knew perfectly well what it meant. The Gospel presented in John's message is for all men—Jews, Gentiles, rich, poor, bond or free, "whosoever."

The fact that these men wanted to go home with Jesus denotes that they wanted fellowship with Him. They wanted to talk with Him and ask Him questions. They sought communion with this Person whom John had declared to be "the Lamb of God who taketh away the sin of the world." There is a lesson for us in this passage. It is scriptural and profitable to invite inquirers into the home, which is one of the finest places to win souls. In these closing days of this Dispensation of Grace, the greater percentage of those who are being saved are being won for Christ in the home. The true ministers of Jesus readily confess that unsaved people are not attending churches today. Through my years as an evangelist I have seen the tremendous decline in the number of sinners who attend revivals—even city-wide campaigns held in auditoriums and in tents, as well as in churches. If we would win the unbelievers for Christ today we must go where they are, and in the quietness of their homes lead them to Him.

These two disciples who followed Jesus wanted to know more about Him, evidently they wanted to talk with Him alone in privacy, and it may be that they felt unworthy to invite Him into their homes. When they asked Him where He lived He did not give them a street address. He simply invited, *"COME AND SEE."*

Here is something extremely interesting to me, rich food for my soul: Insofar as we know, the first words spoken by the Lord Jesus Christ in His public ministry are recorded here in John 1:38. The first words spoken in the

presence of men after his baptism and temptation were,
"What seek ye?"—a question; and the second words were,
"Come and see!"—an invitation.

Today He asks you and me, "What are YOU seeking?"
Friend, what IS your aim in life? What is your first love?
Day by day as you live and work, what are you seeking?
If you do not have peace, joy, assurance, and hope, then
Jesus invites you to come to Him. "Come and see" for
yourself who He is, what He is, what He has to offer you,
and what He will do for you. The most reasonable thing
any man has ever done is come to Jesus; SEE what He
is able to do for a poor, helpless, hopeless human being
who will hear His words and have faith in His finished
work and shed blood. To the seeking soul today, as in
the day of John the Baptist, the invitation of Jesus is simple: *"Come and see!"*

There is no record as to where Jesus was dwelling at
that time. If He lived in a house it was certainly only a
temporary residence somewhere near Bethabara. His testimony in Matthew 8:20 was, "The foxes have holes, and
the birds of the air have nests; but the Son of man hath
not where to lay His head." His abode was no doubt a
very humble place, possibly a cave, for He had nothing of
this world's goods. He borrowed a boat to use as a pulpit
on one occasion, and another time, when He had five thousand guests to feed, He borrowed a lad's lunch with which
to feed them. When He died, He was buried in a borrowed tomb. He who was rich in glory laid aside His riches and became poor, that WE, through HIM, might be
rich.

The Scripture does not tell us where Jesus and the two
disciples went nor where they spent the rest of that day,
but wherever it was, the two men never got over it. Something happened to them that day that changed their lives.
*"They came and saw where He dwelt, and abode with
Him that day: for it was about the tenth hour."* The
Jewish day began at six o'clock in the evening. "The tenth

hour" would have been about four o'clock in the afternoon.
At such a late hour (two hours before nightfall) we doubt
not that the two disciples spent the night with Jesus, although it is not expressly stated.

We are not told what these men asked of Jesus, we do
not know the answers He gave them; but there are no de-
ficiencies in the Word of God and if it had been for our
good and our edification you may rest assured God would
have told us.   All Scripture is profitable, all Scripture is
given by inspiration, and the man of God is perfectly fur-
nished with all that he needs.   Had he needed more, God
would have given more.   We have the perfect law of liberty, the complete Word of God—all that we need to prepare
us for time and for eternity.   Certainly the hours these two
disciples spent with Jesus were blessed hours.

Andrew was not an ordinary man.   Other men became
outstanding generals in the army of the Lord, but Andrew
planned the campaigns, removed the difficulties, prepared
the way for battle.   He heard the message of John the Baptist, he believed that message, and he followed Jesus.   He
spent the day with the Lord, and then *"findeth his own
brother Simon, and saith unto him, We have found the
Messiah . . . and he BROUGHT HIM TO JESUS."*   Andrew had not the slightest doubt that the Person with whom
he had spent the day was the Messiah.   He did not say
to Peter, "We *think* we have found the Messiah," or "We
believe we have found the Messiah."   He simply announced,
with perfect assurance, "We *have found* the Messiah!"   To
be an effective soul-winner, one must have such assurance
as Andrew had.   His testimony assured Peter that Andrew
KNEW the Messiah, and influenced *him* to come to Jesus.

John 6:1—14 records another incident which shows Andrew to have been a very extraordinary man.   A great company of people attended the Bible classes of Jesus, and on
this particular day there were five thousand men, not counting women and children.   Jesus looked out over this great
multitude, and then asked of Philip, "Whence shall we buy

bread, that these may eat?" Philip replied, "Two hundred pennyworth of bread is not sufficient for them, that every one of them may take a little." Philip's mind immediately went to *money* and the amount needed to buy bread for so great a number of people; but while Philip and the other disciples were counting pennies, Andrew was searching for bread—and he found it. He found a lad with five barley loaves and two small fishes—and the fact that he convinced the boy that Jesus needed his lunch bears out the unusual character of Andrew. Have you ever attempted to persuade a little boy to give you his lunch? Try it sometime. Andrew had great persuasive power, and he used that power for Jesus. He and the small boy got together, pooled their resources, and surrendered them to Jesus, leaving the rest to Him. Andrew was fully convinced that Jesus was equal to the occasion. Like Mary when she anointed Jesus with the costly perfume, *he did what he could* and left the results with the Master. When we as believers do what we can, when we do our best to the glory of God, we can leave our efforts in the hands of Jesus and fear not for the outcome.

John 12:20—22 records another incident in the life of Andrew, again revealing his resourcefulness and his complete assurance that Jesus was capable of handling any situation:

"And there were certain Greeks among them that came up to worship at the feast: The same came therefore to Philip, which was of Bethsaida of Galilee, and desired him, saying, Sir, we would see Jesus. *Philip cometh and telleth Andrew: and again Andrew and Philip tell Jesus.*" Philip did not know what to do. Although these Greeks were proselytes, they were *Gentiles*—and up to this time Jesus had instructed the disciples to go only to the lost sheep of the house of Israel, NOT into the way of the Gentiles. This was something entirely new, and Philip did not know what steps to take nor what suggestions to make to the Greeks—but he knew someone who *would* know!

He immediately sought Andrew.

Andrew did not know the answer to Philip's problem, but he knew *Jesus,* the One who holds ALL answers to all problems. Without hesitation Andrew and Philip went to Jesus and told Him that the Greeks wanted to see Him. The solution Jesus offered is found in verses 23 and 32 of the same chapter. He said, "The hour is come, that the Son of man should be glorified. . . And I, if I be lifted up from the earth, will draw ALL men unto me" — yea, Greeks, Gentiles, *"whosoever."* So it was Andrew, that extraordinary soul-winner, who had the great privilege of bringing those Gentiles to Jesus.

Andrew's proclamation, *"We have found the Messiah, the Christ"* indicates a joyful discovery, suggesting that he had been *expecting* to see the Messiah. Even though Andrew probably came from a poor and humble family, he had knowledge of the Old Testament prophecies concerning the coming of Messiah. When Jesus came, the poor and humble people knew more about His coming than did the religious leaders of the nation Israel. The same is true in many instances today. It is the humble saints of God who understand the signs of the times and who are looking for that glorious appearing of the great God and our Saviour Jesus Christ, when He comes the second time to put down evil and set up the glorious kingdom promised throughout the Old Testament.

Andrew brought Simon Peter to Jesus, *"and when Jesus beheld him, He said, Thou art Simon the son of Jona: thou shalt be called Cephas, which is by interpretation, A stone."* Here our Lord declared His omniscience and displayed perfect knowledge of all persons, names, and things. Jesus "knew all men, and needed not that any should testify of man: for He knew what was in man" (John 2:24,25). The Israelites should have recognized such knowledge as an attribute of the Messiah, because Isaiah 11:3 prophesied that He would be "of quick understanding." Only God knows the thoughts of men and the intent of their hearts, and the perfect knowledge Jesus had concerning Simon Peter plainly declared that He was more than man. It offered plain proof of His divinity. He displayed that same knowledge in speaking of Nathanael(v. 47 of our present chapter) and in speaking with the Samaritan woman in John 4:18.

When Andrew brought Simon Peter to Jesus, the Lord's acknowledgement of Peter was unmistakable evidence that He was thoroughly acquainted with his character and fully aware of Peter's impetuous, unstable, fiery nature; yet He said to him, "Thou shalt be called *a stone.*" In other words, "Thou art Simon (meaning unstable and impetuous) but thou shalt be called Cephas (meaning a rock). In spite of your natural temperament of impetuousness and instability, you will become stable and fixed." He gave Simon this new name to signify that through the work of grace in his heart he would become a new creation in Christ — and we know from the scriptural record that this is true. This man who was naturally impulsive and unstable became a firm, solid stone in the New Testament Church. (According to I Peter 2:5, *all* born again believers become "lively stones, are built up a spiritual house, an holy priesthood, to offer up spiritual sacrifices, acceptable to God by Jesus Christ.")

There are some who believe that Jesus gave Simon a new name at this specific time to show that He Himself was the great "I AM" of the Old Covenant, the One who changed Abram to Abraham, Sarai to Sarah, the One who changed Jacob's name to Israel.

As we study these verses you will notice that Jesus selected humble, unlearned men to be the first soul-winners, preachers, and apostles; the first to declare the Gospel message which is the power of God unto salvation. This is strong proof of the truth of the Christian religion. In the first century, Christianity encountered opposition from the chief priests and the religious rulers of that day; the early Christians were persecuted beyond imagination—and yet, in the face of such great odds, Christianity grew and spread throughout the known world—ample proof that Almighty God was in it and behind it.

Nathanael's Confession

Verses 43—51: *"The day following Jesus would go forth into Galilee, and findeth Philip, and saith unto him, Follow me. Now Philip was of Bethsaida, the city of Andrew and Peter. Philip findeth Nathanael, and saith unto him, We have found Him, of whom Moses in the law, and the prophets, did write, Jesus of Nazareth, the son of Joseph. And Nathanael said unto him, Can there any good thing come out of Nazareth? Philip saith unto him, Come and see.*

"Jesus saw Nathanael coming to Him, and saith of him, Behold an Israelite indeed, in whom is no guile! Nathanael saith unto Him, Whence knowest thou me? Jesus answered and said unto him, Before that Philip called thee, when thou wast under the fig tree, I saw thee. Nathanael answered and saith unto Him, Rabbi, thou art the Son of God; thou art the King of Israel.

"Jesus answered and said unto him, Because I said unto thee, I saw thee under the fig tree, believest thou? thou shalt see greater things than these. And He saith unto him, Verily, verily, I say unto you, Hereafter ye shall see heaven open, and the angels of God ascending and descending upon the Son of man."

"The day following . . . ." On the *first* day, Christ was proclaimed (vv. 15—18). On the *second* day, He was specifically pointed out: "Behold the Lamb of God, which taketh away the sin of the world" (v. 29). On the *third* day, He was followed by disciples (vv. 35—37). Now we read of "the day following," which is the *fourth* day. It was on that day that Jesus *"findeth Philip, and saith unto him, Follow me."*

We do not know whether or not Philip heard John the

Baptist announce Jesus as the Lamb of God, but if he *did* hear he did not follow Him that day. Andrew led Peter to Jesus, and Philip was invited by the Lord Himself; but they belonged to the same disciple band, they believed the same truths concerning Jesus, they were led by the same Spirit just as all believers today are led by one Spirit. There is one Lord, one faith, one baptism. There is only one Saviour, one Door, one Shepherd. Not all are converted in the same manner, not all have the same emotional experience; *but all are converted by hearing and believing the Word and receiving the Lord Jesus Christ by faith.*

"Jesus would go forth into Galilee." This has the same meaning as John 4:4, where Jesus "must *needs* go through Samaria." That is, He *willed* to go through Samaria, knowing that He would lead the Samaritan woman to the living water, she would drink, and would become a great soul-winner. The same is true in our present verse. Jesus knew that He would encounter Philip and that Philip would follow Him.

We are not told where Philip was when Jesus said to him, "Follow me." He could have been at Bethabara among the disciples of John, he could have been traveling from Bethabara to Galilee, or he could have been in his hometown of Bethsaida, *"the city of Andrew and Peter."* Since Andrew and Peter had found Jesus and were then traveling with Him, it is not unreasonable to suppose that they invited Him to go by way of their hometown, hoping that some of their friends would follow Him when they heard Him speak. But regardless of where Philip might have been at the time Jesus called him, the invitation was simple: Jesus said to him, *"Follow me."* In John 6:63 Jesus said, "The words that I speak unto you, they are spirit, and they are life." Faith comes by hearing, and hearing by the Word of God. When Jesus invited Philip, "Follow me," the words, accompanied by the Holy Ghost, led Philip to leave everything to follow Jesus and become His disciple.

Philip, like Andrew, seemed to have expected the coming of Messiah. He found Nathanael and said to him, *"We have found Him of whom Moses in the law, and the prophets, did write."* Philip knew that according to the prophets and the books of Moses, a Redeemer would come, the Messiah who would be a Priest, Prophet, and King superior to anyone Israel had ever known. If all the Jews—especially the religious rulers—had understood the Old Testament Scriptures as Andrew and Philip did, they would never have nailed their Messiah to the cross. Even the Samaritan woman testified, "I know that Messias cometh, which is called Christ: when He is come, He will tell us all things" (John 4:25). In spite of the spiritual ignorance of the religious leaders in Israel, there were many who were expecting Messiah to come, and Philip and Andrew were among them.

Notice that Philip called Jesus *"the son of Joseph."* It was commonly reported that Jesus was the son of Joseph, and we know that many of the Jews did accuse Him of being a child of fornication, an illegitimate. No doubt Philip was saying what he had heard others say, perhaps from force of habit, perhaps in ignorance, for as yet the miraculous conception of Christ was hidden from him; but it could be that this spiritual ignorance is what prompted Nathanael to ask, *"Can there any good thing come out of Nazareth?"*

Sometimes young converts have more zeal than knowledge, and they make mistakes that stand in the way of sinners and hinder souls from being saved. However, it speaks well of any young believer to be zealous for God, and it is the responsibility of older Christians to instruct them and help them to rightly divide the Word of truth. Philip had a sincere heart and was acting on all the wisdom, knowledge, and understanding he had. Therefore the Holy Spirit overruled any mistake he might have made, and saw to it that his sincere witnessing came out for good.

Evidently when Philip mentioned "Jesus of *Nazareth*"

Nathanael failed to remember any prophecy that the Messiah would come out of Nazareth. The town was small, obscure, with a reputation that was far from good, and it was only natural that Nathanael should wonder how a prophet of God could come out of such an insignificant, contemptible place as Nazareth.

In Matthew 10:16 Jesus instructed His disciples to be "wise as serpents, and harmless as doves." Philip could easily have started a religious argument with Nathanael, but he did not. In answer to the question, "Can any good thing come out of Nazareth?" he simply invited, *"Come and see!"* We do not know if Philip had heard Jesus answer the two disciples who asked Him where He lived, but at any rate he used the *words* of Jesus in leading Nathanael to the door of salvation. Jesus said, "Come and see," and Philip repeated those words—the words of Jesus, the Word of God which is the power of God unto salvation. Faith comes by hearing and hearing by the Word.

We would do well to follow Philip's example. Even well-meaning Christians sometimes enjoy disputing and arguing concerning the Word of God; but little good comes from such practice. We are to give out the Word and let the Word speak for itself. Many times it is not love of truth that causes men to argue about the Bible; more times than not, it is *pride.* Some Christians enjoy advertising their knowledge of the Word, and opportunities to win souls are lost, even though arguments may be won. It is much better to win a soul than to win an argument.

I am not suggesting that we should *compromise* the Word, not at all. We are not to join hands with liberals and modernists. We are to stand on "thus saith the Lord," and in the words of Paul, "Let God be true, but every man a liar." In soul winning, when we do what we can in giving the invitation and sowing the seed, we should leave the rest with Jesus. Philip did that. Whether or not he realized what he was doing is beside the point. Nathanael had put a question mark around the Christ, and Philip did not argue with him. After all, he was trying to lead him to Jesus, so he simply invited, "Come and see!" Jesus took over from there.

When Jesus saw Nathanael coming toward Him He said, *"Behold an Israelite indeed, in whom is no guile!"* The Lord was quoting here from Psalm 32:2: "Blessed is the man unto whom the Lord imputeth not iniquity, and in whose spirit there is no guile." It stands to reason that Nathanael recognized the words of this Old Testament Scripture. Hebrew authorities tell us that the mark of a true Israelite, in spirit, was not sinlessness or "sinless perfection," but pure sincerity. In His omniscience Jesus knew that Nathanael possessed a sincere heart, no hypocrisy was there, and therefore even before Nathanael spoke a word, Jesus announced him as an Israelite "in whom is no guile."

Nathanel was astonished that Jesus knew so much about him since he had never met Him or talked with Him. "Whence knowest thou me?" he asked, and Jesus replied, "Before that Philip called thee, when thou wast under the fig tree, I saw thee."

What was Nathanael doing under the fig tree? The Scriptures do not tell us. Some Bible scholars believe that he was praying and worshipping God. If he was a student of the Old Testament Scriptures, if he expected the coming of Messiah, then it is possible that he had a favorite place of prayer under the fig tree. Many men of God have had special places where they loved to go and pray. Jesus Himself sought the Garden of Gethsemane as a place of prayer and fellowship with His disciples (John 18:2).

It may be that Nathanael thought he was all alone, with no eye fixed upon him; but Jesus was God in flesh, and "the eyes of the Lord are in every place, beholding the evil and the good" (Prov. 15:3). He sees all of us and *knows* us all. The Word of God tells us that the hairs of our heads are numbered (and Jesus knows the number); and that not one little sparrow falls to the ground without His knowledge. In Matthew 10:29—31 Jesus said to His disciples, "Are not two sparrows sold for a farthing? and one of them shall not fall on the ground without your Father. But the very hairs of your head are all numbered. Fear ye not therefore, ye are of more value than many sparrows." (See also Luke 12:6,7.)

Nathanael was disarmed by the courtesy of the Lord Jesus Christ, and the supernatural knowledge evidenced in the Lord's greeting convinced him that this was indeed the Messiah. He confessed, *"Rabbi, thou art the Son of God; thou art the King of Israel!"* Thus Nathanael confessed that Christ, from the *prehistoric* standpoint, was the only begotten of the Father; and, from the *historic* standpoint, He was the Christ. He confessed that Jesus was the divine Person promised in the Old Testament, "that Prophet" who was to come into the world to redeem sinners, "that King" who was to come and gather together the tribes of Israel and rule over them. Whether or not Nathanael clearly understood the *nature* of the kingdom, we do not know; but he confessed that Jesus was both Son of God and King of Israel—and this is true. One day Jesus will sit on the throne of David and reign over the nation of Israel, and the Church will reign with Him.

The restoration of the kingdom to Israel was one of the last things the disciples fully understood about Jesus. They could not understand why He said He would go into Jerusalem, be arrested, tried, and put to death. They believed He was the Son of God—yes; but they also believed that He was the King of Israel, and they expected Him to set up the kingdom at that time: "When they therefore were come together, they asked of Him, saying, Lord, wilt thou at this time restore again the kingdom to Israel?" (Acts 1:6).

In comparing Nathanael's calling to the conversion of the woman of Samaria in John 4 it is interesting to notice that the discovery of the Lord's perfect knowledge of the most secret things in their lives was what caused them both to believe on Jesus and receive Him into their hearts. Jesus knows just as much about you and me as He knew about Nathanael and the Samaritan woman. Sinner friend, Jesus knows everything about you—everything you do, even the innermost thoughts of your heart. Careless Christian, the same is true of you. It is possible to fool men, but there is no such thing as fooling God!

You will note that Jesus did not rebuke Nathanael for calling Him "King of Israel." He never rebuked anyone for referring to Him in that manner, or as "King of the Jews." In the Annunciation Gabriel foretold that God would give to Jesus the throne of David: "He shall be great, and shall be called the Son of the Highest: and the Lord God shall give unto Him the throne of His father David: and He shall reign over the house of Jacob for ever; and of His kingdom there shall be no end" (Luke 1:32,33).

When the wise men came from the east in search of the child Jesus, they asked, "Where is He that is born King of the Jews?" (Matt. 2:2). When He was nailed to the cross the superscription over His head boldly proclaimed, "THIS IS JESUS THE KING OF THE JEWS!" Christ will be King in Zion, He will reign over the restored twelve tribes of Israel. Then the full confession of Nathanael will be completely fulfilled. All men will then acknowledge Jesus as "the Son of God, and King of Israel."

Jesus said to Nathanael, *"Because I said unto thee, I saw thee under the fig tree, believest thou?"* Greek authorities tell us that this verse in the original reads, "Because I said unto thee, I saw thee under the fig tree, THOU BELIEVEST"—a statement, not a question. Jesus did not need to *ask* Nathanael if he believed; He knew the heart of this man and He had no need to ask. So what He really said was, "Because I told you that I saw you under the fig tree, *you believed,* and that is well and good; but one day you will see far greater things than these, far greater proof that I am the Son of God, Messiah, King of Israel."

"Verily, verily, I say unto you . . . ." No other Gospel writer uses a double "verily." It is a term peculiar to John's Gospel, where it is used twenty-five times. *"Verily"*

means "amen," and where we see a double "verily" the Holy Spirit is saying, "Amen, amen!" A double "verily" is always found at the beginning of a statement made by Christ, and in each instance a tremendous truth or heart-searching fact is declared. Such is true here in this verse:

"Hereafter ye shall see heaven open, and the angels of God ascending and descending upon the Son of man." The truth of this verse was not addressed to Nathanael only. In the preceding verse we read, "THOU shalt see," but here Jesus said, "YE shall see," meaning Nathanael and the other disciples.

Here is the Lord's exposition of Jacob's dream at Bethel. In Genesis 28:12 we read, "And (Jacob) dreamed, and behold a ladder set up on the earth, and the top of it reached to heaven: and behold the angels of God ascending and descending on it." The ladder in Jacob's dream is a type of our Lord and Saviour Jesus Christ as "the Son of man." Nathanael had just confessed that the Lord Jesus was the *Son of GOD,* but notice that when Jesus answered him He referred to Himself as *"the Son of MAN."* When Jesus comes the second time He will come to rule and to judge the world. In John 5:27 Jesus declares that the Father "hath given Him authority to execute judgment also, because He is *the Son of man."* In order that Jesus might execute judgment as King of kings and Lord of lords, the incarnation of the Son of God in human flesh *as the Son of man* was imperative. It was also a divine necessity that God take flesh and the Son of GOD become the Son of MAN, in order that the ladder connecting earth and heaven might open the way for man to enter into the presence of God. *JESUS is that ladder:*

"Forasmuch then as the children are partakers of flesh and blood, He also Himself likewise took part of the same; that through death He might destroy him that had the power of death, that is, the devil; and deliver them who through fear of death were all their lifetime subject to bondage. For verily He took not on Him the nature of angels;

but He took on Him the seed of Abraham. Wherefore in all things it behoved Him to be made like unto His brethren, that He might be a merciful and faithful high Priest in things pertaining to God, to make reconciliation for the sins of the people. For in that He Himself hath suffered being tempted, He is able to succour them that are tempted" (Heb. 2:14—18).

Philippians 2:5—11 shows the self-imposed humiliation of the Son of God as He became the Son of man, taking a body *like unto* sinful man; and also the way of His exaltation AS the Son of man, to the place where He now sits at the right hand of the Majesty on high. There is a Man in heaven now, exalted to heaven's highest place—seated at the right hand of Almighty God.

It may be asked how the Son of God could be called the Son of *man* when He was the seed of the woman, made of a woman without human father (Gal. 4:4,5). The answer is simple when we study and rightly divide the Word of truth: Having descended from the first man Adam through a human mother, Jesus became the Son of man in the *generic*—He became the Son of the human race, Son of humanity, Son of all mankind.

Referring again to the passage in Philippians 2, we read, ". . . Christ Jesus . . . being in the form of God, thought it not robbery to be equal with God: but made Himself of no reputation, and took upon Him the form of a servant, and was made in the likeness of men: and being found in fashion as a man, He humbled Himself, and became obedient unto death, even the death of the cross."

"Being in the form of God" was His rank, His place. Remember, "The Word was with God, and the Word WAS God" (John 1:1). Then, "the Word was made flesh" (John 1:14). Jesus was the Word incarnate. He was equal with God, but He willingly laid aside that equality, that place and form, in order that He might take *our* place, that we might be saved through His blood. Therefore, "He made Himself of no reputation, and took upon Him the form of a servant." In other words, *He emptied Himself*—and it is impossible for the mind of man to comprehend the meaning of that statement! Think of the glory Christ had "before the world was" (John 17:5). With the Father in the beginning, He was co-equal with God in power, in honor, in majesty. Then think what it meant for Him to empty Himself, exchanging the form of God, the place and rank of God, for the rank of a bondservant or slave! The mind of man cannot comprehend such humiliation. Yet that was what Jesus did, willingly, that we might be saved. He who was GOD humbled Himself and was made in the likeness of men—there was no other way by which He could become the ladder from earth to God. In order to become the one Mediator between God and men (I Tim. 2:5) it was a divine imperative that He who was God become the Man, Christ Jesus.

The good Samaritan, seeing the man who had been robbed, wounded, and left half dead, "came where he was" (Luke 10:33). In like manner, Jesus came where sinners were. He left the bosom of the Father and came to earth's sorrows, to lay His life down that we might *have* life. He became obedient unto death, even the death of the cross—a form of execution so humiliating and degrading that no Roman citizen was ever crucified. The Son of God, very God in flesh, came all the way from heaven to become the Son of man, to take our place that we might have life and have it abundantly. He did all of this as the Son of man, *"wherefore God also hath highly exalted Him."*

Who is it that God has so highly exalted? It is not the Son of God *as such,* although He never ceased to BE the Son of God. He was the Son of God in the beginning, He was the Son of God here on earth; but the One exalted is *"the Son of MAN"* as such, and He sits at the right hand of the Majesty where a Man never before sat. Yes, there is a Man in heaven now, the ladder from earth to heaven has been set up, and the way into God's presence has been made manifest by Jesus, He who said, "I am the way, the truth, and the life: no man cometh unto the Father, but by me" (John 14:6).

"Wherefore God also hath highly exalted Him, and given Him a name which is above every name: that at the name of Jesus every knee should bow, of things in heaven, and things in earth, and things under the earth; and that every tongue should confess that Jesus Christ is Lord, to the glory of God the Father" (Phil. 2:9–11).

Daniel saw and prophesied this. We find the record in Daniel 7:13,14: "I saw in the night visions, and, behold, One like the Son of man came with the clouds of heaven, and came to the Ancient of days, and they brought Him near before Him. And there was given Him dominion, and glory, and a kingdom, that all people, nations, and languages, should serve Him: His dominion is an everlasting dominion, which shall not pass away, and His kingdom that which shall not be destroyed."

To John the beloved disciple, God revealed the fulfillment of this prophecy, and John penned it down in Revelation 5:11–14:

"And I beheld, and I heard the voice of many angels round about the throne and the beasts and the elders: and the number of them was ten thousand times ten thousand, and thousands of thousands; saying with a loud voice, Worthy is the Lamb that was slain to receive power, and riches, and wisdom, and strength, and honour, and glory, and blessing. And every creature which is in heaven, and on the earth, and under the earth, and such as are in the sea, and all that are in them, heard I saying, Blessing, and honour, and glory, and power, be unto Him that sitteth upon the throne, and unto the Lamb for ever and ever. And the four beasts said, Amen. And the four and twenty elders fell down and worshipped Him that liveth for ever and ever."

When Jesus comes the second time in power and great glory to reign, the words of this text will be literally and fully fulfilled. Heaven will be opened and there will be constant communication between heaven and earth. The tabernacle of God will be with men and the angels will visibly minister to the King of Israel, King of all the earth— the Lord Jesus Christ, Son of God and King of kings.

The words Jesus spoke to Nathanael in verse 51 of our present chapter bear a marked resemblance to what He said to the Pharisees in Matthew 26:64: "Hereafter shall ye see the Son of man sitting on the right hand of power, and coming in the clouds of heaven."

Yes, Jesus was the Son of God—very God; but He became the Son of man, very man. He was ideal manhood, He was man as God intended man to be and as *redeemed men, through HIM,* will one day be.

It is interesting to note that in this first chapter of John's Gospel, Jesus is referred to as "the Word . . . God . . . Light . . . the True Light . . . the only begotten of the Father . . . Jesus Christ . . . the only begotten Son . . . the Lord . . . the Lamb of God . . . Jesus . . . a Man . . . the Son of God . . . Rabbi . . . Teacher . . . Messiah . . . Christ . . . the son of Joseph . . . the King of Israel . . . THE SON OF MAN." Certainly this chapter is full of *Jesus, Son of God, very God in flesh.*

CHAPTER II

1. And the third day there was a marriage in Cana of Galilee; and the mother of Jesus was there:

2. And both Jesus was called, and his disciples, to the marriage.

3. And when they wanted wine, the mother of Jesus saith unto him, They have no wine.

4. Jesus saith unto her, Woman, what have I to do with thee? mine hour is not yet come.

5. His mother saith unto the servants, Whatsoever he saith unto you, do it.

6. And there were set there six waterpots of stone, after the manner of the purifying of the Jews, containing two or three firkins apiece.

7. Jesus saith unto them, Fill the waterpots with water. And they filled them up to the brim.

8. And he saith unto them, Draw out now, and bear unto the governor of the feast. And they bare it.

9. When the ruler of the feast had tasted the water that was made wine, and knew not whence it was: (but the servants which drew the water knew;) the governor of the feast called the bridegroom,

10. And saith unto him, Every man at the beginning doth set forth good wine; and when men have well drunk, then that which is worse: but thou hast kept the good wine until now.

11. This beginning of miracles did Jesus in Cana of Galilee, and manifested forth his glory; and his disciples believed on him.

12. After this he went down to Capernaum, he, and his mother, and his brethren, and his disciples: and they continued there not many days.

13. And the Jews' passover was at hand, and Jesus went up to Jerusalem,

14. And found in the temple those that sold oxen and sheep and doves, and the changers of money sitting:

15. And when he had made a scourge of small cords, he drove them all out of the temple, and the sheep, and the oxen; and poured out the changers' money, and overthrew the tables;

16. And said unto them that sold doves, Take these things hence; make not my Father's house an house of merchandise.

17. And his disciples remembered that it was written, The zeal of

thine house hath eaten me up.

18. Then answered the Jews and said unto him, What sign shew-est thou unto us, seeing that thou doest these things?

19. Jesus answered and said unto them, Destroy this temple, and in three days I will raise it up.

20. Then said the Jews, Forty and six years was this temple in building, and wilt thou rear it up in three days?

21. But he spake of the temple of his body.

22. When therefore he was risen from the dead, his disciples re-membered that he had said this unto them; and they believed the scripture, and the word which Jesus had said.

23. Now when he was in Jerusalem at the passover, in the feast day, many believed in his name, when they saw the miracles which he did.

24. But Jesus did not commit himself unto them, because he knew all men,

25. And needed not that any should testify of man: for he knew what was in man.

Before entering a verse-by-verse discussion of this chapter we should note that we find here two manifestations of the power of the Lord Jesus Christ: the first, in private; the second, in public.

The first manifestation of His power was at a humble wedding in the small Galilaean town of Cana and was performed before a few servants. It came from a heart of love, sympathy, and courtesy, to relieve the embarrassment of friends—although the miracle goes much deeper than merely supplying refreshments for a wedding.

The second manifestation of His power was in the court of the temple at Jerusalem and was performed before the leaders of the Jewish religion. Here, His power was dem-onstrated in righteous indignation as He vindicated the sacredness of His Father's house from the profane indiffer-ence of the priests and leaders. These two manifestations of the power of Jesus are typical of His entire earthly min-istry—mercy and compassion combined with judgment and justice.

Verse 1:   *"And the third day there was a marriage in Cana of Galilee; and the mother of Jesus was there."*

What is *"the third day"* here?   Most probably it was
the third day after the last event described in chapter 1;
the third day after Nathanael was brought to Jesus and became one of His disciples.

"There was a marriage in Cana of Galilee."   John 21:2
tells us that Nathanael lived in Cana, and it is highly
probable that he invited Jesus to visit the place where he
lived, which would account for the Lord's being in Cana
at this time.   The Old Testament does not mention that
village, but Bible authorities tell us that it was not far
from Nazareth.

"The mother of Jesus was there."   It would seem that
Mary was related to the bride or groom in some way, and
because of this relationship she was present.   It stands to
reason that she was even assisting in the arrangements for
the marriage feast since she gave the servants orders concerning Jesus and what they should do.

We note no mention of Joseph here, and some Bible commentators tell us that Joseph had died; but this seems unlikely since John 6:42 tells us that the Jews at Capernaum
called Jesus "the son of Joseph, *whose father and mother
we know,"* and this would suggest that Joseph was still
living.   However, it is not important that Joseph is not
mentioned here.   Had God intended for us to know more
about him it would be recorded in His Word, and it is of
little profit to speculate concerning such things.

Verse 2:   *"And both Jesus was called, and His disciples,
to the marriage."*

Jesus was no doubt invited to the marriage as the son
of Mary, and the disciples were invited as His friends and
companions.   It stands to reason that in this early period
in His ministry He was not known as the Messiah, nor
even as a great teacher—and certainly not as *the Saviour.*
The disciples here referred to would have been only those
who had been called up to this time, though they were
not then known as the leaders in Christianity.

The fact that Christ attended a wedding at the very outset of His ministry sanctions the marriage relationship. We know that marriage was ordained of God in the Garden of Eden, and Jesus here put His stamp of approval upon that institution. His presence at the wedding in Cana was "Amen!" to the first marriage in Eden when God performed the first wedding ceremony for Adam and Eve. Marriage is a sacred institution in the sight of Almighty God, and without the presence of Christ a marriage is not complete. There can be no happy marriage in the true sense of happiness unless Jesus is invited to the ceremony and then invited home with the bride and groom. God cannot bless a marriage where Christ is not present. Remember, "Whether therefore ye eat, or drink, *or WHATSOEVER ye do, do all to the glory of God"* (I Cor. 10:31). That verse means exactly what it says.

Verse 3: *"And when they wanted wine, the mother of Jesus saith unto Him, They have no wine."*

This verse suggests that Mary was careless here. If she recognized the deity of Jesus she knew that He was more than man; she knew that He was God in flesh; and since He was God in flesh, He was omniscient and He *knew* they had no wine. It would seem that Mary, acting in the flesh, was determined to exert her parental authority, and therefore suggested to Jesus what she thought should be done. Did she want Him to perform a miracle and thereby become the center of attraction at the feast? Like all mothers she was naturally proud of her Son, and based on the answer Jesus gave her it is not unreasonable to suppose that she wanted Him to be recognized and acclaimed. Luke 1:28 tells us that Mary was blessed *"among* women," but nowhere are we told that she was blessed *"ABOVE women."* She therefore had no right to suggest to God what He should do, and since Jesus was God in flesh, that was exactly what she was doing. Certainly God does not need our recommendation. Mary erred here. I doubt not that she was sincere in what she did, and that it was with deep affection that she yearned to bring honor and glory to her Son, as any other mother would have done.

Verse 4: *"Jesus saith unto her, Woman, what have I to do with thee? mine hour is not yet come."*

Jesus was not disrespectful to His mother when He called her "woman." In that day the term was not harsh or unkind; it was used when addressing females of all classes and relationships. We find the same form of address in John 19:26 when Jesus spoke to Mary from the cross: "When Jesus therefore saw His mother, and the disciple standing by, whom He loved, He saith unto His mother, Woman, behold thy son!"

Also, in addressing Mary as "woman" He called attention to the fact that He was more than man; He was the Son of Almighty God. If He had called Mary "mother" He would have drawn attention to *human* relationship, but by addressing her as "woman" He showed that it was *God* speaking to her in this instance.

"Woman, what have I to do with thee?" In other words, "What is there in common between us—God in flesh, and you, an ordinary woman?" The same grammatical construction is used here in the Greek as appears in Matthew 8:29 where the demons cried out, "What have we to do with thee, Jesus, thou Son of God? Art thou come hither to torment us before the time?"

Jesus was not angry with Mary, He was not resentful of her suggestion; but by the answer He gave her in gentle rebuke He let her know that she must allow Him to act in His own way and according to divine design. Luke 2:51 tells us that Jesus was subject unto His parents; but now His public ministry had begun and His time of subjection to Mary and Joseph was ended. He was in the world to do the will of God, not the will of man, and henceforth He would take instructions from none save His heavenly Father.

Jesus was omniscient; He knew the end in the beginning, and He knew that in the days to come the system of idolatry would ascribe honors to Mary that no human should have. He knew that she would be called "Queen of Angels . . . Mother of God . . . Holy Virgin," and a score of other names that should never be used with mortal application. He therefore refused to contribute in any way to the system of idolatry which would eventually spring up. It is true that Mary was the mother of our Lord, and God honored and blessed her; but she was only a woman. She was a virgin, yes—but she was not divine, and God never intended that she should be worshipped as she is today by millions!

"Mine hour is not yet come." The "hour" to which Jesus here referred was the hour of His humiliation, the hour of His suffering, the hour when He would take sin and nail it to His cross, the hour when He would die the most shameful death any man could die, that others might live and live abundantly; but why should He make such reference at *the marriage feast* when Mary, in a sense, attempted to tell Him what to do and when to do it? The answer is this: He was speaking of that hour when He would be subject to man's will—when man would lay hands on Him, arrest Him, scourge Him, nail Him to a cross and lift Him up to die between two thieves. In that hour He would be subject to the hands of men. In that hour He would cry out, "My God, my God! Why hast *thou* forsaken me?" But *until* that hour He was not to be ordered by man or woman! He was here to be about His Father's business, to do His Father's will, and to finish the work His Father had sent Him to do.

The Gospel of John contains eight references to that "hour":

1. Our present verse—*"Mine HOUR has not yet come."*

2. John 7:30: "Then they sought to take Him: but no man laid hands on Him, *because His HOUR was not yet*

come."

3. John 8:20: "These words spake Jesus in the treasury, as He taught in the temple: and no man laid hands on Him; *for His HOUR was not yet come.*"

4. John 12:23: "And Jesus answered them, saying, *The HOUR is come, that the Son of man should be glorified.*"

5. John 12:27: "Now is my soul troubled; and what shall I say? Father, *save me from this HOUR:* but for this cause came I *unto this HOUR.*"

6. John 13:1: "Now before the feast of the passover, *when Jesus knew that His HOUR was come* that He should depart out of this world unto the Father, having loved His own which were in the world, He loved them unto the end."

7. John 16:32: "Behold, *the HOUR cometh, yea, is now come,* that ye shall be scattered, every man to his own, and shall leave me alone: and yet I am not alone, because the Father is with me."

8. John 17:1: "These words spake Jesus, and lifted up His eyes to heaven, and said, *Father, the HOUR is come;* glorify thy Son, that thy Son also may glorify thee."

Verse 5: *"His mother saith unto the servants, Whatsoever He saith unto you, do it."*

There is a lesson here for us all: I am sure that most of us, if we will be honest with ourselves, have at times told the Lord what to do, instead of seeking *His will* in our lives. Our duty is to commit our all to Him, trust Him to lead us, and rest securely in the assurance that He will always lead in the right path at the right time and in the right way. Psalm 37:5 tells us, "Commit thy way unto the Lord; trust also in Him; and He shall bring it to pass." Proverbs 3:6 says, "In ALL thy ways acknowledge Him, and He shall direct thy paths." Mary accepted the Lord's rebuke without a word. Evidently she recognized His omniscience, His right to act according to His own will and wisdom, and she committed the need entirely into His hands.

To the servants Mary said, *"Whatsoever He saith unto you, DO IT!"* Most Christians are willing to do *something* Christ says do, but not many are willing to do WHATSOEVER He says. It is the duty of the believer to render simple, wholehearted obedience to Jesus Christ *in ALL things.* We are not our own, we are bought with a price, and we should yield soul, spirit, and body to Him. We *must* do what He says if we hope to have the blessings of God upon our life and stewardship. We should listen to His Word, and "whatsoever He says," we should perform it with all of our heart.

Verse 6:   *"And there were set there six waterpots of stone, after the manner of the purifying of the Jews, containing two or three firkins apiece."*

The presence of several waterpots was not unusual, since this would be a Jewish ceremony, and the Jews' ceremonial washings required much water. Since John's Gospel is the "salvation Gospel," written to Gentiles as well as Jews, John gives details especially for Gentile readers. Mark tells us, "For the Pharisees, and all the Jews, except they wash their hands oft, eat not, holding the tradition of the elders" (Mark 7:3). Therefore we know there was no particular significance in the several waterpots at the feast—they were not brought in for that one occasion. They were often used by the Pharisees and Jews.

But notice that there were not five waterpots, not seven, not ten—there were SIX, and six is the number of man. God created Adam on the sixth day. Revelation 13:18 tells us that the number of the beast who declares that he is God even though he is just a man, is to be six hundred, three score, and six—or, 666. The six waterpots, then, are a symbol of man. Man without God is lost, and these waterpots, apart from the miracle of Jesus, were of no value to the feast. They had been set aside for ceremonial purposes, but they had no value because they were empty, just as every man is empty without the water of life.

Each of the waterpots would hold *"two or three firkins."*
It would be difficult to estimate just how much water these
pots would hold, because there is much uncertainty and
contradiction concerning the precise quantity of liquid contained in the ancient measure of a "firkin." But assuming
that these were especially *large* containers of several gallons each, we must bear in mind that a Jewish marriage
feast lasted several days and a great number of people attended. Thus many gallons of wine would have been
needed.

Verse 7: *"Jesus saith unto them, Fill the waterpots with
water. And they filled them up to the brim."*

These words describe the duty of all believers—especially
ministers, teachers, evangelists, missionaries: We are to hear
and obey the voice of the Lord Jesus. If we hear what
He says and do as He bids, we need not worry about the
results. It is our duty to fill the waterpots, but we cannot
make the water into wine. Only Christ can do that. It
is our duty to sow the seed of the Gospel, but we cannot
save the sinner. Christ alone can change the unbelieving
heart.

Please notice, the servants filled the waterpots *"up to
the brim."* This left no room for any other substance to
be put into the pots to change the water into wine. It
was JESUS who wrought the change, and so it is with the
conversion of a soul. Nothing need be added to God's instruction.

Verse 8: *"And He saith unto them, Draw out now, and
bear unto the governor of the feast. And they bare it."*

I believe it was at this moment that the miracle happened: *simply by an act of His will Jesus changed the
water into wine*—and why should this be thought difficult
for Him? After all, since all things were made by Him and
for Him, since He created the grapevine and made it to

bear grapes, since He created matter out of nothing, certainly it would not be difficult for Him to change one kind of matter into another form.   When we believe in God it is not difficult to believe in the miracles of both the Old and the New Testaments.   To doubt God's miracles is to doubt GOD, because our God is a God of miracles and there is nothing too hard for HIM.

The servants poured water into the waterpots at the Lord's bidding; He then commanded, *"Draw out now,"* and that which was drawn from the waterpots was wine— the best wine the guests had received at the marriage feast. Jesus could have filled the pots with wine *without* first putting water into them, but everything He did on earth was done for a reason and with a purpose.   *Water* is a symbol of the written Word of God.   In John 15:3 Jesus said to His disciples, "Now ye are *clean through the WORD* which I have spoken unto you."   In Ephesians 5:26 we are told that the Church is cleansed *"with the washing of water by the WORD."*   Jesus said to Nicodemus, "Except a man be born of water and of the Spirit, he cannot enter into the kingdom of God" (John 3:5)—and again, the *water* is the WORD.   The Word of God is the living water, the power of God unto salvation.   When we hear the Word, *receive* the Word, then the water of the Word brings salvation to the thirsty soul and springs up into everlasting life in the heart.   So Jesus instructed the servants to put water into the waterpots—and then He changed the water into wine.

Here is a beautiful picture of the regeneration of an unbeliever.   First we see his condition—he is *empty,* like the waterpots.   He has a heart of stone—cold, lifeless, useless. Man without Christ is dead in trespasses and sins.   As the waterpots were empty, so is the unregenerate man.   No man can know real joy until he becomes a believer.   Just as the waterpots were filled with water at the command of Jesus, the unregenerate man is given the water of the Word, he believes the Word, and the miracle of the new birth takes place in his heart.

Jesus told the servants to draw out and bear the wine *"unto the governor of the feast,"* and they did as they were bidden.   We might refer to the governor of the feast as the head waiter, the gentleman in charge.   It was his duty to see that enough food and refreshments were provided.   In verse 9 the same Greek word is rendered *"ruler of the feast."*   Such a person was always present at the feasts of the Greeks and the Romans.

Verses 9 and 10: *"When the ruler of the feast had tasted the water that was made wine, and knew not whence it was: (but the servants which drew the water knew;) the governor of the feast called the bridegroom, and saith unto him, Every man at the beginning doth set forth good wine; and when men have well drunk, then that which is worse: but thou hast kept the good wine until now."*

We know that the ruler of the feast knew nothing of the water having been put in the waterpots.   The servants had not consulted him about a new supply of wine; they had obeyed *Jesus*.   Mary had instructed them to do whatever He commanded, and they did so without asking the governor's permission.   There is nothing here to indicate that the *disciples* knew what had taken place between Jesus and the servants concerning the water and the waterpots.   Only Jesus and the servants knew.   Thus the testimony of the ruler of the feast becomes extremely important: He declared that this was *much better wine* than had been served at the beginning of the feast.   The *reality* of the change from water into wine is proved by the statement made by the ruler of the feast.   Notice, he put the cup to his lips and *"tasted"* the wine, and noticed something unusual about it: It was real wine, but it was better and purer than any wine mortal man had yet tasted.

I am sure that many are wondering just what I believe about this wine.   Was it the kind of wine that can be purchased in liquor stores and wineries today?   Was it the kind of wine that would make a man drunk and cause him to do the things men do in our day under the influence of intoxicants? My answer is according to the Word of God —the only place to find Bible answers to Bible questions:

In the Bible, wine is an emblem of joy. In Psalm 104: 14,15 we read, "He causeth the grass to grow for the cattle, and herb for the service of man: that he may bring forth food out of the earth; *and wine that maketh glad the heart of man,* and oil to make his face to shine, and bread which strengtheneth man's heart." Judges 9:13 speaks of *"wine, which cheereth God and man."*

Speaking of *intoxicating* wine, Proverbs 20:1 tells us, *"Wine is a mocker, strong drink is raging: and whosoever is deceived thereby is not wise."* Then in Proverbs 23:29—32 we read, "Who hath woe? who hath sorrow? who hath contentions? who hath babbling? who hath wounds without cause? who hath redness of eyes? *They that tarry long at the wine; they that go to seek MIXED wine. Look not thou upon the wine when it is red, when it giveth his colour in the cup, when it moveth itself aright. AT THE LAST IT BITETH LIKE A SERPENT, AND STINGETH LIKE AN ADDER!"*

Habakkuk 2:15 warns, *"Woe unto him that giveth his neighbour drink, that puttest thy bottle to him, and makest him drunken* also, that thou mayest look on their nakedness!" Now would you accuse Jesus of doing what God's Word specifically commands us NOT to do? Would you dare accuse the Son of God of putting wine to the lips of those at a marriage feast if that wine would make them drunk? No, my friend—what Jesus made on that day was non-alcoholic, new wine that had no fermentation. Anyone who has visited the Holy Land knows that new wine is nothing more than grapejuice. In that country even the grapes on the vine are sometimes referred to as "wine," and before we judge the Lord and accuse Him of operating a winery we must study the times and the customs of the people. Jesus did not manufacture wine to make the wedding guests drunk; He simply supplied new wine to replenish the refreshments at the marriage supper.

Upon *tasting* the new supply of wine the governor of the feast was so pleased that he called the bridegroom and said to him, "It is customary to serve *good* wine at the beginning of a feast, and inferior wine at the last; but *you* have done a very unusual thing, saving the best until last."

"When men have well drunk" in the Greek means "when men have drunk *sufficiently (or freely)."* It does not mean that they drank until they were drunk. This is another proof that the wine Jesus made was not fermented wine: the people drank FREELY, but were not intoxicated. Jesus came into the world to *deliver* drunkards, harlots, thieves, murderers—He did not come to contribute to *making* them such!

There is a good spiritual lesson in the phrase, *"thou hast kept the good wine until now."* The world gives its best first, and gives its worst last. *Sin is inviting,* there is pleasure in sin—but only for a season. At the end of the way the pleasures of sin turn to heartaches and tears, and in the final analysis will end in everlasting destruction in the lake of fire throughout eternity. The longer a sinner serves the world, the more disappointment he finds. The gifts the world has to offer soon become commonplace; they never satisfy. On the other hand, at the right hand of Jesus are "pleasures forevermore" (Psalm 16:11). He gives "joy unspeakable and full of glory" (I Pet. 1:8). ". . . No good thing will He withhold from them that walk uprightly" (Psalm 84:11). Jesus said to His disciples, "In the world ye shall have tribulation: but be of good cheer; I have overcome the world" (John 16:33). The Christian life is not an easy life, but like Jesus, we look *beyond* this vale of tears to the glory that is set before us (Heb. 12:2). The believer counts it joy to suffer for Jesus because He loved us and laid down His life for us. Yes, the world and sin give the best in the beginning, but "every day with Jesus is sweeter than the day before," and the longer we live for Him the better life becomes!

Verse 11:   *"This beginning of miracles did Jesus in Cana of Galilee, and manifested forth His glory; and His disciples believed on Him."*

This statement is clear: *this was the first miracle our Lord performed.*   There is absolutely no Scripture to substantiate the erroneous teaching of some groups that Jesus worked miracles as a child.   Such teaching is man-made.

It was not by accident that Christ worked His first miracle at a marriage feast. We can name several reasons why this statement is true:

1. *Marriage was the first institution ordained and set up by Almighty God.*   God is the author of marriage; He performed the first marriage in the Garden of Eden, between the first man and woman who ever lived on this earth.   It is therefore fitting that Christ (who was God in flesh) should perform *His first miracle* at a marriage feast.

2. *The first miracle performed on earth by man was a miracle of transformation:*   "When Pharaoh shall speak unto you, saying, Shew a miracle for you: then thou shalt say unto Aaron, Take thy rod, and cast it before Pharaoh, and it shall become a serpent" (Ex. 7:9). The first miracle performed by *the Son of man* was of the same nature—a miracle of transformation.

3. John the Baptist, forerunner of Jesus, was a man of unusual diet—*locusts and wild honey;* but the public appearance of Jesus was at a *feast* where there was food in abundance.

4. Jesus will be present at *another* great marriage feast: "Let us be glad and rejoice, and give honour to Him: for the marriage of the Lamb is come, and His wife hath made herself ready.   And to her was granted that she should be arrayed in fine linen, clean and white: for the fine linen is the righteousness of saints. And he saith unto me, Write,

Blessed are they which are called unto the marriage supper
of the Lamb.   And he saith unto me, These are the true
sayings of God.   And I fell at his feet to worship him. And
he said unto me, See thou do it not: I am thy fellow-
servant, and of thy brethren that have the testimony of
Jesus: worship God: for the testimony of Jesus is the spirit
of prophecy" (Rev. 19:7—10).

5. The miracle at the marriage in Cana was done *that Je-
    sus might manifest forth His glory* (v. 11).   When He
attends the marriage supper in the sky His glory will also
be manifested.   Paul tells us about it in Ephesians 2:4—7:
"But God, who is rich in mercy, for His great love where-
with He loved us, even when we were dead in sins, hath
quickened us together with Christ, (by grace ye are saved;)
and hath raised us up together, and made us sit together
in heavenly places in Christ Jesus: That in the ages to
come He might shew the exceeding riches of His grace in
His kindness toward us through Christ Jesus."

Jesus did not attend the marriage at Cana simply to be
present at a social gathering nor to be a guest at a feast.
He was there for a spiritual reason.   He *"manifested forth
His glory; AND HIS DISCIPLES BELIEVED ON HIM."*
This does not mean that these men had not *believed on
Jesus*—they were already saved, they were already His disciples; but it means that their faith was *increased*.   They
believed more confidently, more implicitly; their faith in
the Lord Jesus Christ was stronger *AFTER witnessing the
miracle* at the marriage in Cana.   There are tremendous
truths to be learned by studying the miracles of Jesus. Modernists and liberals deny the miracles of our Lord, but to
me, *they were designed to prove His divinity!*
This first miracle of Jesus was not a grand parade, it
was not an outstanding display of power and glory.   He
simply supplied the common, ordinary things—refreshment
at a wedding—which proves to me that He is concerned
about the small perplexities of life, the common things. He

is "touched with the feeling of our infirmities. This miracle proves to me that He keeps every promise. He promised to supply all of our human needs—and He will do just that. I am so glad He came to redeem my soul!

Verse 12: *"After this He went down to Capernaum, He, and His mother, and His brethren, and His disciples: and they continued there not many days."*

I believe every word in the Bible was given by the Holy Spirit to holy men, and they penned down the words as God gave them. Here we note that Jesus "went *down*" to Capernaum. The village of Cana was in the hill country; Capernaum was a town on the shore of the Sea of Galilee and was therefore much lower than Cana. It may seem a small thing that the Holy Spirit should tell us that Jesus traveled *down* from Cana to Capernaum, but the Scriptures are inspired and such details prove beyond any shadow of doubt that *man* did not write the Bible.

Some Bible teachers believe that Capernaum was the place where Jesus spent most of His time—we might call it His "home base." Matthew 4:13 tells us that "leaving Nazareth, He came and dwelt in Capernaum." Certainly He did more miracles at Capernaum than at any other place, and there is no other city upon which He declared such severe judgment: *"And thou, Capernaum, which art exalted unto heaven, shalt be brought down to hell: for if the mighty works, which have been done in thee, had been done in Sodom, it would have remained until this day. But I say unto you, That IT SHALL BE MORE TOLERABLE FOR THE LAND OF SODOM IN THE DAY OF JUDGMENT, THAN FOR THEE"* (Matt. 11:23,24).

In the days of our Lord Capernaum was a wealthy and important city; but today it has so completely passed away that its exact location can only be approximated. Archeologists have dug up stones which they believe to have been in the synagogue there in the days when Jesus ministered in the city, and anyone who visits the Sea of Galilee can see the little synagogue which has been reconstructed from those stones; but it is impossible to trace the exact boundaries of what was once the city of Capernaum.

The mother of Jesus went with Him to Capernaum—and again there is no mention of Joseph. It is doubtful that Mary was a constant companion of Jesus throughout His earthly ministry, but she was with Him at Cana and we see her with Him here at Capernaum. In Matthew 12:46 we read, "While (Jesus) yet talked to the people, behold, His mother and His brethren stood without, desiring to speak with Him," and we know that she was present at the crucifixion.

Our present verse tells us that *"His brethren"* and *"His disciples"* also went with Him. God was the Father of Jesus, but it cannot be proved that other children were not born to Mary and Joseph *after* Jesus was born. I personally believe that Mary gave birth to other children, and thus *"His brethren"* would be related to Jesus from the standpoint of the flesh through Mary. They were sons of Joseph; *JESUS* was the Son of God. We read in John 7:5 that some of His relatives did not believe on Him.

In these first twelve verses of the second chapter of John's Gospel we find many rich spiritual lessons. First of all, "this *beginning* of miracles" (His first miracle) "did Jesus in Cana of Galilee." Also from these verses we learn how honorable is the estate of matrimony in the sight of Almighty God and Christ Jesus the Son. Marriage is not a sacrament: it is simply a state of life ordained by God the Father for man's benefit and happiness. God is the author of matrimony; He performed the first marriage, and for a couple to be truly happy, marriage must be undertaken reverently, soberly, and most of all *in the fear of God.* "Marriage is honourable in all, and the bed undefiled: but whoremongers and adulterers God will judge" (Heb. 13:4).

This passage also points out that it is not a sin, it is not unlawful in the sight of God, to rejoice and be merry.

Jesus put His stamp of approval on the marriage feast by attending, and had it been sinful He most assuredly would not have been there.   Christianity does not take the joy out of living.   On the contrary, *Christianity brings life,* and life abundant.

When the disciples witnessed the miracle at Cana, their faith was increased and they trusted Jesus more and became more dedicated than they had been up to that moment.

The First Passover: Jesus Cleanses the Temple

Verses 13 and 14: *"And the Jews' passover was at hand, and Jesus went up to Jerusalem, and found in the temple those that sold oxen and sheep and doves, and the changers of money sitting."*

So long as the dispensation of the Law of Moses continued, Jesus gave all due honor to the law and the old economy regardless of the unworthiness of the hands that administered the rituals and feasts in the days when He cleansed the temple.   If we study the Gospels carefully we will learn that the ministry of Jesus *began* just before a passover feast and *ended* with a passover.   His ministry lasted approximately three years, perhaps a bit more.   If His ministry lasted through four passovers, then it would have been three and one-half years.   John specifically names *three* passovers attended by our Lord—our present passage; John 6:4; and John chapters 18 and 19, which give the account of the crucifixion.   If John 5:1 was also a passover feast (and Bible scholars do not agree on this) then Jesus kept *four* passovers.   The Jews observed many feasts.   John is the only Gospel writer who gives the account of Christ's attendance at this particular one, and all the circumstances which went along with His visit to Jerusalem at this time.

The *oxen, sheep, and doves* were in the temple courts to be sold to the Jews who traveled many miles to come to the passover and other feasts.   Their worship required sacrifices, and therefore the animals were there to be sold for that purpose. The money changers were there to change foreign currency into local money so that the worshippers might purchase the animals for sacrifice. It was not a sin to buy an animal or a dove to be offered in sacrifice. The sin was in the fact that the money changers and those who sold the animals were making *big business* out of what should have been sacred as unto the Lord. Religion is becoming "big business" in *our* day, and many men are making merchandise of the souls of men. Undoubtedly the tendency of the whole system was profane in the sight of the Lord Jesus when He stepped into His Father's temple.

It is not unreasonable to suppose that the priests and religious leaders allowed this because they were connected with the merchants and money changers. They shared in the profits, perhaps they even rented space to them in the house of God. We have almost the same thing going on today in a somewhat different manner. Many churches buy and sell to raise money for various phases of their work— but *that is not God's plan* for supporting His Church and its work. "God loveth a cheerful giver" (II Cor. 9:7), and when a church must sell food and other commodities to pay bills, that church is *spiritually dead!*

The men who sold animals and changed money in the temple had turned the house of God into a place of merchandise. In God's sight, good intentions do not justify unscriptural actions. There is much in organized religion today which is definitely unscriptural, definitely not in the program of the Holy Spirit for this Church Age.

This was Christ's first visit to the temple in Jerusalem after the beginning of His public ministry, and constitutes partial fulfillment of a prophecy in Malachi 3:1: "Behold, I will send my messenger, and he shall prepare the way before me: and the Lord, whom ye seek, shall suddenly come to His temple, even the messenger of the covenant, whom ye delight in: behold, He shall come, saith the Lord of hosts." This prophecy will be literally and *completely* fulfilled when Jesus comes the second time; but here it was fulfilled in part. The Jews were expecting a great *military* leader who would deliver them from the bondage of Rome. They looked for a great and glorious Messiah who would suddenly appear and drive out the oppressors, and they did not recognize the true Messiah when He suddenly appeared in His Father's house.

What Jesus did that day was open testimony to Israel that their first and foremost need was *NOT to be delivered from the rule of Rome* but to be delivered from the form and ceremony of their own religion, to purify their worship and their temple, and to turn their eyes to God instead of to the observance of form and ritual.

Verses 15 and 16: *"And when He had made a scourge of small cords, He drove them all out of the temple, and the sheep, and the oxen; and poured out the changers' money, and overthrew the tables; and said unto them that sold doves, Take these things hence; make not my Father's house an house of merchandise."*

The Greek word here translated *"small cords"* literally means *a cord made of rushes.* (Some Bible scholars believe that these "rushes" were used as bedding for the sheep and oxen which were being sold in the court of the temple.) This entire episode is remarkable. Jesus used more physical exertion and bodily energy here than in any other event in His earthly ministry. Usually He simply spoke a word, or reached out His hand and touched that upon which the miracle or ministry was performed; but it was different here. He did not order the animals and the money changers out of the temple; He made a small whip and literally *drove* them out! He could have spoken a word and every table would have collapsed—but He physically *overthrew* the tables and poured out the changers' money. On no other occasion did He display such strong, outward marks of indignation as when He stepped into the temple and saw what was taking place there in the name of religion.

The entire event is a type of what will happen when

Jesus comes the second time. The *visible* church is made up of wheat and tares, sheep and goats, and when He comes He will separate the wheat from the tares, He will separate the sheep from the goats. They will grow side by side *until* that day, and then when the Rapture of the Church occurs there will be a great separation. "God is love," God is longsuffering, tender, kind, and merciful; but in Revelation 6:16 we see *"the wrath of the Lamb"* revealed. Jesus came the first time as a babe in a manger. He is coming the second time as the Lion of the tribe of Judah. What He did in the temple on that memorable day, He did by virtue of His Sonship—as the Son of Almighty God.

Ministers today have no right to use a scourge. In this day of grace the only whip a preacher is to use is his tongue as he preaches the Word of God! The Word is a hammer, a fire (Jer. 23:29). The Word is "quick, and powerful, and sharper than any twoedged sword, piercing even to the dividing asunder of soul and spirit, and of the joints and marrow, and is a discerner of the thoughts and intents of the heart" (Heb. 4:12). All any minister need do is *preach the Word in all of its purity and power,* and the WORD will take care of those who are abusing the temple of God. The minister of the Gospel should cry aloud and spare not. The sad thing today is that the devil has tied the tongue of many ministers and they do not cry out against evil and corruption in the church.

Notice how Jesus dealt with each category of these things which caused Him displeasure when He walked into His Father's house:

He *drove out* the oxen and sheep (they could be found and rounded up). He *overthrew the tables* and poured the money on the ground (it could be gathered up). But see the tenderness He exercised toward the doves: to those who sold the doves He simply said, *"Take these things hence."* If the doves had been turned loose they would have flown away and their owners would have suffered a monetary loss. Jesus therefore simply instructed them to take the birds out of the temple area. It is wrong to destroy anything that can be used to glorify God or to bring comfort to those who are needy. We should never destroy food, clothing, anything that can be used to God's glory and to make His creatures more comfortable.

When Jesus referred to the temple as *"my Father's house"* He declared His deity, His divine Sonship; and as the Son of God He had a perfect right to vindicate the purity of the temple.   It is not clear whether the Jews noticed this or not.   On other occasions when He declared His Sonship and made Himself equal with God they attempted to stone Him or push Him over a precipice and destroy Him.   In John 5:18 they sought to kill Him because He had not only broken the Sabbath, but also said that God was His Father, thereby making Himself equal with God.

Jesus drove out the cattle and the money changers and reproved the profane custom being practiced in the temple that day, but the Jews *resumed* the custom later.   About three years after the first cleansing of the temple Jesus found the same thing going on again, and again He cast out the buyers and sellers as He had done on *this* occasion.   The fact that they resumed the custom of merchandising *in spite of His rebuke* reveals the total depravity of man and shows just how desperately wicked fallen men are.   The priests and the rulers of the temple did not obey the Lord's rebuke, they turned a deaf ear to His words and refused to obey His instructions; but comparing the two incidents, notice the progressive wickedness: When Jesus first cleansed the temple He said, "Make not my Father's house an house of merchandise," a place where men buy and sell; but when He visited the temple the second time and found the same practice going on, He said, "My house shall be called the house of prayer; but YE HAVE MADE IT A DEN OF THIEVES!" (Matt. 21:13).   Those who had been admonished not to make the house of God "a house of merchandise" did even more than that. Because of their hard hearts and their refusal to obey the Lord, they became not only *merchants,* but *THIEVING merchants!*

The church is *not* a place to buy and sell, a market-place. It is a place where God's people come *to worship and to give* out of a heart of love, thanksgiving, and appreciation for what Jesus has already given for us. According to the Word of God we are to give on the first day of the week, according as the Lord has prospered us (I Cor. 16:2).

Verse 17: *"And His disciples remembered that it was written, The zeal of thine house hath eaten me up."*

They *"remembered."* Old Testament Scripture is quoted here. They remembered the Word of God at the very moment Jesus was casting out buyers, sellers, and animals — and overturning the tables of the money changers. Here again is proof that the disciples and many other poor, unlearned Jews knew much about Old Testament Scripture.

"The zeal of thine house hath eaten me up" is quoted from Psalm 69:9. The New Testament quotes from this Psalm seven times, and it is quoted as the words of the Messiah.

We learn from the actions of Jesus in the temple that it is sometimes justifiable for one to be entirely absorbed, taken over, and "eaten up" by zeal for something in which God's glory is concerned. We find examples of this in Exodus 32:19, Numbers 25:11, and Acts 17:16. Study these verses carefully. Believers should let the zeal of the house of God ever eat their innermost being. By that I mean that we should be zealous to bring glory to God at all times, in all that we do; zealous at all times to *prevent* anything that would dishonor Him.

Verse 18: *"Then answered the Jews and said unto Him, What sign shewest thou unto us, seeing that thou doest these things?"*

These Jews were undoubtedly members of the Sanhedrin, or the assembly of chief priests, scribes, and rulers in the temple, and naturally what Jesus had done reached their ears without delay. Notice what they said to Him: *"What sign shewest thou unto us?"* Their question shows that they admitted that what He had done was *right* and what *they* were doing was not lawful in the house of God. What troubled them was that Jesus had taken upon Himself a grave responsibility—*and He did it independently of those who were in authority in the temple.* They wanted proof of His divine commission to do such a thing. He had not announced Himself as priest, nor was He a Levite; and now the rulers in the temple wanted Him to DO something or PRODUCE something which would prove to them that He was truly a prophet—another like Elijah or Amos. If He would give them this proof, then they would let Him go free without being arrested and punished for what He had done in their house of worship. They asked for a sign of His divine commission, when the Old Testament was *filled* with signs, had they only recognized them. They were familiar with the Scriptures, their Messiah stood in their midst, but they were so blinded by tradition and ceremony that they did not recognize Him.

Verse 19: *"Jesus answered and said unto them, Destroy this temple, and in three days I will raise it up."*

This verse must be rendered as a prophetic statement: "You will destroy this temple if you kill this, my body." Jesus was not *commanding* the Jews to kill Him, He was stating that it would happen. He knew that they would nail Him to a cross, that He would die, but He also knew that He would raise up His body from the grave. He used a manner of speaking which He used on other occasions. In Matthew 23:32 He said, "Fill ye up the measure of your fathers." He was speaking to the Pharisees, but certainly He was not commanding them to do this; the statement is one of prophecy. In Matthew 12:33 He said, "Make the tree good"—not a command, but an hypothesis. Jesus was not commanding the Jews to destroy His body; He was simply speaking words of prophecy which would be literally fulfilled within a matter of months.

". . . *and in three days I will raise it up.*" Here is a prophetical statement concerning the resurrection of Jesus on the third day—but notice: He said, "*I* will raise it up," declaring again His deity and equal power with Almighty God. The Jews would not doubt that *GOD* could raise up a body, but Jesus declared that HE would raise Himself. This is a very remarkable statement, and bears a marked similarity to the statement in John 10:17,18: "Therefore doth my Father love me, because I lay down my life, that I might take it again. No man taketh it from me, but I lay it down of myself. I have power to lay it down, and I have power to take it again. This commandment have I received of my Father."

The fact that Jesus said He would raise up His body does not alter the fact that the Father and the Holy Ghost had part in the resurrection. Certainly God the Father, God the Son, and God the Holy Spirit cooperated and worked in unison in the resurrection; thus Scriptures stating that Christ was raised by the Father and by the Spirit are not inconsistent with Christ's raising Himself. "What things soever (the Father) doeth, these also doeth the Son likewise" (John 5:19b). God the Father, God the Son, and God the Holy Ghost are one in nature, one in operation— *one God* manifest in *three Persons.* There are those in this day of liberalism and modernism who teach that the resurrection of Jesus was the operation of God the Father and God the Holy Ghost, and that Jesus did not rise by His own power; but remember, beloved, *Jesus was GOD in flesh,* and according to His own words, *He DID rise by His own power!* As for me, *I believe Jesus.*

Some might ask, "If the Jews wanted a miracle, why did Jesus not perform a miracle? Why did He not proclaim Himself Messiah at that time?" I would remind you that Jesus did not come into the world to *force* conviction upon men, to force men to follow Him. He knew the hearts of these men, He knew their thoughts and their intentions.

Therefore He answered fools according to their folly (Prov. 26:5).   If He had openly and positively declared that He was the Messiah, if He had worked some miracle to *prove* His messiahship, He would have brought His earthly ministry to an abrupt end and His enemies would have crucified Him before the appointed time.

All these things were planned, programmed, and perfected before the world was, and God's program always works according to "the fulness of time." At the appointed time, it happens—and it cannot happen *until* God's appointed time.

In reality Jesus gave them the greatest sign of all—the fact that He would rise again.   He staked the truth of His mission, His ministry, and His entire earthly sojourn on His bodily resurrection.   In Matthew 12:38—40 the scribes and Pharisees asked Him for a sign, and He replied, "An evil and adulterous generation seeketh after a sign; and there shall no sign be given to it, but the sign of the prophet Jonas: For as Jonas was three days and three nights in the whale's belly; so shall the Son of man be three days and three nights in the heart of the earth."

After the Ascension the apostles consistently preached the bodily resurrection of Jesus and reminded the Jews that Christ *did* rise from the dead and that His resurrection proved beyond all doubt that He was the Messiah.   It is necessary to believe in the resurrection of Jesus in order to be saved: "If thou shalt confess with thy mouth the Lord Jesus, and shalt believe in thine heart that God hath raised Him from the dead, thou shalt be saved" (Rom. 10:9).

Verses 20 and 21:   *"Then said the Jews, Forty and six years was this temple in building, and wilt thou rear it up in three days? But He spake of the temple of His body."*

The Jews were speaking of a literal temple, although Jesus was referring to His body.   They did not understand His meaning; they were thinking only in terms of the natural, and they took His statement literally.

There is some difference of opinion concerning *which* temple they referred to. It could not have been the temple of Solomon because that temple was completely destroyed by Nebuchadnezzar. It is doubtful that it was the temple built by Zerubbabel and his co-workers when Israel returned from the Babylonian captivity. The Bible historian *Josephus* declares that the temple mentioned was the temple Herod rebuilt, and explains that the work on this structure had been going on for forty-six years at that particular time. So extensive were the repairs and reconstruction that 18,000 men were employed in the rebuilding of this temple, and some work was still being done on it when Jesus entered and drove out the money changers. Therefore the Jews, considering the forty-six years of work already expended on the temple, asked Jesus, "Wilt *thou* rear it up in *three days?"* Here is a suggestion of both sarcasm and astonishment. The Jews put emphasis on *"THOU"*—that is, *"This upstart Jesus,* who has just chased out the animals and overturned the money tables—would HE be able to construct such a temple in *three days?"* They were definitely sneering at Him.

But they remembered His words, because at His trial before the Sanhedrin they said of Him, "This fellow said, I am able to destroy the temple of God, and to build it in three days" (Matt. 26:61). Even as He hung on the cross they mocked Him, saying, "Thou that destroyest the temple, and buildest it in three days, save thyself. If thou be the Son of God, come down from the cross" (Matt. 27:40).

The Jews were not the last to worship a building, a program, a system. There are tens of thousands of church members today who reverence the building and the denominational program much more than they reverence the Son of God and "thus saith the Lord"! Thousands think more of the beautiful edifice, the church building, than they do of the God who should be worshipped there.

In the Gospel of John there are several statements along the line of verse 21, statements of explanation given by the

Holy Spirit in order that Gentile readers might thoroughly understand the Gospel message. John makes it plain that Jesus was not speaking of the temple built by human hands, but *"of the temple of His body."* The Apostle Paul, under inspiration of the Holy Spirit, declares that believers are the temple of the Holy Ghost: "What? know ye not that your body is the temple of the Holy Ghost which is in you, which ye have of God, and ye are not your own? For ye are bought with a price: Therefore glorify God in your body, and in your spirit, which are God's" (I Cor. 6:19,20). If it was sinful to desecrate and defile the temple made of stone in the days when Jesus was on earth, how much *more* sinful it is for a believer to defile the body, the temple of God!

Both Paul and Peter refer to the body of a believer as our "tabernacle":

"For we know that if our earthly house of this tabernacle were dissolved, we have a building of God, an house not made with hands, eternal in the heavens" (II Cor. 5:1).

"Yea, I think it meet, as long as I am *in this tabernacle,* to stir you up by putting you in remembrance; knowing that shortly I must *put off this my tabernacle,* even as our Lord Jesus Christ hath shewed me" (II Pet. 1:13,14).

The temple authorities did not question the *moral* right of what Jesus did in cleansing the temple; they were surprised at the display of His *power and authority.* That is why they asked Him for a sign. They failed to see that the very character of the things He had done was the greatest possible sign that He was their Messiah. They asked for a sign—and He gave them a sign, but not according to their expectations: *"Destroy this temple, and in three days I will raise it up . . . the temple of His body"*—and His body was exactly that, for in Him shown the abiding Shekinah glory of the Lord, "in HIM dwelt all the fulness of the Godhead bodily."

Verse 22: *"When therefore He was risen from the dead, His disciples remembered that He had said this unto them;*

and they believed the Scripture, and the word which Jesus had said."

In this verse we find divine proof of two things: First, it shows how much light was brought to the minds and hearts of the disciples of Jesus by our Lord's resurrection, how many of His hard sayings were immediately made plain; and second, it reveals the fact that pure truth may long remain dormant in the minds of men without their *understanding* the truth, without its doing them any good. The Holy Spirit helps the believer to *hear,* and one of the special offices of the Spirit in this Dispensation of Grace is to bring things to our mind and remembrance: "The Comforter, which is the Holy Ghost, whom the Father will send in my name, He shall teach you all things, and *bring all things to your remembrance,* whatsoever I have said unto you" (John 14:26).

The Word of God will not return void but will accomplish that whereunto it is sent. Good seed sown in good ground will eventually bring forth a harvest. Sometimes one person sows the seed, another waters, and still another gathers the fruit; but there *will be* a harvest. The fruit does not always come immediately—or as quickly as we think it should—but we should not become discouraged nor feel that we have failed; for when we deliver God's message, when we sow the seed of His Word, that message WILL bring forth fruit, sometimes even after the one who gave it has passed on to his or her eternal reward. We rest from our labors but our works follow; so if you are a sower of good seed (the Word of God) do not be discouraged if you do not see fruit immediately, or if you do not see as *much* fruit as you would like to see. Keep sowing the seed and *in due season* you will reap.

The disciples *"believed the Scripture, and the word which Jesus had said."* This includes the entire record in the Word of God concerning the Messiah. After the resurrection of Jesus, the disciples were fully convinced that the prophecies concerning the coming of the Messiah were fulfilled in the Lord Jesus Christ. This does not mean that they here believed for *the first time;* this was not when they believed *unto salvation.* It simply means that they were *fully persuaded,* there was no doubt in their minds that the crucified, buried, risen Jesus was their promised Messiah. His bodily resurrection removed any trace of doubt that might have lingered in the heart of any of them. The statement here simply signifies that the disciples believed fully and never again doubted.

Verse 23: *"Now when He was in Jerusalem at the passover, in the feast day, many believed in His name, when they saw the miracles which He did."*

It seems that the *"many"* who "believed in His name" believed only with the mind, not with the heart. They were convinced in their *understanding,* not in their hearts. They had an intellectual belief, not saving faith. James tells us that *the devils* "believe and tremble" (Jas. 2:19), so it is not unscriptural to say that the demons have faith; but they do not have *saving* faith, which means to believe with the heart (Rom. 10:9,10). *"Many"* believed—but it was only an intellectual belief, not saving faith from the heart.

We read of one such person in the eighth chapter of Acts: "There was a certain man, called Simon, which beforetime in the same city used sorcery, and bewitched the people of Samaria, giving out that himself was some great one . . . And to him they had regard, because that of long time he had bewitched them with sorceries. But when they believed Philip preaching the things concerning the kingdom of God, and the name of Jesus Christ, they were baptized, both men and women. *Then Simon himself believed also: and when he was baptized, he continued with Philip, and wondered, beholding the miracles and signs which were done. . .* And when Simon saw that through laying on of the apostles' hands the Holy Ghost was given, he offered them money, saying, Give me also this power, that on whomsoever I lay hands, he may receive the Holy Ghost. But Peter said unto him, Thy money perish with thee, because thou hast thought that the gift of God may be purchased with money. Thou hast neither part nor lot in this matter: FOR THY HEART IS NOT RIGHT IN THE SIGHT OF GOD" (Acts 8:9—21).

The "many" believed *"when they saw the miracles which He did."* These miracles are not named or described here, but we know from God's Word that Jesus performed many miracles and did many things not recorded in the Word: "And *many other signs truly did Jesus in the presence of His disciples, which are not written in this book:* but these are written, that ye might believe that Jesus is the Christ, the Son of God; and that believing ye might have life through His name" (John 20:30,31). *"And there are also many other things which Jesus did, the which, if they should be written every one, I suppose that even the world itself could not contain the books that should be written"* (John 21:25).

If God the Father had wanted us to have a record of those miracles He would have *given* us such record. He has given us enough Scripture to perfectly furnish us with the Gospel message needed by men, and if we study the Word, believe, receive, and live by what is recorded there, we need not worry about things not recorded or not revealed to us. Jesus worked many miracles in Jerusalem and all around that city, but His mighty miracle-working power did not convince the Jews of His identity. They lived in unbelief and hardness of heart, and eventually they demanded the crucifixion of their Messiah.

Verses 24 and 25: *"But Jesus did not commit Himself unto them, because He knew all men, and needed not that any should testify of man: for He knew what was in man."*

Jesus did not *"commit Himself unto them,"* He did not trust Himself into their hands, because *"He knew all men."* This declares the divine omniscience of Jesus Christ. In the same way that God the Father knew all men, *Jesus* knew all men. He knew that these who *professed* to be believers did not believe with the heart; they believed with the head. Theirs was not the faith that saves, the faith that looks to Jesus for cleansing and salvation.

Jesus did not need to be told about man; He needed no information concerning those who professed to believe in Him. He knew their hearts, their real character, and He did not need the testimony of other men.

"He knew what was in man." Jesus was God in flesh, and He therefore had perfect knowledge of the *inner nature* of man. He was a discerner of the thoughts and intents of the hearts of men. In Solomon's prayer of dedication we read, "Then hear thou in heaven thy dwelling place, and forgive, and do, and give to every man according to his ways, whose heart thou knowest; *(for thou, EVEN THOU ONLY, knowest the hearts of all the children of men)"* (I Kings 8:39).

We can be deceived by men, we consistently err in our estimate of people; but the Lord Jesus Christ was never deceived by any man. He knew what was in the heart of *every* man—yes, even when He permitted *Judas* to join the disciple band. He said to Peter, "Have I not chosen you twelve, and one of you is (devil)? He spake of Judas Iscariot the son of Simon: for he it was that should betray Him, being one of the twelve" (John 6:70,71). Jesus was perfectly acquainted with the character of Judas Iscariot, and it is not for us to speculate as to why He allowed him to join the disciple band. God's ways are not our ways. He has a plan, He knows the end in the beginning, and "He doeth all things well."

There are several places in John's Gospel which show the unusual and peculiar way in which the Holy Spirit declares divine knowledge of persons and things. In addition to our present verses, notice these other accounts:

In John 6:64 Jesus said, "There are some of you that believe not. For *Jesus knew from the beginning* who they were that believed not, and who should betray Him."

John 7:37—39:   "In the last day, that great day of the feast, Jesus stood and cried, saying, If any man thirst, let him come unto me, and drink.   He that believeth on me, as the Scripture hath said, out of his belly shall flow rivers of living water.   *(But this spake He of the Spirit,* which they that believe on Him should receive: *for the Holy Ghost was not yet given;* because that Jesus was not yet glorified.)"

John 8:26,27:   "I have many things to say and to judge of you: but He that sent me is true; and I speak to the world those things which I have heard of Him.   *They understood not that He spake to them of the Father.*"

John 12:32—37:   "And I, if I be lifted up from the earth, will draw all men unto me.   *This He said, signifying what death He should die.*   The people answered Him, We have heard out of the law that Christ abideth for ever: and how sayest thou, The Son of man must be lifted up? who is this Son of man?   Then Jesus said unto them, Yet a little while is the light with you.   Walk while ye have the light, lest darkness come upon you: for he that walketh in darkness knoweth not whither he goeth.   While ye have light, believe in the light, that ye may be the children of light.   These things spake Jesus, and departed, and did hide Himself from them.   But though He had done so many miracles before them, yet they believed not on Him."

John 13:10,11:   "Jesus saith to (Peter), He that is washed needeth not save to wash his feet, but is clean every whit: and ye are clean, but not all.   *For He knew who should betray Him;* therefore said He, Ye are not all clean."

John 21:17:   "(Jesus) saith unto him the third time, Simon, son of Jonas, lovest thou me?   Peter was grieved because He said unto him the third time, Lovest thou me?   *And he said unto Him, Lord, THOU KNOWEST ALL THINGS; thou knowest that I love thee.*   Jesus saith unto him, Feed my sheep."

If we are ever inclined to think highly of ourselves, if

we become bold, braggadocio, and in our own eyes we seem
to be righteous and godly, all we need do to humble our
hearts and put us back in our proper place is to read the
message of these last two verses in the second chapter of
John's Gospel. Jesus "knew ALL men, and needed not
that any should testify of man: for He knew what was in
man." Let all men know for sure that the cloak of religion
does not hide the inward rottenness which, though possibly
hidden from man, is plainly visible to the eyes of Almighty
God; and He thunders out, *"I KNOW THY WORKS, that
thou hast a name that thou livest, and art dead!"* (Rev. 3:1).

There should be no doubt in our minds that the Lord
Jesus Christ disapproves of unholy, irreverent behaviour in
the house of God today, even as He did in the days when
He cleansed the temple. The church is only a building,
but that building is sanctified and set apart unto God, a
place where believers gather to worship and fellowship. We
are commanded to forsake not "the assembling of ourselves
together, as the manner of some is; but exhorting one another: and so much the more, as ye see the day approaching" (Heb. 10:25); but the assembling is to be for worship
and the exhortation is to be to the glory of God. The command of Jesus remains, "Take these things hence; make not
my Father's house an house of merchandise!" Thousands
of professed believers attend church on Sunday and behave
just as badly as did the Jews in the day of our Lord. They
come to the house of God—but they bring their money,
their lands, their stocks and bonds. Their mind is so per-
meated with worldly affairs that even though they are *bodily* in the house of worship, their hearts are far from God.

Ecclesiastes 5:1 admonishes, "Keep thy foot when thou
goest to the house of God, and be more ready to hear, than
to give the sacrifice of fools: for they consider not that
they do evil."

CHAPTER III

1. There was a man of the Pharisees, named Nicodemus, a ruler of the Jews:

2. The same came to Jesus by night, and said unto him, Rabbi, we know that thou art a teacher come from God: for no man can do these miracles that thou doest, except God be with him.

3. Jesus answered and said unto him, Verily, verily, I say unto thee, Except a man be born again, he cannot see the kingdom of God.

4. Nicodemus saith unto him, How can a man be born when he is old? can he enter the second time into his mother's womb, and be born?

5. Jesus answered, Verily, verily, I say unto thee, Except a man be born of water and of the Spirit, he cannot enter into the kingdom of God.

6. That which is born of the flesh is flesh; and that which is born of the Spirit is spirit.

7. Marvel not that I said unto thee, Ye must be born again.

8. The wind bloweth where it listeth, and thou hearest the sound thereof, but canst not tell whence it cometh, and whither it goeth: so is every one that is born of the Spirit.

9. Nicodemus answered and said unto him, How can these things be?

10. Jesus answered and said unto him, Art thou a master of Israel, and knowest not these things?

11. Verily, verily, I say unto thee, We speak that we do know, and testify that we have seen; and ye receive not our witness.

12. If I have told you earthly things, and ye believe not, how shall ye believe, if I tell you of heavenly things?

13. And no man hath ascended up to heaven, but he that came down from heaven, even the Son of man which is in heaven.

14. And as Moses lifted up the serpent in the wilderness, even so must the Son of man be lifted up:

15. That whosoever believeth in him should not perish, but have eternal life.

16. For God so loved the world, that he gave his only begotten Son, that whosoever believeth in him should not perish, but have everlasting life.

17. For God sent not his Son into the world to condemn the world; but that the world through him might be saved.

18. He that believeth on him is not condemned: but he that believeth not is condemned already, because he hath not believed in the name of the only begotten Son of God.

19. And this is the condemnation, that light is come into the world, and men loved darkness rather than light, because their deeds were evil.

20. For every one that doeth evil hateth the light, neither cometh to the light, lest his deeds should be reproved.

21. But he that doeth truth cometh to the light, that his deeds may be made manifest, that they are wrought in God.

22. After these things came Jesus and his disciples into the land of Judaea; and there he tarried with them, and baptized.

23. And John also was baptizing in Aenon near to Salim, because there was much water there: and they came, and were baptized.

24. For John was not yet cast into prison.

25. Then there arose a question between some of John's disciples and the Jews about purifying.

26. And they came unto John, and said unto him, Rabbi, he that was with thee beyond Jordan, to whom thou barest witness, behold, the same baptizeth, and all men come to him.

27. John answered and said, A man can receive nothing, except it be given him from heaven.

28. Ye yourselves bear me witness, that I said, I am not the Christ, but that I am sent before him.

29. He that hath the bride is the bridegroom: but the friend of the bridegroom, which standeth and heareth him, rejoiceth greatly because of the bridegroom's voice: this my joy therefore is fulfilled.

30. He must increase, but I must decrease.

31. He that cometh from above is above all: he that is of the earth is earthly, and speaketh of the earth: he that cometh from heaven is above all.

32. And what he hath seen and heard, that he testifieth; and no man receiveth his testimony.

33. He that hath received his testimony hath set to his seal that God is true.

34. For he whom God hath sent speaketh the words of God: for God giveth not the Spirit by measure unto him.

35. The Father loveth the Son, and hath given all things into his hand.

36. He that believeth on the Son hath everlasting life: and he that believeth not the Son shall not see life; but the wrath of God abideth on him.

This chapter includes the conversation between Jesus and Nicodemus, the dispute between the Jews and the disciples of John the Baptist, and the closing testimony of John the Baptist concerning Christ.

The Gospel of John records eleven interviews between Jesus and individuals.   His conversation with Nicodemus is one of the most important passages in all of the Word of God; nowhere else in the entire Bible can we find clearer, stronger statements about the new birth and salvation by faith in the shed blood and finished work of Jesus the Son of God.

One can be ignorant concerning many things pertaining to the Christian religion and still be saved—no one will ever know ALL about Christianity; but one cannot be ignorant concerning the things set forth in this chapter and hope to enter the Pearly White City, because it is a divine imperative that the unbeliever be born again if he hopes to enter the portals of heaven.

Verse 1:   *"There was a man of the Pharisees, named Nicodemus, a ruler of the Jews."*

In the original Greek the opening phrase here reads, *"BUT there was a man,"* thus connecting this verse with the last verse of the preceding chapter. There is a definite and distinct connection here, because in the last two verses of chapter 2 we read that Jesus did not trust Himself unto men "for He knew all men"; but Nicodemus was *a different kind* of man.   He was not like those who believed intellectually.

True, he acknowledged the facts concerning the signs and the miracles Jesus wrought, but he went beyond that. His conscience was touched, he was moved, he felt a thirst and a hunger in his soul.   He was strictly "religious" and dedicated to Judaism, but he opened his hungry heart to Jesus, listened to Him, and *with his heart* he believed the words Jesus spoke.   He undoubtedly thought that the miracles of Jesus were definite indications of the coming *earthly* kingdom, but he had a hungry heart, a willing mind, and he listened attentively, asking questions and hearing the answers Jesus gave. He believed, he became a follower of the Saviour—secretly at first, but later openly making his confession of faith in Jesus as Messiah and Saviour.

It is interesting to note the different people who came to Christ and believed on Him during His earthly ministry. His disciples did not come from one class only. This man who was different was *"of the Pharisees . . . a ruler of the Jews,"* and the general rule was that the Pharisees were bitterly opposed to Jesus; they refused to receive His doctrine, they called Him an imposter and even an illegitimate. The most slanderous words spoken about the Lord while He walked this earth were spoken by the Pharisees; but we see here that God's grace is greater than *all* sin. Even a Pharisee could be touched and converted to Jesus. Consider the Apostle Paul, also a Pharisee, persecuting the Church and putting Christians to death. Paul later referred to himself as "chief of sinners"—and his conversion is proof positive that no heart is too sinful, too hard, or too calloused to be moved by the Gospel and turned to the Lord Jesus Christ.

The fact that Nicodemus was "a ruler of the Jews" does not mean that he was a ruler in civil government. (The government was controlled by the Romans at that time.) It simply means that he was an outstanding person in the religion of the Jews, a high ecclesiastical officer and a famous teacher. He held a master's degree in the religion of Israel, and undoubtedly was one of the most respected people in the realm of Judaism. In addition to the high position he held in the religion of his fathers, there is no doubt that his reputation was above reproach, he had a marvelous education, he was what we might call "a leading citizen"; but those honors did not satisfy his hungry heart and his thirsty soul. He wanted to know more about this Teacher whom he had seen in Jerusalem, this Jesus who wrought miracles that no mortal could have performed apart from Almighty God. Nicodemus was not controlled by the prejudices of his own people; he believed in dealing honestly with plain facts, as shown in John 7:51 when he said to the Pharisees, "Doth our law judge any man, before it hear him, and know what he doeth?" He was a member of the Sanhedrin, but he was modest, he had a receptive heart, and he was willing to receive truth from this Galilaean Teacher.

Verse 2: *"The same came to Jesus by night, and said unto Him, Rabbi, we know that thou art a teacher come from God: for no man can do these miracles that thou doest, except God be with him."*

The Scripture does not tell us *why* Nicodemus came to Jesus by night. Some Bible scholars believe that he feared the Sanhedrin—the chief priests and the Jewish leaders— and this is quite possible. It could also be that his business affairs were so pressing and kept him so busy during daylight hours that he had no time to visit Jesus until evening. It is pointed out three times in the Gospel of John that Nicodemus came to Jesus by night (see also John 7:50 and 19:39), which would seem to indicate that he *did* fear the Jews.

Out of respect for the Lord Jesus Christ Nicodemus addressed Him as "Rabbi"—and then he said, *"We KNOW that thou art a teacher sent from God."* Nicodemus was already convinced of this. He did not say, "We *think,"* or "We *suppose."* He KNEW that only someone sent from God could do the miracles Jesus did.

Some Bible scholars believe that because Nicodemus said, "WE know" some of the other members of the Sanhedrin were like-minded but lacked the courage to come and talk with Jesus personally, and therefore Nicodemus became the spokesman for others as well as for himself. It could have been that more than one member of the Sanhedrin was convinced that Jesus was more than an ordinary man. Or perhaps Nicodemus was afraid—and he might have said "we," knowing that this would make his statement vague as to who was asking the questions. Even today some of us use the term "we" when we should say "I." This is the tendency of weak faith, and those who feel that they are failures are prone to hide in the crowd. This should not be. We should stand for Jesus even if we stand alone.

"No man can do these miracles that thou doest, except God be with him." Here is stated one of the great purposes of the Lord's miracles. Let it be remembered that Jesus never performed any miracle simply for the display of His power, to bring personal glory to Himself, or simply to bring *comfort* to those He healed and blessed. His every miracle had deep spiritual significance. His miracles caused men to pay attention to what He was saying, declared that He was divine and that His mission was divinely ordered. His mighty miracles testified to ordinary men that He was *extraordinary.*

Of His miracles Jesus said, "I have greater witness than that of John: for the works which the Father hath given me to finish, the same works that I do, bear witness of me, that the Father hath sent me" (John 5:36).

In John 10:25 He said, "I told you, and ye believed not: the works that I do in my Father's name, they bear witness of me."

In John 15:24 He said, "If I had not done among them the works which none other man did, they had not had sin: but now have they both seen and hated both me and my Father."

From II Thessalonians 2:9 and Revelation 13:13,14 we know that Antichrist will perform signs and wonders; but notice that Nicodemus points out *"these* miracles"—that is, the *quality* of the miracles performed by the Lord Jesus proved that He was divine. The devil can do mighty things, but there is a *limit* to what he can do. *There is NO limit to what God can do!* False teachers can work miracles—the magicians in Moses' day were miracle workers; but there is a place where magicians, false teachers, and antichrists must stop; God will permit them to go no further. The very *character* of the miracles Jesus performed declared that His miracles were wrought by the hand of Almighty God. Peter preached this in Acts 10:37,38:

"That word, I say, ye know, which was published throughout all Judaea, and began from Galilee, after the baptism which John preached; how God anointed Jesus of Nazareth with the Holy Ghost and with power: who went about doing good, and healing all that were oppressed of the devil; FOR GOD WAS WITH HIM."

Verse 3: *"Jesus answered and said unto him, Verily, verily, I say unto thee, Except a man be born again, he cannot see the kingdom of God."*

Jesus knew the heart of Nicodemus. He knew that in spite of a hungry heart Nicodemus was a religionist, a dedicated and devout Pharisee; but He also knew that this master in Israel, like many other Jews, was looking for the coming of Messiah, thinking that he had *found* Him. Therefore Jesus explained that His was not a temporal kingdom at that time, it was not a kingdom in which all of the seed of Abraham would become subjects because of their birth. The kingdom into which He was calling men at that particular time was a *spiritual* kingdom and could be entered only by grace through faith. There is no doubt that Nicodemus, like all other Jews in his day, honored Abraham very highly, was proud to be of the *seed* of Abraham, proud to be a member of the religion of his fathers. Jesus pointed out to him that he must be willing to renounce all blood ties, all honor from the standpoint of the blood of Abraham, and be *"born again"* if he would enter the kingdom of God!

Notice that Jesus spoke of "the kingdom of *God.*" There is a distinct difference between the *kingdom of God* and *the kingdom of HEAVEN.* The kingdom of heaven will be right here on earth. The disciples were taught to pray in the kingdom: "Give us this day our daily bread." At that time there will be peace on earth, good will toward

men.   *The kingdom of GOD* is not meat and drink; the
kingdom of God is within the heart, and it is entered only
through the new birth.   All who enter the kingdom of God
must be *born into* that kingdom, born anew, born from
above, born of the Spirit.   It is a *spiritual* birth, not concerned with the blood of our ancestors but with *the blood
of JESUS.*

"*Verily, verily, I say unto thee . . . .*"   I refer to this
expression as a "double verily," and I repeat for emphasis
that the Holy Spirit does not need to say anything but once
in order for it to be true; therefore when we read the same
word twice in one verse we should recognize the importance of what is about to be said.   We find twenty-five
"double verilies" in John's Gospel, always in connection
with a tremendously important fact.

"Verily, verily, I say unto thee, *EXCEPT A MAN* (any
man, all men) *BE BORN AGAIN, he cannot see the kingdom of God.*"   Greek scholars tell us that "born again"
can be read with perfect correctness, "*born from ABOVE,*"
born from heaven, or from God.   In chapter 1, verses 12
and 13 we read that to as many as received Jesus, God gave
the power to become the sons of God, "even to them that
believe on His name; *which were born,* not of blood, nor
of the will of the flesh, nor of the will of man, but *of
GOD.*"   It is God who does the "borning," therefore the
new birth is from above.   Please read John 1:13; 3:3,5,6,8;
I Peter 1:23; I John 2:29; 3:9; 4:7; 5:1,4,18.   The expressions
"born again . . . born from above . . . born of the Spirit
. . . born of God" are intimately connected one with the
other and mean the same thing.   The important thing is
to know that we have been born again.   What about YOU?

Sermons on the new birth are few and far between in
some churches today.   What tragedy!   Ministers need to
use this text often and emphasize it heartily, because it is
a divine imperative that men be born again or spend eternity in hell.   There is no way to enter the kingdom of God
except to be born again.

What does it mean to be born again? It means a complete change of heart: "And I will give them one heart, and I will put a new spirit within you; and I will take the stony heart out of their flesh, and will give them an heart of flesh" (Ezek. 11:19).

To be born again is to become a new creation: "Therefore if any man be in Christ, he is a new creature: old things are passed away; behold, all things are become new" (II Cor. 5:17).

To be born again is to become partaker of divine nature: "Whereby are given unto us exceeding great and precious promises: that by these ye might be partakers of the divine nature, having escaped the corruption that is in the world through lust" (II Pet. 1:4).

To be born again is to truly repent, believe the Gospel and trust Christ. Jesus declared, ". . . except ye repent, ye shall all likewise perish" (Luke 13:3,5). Repentance is godly sorrow and turning from sin, turning "face about" with a definite and distinct change of direction. The unbeliever is traveling toward hell. When he truly repents he turns face about and travels in the opposite direction. In Acts 3:19 Peter exhorts, "Repent ye therefore, and be converted, that your sins may be blotted out, when the times of refreshing shall come from the presence of the Lord."

In Romans 6:13 Paul speaks of converts as being "alive from the dead." In Ephesians 2:1 he speaks of them as being "quickened" from the dead. In Colossians 3:9,10 he speaks of the new birth as having "put off the *old* man" and put on the "*new* man." In Titus 3:5 he speaks of it as "the washing of regeneration, and renewing of the Holy Ghost," and in I Peter 2:9 we read, "But ye are a chosen generation, a royal priesthood, an holy nation, a peculiar people; that ye should shew forth the praises of Him who hath called you *out of darkness into His marvellous light.*" I John 3:14 refers to the new birth as passing "from death unto life." All of these Bible statements mean the same thing and declare the same truth.

Notice, Jesus declares that except a man be born again *"he cannot SEE."* The lost person is blind, spiritually speaking. In II Corinthians 4:3,4 we read, *"If our Gospel be hid, it is hid to them that are lost: in whom the god of this world hath blinded the minds of them which believe not,* lest the light of the glorious Gospel of Christ, who is the image of God, should shine unto them." Also in I Corinthians 2:14 Paul tells us that "the natural man receiveth not the things of the Spirit of God: for they are foolishness unto him: neither can he know them, because they are spiritually discerned."

No matter how brilliant, profound, or sincere a person may be, he *must* be born of the Spirit before he can see the kingdom of God or receive the things of the Spirit of God. This is not figurative language—the new birth is definitely and distinctly *birth*. In our natural birth we were begotten of our earthly parents, who by *generation* transmitted to us their very own life and nature. The same is true in the spiritual birth. He who believes in the shed blood and finished work of Jesus is begotten again unto a living hope—begotten of God, who by *re-generation* transmits to us His own life and His divine nature.

We find similar statements in other places in the Scriptures. In John 3:36 Jesus says, "he that believeth not the Son shall not *SEE life.*" In John 8:51 He said, "if a man keep my saying, he shall never *SEE death.*" In Psalm 16:10 we read, "For thou wilt not . . . suffer thine Holy One to *SEE corruption.*" Revelation 18:7 speaks of seeing sorrow.

"The kingdom of God" is the spiritual kingdom which Jesus came into the world to set up, and all believers are subjects of that kingdom. Under the law, the only thing necessary for a Jew to come under the blessings of the covenant of Israel, with all of its temple privileges and blessings, was that he be born of Jewish parents. He then belonged to the covenant, the promises were his. But to

become a subject of the kingdom of God, one must be born again, born of the Spirit, a new creation in Christ. *"For we are His workmanship, created in Christ Jesus* unto good works, which God hath before ordained that we should walk in them" (Eph. 2:10). The new birth is not "doing" or *refraining* from doing. Believers are the product of the miracle of Almighty God.

Nicodemus was thinking in terms of the things Jesus was *doing.* He was working miracles, and those miracles gave strong bodies and fed hungry stomachs; *but Jesus came to change the heart.* He came into the world to die for the sins of mankind, and if He had continued living here—sinless, perfect, powerful, miracle worker that He was— we would still be without a Saviour!

Verse 4: *"Nicodemus saith unto Him, How can a man be born when he is old? Can he enter the second time into his mother's womb, and be born?"*

This was a natural question for Nicodemus to ask. Even though he was a master in Israel and was well versed in the religion of the Jews, he was in ignorance concerning spiritual things. The natural man cannot receive the things of the Spirit of God until he is *born* of the Spirit. In every age of the world's history there has been nothing so hard for the heart of the natural man to understand and receive as the miracle of the work of the Holy Ghost and the power of the Word of God. Man wants to see things, touch things, understand things, whereas *faith* receives and believes *without* seeing, feeling, touching, or tasting. Until the finite mind is quickened by the Holy Spirit, it cannot conceive of a spiritual birth, a spiritual operation whereby God puts a new heart and a new spirit into the bosom of man.

"How can a man be born when he is old?" We do not know the age of Nicodemus at that time, but this suggests that he was not a *young* man. Whatever age he might have been, it is a matter for rejoicing that a person does

not become too old to be born again. It is true that the
older one gets, the slower he is to receive the message of
the Word of God, and it is much more difficult to reach
an old, hardened sinner than it is to reach a youth or a
tender child who has not known the dregs of sin; but there
is no age beyond which God's love and salvation will not
reach if the person will only believe.

*"Can he enter the second time into his mother's womb
and be born?"* Here, too, Nicodemus was thinking in terms
of the physical; and before one can be born again he must
think in terms of the supernatural, because it is GOD who
does the "borning." There must be *seed* to produce new
life, and the incorruptible seed (the Word of God) is the
life-producing power that only God Almighty CAN give.
We did not "born" ourselves into this life, and we cannot
"born" ourselves into the family of God. We must think
beyond the natural, beyond man's power, and look to the
supernatural and the power of God if we are to be born
again. Where there is birth there must be life, strength,
power. *God is life,* He has *all* power, and when we receive Jesus we are given power to become sons of God,
born of God.

The words of Jesus were searching the heart of Nicodemus. His words were the words of God, quick and powerful, sharper than any twoedged sword, dividing asunder
soul and spirit, bones and marrow. The Word of God is
the only thing that will jar the natural man out of his own
security and show him that he needs a Saviour. Nicodemus
came to question Jesus about Himself—but now instead of
asking questions about *Jesus,* he is asking questions about
his own soul: how can an old man change the character
which years have formed and molded?

Verse 5: *"Jesus answered, Verily, verily, I say unto thee,
Except a man be born of water and of the Spirit, he cannot
enter into the kingdom of God."*

This is a very important verse from God's holy Word,

and there are many interpretations of it. The only way to understand difficult or controversial passages is to compare Scripture with Scripture, "spiritual things with spiritual" (I Cor. 2:10−13). This is the same truth declared in verse 3, but it is given here in greater fulness.

"Except a man be born of water . . . ." This is the only time this statement appears in the Word of God. It is a singular declaration, and it is of tremendous importance. What does Jesus mean—*"born of water"*? We know that no one can be literally born of water, therefore the "water" here would have a spiritual meaning, symbolic of some power—the power that "borns" us into the family of God.

Tens of thousands teach that Jesus is declaring that a man must be baptized before he can enter the kingdom of God. This is the teaching of "water regeneration," and if it be true then we are not saved by grace through faith: we are saved by grace through faith *plus baptism*—and such is not the teaching of the Word of God! Jesus did not say to Nicodemus, "If you want to become a subject of my kingdom you must be born again *and baptized in water,"* yet this is the doctrine taught by many religious leaders in various denominations around the world. It is a false doctrine. Water baptism does not wash away sins.

> "There is a fountain filled with blood
> Drawn from Immanuel's veins;
> And sinners plunged beneath that flood
> Lose all their guilty stains."

The blood of Jesus Christ cleanses from all sin (I John 1:7). Paul was appointed God's minister to the Gentiles (Rom. 11:13). He was anointed, Spirit-filled and Spirit-led, a minister of the grace of God, the minister whom God gave to the Church; yet Paul said, "Christ sent me NOT TO BAPTIZE, but to preach the Gospel: not with wisdom of words, lest the cross of Christ should be made of none effect" (I Cor. 1:17).

Baptizing is righteous work, it is an ordinance of the

New Testament Church; but it does not wash away sins. In Ephesians 2:8,9 Paul says, "For *by grace are ye saved through faith;* and that not of yourselves: it is the gift of God: not of works, lest any man should boast."

Titus 3:5 tells us, "Not by works of righteousness which we have done, but according to His mercy He saved us, *by the washing of regeneration,* and renewing of the Holy Ghost."   Jesus said to His disciples, *"Now ye are clean through the WORD which I have spoken unto you"* (John 15:3).   It is the Word of God that cleanses, not water in a baptistry or in the river Jordan.

In Ephesians 5:25,26 we read, "Husbands, love your wives, even as Christ also loved the Church, and gave Himself for it; *that He might sanctify and cleanse it with the washing of water by the Word."*

For those who want to know the truth, those who are not more interested in defending a denomination or a "religion" than in understanding the Word of God, I Peter 1:23 settles it: *"Being born again, not of corruptible seed, but of incorruptible, BY THE WORD OF GOD, which liveth and abideth for ever!"*

Someone may ask, "If the Word of God is the 'water' in John 3:5 why did Jesus not *say,* 'Except a man be born of *the Word* and of the Spirit'?"   Jesus Himself answers: In Luke 10:21 we read that "Jesus rejoiced in spirit, and said, *I thank thee, O Father, Lord of heaven and earth, that thou hast hid these things from the wise and prudent, and hast revealed them unto babes: even so, Father; for so it seemed good in thy sight."*   God is not found by searching.   God is not found in the laboratory in a test tube or under a microscope.   God is found *in His WORD.* When we put childlike faith in "thus saith the Lord," the incorruptible seed brings the new birth.

James 1:18 tells us, "Of (God's) own will begat He us *with the WORD of truth,* that we should be a kind of first-fruits of His creatures."

If you will study the tenth and eleventh chapters of Acts

you will find that the house of *Cornelius* was born of the water and of the Spirit—but the water was the WORD. God told Cornelius to send to Joppa for Simon Peter, who would tell him WORDS whereby he and all his house could be saved (Acts 11:14). When Peter arrived at the house of Cornelius he spoke "words"—the Word of God, "the WORD which God sent unto the children of Israel, preaching peace by Jesus Christ (He is Lord of all)" (Acts 10:36).

"While Peter yet spake these WORDS, the Holy Ghost fell on all them which heard the WORD" (Acts 10:44). Peter preached the death, burial, and resurrection of Jesus, proclaiming that *"through HIS NAME whosoever believeth in Him shall receive remission of sins."* Notice: *"through His name,"* not "through baptism." *"Whosoever believeth,"* not "whosoever is baptized." Cornelius and his household were born again, the Holy Ghost came upon them, and then they were baptized—not *to be* born again, but because they had *already been* born again. Water baptism is a New Testament ordinance, an ordinance of the Church. It signifies death, burial, and resurrection—but it does not save, it does not *help* save, nor does it make men *better* saved. Water baptism has to do with obedience; it has nothing to do with redemption.

"Water . . . washing . . . cleansing . . . purifying" are expressions used many times in the Word of God, in both the Old and New Testaments. Please study Psalm 51:7—10; Isaiah 44:3; Jeremiah 4:14; Ezekiel 36:25; John 4:10; 7:38,39.

God is no respecter of persons; and if "water" in our present verse means *baptism,* then all persons who have been baptized have been born again—but we know that such is not true. In Acts 8:9—24 we read where only a few days after Simon Magnus was baptized, Peter said to him, *"Thou hast neither part nor lot in this matter: for thy heart is not right in the sight of God. Repent therefore of this thy wickedness, and pray God, if perhaps the thought of thine heart may be forgiven thee. For I perceive that thou art in the gall of bitterness, and in the bond of iniquity."*

If the water in our present verse speaks of baptism, then all who have died *without* baptism are in hell; yet Jesus said to the thief on the cross, *"Today shalt thou be with me in paradise!"* (Luke 23:43)—and he was never baptized. If the water in our present verse refers to baptism, then all the babies who have died in their innocence—but without baptism—are lost.   But such is not true.   Babies and innocent little ones are protected by the grace of God, and there are no babies in hell, despite the teaching of some religionists.

If "born of water" means water baptism, why did Jesus rebuke Nicodemus by saying, "Knowest thou not these things?"   How *could* Nicodemus have known about water regeneration when there had been no such thing taught in the Old Testament Scriptures—and that was all Nicodemus had.   Therefore he had no way of knowing the doctrine of baptism.   The Old Testament Scriptures *do* teach that God gave a new heart and a new spirit to those who repented, and that Jehovah forgave sins when the penitent soul brought an offering, a sacrifice, to the temple.   Baptismal regeneration was not taught in the Old Testament (nor is it taught in the New) because it is not Scripture.   It is a man-made doctrine.   The Old Testament saint was saved exactly as the New Testament saint is saved—through the blood of Jesus Christ. The blood began to flow in the Garden of Eden and flowed all the way to Calvary where the Lamb without spot or blemish laid His life down, gave His own blood, and offered one sacrifice for all, forever, never to be repeated.   The Old Testament saint looked forward to Calvary; we on this side of the cross look back to Calvary to the shed blood of Jesus—and apart from the blood there is no cleansing, no remission of sins.

Denominations and ministers who teach water regeneration—(baptism essential to salvation)—should study the epistles.   They should study and rightly divide the Word of truth instead of studying to prove their religious points and denominational dogma. All of the Bible is the Word of God, and all Scripture is given by inspiration; but the epistles are for the Church and for this day of grace. Very little is said about baptism in the epistles. In Romans—the tremendous book that teaches salvation by grace through faith—baptism is mentioned only twice. In I Corinthians it is mentioned seven times, and it is mentioned but once in each of the epistles of Galatians, Ephesians, Colossians, Hebrews, and I Peter. In thirteen of the other epistles, baptism is not named or referred to. Certainly we would expect baptism to be taught in the epistles to Timothy, but neither of those writings say one word about baptism. Titus was a young minister, and to him, through the Apostle Paul, the Holy Ghost directed an epistle—but baptism is not mentioned. However, in Titus 3:5 we read, "Not by works of righteousness which we have done, but *according to His mercy He saved us, BY THE WASHING OF REGENERATION, and renewing of the Holy Ghost.*"

If baptism were essential to salvation, would Paul have thanked God that he had baptized only Crispus, Gaius, and the household of Stephanas? (See I Corinthians 1:14—17.) If baptism were essential to salvation, you may rest assured that the Apostle Paul would have been busy baptizing people instead of thanking God that he had baptized so few! He plainly said to the Corinthians, "In Christ Jesus I have begotten you THROUGH THE GOSPEL" (I Cor. 4:15).

Verse 6: *"That which is born of the flesh is flesh; and that which is born of the Spirit is spirit."*

Here, Jesus continues with His reply to the question Nicodemus asked in verse 4, showing that even if it were *possible* for a man to be born again by his mother, such birth would not bring him salvation or make him fit for the kingdom of God. *"That which is born of the flesh IS flesh"*—and God gave up flesh in the Garden of Eden. Through the seed of the woman He provided redemption

for the soul, but He made no provision for repairing the
flesh. He said to Adam, "Dust thou art, and unto dust
shalt thou return" (Gen. 3:19). Ecclesiastes 12:7 tells us
that the dust shall "return to the earth as it was: and the
spirit shall return unto God who gave it." In the glorious
resurrection morning God will give us a glorified body like
unto the body of Jesus. (Read Luke 24, the entire chapter,
and I John 3:2.) All members of the human race are by
nature the children of wrath—corrupt, sinful, blind, alien-
ated from God. "So then they that are in the flesh cannot
please God" (Rom. 8:8). Flesh has never pleased God and
never will. The only man who ever satisfied God in the
flesh was the Man Christ Jesus, and Jesus was GOD in
flesh.

"That which is born of the Spirit is spirit." When an
unbeliever is transformed into a child of God it is the inner
man (the heart and spirit), not the flesh, that is transformed.
It is true that the flesh *behaves* differently because the
born again man has a new heart, and it is from the heart
that the issues of life proceed. The heart controls the habits
of the flesh, and therefore believers live differently after they
become believers. That does not mean that the old nature
is completely eradicated, although there are some who teach
this erroneous doctrine. (But if you will check on their
lives for a long enough period of time, you will notice that
they are still very much in the flesh!)

"The carnal mind is enmity against God: for it is not
subject to the law of God, neither indeed can be" (Rom.
8:7). The unregenerate man is utterly fallen, carnal, corrupt, unrighteous, ungodly, blind, and hopelessly lost—and
flesh can produce no better than more flesh. The law of
God is "holy, and just, and good" (Rom. 7:12), but "what
the law could not do, in that it was weak through the flesh,
God sending His own Son in the likeness of sinful flesh,
and for sin, condemned sin in the flesh: that the righteousness of the law might be fulfilled in us, who walk not after
the flesh, but after the Spirit" (Rom. 8:3,4).

David, a man after God's own heart, cried out, "Behold, I was shapen in iniquity; and in sin did my mother conceive me!" (Psalm 51:5).

In Galatians 5:17 the Apostle Paul declared, "The flesh lusteth against the Spirit, and the Spirit against the flesh: and these are contrary the one to the other: so that ye cannot do the things that ye would."

In the first part of our present verse the word "flesh" means the natural *body* of man; in the last part of the verse it means the *corrupt nature* of man as described in the verse just quoted from Galatians.

The same is true of the word *spirit.* The first "spirit" named is the *Holy Spirit;* the last spirit named is the spirit of man, *the inner man.* The offspring of the Holy Spirit is spiritual; the offspring of the flesh is carnal and fleshly. A baby born to *believers* is born in sin and when that baby reaches the age of accountability it must be born of the Spirit or be hopelessly lost. There is no power that will make us spiritual and fit for the kingdom of God except the power of the new birth—being born of the Word of God and of the Holy Spirit.

Jesus was in all things "made like unto His brethren" (Heb. 2:17), which means that He had a body like our own; but He was not *"born of the flesh"* by natural generation as men are. Jesus was conceived by the miraculous operation of the Holy Ghost. He was the Son of God—flesh, yes, but He was the God-Man, GOD in flesh.

Verse 7: *"Marvel not that I said unto thee, Ye must be born again."*

Jesus knew that what He had just said astonished this educated religionist. Nicodemus had no doubt lived above reproach, had discharged his duties well, and had been faithful to the religion of his fathers. He marveled that this Teacher should say, *"YOU, Nicodemus, must be born again!"* There are people today who say that they are good, they have never done wrong, they have always lived a good

life—but men do not go to hell because they are bad, nor
do they go to heaven because they are good. People go to
hell because they reject Jesus (John 3:18). Those who go
to heaven go there because they *receive* Jesus (John 1:12,13).
The all-important question is not "Are you good? or are
you bad?" but "Are you BORN AGAIN? What think ye
of *Christ?* Whose Son is He?" Do YOU have a new heart
through the miracle of His saving grace and His cleansing
blood? If you have not, regardless of how "good" you are
or how much good you have done, you are not fit for the
kingdom of God and you cannot enter there!

How long has it been since you heard a sermon in your
church on being born again? It is said that the great English preacher, George Whitfield, preached on the new birth
three hundred times in the city of London. Some of his
friends asked him why he repeated the same sermon so many
times, and he replied, *"Ye must be born again!!"* Since
men must be born again or burn in hell, ministers should
preach often on this subject.

No person has ever "grown into" salvation. We do not
gradually become Christian. The new birth happens instantaneously the split second one believes on the Lord Jesus Christ and by faith receives His finished work. We do
not become Christian by living a good life; we live a good
life because we ARE Christian. We do not become Christian by abstaining from evil; Christians abstain from evil
because they have a new heart—but to have a new heart
one must be born again. All have sinned and come short
of the glory of God, there is none righteous—no, not one.
There is none that seeketh after God, ALL have gone astray,
but God laid on Jesus the iniquity of us all, and all who
will believe on Him and receive Him are then born into the
family of God.

Verse 8: *"The wind bloweth where it listeth, and thou
hearest the sound thereof, but canst not tell whence it cometh, and whither it goeth: so is every one that is born of
the Spirit."*

In explaining to Nicodemus the work of the Holy Ghost in the new birth, Jesus uses a familiar illustration: He speaks of the *wind* that blows where it chooses. We know not from whence it blows nor where it goes; but when we hear the *sound* of it and see the trees moving, we do not question the fact that the wind is *blowing.*

"*So is everyone that is born of the Spirit.*" As it is with the wind, so it is with the operation of the Holy Spirit in the new birth. The spiritual birth is incomprehensible to the mind of man; but it is God's miracle and must be received by faith. We cannot understand it, we cannot explain it, but we know it has happened and by faith we accept it.

To me there is a distinct and peculiar beauty in the Lord's selecting the wind as an illustration of the work of the Holy Spirit in the heart of one who is born again. Everyone knows of the *existence* of the wind, but none can explain where it originates nor where it finishes its course; we simply feel and experience the results of its blowing. In the same sense we cannot, in the language of man, explain the operation of the Holy Spirit, but we see the effects of that operation and we know that the Spirit convicts, convinces, and draws men to God.

The wind is used to illustrate the Spirit's work in many other places in the Word of God. All Bible scholars are familiar with Ezekiel's account of the valley of dry bones, and in Ezekiel 37:9,10 we read, "Then said He to me, Prophesy unto the wind, prophesy, son of man, and say to the wind, Thus saith the Lord God: Come from the four winds, O breath, and breathe upon these slain, that they may live. So I prophesied as He commanded me, and the breath came into them, and they lived, and stood up upon their feet, an exceeding great army."

We find another illustration in Acts 2:2 when the Holy Spirit came on the Day of Pentecost: "And suddenly there came a sound from heaven as of a mighty rushing wind, and it filled all the house where they were sitting."

The Holy Spirit is in the world today; He came on the Day of Pentecost, and He will go out with the Church when the Church is raptured. Just as we hear the sound of the wind and see its effects, so is the work of the Spirit in the life of the born again person. In appearance that person is the same—yet he is a new creation, his aim in life is changed, his motives are changed. The spiritual man draws the inspiration of his daily life from a source men cannot see—that is, from the Holy Spirit. The born again person bears the *fruit* of the Spirit—love, joy, peace, contentment, assurance. Such fruits do not grow on the tree of human nature, they are not produced by the limbs of the flesh.

Verse 9: *"Nicodemus answered and said unto Him, How can these things be?"*

This question displays the spiritual ignorance of ALL unbelievers. Jesus had instructed Nicodemus thoroughly. First of all He had clearly declared that every man must be born again if he is to see the kingdom of God. He repeated the same divine imperative even more fully by explaining, "Except a man be born *of water and of the Spirit,* he cannot enter into the kingdom of God." Water was used often in the ceremonies in the temple, and Nicodemus should have known that "water" was used here in speaking of the Word. Jesus then explained how flesh could produce no better than flesh, and for one to be prepared and fit for the kingdom of God he must be born anew, born from above, and delivered from the corruption of the natural man. By way of further explanation He gave Nicodemus a down-to-earth illustration by using the wind in comparison to the work of the Holy Spirit, showing that it is the *spirit* of man that is born of the Spirit of God. But even then, after He had gone through all of these explanations, Nicodemus asked, *"How can these things BE?"* He was still in the dark, spiritually, and was ignorant of saving grace.

Verse 10: *"Jesus answered and said unto him, Art thou*

a master of Israel, and knowest not these things?"

Note that Jesus did not answer Nicodemus with *further explanation* of how these things could be, but kindly rebuked him for his gross ignorance: "Art thou *a master of Israel,* and knowest not *these things?"* Greek authorities tell us that the original language here reads "THE master of Israel," indicating that Nicodemus was the most outstanding teacher in all of Israel—and yet he did not know the simple things pertaining to salvation.

There are many so-called "teachers" today who are blind, leading the blind, dedicated to a denomination and its doctrine but denying the blood-bought salvation of Calvary. They may have a master's degree in theology and be honored as great religious leaders—but they do not know how to instruct others in the new birth because they have never been born again themselves.

"Art thou a master of Israel, AND KNOWEST NOT THESE THINGS?" In other words, "Nicodemus, you who mastered the Old Testament Scriptures do not know that you must have a clean heart and a new spirit in order to enter the kingdom of God?" As a master in Israel surely Nicodemus would have known many Old Testament Scriptures that pointed to the Messiah and the new birth, such as the familiar passage from Psalm 40:10: "I have not hid thy righteousness within my heart; I have declared thy faithfulness and thy salvation: I have not concealed thy lovingkindness and thy truth from the great congregation." He knew Jeremiah 4:4: "Circumcise yourselves to the Lord, and take away the foreskins of your heart, ye men of Judah and inhabitants of Jerusalem: lest my fury come forth like fire, and burn that none can quench it, because of the evil of your doings."

What religious leader in Israel would not have read Ezekiel 18:31? "Cast away from you all your transgressions, whereby ye have transgressed; and make you a new heart and a new spirit: for why will ye die, O house of Israel?"

Surely Nicodemus had read Ezekiel 36:26: "A new heart also will I give you, and a new spirit will I put within you: and I will take away the stony heart out of your flesh, and I will give you an heart of flesh (*a new heart*)."

Jesus did not abuse Nicodemus when He rebuked him for his ignorance. We notice many times in the epistles of the Apostle Paul that he begs believers to "be not ignorant." No one will ever understand *everything* about the Bible, but the Holy Spirit does reveal the deep things of God to those who are willing to search, study, and trust, in faith believing.

Verse 11: *"Verily, verily, I say unto thee, We speak that we do know, and testify that we have seen; and ye receive not our witness."*

Here is another "double verily," indicating that a tremendous truth follows. Notice, Jesus said, *"WE speak."* There is much discussion and division among Bible scholars concerning just who this "we" might be. Without a doubt Jesus referred to *Himself,* but He used the plural to give weight and divine dignity to His statement. In the spiritual sense it is impossible to separate Father, Son, and Holy Ghost; yet the Godhead is made up of *three* distinct Persons. Jesus used the plural here to assure Nicodemus that what the Son was saying, Father and Holy Spirit were also saying. In other words, "The Godhead knows whereof WE speak." Jesus declared, "I am in the Father, and the Father in me" (John 14:10). He also declared, "I and my Father are one" (John 10:30). Paul tells us that God was in Christ (II Cor. 5:19). There are other instances where Jesus spoke in the plural, speaking for the Godhead—as in Mark 4:30 when He asked, "Whereunto shall WE liken the kingdom of God? or with what comparison shall WE compare it?"

What Jesus said to Nicodemus was simply this: "I speak with authority, I speak truth which I have known from eternity. I was with the Father in the beginning, I have seen and known all that the Father and Holy Ghost have seen and known. I am not speaking as the prophets spoke to the fathers in times past. I do not speak as one *ordained* of God—*I AM GOD in flesh.* God is truth, therefore what I speak is truth. I do not testify what others have *told* me, I speak that which I have received as God's Son, *the Word Incarnate.* My words are God's words. I speak what I have seen and known with my Father from the beginning, before the world was created." Jesus did not come into the world that there might be a Gospel: He WAS the Gospel. He did not come that there might be a Word of God: He WAS the Word of God.

"Ye receive not our witness." This does not mean that not even *one person* believed or received the testimony of Jesus. It simply means that the *masses* did not believe Him—and the same is true today. John the Baptist used almost these same words in verse 32 of this chapter: "And what He hath seen and heard, that He testifieth; and no man receiveth His testimony."

"Ye" applies not only to Nicodemus, but to all the Jews who had heard Jesus teach since He entered the temple and cleansed it just after His first miracle in Cana.

Verse 12: *"If I have told you earthly things, and ye believe not, how shall ye believe, if I tell you of heavenly things?"*

In other words, "Nicodemus, you ask 'How can these things be?' when I talk of earthly things such as the wind. How then could you *possibly* believe if I told you things that are from heaven, through heaven's miracle? I have given you simple truth and you have not received it; how can you receive *deeper* truth that originates in heaven?"

"Earthly things" here refers to the doctrine of the new birth; *"heavenly things"* refers to the truths Jesus is preparing to make known to Nicodemus—the truth concerning His deity, the plan of redemption through His own blood; His sacrificial death on Calvary, God the Father's love for

the whole world, and the divine fact that simple faith in the finished work of the Son of God is the only door to heaven and the only escape from hell. If Nicodemus refused to believe the simple things of earth, how could he hope to receive the tremendous truth concerning who is saved and why, who is lost and why, and that willful rejection of the True Light is the one cause of man's condemnation?

Can we really refer to the new birth as *"earthly"*? It IS earthly when compared to Christ's divinity and His atonement. It is earthly in that it takes place here on earth while man *dwells on earth*. Men who are not born again before they die are certainly not regenerated *after* death! One cannot be born again after he departs this life.

Jesus was in the beginning with the Father, in the bosom of the Father. He became flesh and took a body like unto the body of man, in order that He might taste death for every man. He paid the sin-debt here on earth and purchased our redemption through His precious blood. Provision for the new birth was made on earth; the blood of Jesus was shed here on earth. In *regeneration* God comes down to man—and when one is regenerated by the shed blood of Jesus, *God dwells IN man,* man becomes partaker of divine nature here on earth. In the *atonement* Christ takes man's nature as man's representative, and He becomes man's forerunner in heaven where He is seated at the right hand of God the Father, making intercession for believers.

The divinity of Christ, the Incarnation, the atonement He made, the justification by faith which He makes possible—these are *"heavenly things,"* so heavenly that mortal man cannot comprehend them. These are things that go beyond our thinking, beyond our ability of reason and understanding. The atonement transaction performed by Jesus *for* man is of special effect on man's position before God in heaven. Because of the atonement, believers are hid with Christ in God (Col. 3:3); we sit together in heavenly places in Christ Jesus (Eph. 2:6); we are in Christ (Rom.

8:1); Christ is in us (Col. 1:27). To be justified before God means to be just as just as *Jesus* is just, just as though we had never sinned. We are justified in the sight of God by faith in the shed blood of Jesus (Rom. 5:1). When God looks at us He sees Jesus, He sees righteousness, purity, holiness—all because He sees the believer justified by faith in the finished work of His only begotten Son. How can finite mind comprehend such truth?

Christ is our atonement, He is our Mediator, and as the Man Christ Jesus He is seated at the right hand of the Majesty on high. When we appear before God, Jesus will confess us as His children because, *while here on EARTH*, we believed on Him and received His shed blood through which we have received the atonement:

"Therefore being justified by faith, we have peace with God through our Lord Jesus Christ: by whom also we have access by faith into this grace wherein we stand, and rejoice in hope of the glory of God. And not only so, but we glory in tribulations also: knowing that tribulation worketh patience; and patience, experience; and experience, hope: and hope maketh not ashamed; because the love of God is shed abroad in our hearts by the Holy Ghost which is given unto us. For when we were yet without strength, in due time Christ died for the ungodly. For scarcely for a righteous man will one die: yet peradventure for a good man some would even dare to die. But God commendeth His love toward us, in that, while we were yet sinners, Christ died for us. Much more then, being now justified by His blood, we shall be saved from wrath through Him. For if, when we were enemies, we were reconciled to God by the death of His Son, much more, being reconciled, we shall be saved by His life. And not only so, but we also joy in God through our Lord Jesus Christ, *by whom we have now received the ATONEMENT*" (Rom. 5:1−11).

Verse 13: *"And no man hath ascended up to heaven, but He that came down from heaven, even the Son of man which is in heaven."*

Here Jesus began to tell Nicodemus of *"heavenly things."* He declared His deity, reminding Nicodemus that no son of Adam had ever ascended into heaven where God the heavenly Father dwells, but He in whose presence Nicodemus was standing had come down FROM heaven, and one day in the near future He would again *ascend TO heaven.* In His divine nature He was actually in heaven at that moment—one with the Father, co-equal with the Father, having dwelt with the Father from all eternity.

"Even the Son of man which is in heaven." Certainly this could be said by no ordinary man. It would be absurd for any mortal to testify, "I am speaking here on earth —and *at the same time* I am in heaven." But Jesus could make that statement in perfect truth. He never ceased to be God when He became incarnate. He was *with* God, He *was* God—but at the same time He was MAN. Thus, as God dwelling in a tabernacle of flesh, He was in heaven even at the very second He was speaking these words to Nicodemus.

Verses 14 and 15: *"And as Moses lifted up the serpent in the wilderness, even so must the Son of man be lifted up: That whosoever believeth in Him should not perish, but have eternal life."*

Here, too, Jesus presents *"heavenly things."* Here we see the crucifixion of the Lamb of God. It is not unreasonable to suppose that Nicodemus, like most of the Jews, thought that when Messiah appeared He would come in power and great glory, exalted and honored by men, a great military leader who would lead them to victory over the Roman oppressors.

In that day, the most disgraceful way any person could die was by crucifixion. Jesus had just declared His deity, and now He is telling Nicodemus that the Messiah must be lifted up as Moses lifted up the serpent of brass in the wilderness! Nicodemus knew well this event in the history of Israel's wanderings: "And Moses made a serpent of brass, and put it upon a pole, and it came to pass, that if a serpent had bitten any man, when he beheld the serpent of brass, he lived" (Num. 21:9).

What Jesus is saying here is, "Moses, in whom you trust, has given us a vivid type of the work that I have come to do." Without a doubt, Nicodemus paid much closer attention the moment Moses was mentioned, because the Pharisees regarded Moses very highly.

"Even so must the Son of man be lifted up." The Greek word here translated "must" signified "it is necessary that." There was no other way. The Son of man MUST be lifted up—and a "must" with God is a MUST.

When Jesus used the term "Son of man" Nicodemus undoubtedly remembered Daniel's prophecy of the coming Messiah (Dan. 7:13,14). God's promises of the Redeemer must be fulfilled. God cannot break His promise, He cannot alter His Word. All the types of the Old Testament system, the sacrifices and offerings, would be to no avail if THE sacrifice did not come! The law of God must be satisfied, God's holiness must be satisfied, and a way must be provided whereby God could be just and yet justify the ungodly. The only way to provide such a sacrifice was that Messiah, the Lamb of God, suffer and be hanged on a tree. He must take our place; He who knew no sin must become sin for us: "For He (God) hath made Him (Jesus) to be sin for us, who knew no sin; that we might be made the righteousness of God in Him" (II Cor. 5:21).

The Son of man must die, and He must die in a singular way—He must be *"lifted up."* This points to the cross: "And I, if I be lifted up from the earth, will draw all men unto me. This (Jesus) said, signifying what death He should die" (John 12:32,33).

Some Bible scholars have suggested that for Jesus to be "lifted up" simply means that He must be lifted up by *ministers*—His Incarnation, His sacrificial death, and His resurrection must be lifted up; but that is definitely NOT the meaning here. Jesus used the illustration of Moses and the serpent of brass, which makes it very clear that He was declaring that *He* must be lifted up on the cross as the serpent of brass was lifted up by Moses in the wilderness. It is true that ministers must lift up the Incarnation, the shed blood, the atonement, the bodily resurrection of Jesus, but that is not the meaning of this Scripture.

It was not by accident or chance that Jesus used this particular illustration here. We need to study this portion of God's holy Word very carefully. Just what do we have here? What are the exact points at which the *type* (the serpent of brass) and the *antitype* (Jesus on the cross) meet?

To me, we have this picture: When Moses cried out to God on behalf of the Israelites who had been bitten by the fiery serpents, that nation was in sore distress; they were dying by hundreds from the bites of the poisonous snakes. Unregenerated man is in great *spiritual* distress and danger; he has been bitten by the serpent of sin, he is dying from *the poisonous effects* of sin: "When lust hath conceived, it bringeth forth sin: *and sin, when it is finished, bringeth forth DEATH*" (James 1:15). Sin and death are synonymous. The unbeliever is helpless, hopeless, *sure* to die, for God has decreed that *"the wages of sin is death"* (Rom. 6:23). As the Israelites were in sore distress, dying from the poisonous serpents' bite, *unbelievers* are in sore distress, dying from the poison of sin.

The serpent of brass was lifted up on a pole, in the sight of all the nation of Israel. In like manner Christ was lifted up on the cross *publicly*. (His cross was lifted on Calvary, one of the most public of places. It was the place where criminals were crucified; everyone knew where it was, and it could be seen from every side. Thus it was possible for great throngs of people to stand around Calvary, "the place of the skull," and see Jesus as He hung on the cross. To make it even *more* public, He was crucified at the time of the Passover, a time when Jews came to Jerusalem from all over the known world. Therefore a great part of the nation of Israel was present when Jesus was lifted up on the cross in the same manner that Moses lifted up the serpent in the wilderness in the presence of all the *camp* of Israel.

It may have seemed strange to the Israelites that God had told Moses to make a *serpent*—an object made in the likeness of the poisonous snakes that were biting them and bringing death upon them. If MAN had chosen the emblem to be lifted up you may rest assured it would not have been a serpent; the Israelites would have chosen almost any *other* symbol. But *God* instructed Moses what to do, and the serpent lifted up on the pole was in the exact image of the snakes that were bringing death to the children of Israel.

In the same manner, *Christ who knew no sin,* in whom *was* no sin, was made in the likeness of sinful flesh (II Cor. 5:21; Rom. 8:3). The serpent of brass was without poison, without venom. Christ the Man, made in the *likeness* of man, was without sin—the only man who ever lived without sin. Jesus on the cross was heaven's best for earth's worst. He was counted as a sinner, He took our place though HE had no sin. He was hanged on a tree, and our sin was laid upon HIM: "Who His own self bare our sins in His own body on the tree, that we, being dead to sins, should live unto righteousness: by whose stripes ye were healed" (I Pet. 2:24). On that crucifixion day thousands of Israelites looked upon Him *literally.* Believers today see Him with the eye of faith; we see Him on the cross, *our sins* carried to the cross by Jesus our Redeemer—Lamb of God and only begotten of the Father.

Notice that God told Moses exactly what to do, and Moses obeyed. God also told the Israelites what to do: they were simply to "Look, and *live.*" The only way a dying Israelite could be healed and have life was to look to the brazen serpent. He was not to touch it nor speak to it; He was simply to LOOK upon it. The only way the unbeliever can benefit from Christ's death on Calvary is to

look to Him in faith. No matter how near death an Israelite was, if he had strength enough to open his eyes and
look upon the serpent of brass he was instantly healed. In
the same manner, regardless of how weak one's faith may
be, any poor sinner who will look to Jesus and sincerely
believe and trust *will be saved.* Sincere faith brings salvation.

We are saved by grace through faith, but faith does not
come in inches, feet, yards, ounces or pounds. Faith is
faith; and if one has enough faith to simply look to Jesus
and *yield* to Him in faith, that faith will bring salvation.
Christ on the cross becomes our substitute when we believe
on Him personally. He was our representative, He was
punished in our place through the imputation of our sins
(II Cor. 5:21).

When Moses at the command of God made the serpent
of brass and put it on a pole, the Israelites saw the image
of the very serpent that bit them; and yet when they *looked*
at the serpent of brass as they were commanded to do,
they were healed. When the sin-sick unbeliever looks to
Calvary, in faith believing, he sees on the cross the divine
Son of God, made in our image, *sinless,* but made to be
sin for us. He bore *all* sin, all the *poison* of sin, and all
the *death* sin could bring.

Verse 15 declares the *purpose* of the lifting up of the
Son of man, and the *results* of His being lifted up. Thank
God for the *whosoever!* *"Whosoever believeth in Him,"*
whosoever looks to Him with the eye of faith shall not
perish, *"but have eternal life."* The promise of salvation
is to ALL: *"All we like sheep have gone astray; we have
turned every one to his own way; and the Lord hath laid
on (Jesus) the iniquity of us ALL"* (Isa. 53:6).

The "believing" here is with the heart; it is not an *intellectual* belief. It does not mean whosoever believes there
IS a God, or that there IS a Christ, or even that He is
THE Saviour and is able to save. The believing here is
heart belief. When one realizes that he has been bitten

by sin and that the poison of sin will eventually bring death—*eternal* death; when that person feels the deep need for being healed spiritually and saved for all eternity, and turns to Jesus for forgiveness of sin and commits himself entirely to Jesus, he will be healed, he will be saved—but only through faith in the Lamb of God who made the vicarious atonement at Calvary. Righteousness is imputed. Christ is our righteousness, our holiness, our sanctification— and apart from Him there IS no righteousness, no salvation.

ALL in the Israelite camp were invited to look and live. Those who *looked, LIVED.* Those who *refused to look, DIED.* The invitation to the sinner is to "whosoever"— no one is excluded. No matter how feeble the faith may be—(it is not the quantity of faith, but in WHOM we believe); no matter how sinful and wretched the person may be, *if he believes* he has everlasting life. If an Israelite died it was because he refused to look at the serpent of brass; and if you, dear reader, spend eternity in hell it will be because you refused to look to Jesus, believe on Him and trust in His shed blood.

Please notice that this promise did not end with *"should not perish"*; there is more: *"but have eternal life."* Jesus not only delivers from hell—He gives life eternal, life abundant. We become partakers of divine nature and sit together in heavenly places in Him. He who believes on Jesus not only escapes the damnation of hell, he at once receives eternal life. He receives a title to a home in glory, a title to all the blessedness of the Pearly White City when this life ends.

When a minister preaches a sermon on hell, the average person in the pew thinks of salvation as a way of escape, a way to keep from entering hell; but salvation is more than that: it is full, as well as free; it is the door to the Pearly White City and to everlasting life with Jesus.

Some people refuse salvation because they say, "There is too much to give up, I will lose too much if I become a Christian." But they are wrong. Salvation is not losing;

it is *gaining*.   Jesus said, "Whosoever will save his life
shall lose it: and whosoever will lose his life for my sake
shall find it.   For what is a man profited, if he shall gain
the whole world, and lose his own soul? or what shall a
man give in exchange for his soul?" (Matt. 16:25,26).

Verse 16:   *"For God so loved the world, that He gave
His only begotten Son, that whosoever believeth in Him
should not perish, but have everlasting life."*

John 3:16 is often referred to as "the Gospel in a nut-
shell."   There is enough Gospel in this verse to save the
world if the *world* would hear and believe it.

Nicodemus might have thought that the Messiah would
come only to Israel and that the benefit of His coming
would be enjoyed only by the Jews; but Jesus here announced that God loves the entire world—Jew, Gentile, rich,
poor, bond or free, without exception.   The only begotten
Son of God is God's gift to the entire family of Adam!   He
came from the Father's bosom to reclaim and redeem all
that the first Adam lost.

There is no more wonderful announcement in all of the
Word of God than what we read in this verse.   Think of
it, beloved!   God is love and pure righteousness; yet He
could love a world that hated Him and hated His Son, a
world that demanded the *death* of His Son, nailed Him to
a cross, and mocked Him while He died.   He not only
loved the world, He also provided salvation at the greatest
cost that even HE could know!   There is no way to estimate the cost of this, our "great salvation."   God did not
send angels, cherubim, or any heavenly creature to pay the
price of redemption: *He gave His only begotten Son.*   There
was no other way.

What is meant by the statement, *"God so loved the
WORLD"*?   Some teach that "God so loved *the elect* out
of every tribe and nation"—not all mankind, but a select,
elect few.   But if *that* be true, then John 3:16 should read,
"For God so loved the world that He gave His only be-

gotten Son that *the world* through Him should be saved";
but it does not read that way. It says, *"Whosoever BE-
LIEVETH."* That means *whosoever* out of all the world,
from every tribe and nation, of every language and color.
"Whosoever believeth" becomes a child of God. It is straining the language to make "world" mean the elect only,
for *"the world"* in Scripture refers to the wicked. The
Word of God *never* speaks of the saints as "the world."

Not only did God *love* the world (and every person IN
the world), but in I John 2:2 we are told that Christ is the
propitiation for the sins of the whole world. To teach that
the love of God is shed only upon the elect is to slander
God Almighty and take a very narrow view of His character. If God loved an elect group, if He did not love all
the world, how can He be righteous, just, and holy? How
can He judge the world? I believe in the sovereignty of
God, I believe in Bible election; but I also believe that
"whosoever will" is invited to drink of the water of life
freely. I do not believe the doctrine of hyper-Calvinism, I
do not believe the doctrine of limited atonement. John 3:16
teaches that God so loved *the WORLD* that He gave the
most precious Jewel heaven afforded, that *whosoever IN
the world* believes in God's Son "shall not come into condemnation but is passed from death unto life."

The love spoken of in John 3:16 (God's love for the whole
wide world) definitely clears Almighty God of injustice and
respect of persons in judging the world—and He WILL judge
the world by Jesus Christ. "Wherefore God also hath highly
exalted Him, and given Him a name which is above every
name: That at the name of Jesus every knee should bow,
of things in heaven, and things in earth, and things under
the earth; and that every tongue should confess that Jesus
Christ is Lord, to the glory of God the Father" (Phil. 2:
9—11).

God could not righteously judge the world if He had no
love, no pity, no compassion for the world. If we had justice from God we would all spend eternity in hell. There

is no one in this world who is worthy of God's love, favor, and grace; yet when we were helpless, hopeless, without strength, God commended His love toward us in that Christ died for our sins.

Please notice the following Scriptures; study them carefully:

Ezekiel 33:11: "Say unto them, As I live, saith the Lord God, *I have no pleasure in the death of the wicked; but that the wicked turn from his way and live: turn ye, turn ye from your evil ways; for why will ye die, O house of Israel?"*

John 1:10 and 29: "He was in *the world,* and *the world* was made by Him, and *the world* knew Him not. . . The next day John seeth Jesus coming unto him, and saith, Behold the Lamb of God, which taketh away the sin of *the world.*"

John 6:33 and 51: "For the bread of God is He which cometh down from heaven, and giveth life unto *the world.* . . . I am the living bread which came down from heaven: if any man eat of this bread, he shall live for ever: and the bread that I will give is my flesh, which I will give for the life of *the world.*"

John 8:12: "Then spake Jesus again unto them, saying, I am the light of *the world*: he that followeth me shall not walk in darkness, but shall have the light of life."

Romans 3:19: "Now we know that what things soever the law saith, it saith to them who are under the law: that every mouth may be stopped, and *all the world* may become guilty before God."

II Corinthians 5:18,19: "And all things are of God, who hath reconciled us to Himself by Jesus Christ, and hath given to us the ministry of reconciliation; to wit, that God was in Christ, reconciling *the world* unto Himself, not imputing their trespasses unto them; and hath committed unto us the word of reconciliation."

I John 2:2: "And He (Jesus) is the propitiation for our sins: and not for our's only, but also for the sins of *the whole world.*"

I John 4:4 and 14: "Ye are of God, little children and have overcome them: because greater is He that is in you, than he that is in *the world* . . . And we have seen and do testify that the Father sent the Son to be the Saviour of *the world.*"

II Peter 3:9: "The Lord is not slack concerning His promise, as some men count slackness; but is longsuffering to us-ward, *not willing that ANY should perish, but that ALL should come to repentance!*"

I Timothy 2:3 and 4: "For this is good and acceptable in the sight of God our Saviour; *who will have ALL men to be saved,* and to come unto the knowledge of the truth."

"*God SO loved the WORLD . . . .*" That little word "so" signifies that there are not enough words in all the languages of all the world to explain the depth, the height, the length, or the breadth of the great love God bestowed upon man. How much "so" means in John 3:16, the wisdom of man can never reason out and the tongue of man can never tell. Only God, in eternity, can explain to us just how much He loved us when He "SO loved" that He gave Jesus to die for us that we might have life, and have it abundantly.

"*God SO loved the WORLD that He GAVE . . . .*" God proved His love by giving His very best. Christ on the cross is the *result* of God's love for the world, not the *cause* of His love. God does not love us *because* Jesus died on the cross; but rather, Jesus died on the cross *because God LOVED us* while we were yet sinners. To preach that God loves us because Jesus shed His blood on the cross is gross ignorance. The truth set forth in the Gospel is that God gave Jesus to the world *because He SO LOVED the world.* The suffering of Jesus on the cross did not cause God to fall in love with man; *the love of God ALLOWED Jesus to suffer on the cross.*

God gave Jesus to a lost, sinful world, a world that deserved no better than hell with all of its sorrow and misery.

He gave Jesus to pay the sin-debt:

"But now the righteousness of God without the law is manifested, being witnessed by the law and the prophets; even the righteousness of God which is by faith of Jesus Christ unto all and upon all them that believe: for there is no difference: *for all have sinned, and come short of the glory of God;* being justified freely by His grace through the redemption that is in Christ Jesus: Whom God hath set forth to be a propitiation through faith in His blood, to declare His righteousness for the remission of sins that are past, through the forbearance of God; to declare, I say, at this time, His righteousness: *that He might be just, and the Justifier of him which believeth in Jesus.* Where is boasting then? It is excluded. By what law? of works? Nay: but by the law of faith. *Therefore we conclude that a man is justified by faith without the deeds of the law.* Is He the God of the Jews only? Is He not also of the Gentiles? Yes, of the Gentiles also: Seeing it is one God, which shall justify the circumcision by faith, and uncircumcision through faith" (Rom. 3:21—30).

No wonder the Apostle Paul cried out, *"Thanks be unto God for His UNSPEAKABLE GIFT!"* (II Cor. 9:15).

In verse 14 Jesus referred to Himself as *"the Son of man."* In this verse He speaks of Himself as *the only begotten "Son of GOD."* These two verses declare the two natures of Jesus—very man, very God. That is exactly what He was, and it was necessary that Nicodemus believe this if he wanted to be born again. *You and I* must believe it, we must believe that Jesus was God incarnate. It is impossible to be born again and still deny the Incarnation, the deity of Christ. Those who desire to be born of the Spirit and washed in the blood *must* believe in Him as the Son of man and also as the Son of God.

God so loved the world that He gave Jesus *"that whosoever believeth in Him should not perish, but have everlasting life."* God loves ALL—but He saves only those who believe in His only begotten Son. He cannot save

those who refuse to believe in Jesus. If He did, He would
cease to be just, He would cease to be holy, He would
cease to be righteous. His plan of salvation was designed
and perfected before the foundation of the world (I Pet.
1:18—23), and God cannot repent concerning that plan.
ALL who believe are saved, all who *refuse* to believe are
lost; but this does not alter the fact of God's great love,
mercy, and goodness.

Verse 17: *"For God sent not His Son into the world
to condemn the world; but that the world through Him
might be saved."*

Here Nicodemus learns another "heavenly thing"—the
main object of Messiah's coming into this sinful world. In
spite of the fact that the world deserved judgment and condemnation, Jesus did not come to condemn or judge men.
He came to lay His life down that they might be saved.

No doubt Nicodemus was familiar with the prophecy of
David concerning Messiah: "I will declare the decree: the
Lord hath said unto me, Thou art my Son; this day have
I begotten thee. Ask of me, and I shall give thee the heath-
en for thine inheritance, and the uttermost parts of the earth
for thy possession. *Thou shalt break them with a rod of
iron;* thou shalt dash them in pieces like a potter's vessel"
(Psalm 2:7—9). Surely Nicodemus knew Daniel's prophecy
concerning the judgment that will be meted out to the nations—(please study Daniel 7:9—22)—and perhaps this is
how he expected the Messiah to come—with power and
great glory, a mighty Judge, to judge the nations with a
rod of iron and cast down the enemies of the Jews; but
Jesus declared that He had come, *NOT to condemn the
world,* but to save people from their sins. He WILL come
as King of kings and Lord of lords, the Lion of the Tribe
of Judah; and He WILL judge the nations with a rod of
iron and cast down thrones; but that will be when He
comes in power and great glory. He came the first time
as the meek and lowly Lamb of God, JESUS, Saviour.

"That the world through Him might be saved" does not mean that every person in the world will finally be saved. This could not be, because Jesus clearly states in the next verse that those who believe not are *"condemned already."* Jesus *loved* the whole world, and He carried the sins of the whole world to the cross and took them away. He is the propitiation for the sin of the whole world —but only those who believe on Him are saved. In John 5:40 He said to the unbelieving Jews, *"Ye WILL NOT come to me, that ye might have life!"*

Jesus opened the door of salvation to all the world: *"I am the door: by me if any man enter in, he shall be saved, and shall go in and out, and find pasture"* (John 10:9). There is enough grace to save every sinner who has ever been born or ever will be born, for *"the Father sent the Son to be the Saviour of the WORLD"* (I John 4:14).

Verse 18: *"He that believeth on Him is not condemned: but he that believeth not is condemned already, because he hath not believed in the name of the only begotten Son of God."*

To me, this is one of the greatest verses in all of the Bible. It clearly sets forth three things:

1. Who is saved—and *why*.

2. Who is lost—and *when*.

3. *Why* the lost are lost.

"He that believeth on (Jesus) is not condemned." Anyone who reads these words can understand them. To *believe on Jesus* is to trust Him, have faith in Him, rely upon Him. To believe on Jesus is to believe everything the Bible says about Him—that He was in the beginning with the Father, in the bosom of the Father, born of a virgin, lived a sinless life on earth, died, was buried, and rose again *according to the Scriptures.* When we receive Christ and believe on Him as He is revealed in the Word of God, *con-*

demnation is removed.

This is the third time in four verses that Jesus has spoken of our believing on Himself. Here is the divine declaration concerning the importance of faith—faith that believes in Jesus as having to do with justification. Apart from believing on Him there IS no justification, no life eternal. Any and all who hear the Gospel message can believe if they *will*. Salvation on the basis of faith in God makes salvation possible for all. The worst sinner who ever lived can be saved by *believing*. The little child who has just reached the age of accountability is also saved by *believing*. Whether murderer, drunkard, harlot, chief of sinners, or tender child, all are saved in the same way—the *only* way to become a child of God: by believing on Jesus and accepting His finished work.

The believer, then, is not condemned. He is pardoned, justified, cleared of all guilt and acquitted. Why? *Because he has received the One who carried all his guilt to the cross and nailed it there!* In Christ, the believer is delivered from the curse of the broken law and reckoned righteous in the sight of a holy God (I Cor. 1:30).

Now let us read that statement again: "He that believeth on Him *IS NOT condemned.*" It does not say, "he will not *be* condemned when he dies, or at the judgment." It clearly states that the believer is free from condemnation NOW—the split second he believes. "By Him all that believe are justified from all things . . ." (Acts 13:39). The moment the sinner believes on Jesus, his iniquities, sins, and unrighteousness are taken away and he is immediately counted righteous. We do not become righteous by living a good life; we become righteous by believing on Jesus. When we believe from the heart, *His* righteousness is imputed to us.

"He that believeth NOT is condemned already." Ministers should often use this statement as a text. Unbelievers ARE condemned, they are condemned NOW. There is no need to say, "I hope I will not be lost when I die."

If you are not a *believer,* you are lost NOW; *the wrath of
God* abides on you NOW. "He that believeth on the Son
hath everlasting life: and he that believeth not the Son
shall not see life; *but the wrath of God ABIDETH ON
HIM*" (John 3:36). If you are an unbeliever, even *while
you live* you are under the condemnation of God and the
curse of His broken law hangs over your head. The unbeliever is reckoned guilty before God, dead in trespasses
and sins (Rom. 3:19; Eph. 2:5). Every unbeliever is under
the condemnation of God NOW. One heartbeat is all that
stands between the sinner and hell!

He who believes *not* is condemned already *"BECAUSE
he hath NOT believed in the name of the only begotten
Son of God."* Here is divine proof that there is no sin so
great and so damning as the sin of unbelief. Every soul
in hell is there because of unbelief; every soul that will
ever *be* in hell will be there because of unbelief. Drunkenness, gambling, lying, murder—all these are *fruits* of unbelief. It takes only one sin—the sin of unbelief—to damn
the soul. A man need not get drunk, commit murder, lie,
cheat, or steal in order to be lost; he can be honest, up-
right, sincere, and morally straight and still go to hell if
he does not have faith in the finished work of Jesus. It
is the sin of unbelief that damns the sinner, but sins of
omission (and sometimes sins of commission) rob the believer of his spiritual birthright of full joy and a full reward.

The man who refuses to believe on Jesus is sure for an
everlasting hell; there is no hope for such a one. If he per-
sists in his unbelief he positively *cannot* be saved. There
is no sin so insulting, so offensive, so provoking to a holy
God as for man, created *in the image of God,* to refuse the
glorious gift of salvation which was provided at the unknowable cost of God's only begotten Son. To refuse to
believe on Him is the capstone of the pyramid of sin. To
refuse to believe on Him is to lock the door to heaven and
shut one's self out from the Pearly White City. *Jesus* is
the only name "under heaven given among men, whereby

we must be saved" (Acts 4:12).

Verse 19: *"And this is the condemnation, that light is come into the world, and men loved darkness rather than light, because their deeds were evil."*

This statement was directed primarily to the nation Israel, the unbelieving Jews of that very day; but it also has to do with all who are under the condemnation of God. There was no reason why the Jews should not have recognized their Messiah; He was plainly revealed to them in prophecy—but when He came, Satan darkened their minds and they refused to see and believe. Today—as in the days when Jesus walked this earth—the real reason men are lost is not that they do not have the light and cannot know the way of salvation, nor is it because God is not willing and ready to save.   Men go on in sin *because they love their own way.*   They love sin, they will not come to Jesus that they might be *delivered* from sin and have righteousness imputed to them.   It is the nature of the natural man to love darkness rather than light.   Therefore men go on in darkness, refusing to *see* the light and allow the love of God to come into their hearts by faith.

"This is THE condemnation"—that is, this is the *cause* of the condemnation, the true *account* of condemnation. Men are not condemned because they are sons of Adam through no choice of their own.   It is true that Adam's sin is born into every man, *and death BY sin;* but *"light is come into the world,"* and there is no excuse for condemnation except by the free-will choice of the individual. Those who are condemned are condemned because they refuse to come to the light.   Light and love are provided, and salvation is the gift of God; but men, knowing all this, still go on in darkness because they love sin.   *"Therefore thou art inexcusable, O man . . ."* (Rom. 2:1).

"Light is come into the world."   In I John 1:5—7 we read, "This then is the message which we have heard of Him, and declare unto you, that GOD IS LIGHT, AND

IN HIM IS NO DARKNESS AT ALL. If we say that we
have fellowship with Him, and walk in darkness, we lie,
and do not the truth: but if we walk in the light, as HE
is in the light, we have fellowship one with another, and
the blood of Jesus Christ His Son cleanseth us from all
sin." *God* is light, and Jesus was God Incarnate. To the
Pharisees He said, "I am the Light of the world" (John
8:12).

I believe the statement in this phrase has a twofold meaning: I believe it refers to Christ Himself, His Person; and
I believe it also means the *Gospel* of Christ. The Word is
a lamp unto our feet, a light unto our pathway, and the
entrance of the Word brings light. Jesus came, therefore
light is come into the world. We now have the perfect
law of liberty, the perfect message of the Gospel. God is
light, and Jesus declared God to man.

*"Men loved darkness rather than light, because their
deeds were evil."* "Darkness" here speaks of *mental and
moral darkness,* the darkness of sin—or should I say the
darkness of the *fruits* of sin? Men love the lust of the eye,
the lust of the flesh, and the pride of life. The natural
man cannot love the things of God because his very nature
is sinful. Before we can love God as we should, we must
experience the miracle of the new birth and have a new
heart and a new spirit. Man apart from God is totally depraved—superstitious, ignorant, blinded by the god of this
age.

The *evil deeds* spoken of in this verse have reference to
evil habits of life. Men do not change their wicked habits
apart from the miracle of God's grace in the heart. Man
in flesh has *never* been willing to obey God and follow His
commands. Apart from God's grace, men (including Adam)
have loved darkness and corruption. As long as this world
stands, the natural man will love sin. Even little children
do not need to be taught to do things that are wrong. It
is born in them, it is their nature. Do not misunderstand
me—*the grace of God takes care of the innocent;* but even

little children are prone to do things which testify that man in his natural state is not fit for the kingdom of God.

Through the inspired pen of the Apostle Paul the Holy Spirit gives the final verdict for the entire world, the whole human race:

"As it is written, There is none righteous, no, not one: There is none that understandeth, there is none that seeketh after God. They are all gone out of the way, they are together become unprofitable; there is none that doeth good, no, not one. Their throat is an open sepulchre; with their tongues they have used deceit; the poison of asps is under their lips: Whose mouth is full of cursing and bitterness: Their feet are swift to shed blood: Destruction and misery are in their ways: and the way of peace have they not known: There is no fear of God before their eyes. Now we know that what things soever the law saith, it saith to them who are under the law: that every mouth may be stopped, and all the world may become guilty before God. Therefore by the deeds of the law there shall no flesh be justified in His sight: for by the law is the knowledge of sin" (Rom. 3:10–20).

In Isaiah 53:6 we are given the same truth—but Isaiah adds *hope:* "All we like sheep have gone astray; we have turned every one to his own way; *and the Lord hath laid on HIM the iniquity of us all!*"

Our present verse clearly reveals why men are lost, why they miss heaven and spend eternity in hell. There is not one iota of suggestion that God *predestines* men to destruction. There is no suggestion that God's love and Christ's atonement do not include *everyone.* God has revealed His love, His grace, and the way of salvation to all who will come to the light; therefore those who *refuse* to come to the light are inexcusable; they have no one but themselves to blame for their lost condition. If *you,* dear reader, spend eternity in hell it will not be God's will; it will be because of your own stubbornness in refusing to come to Jesus! God laid on Jesus the iniquity of us all, and the light shines for all who will come TO the light.

In the first chapters of Genesis we read how God created man in His own image, gave him a perfect wife, and placed the two of them in the beautiful Garden of Eden. He told Adam what to do—and also clearly instructed him as to *the one thing* he was NOT to do: *"Of the tree of the knowledge of good and evil, thou shalt not eat of it: for in the day that thou eatest thereof thou shalt surely die"* (Gen. 2:17). In other words, God gave Adam the right to choose.

Adam was innocent—but innocence is negative, righteousness is positive. Righteousness is imputed, and the only way to become righteous in the sight of God is by faith. When we exercise faith in Jesus' shed blood, righteousness is imputed—Christ in YOU is righteousness.

But Adam was not willing to obey God and walk in His commandments. He listened to Eve (who had listened to Satan), they ate of the forbidden fruit, "and the eyes of them both were opened." They made fig-leaf aprons to cover the shame of their nakedness, and then hid among the trees in the garden—but God found them. Their hiding place was inadequate, their covering was inadequate, their excuses were of no avail. God judged them—and judged all creation. He drove the first man and woman from the Garden of Eden—but that is not all:

God in His wisdom knew that Adam would return to the garden, therefore "He placed at the east of the Garden of Eden cherubims, and a flaming sword which turned every way, to keep the way of the tree of life" (Gen. 3:24). God knew that if Adam ate of the tree of life he would live forever in a body of sin—the body in which he had rebelled against his Creator; so He saw to it that Adam did not re-enter the garden and eat of the tree of life.

Salvation is of the Lord. He thought it, planned it, perfected and provided it. The true Light is come into the world to guide all who want to know the way to heaven, and those who refuse to come TO the Light do so because

they love their own dark, corrupt, sinful ways more than
they love righteousness, purity, holiness, and the way of
God. Therefore, like Adam, they reap the fruit of their own
ways; and if they continue to refuse to come to the Light
they will spend eternity in outer darkness where there is
weeping and wailing and gnashing of teeth. Those who
do not like the Light here on earth cannot live in heavenly
light, and if they choose to walk in darkness here, they
are automatically shut out from the eternal light in the
Pearly White City.

We cannot help being born in sin, we cannot help the
corruption of the flesh and the blindness of the natural
mind and heart; but what brings condemnation and damnation is rejecting the Lord Jesus Christ who came to lay His
life down that we might have life. The tragedy of all trag-
edies is for a man or woman to plunge over the precipice
of unbelief, into the lake of fire that burns with brimstone,
when their sins have been paid for, their redemption has
been purchased, and all they need do is come to Jesus!

Verses 20 and 21: *"For every one that doeth evil hateth
the light, neither cometh TO the light, lest his deeds should
be reproved. But he that doeth truth cometh to the light,
that his deeds may be made manifest, that they are wrought
in God."*

In these two verses we find a practical application of
all that Jesus has been saying in His discourse with Nicodemus. Here is the logical consequence of the truth declared in verse 19.

The message of these verses applies directly to the Jews
in that day, but it also applies to the Gentile nations—to
you and to me.

"Every one that doeth evil" (every unbeliever, every person who is not born again) *"hateth the light, neither cometh to the light."* The unbeliever does not love Christ, he
does not love the Gospel. If he came to the light the Gospel would reprove and rebuke him, and he would be forced

to face his lost condition. He does not want his wicked ways and evil deeds exposed and revealed, he does not want to be reproved. He fears the day when he will stand before God, when his every evil deed will be brought to light and judged; but since he loves sin and loves his own wicked way he will not come to the light, he will not seek Christ nor receive the Gospel in order to be saved.

There are two groups of unbelievers: those who hate the Gospel, hate the Church, and display their hatred without apology—(they even insult people who invite them to church and to evangelistic meetings)—and those who seem to *appreciate* the Gospel, they sometimes attend church and seem to appreciate good services. In reality, however, this second group is no better than the first, because deep down inside there is something they love more than they love God, otherwise they would yield to Jesus and serve Him. They remind us of the crowd who followed Jesus for the loaves and fishes, but when He was led away to Calvary they fled and left Him to face the cross alone. One day, when their true nature will be brought to light, they will hear Jesus say, "Depart! I never knew you."

"He that doeth truth cometh to the light." This speaks of the believer, the man who is truly born again. He may be weak, he may be just a babe in Christ, he may be spiritually ignorant; but with his heart he has believed unto righteousness: "For with the heart man believeth unto righteousness; and with the mouth confession is made unto salvation" (Rom. 10:10).

Similar expressions to the words found in verse 21 are also found in John 18:37; I John 1:6,8; 2:4; 3:19; and II John 3,4. "He that doeth truth" does not run from the light. He who lives in truth and walks in the light is always willing for his deeds to be known, he is not ashamed of what he does or of where he walks. He comes to the light *"that his deeds may be made manifest, that they are wrought in God."*

Nathanael is a good example of the truth of this verse.

He was a man "who did truth" *insofar as truth had been revealed to him* through the obscure light of the Mosaic system as it was administered under the scribes and Pharisees; and the very moment he came in contact with Jesus he believed on Him, received Him, and followed Him. The Gospel is a magnet to the believer. It has drawing power, it attracts those who have been born again; and when a person refuses to walk in the light you may rest assured that that person is not born again.

Nicodemus came to Jesus with a hungry heart, and Jesus turned on the light by instructing him in the new birth. We know from the later testimony of Nicodemus before the Sanhedrin and by his actions at the crucifixion that he *received* the light and accepted the truth given him that day. It is my personal belief that he was born again that very day; but if not, then certainly he became a *learner* of the truth, and somewhere, sometime, he was born again. I believe this because he came to the defense of the Messiah before the Sanhedrin (John 7:50,51) and along with Joseph of Arimathea he claimed the body of Jesus at the cross and helped to place it in Joseph's tomb. He proved his faith by his deeds.

The person who comes to Jesus for salvation and sincerely *receives* Jesus will begin to walk in the light and will go on walking in the light. If he is *not* sincere he will eventually turn back. Those who "profess" but do not "possess" may seem for awhile to be walking in the light, but it will soon be evident that they are not genuinely born again. Life *produces;* life is never stagnant or stationary. Life that does not grow is not life. Those who truly receive the Gospel and are born again will continue to walk in the truth of the Gospel, they will press closer to the Lord Jesus and will become more fully surrendered to His will; but if they are not truly born again they will eventually drift back into darkness and the lust of the flesh.

Is it not interesting to note that in this entire passage about Nicodemus there is not one word about his being baptized? Those who teach that the "water" in verse 5 is water baptism should give this serious consideration. I believe if water baptism were essential to redemption, Jesus would have baptized Nicodemus that day—and I further believe the Holy Spirit would have recorded it here. There is no suggestion that Nicodemus was baptized at this time— or ever. Every born again believer ·should follow Christ in baptism, but baptism is not essential to redemption. It is the precious blood of Jesus that washes away our sins.

Tremendous verses, these first twenty-one verses of the third chapter of the Gospel according to John! I doubt that there are twenty-one verses anywhere else in all of the Word of God that are more important in this day in which we live. We need to read them, re-read them, study them, and receive them with our whole being. In these verses we have seen the work of the Father, Son, and Holy Ghost. We learned of the Father's great love for mankind; we learned that the crucifixion was a divine "must"—the Son of man MUST be lifted up on the cross. We learned of the operation of the Holy Spirit in the new birth—"Except a man be born of the Spirit . . . ." These verses teach us that the natural man is corrupt, his nature is sinful, and he MUST be born again if he would enter the kingdom of God. Then we read of the "how" of regeneration, and that faith in Christ removes all condemnation. He who believes not is condemned already *because* he has not believed in the name of the only begotten Son of God. Those who are truly born again are anxious to come to the light, and those who refuse to come to the light are giving proof positive that they have NOT been born again.

A greater sermon has never been preached. Jesus Christ, the virgin-born Son of God, delivered this tremendous sermon, and it is interesting to note that it was preached— not to the multitudes, but to *one man.* Not one single point in the fundamentals of the faith goes untouched here. It is a *full* sermon—and no wonder! It was delivered by the greatest Preacher who ever lived.

Final Testimony of John the Baptist

Verse 22: *"After these things came Jesus and His disciples into the land of Judaea; and there He tarried with them, and baptized."*

The interview between Jesus and Nicodemus probably took place in the city of Jerusalem. Shortly thereafter, He left the city and went out into the rural areas of Judaea, into the countryside, and His disciples went with Him.

"He tarried there" (according to the Greek) indicates that He "spent some days" there. In other words, He continued there for a time, He did not simply pass through. The Scriptures reveal that Jesus loved the country; He traveled much in the countryside and in the mountains.

He tarried in Judaea *"and baptized."* The Bible teaches that Jesus Himself did not baptize (see chapter 4, verse 2). John the Baptist said to Him, "I have need to be baptized of thee"—but Jesus did not baptize him (Matt. 3:13—17). Someone might suggest that this is a contradiction since the passage here plainly says that "He tarried with them and baptized." But the correct interpretation of this is clear if we are willing to study and rightly divide the Word. When ordained men of God, men whom God has called and commissioned, perform the ordinances of the Christian religion, the work they do is HIS work. Thus when the *disciples of Jesus* baptized converts, it is perfectly correct to say that they administered HIS baptism.

Verse 23: *"And John also was baptizing in Aenon near to Salim, because there was much water there: and they came, and were baptized."*

Before the public announcement of the Messiah, John baptized "unto repentance," but after that there is no doubt that he was baptizing *in the name of Jesus.* However, this does not mean that John's baptism was worthless. I believe *John's* baptism and *Christian* baptism were the same in substance and that a person who truly repented and was

baptized by John needed not to be rebaptized after Pentecost. Unless we *do* take this view, there would be a question as to the baptism of the apostles.

The passage in Acts 19:1—6 does not contradict what I
have just said. For one thing, the persons described in
that passage seem to be ignorant of the first principles of
Christianity. They said, "We have not so much as heard
whether there be any Holy Ghost." This shows that they
had not been hearers of John Baptist, who frequently spoke
of the Holy Ghost (Matt. 3:11), nor had they been baptized
by John himself. They were most probably inhabitants of
Ephesus who had heard Apollos preach and who knew less
than their teacher.

It seems very clear that the only baptism the *apostles*
ever had was the baptism of John, and there is no Scripture to suggest that those who were baptized by him at
the beginning of his ministry were ever baptized again, or
that they *needed* to be.

John was baptizing *"in Aenon near to Salim."* Bible
scholars declare that today it is impossible to pinpoint the
location of this place. It was undoubtedly somewhere in Judaea. In Joshua 15:32, in the list of cities given to the tribe
of Judah, we find the names *Shilhim* and *Ain.* It is very
possible that this is the place where John was baptizing,
since translating from one language to another often con-
fuses names and their spelling.

We are told *why* John was baptizing in this particular
place—*"there was much water there."* I believe John the
Baptist baptized by immersion. Otherwise why would the
Holy Spirit point out that there was "much water"? If
John had been baptizing by other methods such as sprink-
ling or pouring, certainly there would have been no necessity for "much water."

I would digress here long enough to explain that I have
never made a point of breaking fellowship with other believers over the mode of baptism used. Water does not
save us, it has nothing to do with our salvation; but I do

emphatically believe that Jesus was immersed in Jordan (the Scripture says that He "went up straightway *out of the water*"—Matt. 3:16); and since I believe the Saviour was baptized by immersion, I have been baptized by the same method and I believe immersion to be the New Testament mode of baptism. But I do not break fellowship with other believers who differ with me on that point, because water baptism has nothing to do with salvation.

"They came, and were baptized." I believe that many who heard John preach believed on Jesus and were baptized.

Verse 24: *"For John was not yet cast into prison."*

It is my belief that John knew his ministry was fulfilled when he publicly announced Jesus and pointed Him out as the Messiah, but that did not cause him to be less diligent. He preached, he taught, he pointed men to Jesus, he baptized—he labored on to the very end of his earthly life. He continued diligently preaching and turning men to the Saviour until Herod demanded his head. "Who then is a faithful and wise servant, whom his lord hath made ruler over his household, to give them meat in due season? Blessed is that servant, whom his lord when he cometh shall find so doing" (Matt. 24:45,46).

Verse 25: *"Then there arose a question between some of John's disciples and the Jews about purifying."*

The Bible does not tell us the nature of the discussion, but judging from the preceding verses the "question" probably had to do with baptism. No doubt the people disputed with some of John's disciples over which was the most purifying, comparing the two baptisms—the baptism of John the Baptist and the baptism of Christ.

There has always been (and probably always will be) more controversy about baptism in Christian circles than any other doctrine or ordinance having to do with Christianity. Much harm has been done by believers' arguing

over baptism.   It is a pity some folk are not as zealous
over the winning of souls as they are over the method of
baptism.   Water has never washed away one sin—and never
will.   It is the blood of Jesus Christ that cleanses from sin.
The person who has hope in water baptism is building on
sand, and one day when the floods come his house will
surely fall.   Those who have their hope in "nothing less
than Jesus' blood and righteousness" will stand when the
world is on fire!

Verse 26:   *"And they came unto John, and said unto
him, Rabbi, He that was with thee beyond Jordan, to whom
thou barest witness, behold, the same baptizeth, and all
men come to Him."*

"They came unto JOHN."   You will notice that John
the Beloved did not refer to John the Baptist as "the Baptist."   It has been suggested that the reason for this is
that when John the Beloved wrote, John's baptism had
passed away.

The disciples of John were guilty of the same party spirit
for which Paul rebuked the Corinthians when they were
disputing among themselves, some saying, "I am of Paul,"
others saying, "I am of Apollos."   (Read the entire third
chapter of I Corinthians.)   The disciples of John were jealous because Jesus was making more disciples than John;
the ministry of Jesus was growing by leaps and bounds
while the ministry of John was diminishing.   They referred
to Jesus as *"He that was with thee beyond Jordan, to whom
thou barest witness."*   This statement shows that John's
testimony proclaiming Jesus as Messiah was far reaching.
He had made it clear publicly and in the hearing of his
disciples that he was not "that Light," but only "a voice."
In the light of this verse his words seem to have had little
effect on the minds of his disciples.   They did not trust in
their Messiah even though John plainly pointed them to
Jesus instead of to himself.

"Behold, the same baptizeth, and all men come to Him."

The ministry of Jesus was attracting so many people, so many were being baptized by His disciples, that the disciples of John cried out, "ALL men come to Him!" We know that not all men came to Jesus—and even of those who *did* come, very few believed unto salvation. The statement simply means that a great number had flocked to Jesus and were being baptized by His disciples. Many followed Him for the loaves and fishes, and because of His miracles.

In many instances, the Holy Spirit can *use* an unkind saying such as these statements of John's disciples, and can give a Christian an opportunity to give tremendous testimony. John the Baptist was not provoked by the success of the ministry of Jesus, his spirit was not vexed. He KNEW that he must decrease and Jesus must increase. His answer expressed divine truth concerning success, growth, influence, and promotion in spiritual things:

Verse 27: *"John answered and said, A man can receive nothing, except it be given him from heaven."*

God the Father knows who can stand promotion and spiritual growth. Spiritual gifts are in His hands and He controls them. If we walk in the light He has given us and fulfill the stewardship He lays out for us, at the end of life's journey we will hear Him say, "Well done, thou good and faithful servant. Enter into the joys of thy Lord." A true and faithful minister of God does not grumble if his popularity wanes while the popularity of another minister increases. *"For promotion cometh neither from the east, nor from the west, nor from the south. But God is the judge: He putteth down one, and setteth up another"* (Psalm 75:6,7).

John's statement in this verse plainly declares to his disciples that what he had, he received from God; and if God should see fit to give him more, God was able to do so; but if it were God's will for him to decrease while Christ increased, that was God's business. Man can receive nothing except that which is given to him from heaven; all spiritual gifts and all spiritual ministry are ordained of God and provided by Him.

This verse is a marvelous cure for jealousy in the heart of a Christian worker when a brother seems to be prospering more than himself. We should rejoice when our fellow workers prosper; all true ministers are ministers of the same Gospel, and we should be ministering to the glory of God, not to the glory of self. If what we are doing in the name of Christianity is done to bring honor and prosperity to ourselves, then we *have* our reward and there will be no reward at the end of life's journey. God is the giver of every good and perfect gift, and we have nothing to boast about. To God be the glory! He is worthy.

Verse 28:   *"Ye yourselves bear me witness, that I said, I am not the Christ, but that I am sent before Him."*

Here John reminds his disciples that he repeatedly pointed them to Christ, not to himself. He had declared again and again that he was only a voice, the forerunner sent to announce the coming of Messiah; and if they had remembered his testimony they would not have been surprised when Jesus made and baptized more disciples than John did. If they had believed John's testimony they would have *expected* Jesus to surpass John; but they had listened with the ear, not with the heart.

The truth of this verse is a divine illustration that men are easy to forget—they hear, but they do not remember. John had constantly laid it upon the hearts of the people that the One whom he had come to announce was superior to himself; but when Christ began to increase and John the Baptist began to fade into the background, they became jealous and envious. They forgot that John had told them repeatedly that what they were witnessing would happen exactly as they had witnessed it.

Verse 29:   *"He that hath the bride is the bridegroom:*

*but the friend of the bridegroom, which standeth and hear-
eth him, rejoiceth greatly because of the bridegroom's voice:
this my joy therefore is fulfilled."*

Here John the Baptist used a very familiar illustration
to explain the relative positions occupied by Christ and
himself. "The bride" is the whole company of born again
believers—the Lamb's wife (Rev. 21:9). *"The bridegroom"*
is Christ Jesus the Lord. *"The friend of the bridegroom"*
refers to John himself, and to other faithful ministers of
Christ.

John's illustration here is according to the customs of
the Jews in a marriage in that day. The bridegroom's friends
were the means of communication between the bride and
groom before they were united in marriage, and it was the
duty of these friends to remove any and all hindrances to
a speedy marriage. Through this illustration John the Baptist showed his disciples that his work was to announce
the Messiah and promote a good understanding between
the Messiah and men. Therefore he rejoiced even though
his ministry was diminishing. The ministry of "the Bridegroom" was *increasing,* and this was John's mission on
earth.

The bridegroom *"hath the bride."* The Greek word translated "hath" literally means "to possess as one's own"—
i. e., the bridegroom possesses the bride; she is bone of his
bone and flesh of his flesh (Gen. 2:23).

The bride is possessed by the bridegroom, but the *friend*
of the bridegroom *"standeth,"* an expression surely suggesting inferiority. The Jewish priest *"standeth daily"* as he
ministered and offered sacrifices, many times the same sacrifice over and over again; but Christ *"sat down* on the
right hand of God" after He had offered one sacrifice (Heb.
10:11,12).

In Matthew 9:15, speaking to the disciples of John the
Baptist, Jesus refers to Himself as the bridegroom: "And
Jesus said unto them, Can the children of the bridechamber
mourn, as long as the bridegroom is with them? but the

days will come, when the bridegroom shall be taken from
them, and then shall they fast."

Verse 30: *"He must increase, but I must decrease."*

John here tells his complaining followers that it is the
will of God that Christ Jesus grow in popularity and dignity, while he and his following should diminish. This,
too, is but a repetition of what he had said in the beginning of his ministry. He was simply the forerunner; *Christ*
was the King.

The true minister must always be content to take second
place. He wants to be loved and appreciated, certainly;
but he also wants his followers to love Jesus supremely.
It is *right* for us to love those who pointed us to Jesus—
those who prayed for us, those who witnessed to us, those
who kept on insisting until we received Jesus and were
saved; but we should remember that they only pointed us
to the Lamb of God. It was HE who saved us, and therefore He is to hold the supreme place of love, adoration,
and worship in our hearts.

Jesus Above All

Verse 31: *"He that cometh from above is above all: he
that is of the earth is earthly, and speaketh of the earth:
He that cometh from heaven is above all."*

Here is declared the infinite superiority of the Lord Jesus
Christ over all mortals. Christ is "from above"—the only
begotten of God—and as God in flesh He is far above any
and all men. The Creator is greater than the creature created by Him; therefore Christ is "far above all principality,
and power, and might, and dominion, and every name that
is named, not only in this world, but also in that which
is to come: (God) hath put all things under His feet, and
gave Him to be the head over all things to the Church,
which is His body, the fulness of Him that filleth all in
all" (Eph. 1:21—23).

"He that is of the earth is earthly." All ministers except Jesus are of this earth. Even John the Baptist, forerunner of the Christ, was conceived and born like any other baby. But Jesus was conceived of the Holy Ghost, He was God in flesh. All ministers—then and now—are subject to mistakes *because* we are of the earth; but Jesus could not err, and the words He spoke were words that brought life.

"He that cometh from heaven is above all." Under the inspiration of the Holy Ghost, John here repeats what he said in the first part of the verse, thus emphasizing that Christ Jesus came from heaven; and since by nature He is God in flesh, He is far above all ministers of earth. We are limited because we *are* of the earth, but Jesus is not limited. He came from God, and though He is man He is the *GOD-Man* and is therefore superior to all earthly ministers.

Verse 32: *"And what He hath seen and heard, that He testifieth; and no man receiveth His testimony."*

Again John the Baptist declares the divinity of Christ. All earthly ministers speak what the Holy Spirit gives to them; they deliver the message of the Word; but Christ WAS the Word and He delivered what He had *"seen and heard"* with the Father from the beginning. Christ (as God) declared with authority truths He had heard and known from all eternity. (Study John 5:19—30 and 8:38.) Even though on earth Jesus tabernacled in a body of flesh, He was with the Father in the beginning, He had seen and heard all that the Father had seen and heard. He possessed perfect knowledge, and the words He spoke were the living words of Almighty God.

"And no man receiveth His testimony." This speaks comparatively, considering the masses that followed Jesus during the height of His ministry. There were five thousand men (not counting women and children) who were fed with the loaves and fishes; and yet when Jesus was led away to Calvary, Simon the Cyrenian was *forced* to carry His cross!

The disciples of John had complained that the *whole world* had gone after Jesus, and John used these words to show them that they had been guilty of gross exaggeration, and in reality, compared to the crowds that had heard the Messiah speak, very few had followed Him.

Oh, yes, the masses did come to hear Jesus preach, many desired baptism, but few believed with the heart unto righteousness and became *true disciples*. His ministry was popular for a season, but many who followed Him did not follow for the right purpose. Multitudes followed Him—but when He hung on the cross, that same multitude mocked Him! Only a very small group believed on Him and loved Him. When He was dying on the cross, even His disciples (with the exception of John the Beloved) were in hiding for fear of the Jews.

Verse 33:   *"He that hath received His testimony hath set to his seal that God is true."*

The meaning here is that those who *received* the testimony of Jesus publicly announced their faith in Him and formally declared that they believed He was the Son of God. The truth of this verse shows the importance of receiving the testimony of Jesus, which is the only way to be born again. Jesus came into the world to declare God—and that is the only authentic declaration of God that we have. Those who truly received the testimony of Jesus thereby declared *"that God is true."*   They publicly declared their belief that God sent Christ, that Christ was the Messiah—"that Prophet" foretold in the Old Testament. "He that believeth on the Son of God hath the witness in himself: he that believeth not God hath made Him a liar; because he believeth not the record that God gave of His Son" (I John 5:10).

Verse 34:   *"For He whom God hath sent speaketh the words of God: for God giveth not the Spirit by measure unto Him."*

"He whom God hath sent" again declares the deity of

Christ and makes it clear as to who Jesus was and from whence He came. The meaning here is that Christ was "the sent One," the One whom God sent into the world according to His promise, the One promised to Adam in the Garden of Eden, the One who was promised throughout the Old Testament Scriptures. John was God's ordained minister, and his words were true—but he was only a man. The words JESUS spoke were not the words of man; they were the words of God. When the multitudes heard Jesus speak, they were hearing *God* speak. When they listened to the words of Jesus they were listening to the words of Almighty God. Christ the Son and God the Father are so close, so perfectly united, that he who listens to the teaching of Jesus is listening to the teaching of God the Father. Please study John 7:16—18; 8:28; 12:49; 14:10,11.

All earthly ministers are taught of God the Father through the ministry of the Holy Spirit. We look to God, we search His Word, and then we rely upon the Holy Spirit to lead us when we deliver a message; but Jesus did not *need* to be taught, because whatever God the Father knows, Christ the Son knows; and whatever the Holy Ghost knows, the Son knows. Therefore when Jesus spoke He spoke as God. He was the Word Incarnate (John 1:14).

In Deuteronomy 18:18 we read, *"I will raise them up a Prophet from among their brethren, like unto thee, and will put my words in His mouth; and He shall speak unto them all that I shall command Him."*

"God giveth not the Spirit by measure unto Him." To all descendants of Adam—yes, even the outstanding prophets and men of God—the Holy Spirit is given *"by measure."* In I Corinthians 13:9 Paul said, "We know in part, and we prophesy in part." But Christ is different: to HIM God gave the Holy Ghost *"WITHOUT measure,"* in divine, infinite fulness, divine completeness. "Without measure" He was anointed with the Holy Ghost, fitted for His office as Priest, Prophet, and King, anointed to a degree never granted to any other prophet, priest, or king: "God anointed

Jesus of Nazareth with the Holy Ghost and with power: who went about doing good, and healing all that were oppressed of the devil; for God was with Him" (Acts 10:38).

We must be careful lest we forget the divine truth that Christ Jesus our Saviour and Lord did not for one moment cease to be God when He dwelt in a body of flesh. His deity remained the same as it was in the beginning with the Father; and since He was God in flesh He was never separated from the Spirit.

I believe John's aim here was to lead his disciples step by step into the highest, noblest view of the divinity and dignity of the Lord Jesus Christ. He wanted his disciples to recognize *in Christ* the One who was very God as well as very man, which was exactly what Jesus was. John the Baptist knew this, and in his last testimony he was attempting to get this tremendous truth across to his followers.

Verse 35: *"The Father loveth the Son, and hath given all things into His hand."*

The Man Christ Jesus is God's eternal Son, He was with the Father in the beginning, God has loved Him from all eternity, and by an everlasting covenant He has intrusted into the Son's hands *all things* pertaining to salvation. Before ever the world was, before anything was created, it was foreordained that Christ would shed His blood for the remission of sins, that men might be redeemed (I Pet. 1: 18—23). It was this eternal Son to whom God the Father said, "I shall give thee the heathen for thine inheritance, and the uttermost parts of the earth for thy possession" (Psalm 2:8).

"The Father loveth the Son." These are words far too deep for mortal mind to comprehend. This is the love to which Jesus referred when He said, "Thou lovedst me before the foundation of the world" (John 17:24). This is the love which the Father had in His heart for the Son and which He declared at the baptism of Jesus at the very beginning of His ministry when He said, "This is my beloved

Son, in whom I am well pleased" (Matt. 3:17). God never spoke these words to or about any other person, and the only time they were repeated was when God the Father repeated them on the Mount of Transfiguration when Peter put Jesus on the same level with Moses and Elijah. God blacked out the mountain, and His voice from the shadows said, "This is my beloved Son, in whom I am well pleased; hear ye Him" (Matt. 17:5).

"The Father hath given all things into His hand." By and through the terms of the everlasting covenant (made between the Persons of the Godhead in the eternity behind us), God the Father has given to Jesus the Son all power over all flesh. The Son has power to quicken whom He will; He has power to justify, make righteous, sanctify and set apart whom He will; He has power to save, deliver, keep, and glorify His people, and *all judgment* has been committed unto Him. He is the Righteous Judge; He will judge the quick and the dead, and *finally* He will punish the wicked, the unbelieving (Rev. 21:7,8). Then He will sit on the throne of His father David, He will reign over all the world, He will put down every enemy and His enemies will become His footstool.

These are *"all things"* that the Father has given into the hands of the Son of His love. Jesus holds the key to death and hell; he conquered the world, the flesh, the devil, death, hell, and the grave. He is the only One to whom poor unbelieving sinners can go; He is the One to whom they MUST go if they hope to hear God say in that final day, "Enter thou the joys of thy Lord!" God has made Christ the Son the head of His Church, the High Priest of good things to come, and the Steward of all good gifts that can be ours because of God's grace. Precious truth! It should cause us to rejoice exceedingly.

We are "hid with Christ in God" (Col. 3:3).

We "sit together in heavenly places in Christ Jesus" (Eph. 2:6).

Therefore, the love which God the Father has for the

Son is the same love with which He also embraces US *because we are hidden with Christ in God.* This singular, peculiar love with which the Father loves the Son is ours because Christ is in us and we are in Christ, hid with Him in God.

Man cannot save himself, he cannot make himself righteous, he cannot sanctify himself, he cannot keep himself; and if God should commit salvation into OUR hands *we would lose ALL,* and lose it much more quickly than Adam did in Paradise! Jesus did not commit Himself to man because He knew what was IN man (John 2:24,25). We must trust HIM for salvation and commit our all to Him. Then we can say with Paul, "I KNOW WHOM I HAVE BELIEVED, and am persuaded that He is able to keep that which I have committed unto Him against that day" (II Tim. 1:12).

Since God the Father has committed all things into the hands of Jesus the Son, the destiny of every living mortal is under His control; but the destiny of each and every mortal *also* depends upon that individual's attitude toward God's Son. Jesus came into the world to declare God; He spoke the words of God because He WAS God, and He declared that the words that He spoke were *spirit and life.* He did all that He *could* do, and now it is up to the individual to hear His words and believe on Him. To do this is to have eternal life. He who believes on Jesus "shall not come into condemnation; but is passed from death unto life" (John 5:24).

Verse 36: *"He that believeth on the Son hath everlasting life: and he that believeth not the Son shall not see life; but the wrath of God abideth on him."*

With this clear, solemn declaration of the indescribable importance of believing on Jesus, John the Baptist concludes his testimony concerning his Lord. He makes it very plain that believing on Jesus is the way to heaven, and by contrast, the way to hell is simply to *refuse* to believe on Him.

It is not necessary to murder, lie, steal, get drunk, or commit adultery in order to be eternally lost. All one need do to be lost is refuse to believe on Jesus. *"He that believeth NOT is condemned ALREADY."*

Notice that John says, *"He that believeth on the Son HATH everlasting life."* We who *believe* are saved NOW. We who *believe* possess everlasting life NOW. We will not be pardoned when we die, or when we stand before God; we are forgiven and pardoned *now.* The split second we believe on Jesus, that second we possess pardon, peace, life eternal, and a title to heaven, as well as grace and strength to live the life a believer should live in this world.

"He that believeth not the Son shall not see life." In the Greek, the word here translated *"believeth not"* is much different from the word translated *"believeth"* in the first part of the verse. It means something much stronger than "not trusting." The literal meaning is that the person who "believeth not" does not obey (or is disobedient to) the words of Jesus. Such a person shall not see life.

To *"see life"* does not mean to see with the natural eye, nor even with the spiritual or mental eye. It means to *possess* life, to enter into and taste life, to enjoy life. To say that the unbeliever "shall not see life" simply means that he will spend eternity in outer darkness, he will suffer eternal destruction.

"The wrath of God abideth on him." Again, notice the present tense—*ABIDETH.* The unbeliever is under the wrath of Almighty God NOW—not at death, not at the judgment. The wrath of God *abides* on him *now,* and as long as he continues in unbelief, the wrath of God will "hang heavy" over his head. As long as he continues in unbelief he will be under the curse of God's broken law. Man by nature is born in sin, a child of wrath; and until he becomes a believer the wrath of God hangs over him because he is unpardoned, unforgiven, sin is still in him and upon him.

Spiritually speaking, there are only two classes of people: sons of God and sons of the devil. When we believe on

Jesus we become sons of God and are no longer children of wrath. In John 8:44 Jesus said to the unbelieving Pharisees, *"Ye are of your father the devil,* and the lusts of your father ye will do. He was a murderer from the beginning, and abode not in the truth, because there is no truth in him. When he speaketh a lie, he speaketh of his own: for he is a liar, and the father of it."

God is love, indeed He is — longsuffering and slow to anger; but it is gross error to teach that *God is love, all men will eventually be forgiven, and those who die in sin will be given another chance! THE BIBLE TEACHES NO SUCH DOCTRINE.* God plainly tells us that He hates sin and is angry with the sinner every day (Psalm 7:11), and that "the wicked shall be turned into hell, and all the nations that forget God" (Psalm 9:17). There IS a burning hell, and in Mark 9:43—48 Jesus declared:

"If thy hand offend thee, cut it off: it is better for thee to enter into life maimed, than having two hands to go *into hell, into the fire that never shall be quenched:* where their worm dieth not, and *the fire is not quenched.* And if thy foot offend thee, cut it off: it is better for thee to enter halt into life, than having two feet to be *cast into hell, into the fire that never shall be quenched:* where their worm dieth not, *and the fire is not quenched.* And if thine eye offend thee, pluck it out: it is better for thee to enter into the kingdom of God with one eye, than having two eyes to be *cast into hell fire:* where their worm dieth not, *and the fire is not quenched!"*

Yes, God IS love — but Paul thunders out, *"Our God is a consuming FIRE!"* (Heb. 12:29). We should preach the love of God, the mercy of God, the compassion and longsuffering of God; but we should also preach *the WRATH of God.* In this day of liberalism and modernism, many ministers never mention hell, they never speak of the wrath of God. They preach the *love* of God, the fatherhood of God and the brotherhood of man; but they also preach that since God is a loving, tender God He would never allow His creatures to burn in hell. I would remind you that the hottest sermon ever preached on hell fire was preached by the tender, loving, compassionate Son of God. (In addition to the passage just quoted from the Gospel of Mark, please read the fifth chapter of Matthew.) The term "hell fire" was not coined by some fanatical preacher; it was used first by the Lord Jesus. Preachers today need to cry aloud and spare not. We need to warn sinners that the wrath of God abides on them, and that *"he that believeth not is condemned already!"*

Among the *first* words spoken by John the Baptist in his public ministry were words announcing the coming Messiah, the Lamb of God, the true Light, the Lord Jesus; and among the *last* words of his testimony were words warning men of the wrath of God and the danger of hell. John preached the *love* of God, but he also preached the *wrath* of God because he loved the souls of men. He preached judgment with just as much fervor and compassion as he announced the coming Messiah. God have mercy on the minister who stands in the pulpit Sunday after Sunday and fails to warn the people that there IS an everlasting hell that burns with fire and brimstone, and that all unbelievers will spend eternity there, in the lake of fire!

Never for one moment did John the Baptist doubt who Jesus was. It is true that he sent two of his disciples to ask Jesus if He were the Christ or if they should look for another (Matt. 11:2,3), but the question was not for John himself; he sent the disciples to Jesus for their own sakes, that they might see and hear for themselves.

You will notice in the last testimony of John the Baptist that he speaks of Jesus as "the Christ" (v. 28); "the Bridegroom" (v. 29); He who testifies "what He hath seen and heard" (v. 32); "He that cometh from above" (v. 31); "He whom God hath sent" (v. 34); He who has the Spirit without measure (v. 34); Him whom the Father loves (v. 35); Him into whose hands all things are given by the Father (v. 35); and Him in whom to believe is everlasting life (v.36).

Now hear the testimony of *Jesus* concerning John the Baptist: In Luke 7:26—28 we read, "What went ye out for to see? A prophet? *Yea, I say unto you, and MUCH MORE than a prophet. This is he, of whom it is written, Behold, I send my messenger before thy face, which shall prepare thy way before thee. For I say unto you, AMONG THOSE THAT ARE BORN OF WOMEN THERE IS NOT A GREATER PROPHET THAN JOHN THE BAPTIST...."*

CHAPTER IV

1. When therefore the Lord knew how the Pharisees had heard that Jesus made and baptized more disciples than John,

2. (Though Jesus himself baptized not, but his disciples,)

3. He left Judaea, and departed again into Galilee.

4. And he must needs go through Samaria.

5. Then cometh he to a city of Samaria, which is called Sychar, near to the parcel of ground that Jacob gave to his son Joseph.

6. Now Jacob's well was there. Jesus therefore, being wearied with his journey, sat thus on the well: and it was about the sixth hour.

7. There cometh a woman of Samaria to draw water: Jesus saith unto her, Give me to drink.

8. (For his disciples were gone away unto the city to buy meat.)

9. Then saith the woman of Samaria unto him, How is it that thou, being a Jew, askest drink of me, which am a woman of Samaria? for the Jews have no dealings with the Samaritans.

10. Jesus answered and said unto her, If thou knewest the gift of God, and who it is that saith to thee, Give me to drink; thou wouldest have asked of him, and he would have given thee living water.

11. The woman saith unto him, Sir, thou hast nothing to draw with, and the well is deep: from whence then hast thou that living water?

12. Art thou greater than our father Jacob, which gave us the well, and drank thereof himself, and his children, and his cattle?

13. Jesus answered and said unto her, Whosoever drinketh of this water shall thirst again:

14. But whosoever drinketh of the water that I shall give him shall never thirst; but the water that I shall give him shall be in him a well of water springing up into everlasting life.

15. The woman saith unto him, Sir, give me this water, that I thirst not, neither come hither to draw.

16. Jesus saith unto her, Go, call thy husband, and come hither.

17. The woman answered and said, I have no husband. Jesus said unto her, Thou hast well said, I have no husband:

18. For thou hast had five husbands; and he whom thou now hast is not thy husband: in that saidst thou truly.

19. The woman saith unto him, Sir, I perceive that thou art a prophet.

20. Our fathers worshipped in this mountain; and ye say, that in Jerusalem is the place where men ought to worship.

21. Jesus saith unto her, Woman, believe me, the hour cometh, when ye shall neither in this mountain, nor yet at Jerusalem, worship the Father.

22. Ye worship ye know not what: we know what we worship: for salvation is of the Jews.

23. But the hour cometh, and now is, when the true worshippers shall worship the Father in spirit and in truth: for the Father seeketh such to worship him.

24. God is a Spirit: and they that worship him must worship him in spirit and in truth.

25. The woman saith unto him, I know that Messias cometh, which is called Christ: when he is come, he will tell us all things.

26. Jesus saith unto her, I that speak unto thee am he.

27. And upon this came his disciples, and marvelled that he talked with the woman: yet no man said, What seekest thou? or, Why talkest thou with her?

28. The woman then left her waterpot, and went her way into the city, and saith to the men,

29. Come, see a man, which told me all things that ever I did: is not this the Christ?

30. Then they went out of the city, and came unto him.

31. In the mean while his disciples prayed him, saying, Master, eat.

32. But he said unto them, I have meat to eat that ye know not of.

33. Therefore said the disciples one to another, Hath any man brought him ought to eat?

34. Jesus saith unto them, My meat is to do the will of him that sent me, and to finish his work.

35. Say not ye, There are yet four months, and then cometh harvest? behold, I say unto you, Lift up your eyes, and look on the fields; for they are white already to harvest.

36. And he that reapeth receiveth wages, and gathereth fruit unto life eternal: that both he that soweth and he that reapeth may rejoice together.

37. And herein is that saying true, One soweth, and another reapeth.

38. I sent you to reap that whereon ye bestowed no labour: other men laboured, and ye are entered into their labours.

39. And many of the Samaritans of that city believed on him for the saying of the woman, which testified, He told me all that ever I did.

40. So when the Samaritans were come unto him, they besought him that he would tarry with them: and he abode there two days.

41. And many more believed because of his own word;

42. And said unto the woman, Now we believe, not because of thy saying: for we have heard him ourselves, and know that this is indeed the Christ, the Saviour of the world.

43. Now after two days he departed thence, and went into Galilee.

44. For Jesus himself testified, that a prophet hath no honour in his own country.

45. Then when he was come into Galilee, the Galilaeans received him, having seen all the things that he did at Jerusalem at the feast: for they also went unto the feast.

46. So Jesus came again into Cana of Galilee, where he made the water wine.   And there was a certain nobleman, whose son was sick at Capernaum.

47. When he heard that Jesus was come out of Judaea into Galilee, he went unto him, and besought him that he would come down, and heal his son: for he was at the point of death.

48. Then said Jesus unto him, Except ye see signs and wonders, ye will not believe.

49. The nobleman saith unto him, Sir, come down ere my child die.

50. Jesus saith unto him, Go thy way; thy son liveth.   And the man believed the word that Jesus had spoken unto him, and he went his way.

51. And as he was now going down, his servants met him, and told him, saying, Thy son liveth.

52. Then enquired he of them the hour when he began to amend. And they said unto him, Yesterday at the seventh hour the fever left him.

53. So the father knew that it was at the same hour, in the which Jesus said unto him, Thy son liveth: and himself believed, and his whole house.

54. This is again the second miracle that Jesus did, when he was come out of Judaea into Galilee.

In the first three chapters of the Gospel of John we learned first that the Levitical priesthood was spiritually blind (ch. 1, vv. 19—26).   The Israelites had lost their joy. They had form and ritual, but they had no joy in the heart.

Not only was the priesthood blinded and the joy of the nation gone, but they had desecrated the house of God, they were making merchandise of the souls of men (ch. 2, v. 14).   They despised the Messiah (ch. 3, v. 26), and rejected His testimony (ch. 3, v. 32).

In chapter 4 we will see the self-righteousness of the

Jews, the sad spiritual state of the nation of Israel at the time Jesus tabernacled among men. In the closing verses of chapter 3 the Jews despised Jesus and rejected His testimony, which pointed to their final rejection of Him and to the day when they would demand His crucifixion and death.

Chapter four also contains prophetic truth concerning the future. In verse 3 of this chapter we see where Jesus turned to the Gentiles. He left Judaea and went into Galilee, which Matthew refers to as *"Galilee of the Gentiles"* (Matt. 4:15). In this chapter, Jesus is not occupied with the Jews, but with the Samaritans—and please note: The Samaritans "besought Him that He would tarry with them: and *He abode there TWO DAYS"* (v. 40). This is most interesting. In II Peter 3:8 we read that *"one day is with the Lord as a thousand years, and a thousand years as one day."* Since this is true, *two days* on God's calendar is two thousand years. We are now living nineteen hundred years and more from the day Jesus left Judaea and departed into Galilee— "Galilee of the Gentiles." (In connection with this, please study the entire eleventh chapter of Romans.)

Jesus Returns to Galilee

Verses 1–3: *"When therefore the Lord knew how the Pharisees had heard that Jesus made and baptized more disciples than John, (though Jesus Himself baptized not, but His disciples,) He left Judaea, and departed again into Galilee."*

The controversy between the unbelieving Jews and the disciples of John the Baptist had called the Lord's ministry to the attention of the masses and had become the subject of conversation the countryside over. Naturally such controversy attracted the attention of the religious leaders— the scribes, Pharisees, and chief priests. They had been greatly disturbed by the ministry of John the Baptist and the fact that great crowds had flocked to hear him (John 1:19—28). John had declared to them that One greater than himself would soon appear, and when they heard that Jesus was attracting greater crowds and baptizing more disciples than John, they were disturbed even more! Who could this mysterious, powerful Person be, that He should attract such multitudes?

I do not doubt that these members of the Sanhedrin discussed the facts over and over again, asking among themselves if this miraculous Person could possibly be the Christ, their expected Messiah, and finally agreeing that if He *were* the Messiah, He was certainly not what they had expected— nor was He what they desired. Therefore their feelings were against Him and they decided that the best thing to do was to get rid of Him.

There is no need to wonder how the Lord *knew* what the Pharisees were thinking and saying among themselves, for since He was God in flesh He was omniscient and He knew every thought and every intent of their hearts. In Matthew 12:22—32 we read the account of a group who committed the *unpardonable sin* by thinking! They did not say one word that audibly reached the ears of Jesus; but they thought in their hearts, and their thoughts blasphemed the Holy Spirit. Jesus knows every thought WE have; He knows all things about all people.

Therefore there is a change of scene. Knowing of the Pharisees' attitude and their jealousy, Christ took His ministry outside the Jewish nation, into new territory. But we must remember that *whatever* move He made had significance beyond the mere fact of His moving into another area. When He moved into Samaria, for example, His move pointed to the Gospel of John 3:15—17—*"whosoever"* will believe (whether Jew, Samaritan, or Greek) will be saved. Here is foreshadowed the world-wide message of the Gospel after the crucifixion and ascension of Christ, and the coming of the Holy Spirit on the Day of Pentecost.

"He left Judaea." There is something outstanding here. The Greek word translated "left" signifies much more than simply *departing* from one place to go into another. It

means "He let it go, He left it to itself." In Proverbs 29:1 we read, "He, that being often reproved hardeneth his neck, shall suddenly be destroyed, and that *without remedy.*" Isaiah 55:6 warns, "Seek ye the Lord while He may be found, call ye upon Him while He is near," and in Proverbs 1:24—31 we are told, "Because I have called, and ye refused; I have stretched out my hand, and no man regarded; but ye have set at nought all my counsel, and would none of my reproof: I also will laugh at your calamity; I will mock when your fear cometh; when your fear cometh as desolation, and your destruction cometh as a whirlwind; when distress and anguish cometh upon you. Then shall they call upon me, but I will not answer; they shall seek me early, but they shall not find me: for that they hated knowledge, and did not choose the fear of the Lord: They would none of my counsel: they despised all my reproof. Therefore shall they eat of the fruit of their own way, and be filled with their own devices!" Jesus came unto His own and His own received Him not; therefore He left Judaea, He let it go, He left it to itself.

"Jesus Himself baptized not . . . ." This is the only place in the Gospels where it is stated that Jesus did not actually administer baptism with His own hands. In verse 1 we read that He baptized more disciples than John, but here we are told that He "baptized NOT." It is pointed out, however, that His disciples baptized, and their baptism was as though He did it Himself because they did it at His command. When the minister of God obeys the will of God and ministers according to God's directions, it is as though Jesus ministered.

No doubt the question will be asked, "Why did Jesus refrain from baptizing?" I think there are many reasons, the most outstanding being that He knew there would be quarrels and disputes among His followers if *He* baptized some and the disciples baptized others. Human nature does not change. The Corinthian Christians quarreled among themselves, some saying they were baptized by Paul, others

saying they were baptized by Apollos, still others claiming
baptism by Cephas. Therefore Jesus did not baptize.

I am convinced that another reason He did not personally administer baptism was to show that the *effect and
benefit* of that ordinance are not dependent upon the person
who does the baptizing; it is the *meaning* of baptism that
is important. Without a doubt, *Judas,* as well as the other
disciples, baptized some of the people, and in John 6:70
Jesus plainly said that Judas was "devil." Baptism is for
believers, and we should be baptized by a God-fearing minister; but baptism is NOT essential to salvation, it has
nothing to do with redemption. We are baptized because
we ARE born again, not to BE born again. Therefore it is
not a question of who *administers* the baptism, but whether
or not we accept it in its true meaning.

Verse 4: *"And He must needs go through Samaria."*

While Jesus was here on earth, every step He took and
every word He spoke was by divine counsel and appoint-
ment; His every act was in fulfillment of His mission here—
to do the Father's will. That He "must needs go through
Samaria," and His visit to Jacob's well, did not come about
by accident but was foreordained before the foundation of
the world.

Historians tell us that the usual route from Judaea to
Galilee was through Peraea, across the Jordan; the Jews
traveled this way to avoid going through Samaria. It was
a longer route, but the Jews hated the Samaritans to such
degree that they refused to even travel *through* that country.
The Jews had no dealings with the Samaritans, but Jesus
was a different Jew. He had no hatred, no prejudice or
animosity toward any man. He came to seek and to save
the lost, whosoever would believe on His finished work. It
is true that He came first to the Jews, and in the early
part of His ministry he instructed His disciples to go only
to the lost sheep of the house of Israel; but even in this
journey through Samaria He was teaching them that God's

saving grace is for "whosoever will."

"He MUST needs go through Samaria"—not because that route was nearer, but because there was a thirsty soul waiting to drink of the water of life, and the chances are that she would not have come to Him; so He went where she was, He carried the message of life to her. Such is our duty today. Many church members are so busy with church activities and meetings that they do not have time to get out and win souls. It is our business to carry the good news to those who have never heard, those who are thirsty for the living water.

Verse 5: *"Then cometh He to a city of Samaria, which is called Sychar, near to the parcel of ground that Jacob gave to his son Joseph."*

Most Bible authorities agree that this is the same city as Sichem, Shalem, or Shechem: "And Jacob came to Shalem, a city of Shechem, which is in the land of Canaan, when he came from Padan-aram; and pitched his tent before the city. And he bought a parcel of a field, where he had spread his tent, at the hand of the children of Hamor, Shechem's father, for an hundred pieces of money" (Gen. 33:18,19).

I suppose that Jerusalem is the only city in Palestine that has had more Bible history connected with it than this city. We read in Genesis 12:6 that God first appeared to Abraham there. It was there that Jacob dwelt when he first returned from Padan-aram. The disgraceful history of Dinah centered there and it was there that the Shechemites were murdered because of her. (Study the thirty-fourth chapter of Genesis.) It was at Shechem that Joseph's brethren were feeding their flocks when Jacob sent Joseph to see if all was well with them—and it was the last time he saw his favorite son for many years (Gen. 37:12—27).

Shechem was one of the cities of refuge when the Israelites took possession of the land of Canaan (Josh. 20:7,8), and it was there that Joshua gathered all the tribes and addressed them for the last time (Josh. 24:1). The bones of Joseph and the patriarchs were buried there (Josh. 24:32; Acts 7:16). It was in Shechem that the events in the history of Abimelech took place (Judges 9:1 ff). After the death of King Solomon, Rehoboam met the tribes of Israel at Shechem and gave them the answer which divided the kingdom (I Kings 12). When Jeroboam was made king of Israel, he dwelt in Shechem (I Kings 12:25). Very close by that city was the city of Samaria itself, and the two hills of Ebal and Gerizim; it was there that the solemn blessings and cursings were recited after the children of Israel had entered into Canaan (Josh. 8:30−35). This was without a doubt the place where Jesus sat by Jacob's well when the Samaritan woman came to draw water.

Verse 6: *"Now Jacob's well was there. Jesus therefore, being wearied with His journey, sat thus on the well: and it was about the sixth hour."*

We know this was Jacob's well because the record says so, but no one knows how it got its name. We read in Genesis that Abraham and Isaac digged wells, but we find no record that Jacob ever dug a well. It is interesting that in Palestine today, near the ruins of Shechem, is a well which is supposed to be the place where Jesus met the woman of Samaria—and there is no reason to doubt that it *is* the actual well where the meeting took place, as recorded here.

Jesus was *"wearied with His journey."* I appreciate this statement so very much; it proves the reality of the human nature of Jesus. He had a body that became tired, thirsty, and hungry just as we do. He had a body like our own, subject to all the conditions to which our bodies are subject—except that He was sinless.

Then, too, the account here shows the infinite compassion of Jesus, His humility and condescension. The Man sitting by Jacob's well was the One who made the world and all that therein is. He was the One to whom the cattle on a thousand hills belong. Yet He was content to take a body of flesh and come to earth, travel on foot, walk a dusty road until, in weariness, He sat by a rustic well while His disciples went into the city to buy bread. He was willing to do this that we might be saved; He did it to make our redemption possible.

There is no place in the Bible that tells us Jesus ever rode in a carriage as a *king* might travel, or even that He traveled on horseback. The only record given of His riding was when He rode into Jerusalem on a donkey, as prophesied in the Old Testament.

Wearied with His journey, and coming to the place where Jacob's well was, He *"sat thus on the well."* Like any other man who was tired, Jesus sat down on the stones that were built around the well. He did not seek a cushion or a special, more comfortable place; He simply sat down on the rocks as any weary, thirsty traveler would have done.

"And it was about the sixth hour." According to the time used in those days, this was twelve o'clock—*high noon,* the hottest, sultriest time of the day. It was the time of day when no travelers were on the road, nor did the women come to draw water from the well at that time; they came in early morning just at daybreak, or in late afternoon at sunset. Some Bible scholars try to place the time at six in the evening, but this is very unlikely. Jesus and the Samaritan woman had quite a lengthy conversation, and then after the woman was converted she left her waterpot and ran into the city to tell the people about Jesus. They came out to see Him, and there was much activity. If this had all happened at six in the evening, there would not have been time for all that happened, as recorded here.

We will notice as we continue that Jesus dealt with this Samaritan woman in an altogether different way from His dealings with Nicodemus—one, a self-righteous religionist, ruler of the Jews, with character above reproach, yet *lost;* the other, a woman of the streets, low of morals, steeped in sin, ignorant and carnally minded.

Christ and the Samaritan Woman

Verse 7: *"There cometh a woman of Samaria to draw water: Jesus saith unto her, Give me to drink."*

This part of the ministry of Jesus was a particular fulfillment of Genesis 49:22—"a fruitful bough by a well," a *branch* running "over the wall," and the "wall" in this instance was the wall of Judaism. This was why He "must needs go through Samaria." He knew this dear woman was coming to the well at that time, He knew all about her, and He knew the saving grace of God would be bestowed upon her.

You will notice that even though Jesus knew all about this woman, He did not open the conversation by reproving and rebuking her because of her ungodly living. No, He opened the conversation by asking a favor of her; He said, *"Give me to drink."* And with this request He opened the door to a spiritual conversation which led to the woman's conversion and a great revival among the Samaritans.

If you will study the sermons of Jesus you will see that whether He was speaking to an individual or to a group, He spoke on the level where people lived. He talked about the sparrows, the lilies of the field, the sower and the seed, the vine and the fruit of the vine. He talked of bread, water, salt, light. Who does not understand these things? Asking the Samaritan woman for a drink was an act of marvelous condescension on the Lord's part. He made all things, He created the fountains, the rivers; but even though He had created all the water in the world He was not above asking a drink of a Samaritan woman.

Scripture bears out the fact that the water was drawn and carried to the homes by women (Gen. 24:11; I Sam. 9:11). The community well was the common meeting place for the women, but when this woman of Samaria came to the well there was no one there but Jesus. This is a significant point, and we will discuss it later on.

Verse 8:   *"For His disciples were gone away unto the city to buy meat."*

This bears out the fact that Jesus never performed a miracle in order to supply His personal needs. He could take a small boy's lunch and use it to feed five thousand hungry people, but He did no miracle to satisfy His own hunger. He sent His disciples into the city to buy bread.

Verse 9:   *"Then saith the woman of Samaria unto Him, How is it that thou, being a Jew, askest drink of me, which am a woman of Samaria? for the Jews have no dealings with the Samaritans."*

The Samaritan woman was surprised when Jesus spoke to her; it was an unexpected act of condescension on the part of a Jew to speak to a Samaritan. She did not know who He was, of course, but she knew that He was a Jew, and the fact that He would speak to a Samaritan arrested her attention and stirred her interest.

"How is it that thou, BEING A JEW, askest drink of me . . . ?" This woman immediately recognized Jesus as a Jew—perhaps it was from His general appearance, perhaps He wore the fringe upon His garment as was required by the Mosaic Law (Num. 15:38,39). In His *personal* appearance as He walked this earth—man, yet God—Jesus resembled any other Jewish traveler who became weary on a hot, dusty road and sat down on the edge of a well to rest. There was nothing unusual or peculiar about the way He was dressed; He looked like other Jews in the garments He wore.

"The Jews have no dealings with the Samaritans"—and that was true. Bible antiquity tells us that the devout Jews prayed each morning that Jehovah would deliver them from the sight of the face of a Samaritan that day. Their hatred for the Samaritans surpassed all reason. The enmity and hatred between the Jews and the Samaritans no doubt

originated in the separation of the ten tribes under Jeroboam at the time the kingdom of Israel was established, and *increased* after the Assyrians captured the ten tribes and carried them into captivity. The Samaritans mingled with the Assyrians who were sent to Samaria from Babylon and other places by the king of Assyria, and thus lost the right to be called pure Jews. (Study II Kings 17.) The enmity between these two peoples was deepened still further by the Samaritans' opposition to the rebuilding of the city of Jerusalem after the return from the Babylonian captivity in the days of Ezra. (Read Ezra, chapter 4.) Thus hatred between the Jews and the Samaritans had reached the extreme by the time Jesus came and tabernacled among men. The Samaritans were accounted as foreigners, aliens from the commonwealth of Israel. In John 8:48 the Jews said to Jesus, "Say we not well that thou art a *Samaritan,* and hast a devil?"

However, we will learn in this chapter that the Samaritans were not pagan. They regarded themselves as Jacob's descendants, they believed in the Old Testament religion, and they expected the coming of Messiah.

We need not be too critical of the Jews for their attitude toward the people of Samaria, because the same spirit still exists today between denominations and churches. Many people refuse to fellowship with others because they do not belong to the same denomination. Whether one be Methodist, Baptist, Presbyterian, or whatever, if he is truly born of the Spirit of God and washed in the blood of Jesus Christ we should fellowship with him. Such a spirit of division is wrong among Christian folk—but make no mistake, it brings great joy to the devil because he is the instigator of division! If Satan cannot damn a soul, he will do everything in his diabolical power to rob the believer of his spiritual birthright, and where there is strife among brethren there cannot be full joy and abundant life. The spirit of division and strife among Christians is a stumbling block and hinders the spreading of the Gospel of the grace of God.

When Jesus answered the Samaritan woman, you will notice He did not mention the hatred that existed between the Jews and the Samaritans:

Verse 10:   *"Jesus answered and said unto her, If thou knewest the gift of God, and who it is that saith to thee, Give me to drink; thou wouldest have asked of Him, and He would have given thee living water."*

This was not the time to discuss the conditions that prevailed between the Jews and the Samaritans; therefore Jesus did not answer the woman's question on that subject. He knew her heart, He knew that her curiosity and interest had been aroused, and His reply led her another step toward the gift of God and the living water.

"If thou knewest the gift of God, and who it is that (speaketh) to thee . . . ." The gift of God referred to here is the gift of His saving grace: "But not as the offence, so also is the free gift.   For if through the offence of one many be dead, much more the grace of God, and the gift by grace, which is by one man, Jesus Christ, hath abounded unto many" (Rom. 5:15).   Jesus was "full of grace and truth," and He was offering this dear woman the grace of God.

In other words, He said to her, "If you only knew that you are standing in the presence of Christ Jesus, Messiah and Saviour, and that it is He who speaks to you, if your blinded mind were open to the truth, you would be asking me for *living water."*

"Living water" was especially mentioned in Old Testament prophecies of good things to come, and would cause an Old Testament student to think of the coming Messiah. In Isaiah 12:3 we read, "Therefore with joy shall ye draw water out of the wells of salvation." Life-giving water was mentioned as one of the things Messiah would give.   Isaiah 44:3 tells us, "I will pour water upon him that is thirsty, and floods upon the dry ground: I will pour my Spirit upon thy seed, and my blessing upon thine offspring."

Zechariah 13:1 says, "In that day there shall be a fountain opened to the house of David and to the inhabitants of Jerusalem for sin and for uncleanness," and in Zechariah 14:8 we read, "And it shall be in that day, that living waters shall go out from Jerusalem; half of them toward the former sea, and half of them toward the hinder sea: in summer and in winter shall it be."

Jesus could have said to this woman, "If you only knew who I am, you would ask me and I would have mercy on your poor, adulterous life and save you by grace"; but at this stage of the conversation, if He had mentioned grace, mercy, and the new birth, she would not have known what He was talking about because she was spiritually ignorant. She had not received the light of the Word of God. No doubt she would have turned away because she would not have been interested in the religion of the Jews. But Jesus spoke to her of *living water,* she had come to the well to *draw* water, and her curiosity was increased when He told her that He had water much better than the water she had come to draw from the well. She had a desire to know just what all of this meant.

Verse 11: *"The woman saith unto Him, Sir, thou hast nothing to draw with, and the well is deep: from whence then hast thou that living water?"*

Like Nicodemus, this woman was thinking in the realm of the natural. She was wondering just how Jesus would get water from the depth of the well when He had no visible means of drawing it up; He had no rope, no bucket to lower into the well. I fully understand what this woman meant, because I was reared on a farm, and many, many times I have drawn water from the well to water the stock, and still more water to carry into the house to be used for drinking and cooking. It is understandable that the woman was curious when this Man, sitting beside a well that was a hundred feet deep, spoke of giving her living water when He had absolutely nothing with which to draw water. In the natural realm, she asked a sensible question: *"From whence then hast thou that living water?"*

Verse 12: *"Art thou greater than our father Jacob, which gave us the well, and drank thereof himself, and his children, and his cattle?"*

It is natural for the unregenerate person to put a carnal and material meaning on spiritual expressions. That is the very reason we have so many cults and false religions, so many errors concerning spiritual things. To this woman, Jesus looked like any ordinary Jewish traveler, and she could not understand how an ordinary Jew could suggest that He would provide better and more abundant water than the patriarch Jacob had found sufficient for himself and his family. Could there be another well, a better well, from which He would obtain water?

"Our father Jacob gave us the well." Notice here that the woman claimed kinship with Jacob. This probably refers to the land of the district near the well, land that Jacob gave to Joseph (Gen. 48:21,22). History tells us that the Samaritans were proud to claim relationship to Jacob and to possess the land where Jacob's well was; but they did not follow him in spirit, they did not serve his God.

Jesus could have started a first-class religious argument here. The woman had asked Him if He were greater than Jacob, and He could easily have said, *"Certainly* I am greater than Jacob!" On one occasion He said to the Pharisees, "Before Abraham was, I AM," and He could have said the same to this poor, ignorant, spiritually blind woman —but had He made such a statement to her He would have lost the opportunity to win her to salvation. He would have lost the purpose of the scriptural declaration that "He must needs go through Samaria." But He did not start an argument. Still using figurative expressions, refraining from statements of doctrinal truth, He led the woman gently on to the truth of the glorious salvation that was standing in her very presence. He did not answer her question directly;

He continued to impress upon her the excellence of the "living water":

Verse 13: *"Jesus answered and said unto her, Whosoever drinketh of this water shall thirst again."*

This was a fact the woman well knew, for she came day after day to draw water to quench a thirst that returned again and again.

The waters of Jacob's well are specifically typical of temporal and material things. It was good water—just as there are many material things that are good; but material things do not satisfy the heart and soul. Man is created in the image of Almighty God, and "things" cannot satisfy him. He cannot be satisfied until his heart is right with God. Regardless of how much money he may have, regardless of how many material things he may possess, these cannot satisfy his soul. The only person who has perfect peace and satisfaction of heart is the person who has been born again and has yielded all to Jesus.

Verse 14: *"But whosoever drinketh of the water that I shall give him shall never thirst; but the water that I shall give him shall be in him a well of water springing up into everlasting life."*

The literal Greek here reads, "shall never thirst *unto eternity.*" The same expression is used in John 6:51,58; 8:51; 10:28; 11:26; 14:16. This is a precious promise from the lips of Jesus, the declaration of a glorious truth of the Gospel of the grace of God—and the promise is to everyone. *ALL who are thirsty* are invited to drink, all who are willing to drink may drink freely of the water of life.

This does not mean that the believer will never feel the need of spiritual strength, or feel the need to grow in spiritual things. It simply means that the "living water" Jesus gives is of an enduring and abiding nature which will continue to satisfy the heart day by day, moment by moment. They who drink of the living water are satisfied until they see Jesus face to face.

"The water that I shall give him shall be in him a well of water springing up into everlasting life." The salvation which comes by grace through faith refreshes the believer as the flowing waters of a river refresh the meadow through which it flows. He who receives this "living water" will have a fountain opened in his inner man, a fountain that will never run dry, in this life or throughout all eternity.

Jesus said, "If any man thirst, let him come unto me, and drink. He that believeth on me, as the Scripture hath said, out of his belly shall flow rivers of living water. *(But this spake He of the Spirit, which they that believe on Him should receive: for the Holy Ghost was not yet given; because that Jesus was not yet glorified)"* (John 7:37—39).

Greek scholars tell us that there is a change of tense in these two verses: "Whosoever drinketh" in verse 13 is in the present tense—"drinketh *habitually*"; whereas "whosoever drinketh" in verse 14 is in the perfect tense, *"hath drunk"*—meaning an act with an abiding result. The negative in "shall never thirst" is very strong and means literally, "shall certainly not, no, *never*, thirst forever!"

Verse 15: *"The woman saith unto Him, Sir, give me this water, that I thirst not, neither come hither to draw."*

What Jesus had said to the woman up to this point created in her heart a desire for the living water of which He spoke, and she did what He had wanted her to do from the very beginning of their conversation: She said, *"Give me this water."*

Jesus was God in flesh, and the words He spoke to this woman were certainly the words of God. "Faith cometh by hearing, and hearing by the Word . . ." (Rom. 10:17). As Jesus spoke to this woman about the living water, the Word began to create a thirst within her soul. She still had material things in mind, she was thinking of water like the water that came from Jacob's well; but in her spirit she longed for something that would satisfy her heart. The

life she had lived testified that she had not known satisfaction up to this point, she did not have peace of mind
and heart.

Some Bible teachers have suggested that there was a note
of sarcasm in the woman's request for living water, but I
do not agree. I believe she was sincere. The beautiful
climax to this conversation between Jesus and the Samaritan
woman came with her salvation by simply believing the
Word of God, the words Jesus spoke to her.

Verse 16: *"Jesus saith unto her, Go, call thy husband,
and come hither."*

Up to this point in the conversation, Jesus had dealt
with material things; but here He began to deal with the
woman's conscience, and as He spoke she suddenly realized
that her whole life was open before Him. She was spiritually ignorant, but she now recognized that she was in the
presence of a very unusual Person. From this point on,
Jesus spoke no more of living water, nor did He use figurative language. His words from here on were direct, plain,
and very personal.

He asked the woman to go call her husband because
He wanted her to realize that she was a sinner. She must
be convicted of her sin before she would receive Him as her
Saviour. He knew her besetting sin, and He knew that
when He asked her to go call her husband it would lead
her to the next step in her conversion—it would lead her
to confess the truth. He wanted her to know that she was
standing in the presence of Deity; therefore He revealed to
her that He knew the secrets of her soul and of her life,
even the besetting sin that was robbing her of the peace
and joy she longed for, and which the "living water" would
bring to her heart.

In our soul-winning efforts today, we must first get sinners to realize that they are lost. They must be convicted
of sin, they must realize that Jesus looks upon the heart.
When we are able to get unbelievers to see their *need* for

salvation, when we can get them to see the exceeding sinfulness of sin, then they are in a good position to be born
again.

Verses 17 and 18: *"The woman answered and said, I*
have no husband. Jesus said unto her, Thou hast well
said, I have no husband: for thou hast had five husbands;
and he whom thou now hast is not thy husband: in that
saidst thou truly."

The woman could have said, "Wait a moment and I
will go and bring my husband." But the fact that she did
not go and bring the man with whom she was living proved
that she had realized that she was in the presence of a
messenger of Almighty God, and she confessed, *"I HAVE*
no husband."

"Thou hast well said, I have no husband." Jesus commended her for telling the truth. She did not confess that
she had had five husbands and was then living with a man
to whom she was not married, but she was honest in saying that she had no husband, and Jesus commended her
for her honesty.

It is highly improbable that this woman had married five
times and in each instance the husband had died. Mates
could be divorced for very trivial reasons in those days,
and she had more than likely divorced these five men—or
perhaps they had divorced *her* for reasons of adultery. She
had then taken up with a man whom she had not bothered
to marry.

This was a wicked woman, a notorious sinner as man
looks upon sinners; but notice the kindness with which the
Saviour dealt with her: "Thou hast well said, I have no
husband: for thou hast had five husbands; and he whom
thou now hast is not thy husband: in that saidst thou truly." Twice He commended her because she had confessed
her sin of adultery—"Thou hast well said . . . In that saidst
thou truly." People can be led, but they cannot be driven.
Kindness, sympathy, and compassion on the part of a soul-

winner many times disarms prejudice and helps to gain the confidence and attention of an unbeliever so that the Word of God can be given out. Jesus could have said to this woman, "I know you are wicked, adulterous, ungodly; and unless you repent you will spend eternity in hell!" But He said nothing like that. His gentle words were, "Thou saidst truly."

Verse 19: *"The woman saith unto Him, Sir, I perceive that thou art a prophet."*

Nicodemus said practically the same thing when he came to Jesus and confessed, "We know that thou art a teacher come from God, for no man can do these miracles that thou doest, except God be with him." We see in this verse a great change in the Samaritan woman's mind. In this one statement it is as though she said, "I changed my mind about you. Even though you look like an ordinary Jew, I perceive that you are no ordinary Person. You have told me things you could not have told me had you not been a prophet sent from God. You see my heart, you know my sin, you have shown me that I have a spiritual need."

This woman of Samaria did not have the New Testament as we do. All that she had learned about this Person at the well was what she had learned through His words since their conversation began. She acknowledged Him as a *prophet;* she did not recognize Him as the Messiah, Saviour of mankind. It seems that very few had a clear view of the divine nature of Jesus. The entire Jewish nation was in darkness and ignorance concerning who He was. Even the scribes and the chief priests could not explain how Messiah was to be David's Lord and at the same time be David's son (Mark 12:35—37).

In her spiritual ignorance, this woman asked the wrong question:

Verse 20: *"Our fathers worshipped in this mountain; and ye say, that in Jerusalem is the place where men ought to worship."*

Even though she was under conviction for sin, this woman of Samaria was still in spiritual darkness. She was actually asking Jesus, "Where do you think I should join the church? Which denomination is right for me? Where should I worship?" But she was not ready to worship; she needed to be born again.

She was alarmed when Jesus revealed that He knew all about her life, when her sins were so suddenly brought to light by a Man whom she had never seen before. She realized that she was in the presence of a prophet of God, and for possibly the first time in her life she felt that she was a great sinner and needed spiritual help; but even in that anxious moment she could not forget the hatred that existed between the Jews and the Samaritans, and she remembered that *her* people said to worship in one place, and the *Jews* said to worship in another. This troubled her, and her heart and mind asked the question, "Who is right? Where *should* I worship? What *should* I believe?"

The first thing a poor, blinded sinner thinks of when he is approached by a minister or a personal worker, is uniting with a church and attending services; but uniting with a church—even faithfully attending services and helping to carry on the *work* of the church—will not save anyone. Never has there been a more zealous group of people than the Jews; yet Paul declared, "Brethren, my heart's desire and prayer to God for Israel is, that they might be saved. For I bear them record that they have a zeal of God, but not according to knowledge. For they being ignorant of God's righteousness, and going about to establish their own righteousness, have not submitted themselves unto the righteousness of God" (Rom. 10:1—3).

This woman was still unregenerated, and it was only natural for her to think in terms of the religion of her fathers and follow the customs and traditions of the Samaritans. There are tens of thousands of people today who belong to certain denominations simply because their parents belonged. There are many denominational people—Baptist,

Methodist, Presbyterian, and others—that do not know what their church believes or teaches. They do not know Jesus; they joined a church because their parents were members of that church, and not because they have been regenerated by the Holy Spirit.

The *"mountain"* referred to was no doubt the hill where the temple of Samaria was built, a rival to the temple in Jerusalem and of no small offence to the Jews. Historians tell us that this rival temple was built by Sanballat in the days of Nehemiah, and that Sanballat's son-in-law (the son of Jodiah) whom Nehemiah "chased" from him, was the first high priest to officiate there: "Remember them, O my God, because they have defiled the priesthood, and the covenant of the priesthood, and of the Levites" (Neh. 13:29).

"YE say that in Jerusalem is the place where men ought to worship." The woman was here speaking of the Jewish nation, not necessarily of the Lord Jesus, for He had not even mentioned worshipping. It was the Jewish nation that claimed Jerusalem as the place of worship.

Satan was attempting to divert the woman's mind from salvation to a place of worship, to sidetrack the issue, but Jesus did not allow him to do it. Instead of starting an argument as to which place to worship, Jesus continued to lead her to the door of salvation.

Verse 21: *"Jesus saith unto her, Woman, believe me, the hour cometh, when ye shall neither in this mountain, nor yet at Jerusalem, worship the Father."*

Our Lord is declaring here that a new dispensation was about to be ushered in—the Dispensation of the Gospel of Grace. Under grace there was to be no more distinction of places such as Jerusalem (the temple) or Samaria (the mountain). The old dispensation where the Jews had to go up to Jerusalem to worship and attend feasts was to pass away. All questions about the superiority of Samaria or Jerusalem were about to come to an end, for under the Gospel of grace believers would find access to the Father anywhere and

everywhere without the temple services, priests, or altars.
Under the Gospel of grace, all places would be alike.

Verse 22:   *"Ye worship ye know not what: we know
what we worship: for salvation is of the Jews."*

Here Jesus clearly and unmistakably condemned the religion of the Samaritans as compared to the religion of the
Jews.   History tells us that the Samaritans believed and
taught that Mount Gerizim was the place where Abraham offered up Isaac and where he met Melchizedec; but there is
no Scripture to substantiate this belief.   Abraham offered
Isaac on Mount Moriah where the temple of Solomon was
later built.

The Samaritans had no scriptural background or authority
for either their religion or their place of worship.   They
had no revelation, no commandments from Almighty God.
Their worship was of man, and God had never sanctioned it.
They had no right to believe that their prayers were heard
or that their offerings were accepted. Theirs was a religion
of uncertainty; it did not bring peace to the heart.   They
were worshipping what Paul referred to as an "unknown
god."   They emphasized the *place* of worship instead of
the Person they worshipped.

"We know what WE worship."   Notice that Jesus identi-
fies Himself with the Jews.   It was to the Jews that Jehovah gave the commandments, and they had divine sanc-
tion as well as scriptural authority for their religion.   They
could give a reason for their hope: They knew the God of
Abraham, Isaac, and Jacob, even though they refused to
recognize and receive their Messiah.

"Salvation is of the Jews."   If Jesus had *opened* His
conversation with these words He would have lost a convert; but in His omniscience He began at the right place—
discussing *water,* not the salvation that had come through
the lineage of David; and having led the woman gently
step-by-step to this point, He could clearly declare that the
Saviour was promised especially to the Jews. On this point

at least the Samaritan had no right to claim equality with the Jew. The Jews were descendants of the tribe of Judah, and to them belonged the promises made to the house and lineage of David. Jesus came to the Jew first (Rom. 1:16); but in this marvelous day of grace, that middle wall of partition has been broken down and in the Church of the living God there is neither Jew nor Gentile. We are ONE in Christ. In Ephesians 2:11−18 we read:

"Wherefore remember, that ye being in time past Gentiles in the flesh, who are called Uncircumcision by that which is called the Circumcision in the flesh made by hands; that at that time ye were without Christ, being aliens from the commonwealth of Israel, and strangers from the covenants of promise, having no hope, and without God in the world: But now in Christ Jesus ye who sometimes were far off are made nigh by the blood of Christ. For He is our peace, who hath made both one, and hath broken down the middle wall of partition between us; having abolished in His flesh the enmity, even the law of commandments contained in ordinances; for to make in Himself of twain one new man, so making peace; and that He might reconcile both unto God in one body by the cross, having slain the enmity thereby: and came and preached peace to you which were afar off, and to them that were nigh. For through Him we both have access by one Spirit unto the Father."

"Salvation is of the Jews" means literally that the Saviour Himself has come through the Jewish nation from the standpoint of the flesh. Greek authorities say that this should read "THE salvation (or the Saviour)," because Jesus IS salvation. He said to Zacchaeus, "This day is salvation come to this house," and of course it was Jesus who came to the house of Zacchaeus that day (Luke 19:1−10).

Verse 23: *"But the hour cometh, and now is, when the true worshippers shall worship the Father in spirit and in truth: for the Father seeketh such to worship Him."*

"The hour cometh, and now is" means the hour of salvation for "whosoever will"; the hour when Jesus would settle the sin-question once and forever; the hour when He would make the one sacrifice never to be repeated; the hour which is later referred to in John 13:1: "Now before the feast of the passover, *when Jesus knew that His hour was come that He should depart out of this world unto the Father,* having loved His own which were in the world, He loved them unto the end."

"The hour cometh" was fully brought in by the New Testament Church, made up of born again believers—not a building, not a mountain, not a temple. That hour came on the Day of Pentecost when one hundred and twenty people in the upper room were baptized into the body of Christ by the Holy Spirit. Now ALL believers are baptized into the body of Christ: "For as the body is one, and hath many members, and all the members of that one body, being many, are one body: so also is Christ. For by one Spirit are we all baptized into one body, whether we be Jews or Gentiles, whether we be bond or free; and have been all made to drink into one Spirit" (I Cor. 12:12,13).

So the "hour" was beginning at the very moment Jesus uttered those words, the hour when true worshippers would worship—not necessarily in a mountain or in a temple, but in spirit and in truth. It is perfectly scriptural to have a building in which to meet—but that is the meeting house, not the Church. The born again believers make up the Church, with Jesus as the head and the foundation. The Samaritans put great emphasis on the mountain, and the Jews put emphasis on the temple; but now the external part of worship (the building or the place) is of little or no consequence. What counts in our worship is the internal state of the individual worshipper, the condition of the heart. True worshippers worship in spirit and in truth, thinking nothing of the building or the beauty of the surroundings. They are concerned with the beauty of holiness in the finished work and shed blood of Jesus.

"Spirit" in this verse does not mean the Holy Spirit, but the intellectual or mental part of man, in contrast with the material and carnal part of man. "The natural man receiveth not the things of the Spirit of God: for they are foolishness unto him: neither can he know them, because they are spiritually discerned" (I Cor. 2:14).

To worship "in spirit" is to worship from the heart—not in form, not a carnal worship consisting of ceremonies, offerings, sacrifices, feasts, and keeping of days.

To worship "in truth" means to worship by and through the one way to God. We do not worship today through sacrifices of lambs, doves, bullocks; we worship God through truth. Jesus said, "I am the Truth." He is the truth concerning God, He is the life of God, He is the way TO God. Therefore we worship God through Jesus Christ. The only way we can approach God is in the name of Jesus; He is the only Mediator between God and men (I Tim. 2:5).

Before Jesus shed His blood, men worshipped through emblems, figures, types, and ceremonies; but *when Jesus died* the veil was rent from top to bottom and the holy of holies laid bare. Then men began to worship *"in truth."* We worship "in spirit"—and spirit is opposed to flesh. Spirit is heart-service contrasted with lip-service and formal worship. We worship "in truth"—and truth is opposed to type and shadow. The sacrifices of the Mosaic system pointed TO the truth, to *Jesus,* settling the sin-debt with His own blood—one sacrifice, for all, forever, never to be repeated:

"But this Man, after He had offered one sacrifice for sins for ever, sat down on the right hand of God; from henceforth expecting till His enemies be made His footstool. For by one offering He hath perfected for ever them that are sanctified. Whereof the Holy Ghost also is a witness to us: for after that He had said before, This is the covenant that I will make with them after those days, saith the Lord, I will put my laws into their hearts, and in their minds will I write them; and their sins and iniquities will I remember no more.

"Now where remission of these is, there is no more offering for sin. *Having therefore, brethren, boldness to enter
into the holiest by the blood of Jesus, by a new and living
way,* which He hath consecrated for us, through the veil,
that is to say, His flesh; and having an High Priest over
the house of God; let us draw near with a true heart in
full assurance of faith, having our hearts sprinkled from an
evil conscience, and our bodies washed with pure water"
(Heb. 10:12—22).

"The Father seeketh such to worship Him."   Anyone
who surrenders soul and spirit to God *does* worship Him in
spirit and in truth.   The Greek language here expresses a
deep compassion of the heavenly Father in His desire to
save souls—yes, even a Samaritan harlot! He actually search-
es and seeks for lost souls, He waits for them—and we remember the parable of the ninety-and-nine, where one sheep
was lost and the shepherd left the ninety-and-nine to search
until he found that one and brought it home (Luke 15:3—7).
God is not willing that any should perish; He has a deep
compassion, a tender love, and is willing to save all who
will come to Him by Christ Jesus.

Jesus was attempting to point the Samaritan woman to
"WHOM," not "where."   If she were willing to worship
in spirit, she was invited.   God seeks our worship—think
of it!   God the Creator of heaven and earth and all that
therein is, the great God of the universe, seeks *you* and
seeks *me* to worship Him!   God forgive us for not bowing
our heads more often in worship and humble submission
to Him.

Verse 24:   *"God is a Spirit: and they that worship Him
must worship Him in spirit and in truth."*

Jesus is teaching this Samaritan woman that God is not
like earthly kings, to be found in a temple or in a mountain.   He is teaching her that God is not as we are; He is
an immaterial Being, an eternal Spirit.   There was never a

time when He was not, there was never a *place* where He was not. He does not dwell in temples; He is everywhere; He is not (as we are) confined to one place. We cannot fully understand this great truth. We ask, "Where and when did God originate?" He did not *originate;* He did not come from any place or any thing. He is an *eternal Spirit,* and before this world was created, *God WAS.* In the *beginning* He was GOD: "Lord, thou hast been our dwelling place in all generations. Before the mountains were brought forth, or ever thou hadst formed the earth and the world, *even from everlasting to everlasting, THOU ART GOD"* (Psalm 90:1,2).

I am afraid modern worship attracts the flesh more than it praises and worships God. Too many services are planned and programmed to please the listening ears of the parishioners—attractive services, beautiful surroundings, entertaining music. Oh yes—I believe in music in the church. I love music, and I believe we can praise God in music and song; but today the musical programs in some churches take up more time than the preaching. All too often music is substituted for "the foolishness of preaching" by which God saves men in this dispensation. It is not wrong for Christians to sing with grace in their hearts unto the Lord, but it IS wrong to substitute music and singing for the preaching of the Word of God—not to mention the fact that some of the modern music is a disgrace to the name of Christianity!

Buildings—stained glass windows, costly fittings and furnishings—are getting praise and adoration that should be given to Almighty God. I believe the house of worship should be comfortable and inviting—but I also know that millions of dollars have been wasted on costly, ornate buildings when those dollars should have been spent for missions. I have had the happy privilege of visiting many foreign mission fields. I have been in the jungles of South America, I have even worshipped with converted pygmies, head-hunters. I have heard the testimony of natives who knew the taste of human flesh, for as children they had eaten white men. I worshipped with these converted jungle people, and I must confess that in those services, as I sat on the ground under a thatched roof, I was nearer heaven than I have been in many beautiful edifices in our beloved land!

We say that we beautify and adorn our church buildings because God wants it so—but is it really for *God*? or is it for *ourselves*? We point to Solomon's temple as an example, but that temple has been completely destroyed; not one stone of it remains upon another. I do believe in the local church. I believe in having a comfortable (and, within reason, a *beautiful*) place of worship; but I do know that true worship does not depend upon the elaborate and extravagant ornamentation of a building.

True worship proceeds from the heart, and only from a *regenerated* heart. Jesus said of the Pharisees, "This people draweth nigh unto me with their mouth, and honoureth me with their lips; but their heart is far from me. But in vain they do worship me, teaching for doctrines the commandments of men" (Matt. 15:8,9). We should testify to the saving grace of Jesus, we should praise His lovely name; but since God is a Spirit, they who worship Him *"MUST worship Him in spirit and in truth."*

It is interesting to notice the divine *"must"* in this verse. In John 3:7 Jesus said, "Ye MUST be born again." In John 3:14 He said, "The Son of man MUST be lifted up." Here in verse 24, we "MUST worship Him in spirit and in truth." In these three "musts" we see the Trinity: The first "must" points to the Holy Spirit, for the new birth is OF the Spirit. The second "must" points to Jesus the Son, lifted up on the cross; and the "must" in our present verse points to the Father who so loved the world that He gave Jesus, that we might have the opportunity to be born of the Spirit; and only those who have been born of the Spirit through the shed blood of Jesus Christ can worship the eternal God and Father of our Lord and Saviour. All other worship is an abomination to Him (Prov. 15:8).

True worship to God can proceed only from redeemed, delivered people. As long as the children of Israel were in bondage to Egypt they did not worship; they could only groan and cry: "And it came to pass in process of time, that the king of Egypt died: and the children of Israel sighed by reason of the bondage, and they cried, and their cry came up unto God by reason of the bondage. And God heard their groaning, and God remembered His covenant with Abraham, with Isaac, and with Jacob" (Ex. 2:23,24). But after they passed through the Red Sea, *they sang:* "Then sang Moses and the children of Israel this song unto the Lord, and spake, saying, I will sing unto the Lord, for He hath triumphed gloriously: the horse and his rider hath He thrown into the sea. The Lord is my strength and song, and He is become my salvation: He is my God, and I will prepare Him an habitation; my father's God, and I will exalt Him" (Ex. 15:1,2).

I believe God is a Person, a spiritual Person. He has form, to be sure; we read of "the hand of God . . . the eyes of God . . . the ears of God." He is a personality, but He is Spirit; therefore true worship must be in accord with the nature of Him who is *worshipped.* God is a Spirit and He must be approached by means of that part of our being which is spirit—the new heart that He gives us when we are *born* of the Spirit. God must be worshipped in truth—not in superstition, sectarianism, and ignorance. There must be total submission of feeling, thought, and desire to do His will—yes, even in worship.

Verse 25: *"The woman saith unto Him, I know that Messias cometh, which is called Christ: when He is come, He will tell us all things."*

This woman had a better understanding of the Messiah than most of the Jews had. She was looking for Messiah, she knew His name (Christ), and she was expecting Him to be a great Teacher. The Jews were simply looking for a powerful, glamorous, conquering king who would deliver them from the Roman rule.

This verse clearly shows that at sometime in her life this woman had been exposed to the teaching of the Old Testament prophecies. She knew that when Messiah came He would be omniscient, able to tell them "all things." *This Man* had told her things that as mortal He could not possibly have known because she had never seen Him before. He had first told her of "living water," she had expressed a desire to *receive* the living water. He had then revealed her sin to her, and while He had ignored her question about the place to worship, He had clearly declared the necessity of worshipping God in spirit and in truth. She was now ready to receive a revelation concerning this Man with whom she was conversing.

The Great Revelation

Verse 26: *"Jesus saith unto her, I that speak unto thee am He."*

Here is the clearest and most complete declaration Jesus ever made of His own deity and messiahship; and it was made—not to Nicodemus, not to the rulers of the Jews, not to Herod nor to Pilate; but to a poor, fallen, Samaritan woman. This is one of the most wonderful instances of our Lord's tenderness, humility, grace, and condescension. Now she had the answer to her question, "Art thou greater than our father Jacob?"

Jesus is always ready and anxious to reveal Himself to a poor, seeking sinner. The very moment the woman expressed her *desire* for Messiah, Jesus revealed Himself to her and she received Him as her Saviour. He did not work a miracle for her to see, He did not cause a bright light to shine, there was no thunder or lightning. He simply spoke seven words: *"I that speak unto thee am HE."* Seven words—God's number for perfection. She was standing in the presence of the great "I AM." He had been speaking

with her, and His words were the words of God. The Word
brings saving faith. The words Jesus spoke to her melted
her hard heart, lightened her darkened soul, she believed
and was saved immediately. Proof? She threw down her
waterpot, she forgot temporal things, and ran to the city
to announce that she had found the Messiah (v. 29), proving
that the living water had been poured into her soul and
an artesian well was the result!

This entire account is rich indeed, a most remarkable
passage of Scripture. The love of God and the grace of
God know no racial barriers; all are included. The power
of God knows no human limitation; it is sufficient to pour
living water into the believing heart. There are no secrets
with God; everything is naked before His eyes, He knows
every thought of every heart.

From the Lord's example here we know that we are not
to despise poor, wretched sinners. Few have stepped deeper
into sin than had this woman, yet Jesus did not despise
her. He had come to seek and to save that which was
lost, and in love and compassion He led her to the fountain of life. Let each of us study this account, re-study it,
and then study it again, and pray for God to give us patience, wisdom, compassion, mercy, and love such as Jesus
demonstrated here insofar as it is possible for us to possess
these qualities in Him. By His example we can become
effective soul-winners.

Verse 27: *"And upon this came His disciples, and marvelled that He talked with the woman: yet no man said,
What seekest thou? or, Why talkest thou with her?"*

It was not by accident that the disciples returned just
as Jesus made Himself known to the woman and she received Him. The Holy Spirit ordained it to be that way.
If the disciples had returned while Jesus was talking with
the woman, they would have caused confusion and distrac-
tion, and her conversion would not have been complete;
but the heavenly Father saw to it that the disciple band

did not return until the woman was converted.

The disciples *"marvelled that He talked with the woman."* The disciples did not have such compassion as Jesus had for the Samaritans; but the fact that the Master talked with a woman of Samaria should have impressed them and influenced them in the direction of "whosoever will." However, they were slow to believe, as most folk are in our day. This is something of the same lesson Peter learned in Acts 10:9—15:

"On the morrow, as they went on their journey, and drew nigh unto the city, Peter went up upon the housetop to pray about the sixth hour: and he became very hungry, and would have eaten: but while they made ready, he fell into a trance, and saw heaven opened, and a certain vessel descending unto him, as it had been a great sheet knit at the four corners, and let down to the earth: wherein were all manner of fourfooted beasts of the earth, and wild beasts, and creeping things, and fowls of the air. And there came a voice to him, Rise, Peter; kill, and eat. But Peter said, Not so, Lord; for I have never eaten any thing that is common or unclean. And the voice spake unto him again the second time, *What God hath cleansed, that call not thou common."*

"Yet no man said, What seekest thou? or, Why talkest thou with her?" At this point in the ministry of Jesus the disciples undoubtedly respected Him very highly, and most assuredly they had a deep reverence for Him. They wondered—but they did not question Him. On occasion the disciples did not give expression to the feeling in their hearts concerning some of the things they saw Him do and some of the words they heard Him speak. They did not always understand, but they kept silent and wondered in their hearts.

So should it be with us today. There are many things that we cannot understand. We do not understand Romans 8:28—but we know it is true because God's Word declares it. Many individual things happen that we cannot understand, but we should hold our peace and stand in awe before God, knowing that He doeth all things well. Things we do not understand today (and may *never* understand in this life) God will explain to us in that Great Day. A good servant in the king's court must perform his duty and ask no questions; and just so, born again believers should strive to be good servants of the King of kings. We should listen to His voice, obey His commands, and not question why.

Verses 28 and 29: *"The woman then left her waterpot, and went her way into the city, and saith to the men, Come, see a man, which told me all things that ever I did: is not this the Christ?"*

"Waterpot" here is the same Greek word used in John 2:6. This was not a small vessel from which the household drank, but a large jar. Women in the east still use these large earthen jars which they carry balanced on their heads.

Why did the woman *leave* her waterpot? Why did she not carry it with her? She was in a hurry to spread the good news that she had found the Messiah, and she could make the trip to the city much quicker by leaving the waterpot. We, too, should lay aside anything that would hinder us in spreading the good news and the living waters of salvation. As Paul said to the Hebrew Christians, ". . . Let us lay aside every weight, and the sin which doth so easily beset us, and let us run with patience the race that is set before us, looking unto Jesus the author and finisher of our faith; who for the joy that was set before Him endured the cross, despising the shame, and is set down at the right hand of the throne of God" (Heb. 12:1,2).

The actions of the Samaritan woman remind us of the lame man whose healing is recorded in Acts 3:1—11. When he was healed "he leaping up stood, and walked, and entered with them into the temple, walking, and leaping, and praising God." The same is true in the life of every poor lost sinner who drinks of the living water of salvation by faith. What had happened to the Samaritan woman was so marvelous in her own life, she was anxious to tell others. She forgot all else and ran into the city to spread the good news.

Notice to whom this woman testified: She *"saith to the MEN."* I believe this woman testified to the men because she had no women friends. Undoubtedly every lady in the countryside knew that this was a husband-stealer and a home-wrecker, and the women simply did not keep company with her. That is probably why she went alone at high noon to draw water, instead of going early in the morning or late in the afternoon when the other women went to the well. So when she returned to the city she spoke to the men.

Notice the wisdom of her testimony: She did not try to convince them that there had been a birth in her spirit and soul. Every man in the neighborhood knew the kind of life she had lived. She simply invited them to come and see for themselves. She knew that they would be convinced if they saw the Man who had changed her life.

This woman became a home missionary immediately, but all she did was give her testimony and invite others to come to Jesus. She did not begin to teach a Bible class or conduct evangelistic campaigns. This is an important lesson all church leaders should learn. Young converts should not be placed in important positions in the church— such as Sunday school teachers, deacons, etc. It is not wise to put a novice in a place of responsibility until he (or she) has studied and learned to rightly divide the Word of truth. I have known young converts who wanted to master the books of Daniel and Revelation within thirty days after they were born again; they were immediately zealous to open a Bible conference on prophecy. This is "zeal without knowledge" and will lead to error; but there is not much chance of making a mistake or preaching the wrong doctrine when we shout to the neighborhood, "Come and see Jesus!" If, like the Samaritan woman, we can get people to see Christ, the battle is won. They will believe on Him when they really see Him with the eye of faith. We need no degree from a theological seminary to say, "Come and drink of the water of life." This woman's invitation paid great dividends; many did come to see Christ, and many were saved.

"All things that ever I did" simply means that the woman realized that Jesus knew her past, He knew the innermost secrets of her heart. (See Isaiah 11:2,3.)

"Is not this the Christ?" This is posed as a question, yet it is a declaration—"This can be no other *but* the Christ, for no one but God's Messiah can do what this Man has just done!" Her question certainly aroused the curiosity of the people, and they went out in great numbers to see Jesus. The woman used wisdom in her testimony. Many times it is profitable in soul winning to ask questions of the unbeliever and allow him to ask questions of the personal worker. Asking and answering questions can often keep his attention and deepen his thirst for the living water.

Revival in Samaria

Verse 30:   *"Then they went out of the city, and came unto Him."*

We see that it is not necessarily the long sermon, nor yet the well-outlined sermon, that wins souls. This woman did not deliver a long message, nor did she have points 1, 2, 3, and 4 neatly outlined. She simply said, "Come and see a Man who told me all things that ever I did. Is not this the Christ?" She gave no benediction, her words were not accompanied by soft music, she used no elaborate setting for her message; but a revival broke out and many were saved as a result of her testimony.

It would be well here to give a word of encouragement to the dear women who serve God so faithfully. It is true that Satan uses women, but God also uses them; and a godly woman is a great asset to any church. The first convert in Europe under the preaching of the Apostle Paul was a woman—Lydia, a seller of purple (Acts 16:14,15); and there are many other accounts in the Word of God concerning women and their ministry.

Verse 31: *"In the mean while His disciples prayed Him, saying, Master, eat."*

Between the time the woman gave her testimony and the crowds arrived at the well to see Jesus, the disciples questioned Him about eating. Greek scholars tell us that the word here translated *"prayed"* is a most unusual word which is frequently used to convey the idea of asking or making inquiry, but not in describing any person's address to God in prayer except that of the Son of God, the Lord Jesus Christ. We find the same word in John 14:16; 16:26; 17:9,15,20. I John 5:16 is the only verse where this word is used in seeming to describe a believer's prayer, and this one instance is so entirely alone in the Word of God that probably the meaning here is not *praying* but "making curious inquiry."

The disciples could not understand why Jesus did not eat. They were still ignorant of His real mission; they did not fully understand. He was occupied with souls, but they were thinking of the body. They wanted to satisfy the hunger of the physical body; Jesus longed to satisfy the hunger of the souls of the Samaritan people. The same spirit prevails among believers today. Some are devout soul winners, more interested in dealing with souls than in attending a fellowship supper. There are others who, though truly born again, never participate in visitation, never go out to witness in the homes and win souls; but they attend every fellowship meeting where food is served! The disciples had not yet learned the full lesson of winning souls. Jesus came to seek and to save that which was lost, and at that moment He was not hungry for the food the disciples had bought in the city. Instead, His hunger reached out to the Samaritans.

Verses 32 and 33: *"But He said unto them, I have meat*

*to eat that ye know not of. Therefore said the disciples
one to another, Hath any man brought Him ought to eat?"*

Jesus had become so engrossed in His conversation with
the Samaritan woman and the multitude of folk who were
coming out to hear Him because of her testimony, that His
physical body had lost its desire for food. He was doing
the very thing He had come into the world to do. He had
not come into the world to major on temporal things, but
to give the water of life, to break the bread of life to all
who would come to Him and believe on Him. He came
to seek and save the lost, not to feed hungry bodies with
physical bread.

Too many churches today are so occupied with serving
food in the social hall that they have lost sight of the fields
"white already unto harvest." They spend more time over
the stove in the kitchen than they do at the altar in intercessory prayer for a lost world. When a church wears out
the linoleum on the floor of the social hall more quickly
than it wears out the carpet around the altar, you may
mark that church as carnal; it is feeding on the wrong kind
of meat. That is why the world is in such sad condition
today—churches have become social and recreational centers
instead of spiritual cafeterias where souls can be fed and
satisfied with the Word of God. The Church of the living
God was not commissioned to feed hungry bodies, but to
nourish the souls of men.

The disciples commented *"one to another."* This was a
private (and probably whispered) conversation among the
disciples only. Jesus had said to them, *"I have meat to
eat that ye know not of,"* and they did not understand that
He was speaking of spiritual things. They were unable to
put anything but a carnal meaning on the words He had
just spoken. They did not ask *Him* if someone had brought
Him food; they questioned among themselves, *"Hath any
man brought Him ought to eat?"* They had no recognition
of the spiritual meaning of these wonderful words of our

Lord.

Verse 34:   *"Jesus saith unto them, My meat is to do the will of Him that sent me, and to finish His work."*

To Jesus, doing the will of God the Father was so soul-refreshing and pleasant that He felt no need for physical food.   He had come into the world to do the work of His Father, and at that moment He did not have time to eat. What IS the will of God?   It is *not* His will "that any should perish, but that all should come to repentance" (II Pet. 3:9).   His will is that we carry out the commission Jesus gave in Matthew 28:18−20:   "And Jesus came and spake unto (the disciples), saying, All power is given unto me in heaven and in earth.   Go ye therefore, and teach all nations, baptizing them in the name of the Father, and of the Son, and of the Holy Ghost: teaching them to observe all things whatsoever I have commanded you: and, lo, I am with you alway, even unto the end of the world. Amen."

In this verse Jesus is saying, "The meat that removes *my* hunger is to do the will of God the Father who sent me.   The *work* that I am to finish is to give out the message that *whosoever* believeth on the Son shall not perish. My meat is to obey my heavenly Father and fulfil every jot and tittle of His law."

Ministers today can certainly take a lesson from these words of Jesus.   So much man-made doctrine and routine have crept into the local church until in many instances by the time the pastor finishes with his business duties, recreation, and social activities, he has little time left to witness to souls or even to prepare a soul-nourishing message for his parishioners on Sunday.   We must have some recreation, to be sure—even ministers are human; but in some churches there is so much required of the pastor that preaching has become a sideline.   Woe unto such when they meet Christ face to face at the judgment.   To Jesus, the conversion of a sinner was His meat, His very life.

Verse 35: *"Say not ye, There are yet four months, and then cometh harvest? Behold, I say unto you, Lift up your eyes, and look on the fields; for they are white already to harvest."*

Here Jesus was reminding the disciples of the common saying among the Jews that it was four months from seedtime to harvest. The sower sowed the seed, and in four months the harvest was ready for reaping; but HE said here, "I tell you the spiritual harvest is reaped more quickly. Behold these Samaritans coming out already to hear the Word, on the very day the seed has been sown among them. The fields are already white for the harvest."

This Scripture also points out how much more attentive and zealous the minds of men are concerning earthly things than concerning heavenly. The farmer, from the day he sows the seed until he reaps the harvest, lives in anxiety and labors day by day looking forward to the harvest; but many times soul winners are slothful and lazy; they do not get excited about gathering in heavenly wheat. If the farmer is zealous and attentive about a material harvest, how much more should *we* be concerned about gathering in heavenly wheat to the glory of God!

"Lift up your eyes . . . Look on the fields!" Here the words of Jesus express the vast area where many precious souls are ready to receive the Word of God if only someone would carry the Word to them. The *"eyes"* referred to are both physical and spiritual. Jesus wanted His disciples to see, *literally,* the masses of unsaved—especially the Samaritans who were approaching the place where the disciples were at that time; but He also wanted them to see, with the spiritual eye, the *great need* of the Samaritans.

The fields, *"white already unto harvest,"* served as a natural illustration of the spiritual harvest. Jesus used objects around Him to give vivid power to His wonderful words of life; and by so doing He caused His messages to be pleasant and more quickly received into the mind, from whence they would sink into the heart and bear fruit. Our

Lord was the greatest illustrator who ever lived; even a little child could understand His parables and His illustrations. He put His messages down where people could understand them and grasp His meaning—the sparrows, the lilies, the mother hen gathering her little ones under her wings; who does not understand such language as this?

Verse 36: *"And he that reapeth receiveth wages, and gathereth fruit unto life eternal: that both he that soweth and he that reapeth may rejoice together."*

Here the Lord speaks in general: the field is the world, and His words here are words of encouragement to His disciples and to all who labor for Him. The full meaning of the statement is that he who reaps a spiritual harvest has a far greater, more honorable reward and a far greater joy and satisfaction than he who reaps a natural harvest of wheat, barley, and corn. The man who reaps a *natural* harvest receives wages; but he who reaps the *spiritual* harvest gathers fruit for life eternal as well as for life in this world. Therefore, he who reaps a spiritual harvest has an *eternal* paycheck: "And when the chief Shepherd shall appear, ye shall receive a crown of glory that fadeth not away" (I Pet. 5:4).

Fruit gathered by the soul winner is eternal fruit—souls of men plucked from eternal destruction and saved unto eternal life. Listen to these Scriptures:

Daniel 12:3: "They that be wise shall shine as the brightness of the firmament; and they that turn many to righteousness as the stars for ever and ever."

John 15:16: "Ye have not chosen me, but I have chosen you, and ordained you, that ye should go and bring forth fruit, and that your fruit should remain: that whatsoever ye shall ask of the Father in my name, He may give it you."

I Corinthians 9:17: "For if I do this thing willingly, I have a reward: but if against my will, a dispensation of the Gospel is committed unto me."

James 5:20: "Let him know, that he which converteth the sinner from the error of his way shall save a soul from death, and shall hide a multitude of sins."

It is honorable to sow seed and reap a harvest of grain to provide food for hungry bodies; but it is much more profitable to sow the good seed of the Word of God, the incorruptible seed that will bring forth a harvest of life eternal. We are commanded to pray the Lord of the harvest that He will send forth laborers into the fields, for "the harvest truly is plenteous, but the labourers are few" (Matt. 9:37,38). There are untold millions who have never heard a simple Gospel message of the love of God and the saving grace of our Lord and Saviour, Jesus Christ. What are we doing about it?

"Both he that soweth and he that reapeth may rejoice together." This refers to that great day when the Church will be caught up to meet Jesus in the clouds in the air, when the saints will rejoice together at the marriage supper of the Lamb and the harvest will be reaped. Then will be the rewarding of the saints. "And I heard a voice from heaven saying unto me, Write, Blessed are the dead which die in the Lord from henceforth: Yea, saith the Spirit, that they may rest from their labours; and their works do follow them" (Rev. 14:13).

Beloved, not one servant of God can be rewarded fully until the consummation of all things. Seed sown by John the Baptist are still bringing forth fruit through those of us who are preaching the Gospel today. Many times in my evangelistic messages I have used John's words when he pointed two of his disciples to Jesus; I have emphasized the fact that John said to them, "Behold the Lamb of God," and I have shown how his invitation to those two men led them to follow Jesus and be saved. John the Baptist sowed the seed that gave me the text which I have used many times to see men born again. The seed he sowed are still bringing forth fruit and will continue to do so until the consummation of all things. THEN all saints will rejoice together.

In the temporal, there are times when a farmer sows seed and does not live to see the crop ripen to harvest, but such is not true in the spiritual. When we sow spiritual seed we are sowing unto eternity, and both sowers and reapers are sure to share in the joy of the harvest. They will *"rejoice together"* when they see the results of their sowing and reaping. Hallelujah! There will be no envy, no jealousy, among believers at the marriage supper, the great rewarding day! We will all rejoice together, we will all praise God together. There will be no little groups or "cliques" standing about, pouting at each other. We may not see the result of our sowing in this life, but we are laborers together with God and at the rewarding day we will see the full results of our work.

I was reared on the farm and I have been both sower and reaper in the wheatfield. I have learned that the sowing is not nearly so glamorous and exciting as the reaping. Yet it is an established fact that without the sowing there would be no reaping; both are necessary in the physical, and it would be well if we would remember this in the spiritual aspect. May God forgive Christians who honor and praise one man for bringing great revival to the church, the community, or the city! One man may reap a tremendous harvest, but the seed that *produced* that harvest might have been sown by people who have been dead for many years. It is marvelous to have a pastor or an evangelist who can attract great crowds and lead great numbers to receive Jesus and make confessions of faith; but before we praise *one man* for the harvest, consider the hundreds of men and women—even the shut-in and disabled—who sowed the seed for that harvest, sometimes at great cost to themselves. All too often excessive honor is given to the reapers, and the sowers are overlooked and forgotten. But GOD does not forget; He keeps the record, and in that crowning day all will rejoice together.

Verse 37: *"And herein is that saying true, One soweth,*

and another reapeth."

The sower is not always the reaper. This is true even in the natural realm; one man may sow the seed and another may reap the harvest. Jesus was sending His disciples to reap a harvest the seed of which had been sown by others, such as John the Baptist.

Verse 38: *"I sent you to reap that whereon ye bestowed no labour: other men laboured, and ye are entered into their labours."*

The disciples were sent to reap a harvest on which they had bestowed no labor. Old Testament prophets, John the Baptist and others, had broken the ground, sown the seed, and prepared the way; and now the result of their labor was to be reaped by the disciples as they traveled and preached the Gospel.

"I SENT you to reap"—(past tense), yet Jesus had not actually sent the disciples at that time. This is common in the Scriptures, especially when God speaks about something that is about to be done. There is no uncertainty with God; He is omniscient, He knows the end in the beginning. When He speaks or when He undertakes, the thing spoken or undertaken can be regarded as already accomplished because in His eternal counsels, His perfect wisdom, and His almighty power, *it is certain to BE done.* Nothing can fail if God undertakes. Thus Jesus is saying to His disciples, "I am sending you to Samaria, Judaea, Galilee, Jerusalem, and to the uttermost parts of the earth, and you will reap a harvest where you bestowed no labor. Others sowed the seed for your reaping."

Verse 39: *"And many of the Samaritans of that city believed on Him for the saying of the woman, which testified, He told me all that ever I did."*

Some think that the Samaritans believed only intellectually that day, but it seems to me that theirs was the true faith that justifies the unbeliever before a righteous God.

They were ignorant concerning many truths of the grace of God, their faith was weak, but I believe they were truly saved when they came to Jesus that day. Later, Philip went down to Samaria after Pentecost and preached to them, and they received him with joy, they heard him without prejudice, and accepted his message as the truth:

"Then Philip went down to the city of Samaria, and preached Christ unto them. And the people with one accord gave heed unto those things which Philip spake, hearing and seeing the miracles which he did. For unclean spirits, crying with loud voice, came out of many that were possessed with them: and many taken with palsies, and that were lame, were healed. And there was great joy in that city" (Acts 8:5—8).

The Samaritans believed on Jesus *"for the saying of the woman."* This shows the importance of giving testimony to the saving grace of Jesus. If we are born again, we can certainly give our personal testimony to others. In this instance, the words spoken by one poor, ignorant, Samaritan woman were used of God to bring saving faith to many of her fellow citizens. Her message was not outstanding, there was nothing remarkable about it—except that she said, "Come see a Man who told me all that ever I did." The Samaritans knew the wicked life she had lived; their curiosity was stirred when she declared that a total stranger had told her everything she had ever done. Surely this Man was no ordinary person! They went out to see Him, they were convinced that He was the Messiah, and they believed on Him.

Verse 40: *"So when the Samaritans were come unto Him, they besought Him that He would tarry with them: and He abode there two days."*

The Samaritans were open for instruction, they were willing to listen to the wonderful words of Jesus, they were hungry for the bread of life. Jesus is always ready and willing to spend time with those who invite Him. He waits to be invited; He never intrudes, and if He is not abiding at your house and in your heart it is because you have not invited Him. He will come in if you will open the door.

"He abode there two days." The ministry of Jesus during these two days is not recorded, but I do not doubt that those days were spent in a great Bible conference as Jesus taught and preached to the Samaritans, and they received His teaching with gladness. It is interesting to note that even today Samaria is a flourishing place; but Capernaum, Chorazin, and Bethsaida are almost entirely forgotten. It was in these cities that Jesus did most of His mighty works and miracles, but they rejected Him, and today few traces of them remain.

Verses 41 and 42: *"And many more believed because of His own word; and said unto the woman, Now we believe, not because of thy saying: for we have heard Him ourselves, and know that this is indeed the Christ, the Saviour of the world."*

Here we see the sovereignty of God in saving the lost. One soul may be called in one way, another may be called in another way. Some of the Samaritans believed on Jesus when they heard the testimony of the woman; others did not believe until they saw Christ in person. All souls are redeemed alike (through the shed blood of Jesus Christ); all souls are saved by grace through faith—but not all persons are brought to repentance in the same way. We must not limit the Holy Ghost to one mode of operation. "God moves in mysterious ways, His wonders to perform," and the Holy Spirit works in many ways to bring unbelievers under the sound of the Gospel, put them under conviction, and bring them unto Christ. One person may be used of the Lord to win souls that another could never reach, and the method used to reach one person may not reach another. We are instruments in the hands of Jesus; and in dealing with souls, as in other endeavors, we must be sure that He is leading.

"Now we believe, not because of thy saying: for we have heard Him ourselves." This means that after seeing and hearing Jesus these people had even stronger faith and stood on a much stronger foundation. This is true of a believer when he studies the Word and feeds upon it. The more we dwell on the Word, the stronger we become in the faith. We do not become any more fully saved, but we do become stronger in the spiritual life. The Samaritans had assurance after seeing Jesus. They said, *"We have heard Him ourselves, and KNOW that this is indeed the Christ, the Saviour of the world!"*

Their confession here is singular: *"Saviour of the world"* is not found anywhere else in the Gospels. It is possible that the Samaritans did not clearly understand what they were saying, but they believed that Jesus was the Saviour of the WORLD—and that is exactly what He was. The Jews thought the Messiah would come to *them* only, since they were God's chosen people, the elect; but the *Samaritans* pronounced Him "the Saviour of the *world.*"

God's marvelous saving grace is certainly put on display here, that such a testimony should be given by a mixed race, semi-heathen, mixed with *many* races. It is indeed extraordinary that *they* gave this testimony, instead of the Jews to whom the covenants and promises were given. After two days of Jesus' teaching, the Samaritans made a confession that the Jews did not make even after *many* days of teaching in Jerusalem—nor did they ever make such confession as a nation. His teaching among the Samaritans did not differ from His teaching among the Jews, but the hearts of the Samaritans were opened to the Gospel and they believed, whereas the Jews hardened their hearts and demanded His crucifixion. He worked His greatest miracles among the Jews; all He did for the Samaritans was teach and preach the Word; but they *believed* His word and confessed Him as Saviour. Many times the most ignorant, unenlightened person will receive the Gospel, believe on the Lord Jesus Christ, and be saved; while in the same meeting one who is learned and enlightened will walk away an unbeliever, lost and on the road to hell.

Paul said it this way: "For ye see your calling, brethren, how that not many wise men after the flesh, not many mighty, not many noble, are called: but God hath chosen the foolish things of the world to confound the wise; and God hath chosen the weak things of the world to confound the things which are mighty; and base things of the world, and things which are despised, hath God chosen, yea, and things which are not, to bring to nought things that are: that no flesh should glory in His presence. But of Him are ye in Christ Jesus, who of God is made unto us wisdom, and righteousness, and sanctification, and redemption: That, according as it is written, He that glorieth, let him glory in the Lord" (I Cor. 1:26—31).

Verse 43: *"Now after two days He departed thence, and went into Galilee."*

To me, the *"two days"* Jesus spent in Samaria are very significant from the standpoint of prophecy. When the Jews demanded the death of their Messiah, He turned to the Gentiles, called the Apostle Paul, and revealed to him the mystery that had been hidden from the ages and eternity: "Even the mystery which hath been hid from ages and from generations, but now is made manifest to His saints: to whom God would make known what is the riches of the glory of this mystery among the Gentiles; which is Christ in you, the hope of glory" (Col. 1:26,27).

According to God's days (a thousand years as one day and one day as a thousand years) He has been dealing with the Gentiles now for *almost* "two days." Who knows? The time may be ripe and the hour may be upon us when Jesus will catch away His Gentile bride and turn again to Israel, as Paul declares in the eleventh chapter of Romans:

"I say then, Hath God cast away His people? God forbid. For I also am an Israelite, of the seed of Abraham, of the tribe of Benjamin. God hath not cast away His people which He foreknew. Wot ye not what the Scripture saith of Elias? how he maketh intercession to God against Israel, saying, Lord, they have killed thy prophets, and digged down thine altars; and I am left alone, and they seek my life. But what saith the answer of God unto him? I have reserved to myself seven thousand men, who have not bowed the knee to the image of Baal. Even so then at this present time also there is a remnant according to the election of grace.   And if by grace, then is it no more of works: otherwise grace is no more grace. But if it be of works, then is it no more grace: otherwise work is no more work.

"What then?   Israel hath not obtained that which he seeketh for; but the election hath obtained it, and the rest were blinded (according as it is written, God hath given them the spirit of slumber, eyes that they should not see, and ears that they should not hear;) unto this day.

"And David saith, Let their table be made a snare, and a trap, and a stumblingblock, and a recompence unto them: Let their eyes be darkened, that they may not see, and bow down their back alway.

"I say then, Have they stumbled that they should fall? God forbid: but rather through their fall salvation is come unto the Gentiles, for to provoke them to jealousy. Now if the fall of them be the riches of the world, and the diminishing of them the riches of the Gentiles; how much more their fulness? For I speak to you Gentiles, inasmuch as I am the apostle of the Gentiles, I magnify mine office: If by any means I may provoke to emulation them which are my flesh, and might save some of them. For if the casting away of them be the reconciling of the world, what shall the receiving of them be, but life from the dead? For if the firstfruit be holy, the lump is also holy: and if the root be holy, so are the branches.

"And if some of the branches be broken off, and thou, being a wild olive tree, wert graffed in among them, and with them partakest of the root and fatness of the olive tree; boast not against the branches. But if thou boast, thou bearest not the root, but the root thee. Thou wilt say then, The branches were broken off, that I might be graffed in.

"Well; because of unbelief they were broken off, and thou standest by faith. Be not highminded, but fear: For if God spared not the natural branches, take heed lest He also spare not thee. Behold therefore the goodness and severity of God: on them which fell, severity; but toward thee, goodness, if thou continue in His goodness: otherwise thou also shalt be cut off. And they also, if they abide not still in unbelief, shall be graffed in: for God is able to graff them in again.

"For if thou wert cut out of the olive tree which is wild by nature, and wert graffed contrary to nature into a good olive tree: how much more shall these, which be the natural branches, be graffed into their own olive tree? For I would not, brethren, that ye should be ignorant of this mystery, lest ye should be wise in your own conceits; that blindness in part is happened to Israel, until the fulness of the Gentiles be come in.

"And so all Israel shall be saved: as it is written, There shall come out of Sion the Deliverer, and shall turn away ungodliness from Jacob: For this is my covenant unto them, when I shall take away their sins. As concerning the Gospel, they are enemies for your sakes: but as touching the election, they are beloved for the fathers' sakes. For the gifts and calling of God are without repentance.

"For as ye in times past have not believed God, yet have now obtained mercy through their unbelief: Even so have these also now not believed, that through your mercy they also may obtain mercy. For God hath concluded them all in unbelief, that He might have mercy upon all.

"O the depth of the riches both of the wisdom and knowledge of God! How unsearchable are His judgments, and His ways past finding out! For who hath known the mind of the Lord? or who hath been His counsellor? Or who hath first given to Him, and it shall be recompensed unto him again?   For of Him, and through Him, and to Him, are all things: to whom be glory for ever.   Amen."

We do not know the day or the hour when Jesus will come, but He Himself clearly instructed His disciples:

"Now learn a parable of the fig tree: When his branch is yet tender, and putteth forth leaves, ye know that summer is nigh: So likewise ye, when ye shall see all these things, know that it is near, even at the doors. Verily I say unto you, This generation shall not pass, till all these things be fulfilled. Heaven and earth shall pass away, but my words shall not pass away.   But of that day and hour knoweth no man, no, not the angels of heaven, but my Father only" (Matt. 24:32−36).   (The *fig tree* is symbolic of the nation Israel.   Study the entire twenty-fourth chapter of Jeremiah.)

Israel is a nation today, his branch is tender, he is putting forth leaves−and "all these things" are with us at the same time.   Surely, Jesus is at the door! and we should pray with John the Beloved, "Even so, come, Lord Jesus!"

After two days in Samaria, Jesus *"departed thence, and went into Galilee."*

Verse 44:   *"For Jesus Himself testified, that a prophet hath no honour in his own country."*

Our Lord's testimony in this verse is worthy of notice. There are many interpretations of this verse, and perhaps many questions which will never be answered. For instance, what is the connection between this verse and the preceding verse? Did someone ask Jesus about returning to where He grew up, in the country around Nazareth?   What IS our Lord's *"own country"*? Many believe He meant the whole of Galilee; but if this be true, how do we reconcile verse 44 with verse 45, which says that the Galilaeans received Him?   After much research, and after comparing the Scriptures in Matthew 13:53,54; Mark 6:1−6; and Luke 4:16−32, I believe He meant *Nazareth.* The sense of the verse would then be, "Jesus departed from Samaria into Galilee, but not to His own country (or city) Nazareth, for He testified that a prophet has no honor in his own country."

Even though we cannot answer all the questions in matters surrounding the statement, it is important that we see the truth of what Jesus said here. Some ministers and evangelists have *discovered* that truth through painful and bitter experience. It has always been true (and will always BE true until Jesus comes), that man is a fallen creature, corrupt, placing no value on that with which he becomes too familiar. It is well to remember the old adage, "Familiarity breeds contempt." For that reason, it is unwise for a minister to remain too long in the same community. I believe it is pleasing to the Lord for His servants to move about and minister to new faces in new areas—and most certainly it is refreshing to a congregation to listen to the voice of a new preacher. If we are God's preachers we all preach the same Gospel, but we do not preach it in the same way, and many times one minister can help people that another minister cannot reach. We are all human, but we are not all alike; and it seems that God greatly uses men who move about. Those who remain too long in one pastorate many times have heartaches that would not have come to them if they had listened to the Holy Spirit instead of listening to people who are supposed to be their trusted friends. Usually, it is those who are closest to a pastor during the first few years of his ministry who ask him to resign after a period of years.

Verse 45: *"Then when He was come into Galilee, the Galilaeans received Him, having seen all the things that He did at Jerusalem at the feast: for they also went unto the feast."*

"The Galilaeans received Him" (the Greek language here indicates that they received Him with respect and reverence, they honored Him as a great Teacher and Healer, one who worked great miracles), *"having seen all the things He did at Jerusalem."* John 2:23 tells us, "Now when He was in

Jerusalem at the passover, in the feast day, many believed in His name, when they saw the miracles which He did." Notice that the Galilaeans received Him because of what they SAW, but the Samaritans received Him *because they heard His word.* The Galilaeans received Him as one who was no common person, but there is no reason to suppose that they *all* received Him in saving faith.

The Galilaeans *"also went unto the feast."* Here is scriptural proof that the Jews from all over the known world attended the great religious feasts at Jerusalem—especially the feast of the Passover. Jews who lived a great distance from Jerusalem, in Galilee and other localities, went to the city of worship to attend the Passover. This indicates the publicity that our Lord's ministry received—and not only His ministry, but His death as well, for He was crucified at Passover time. The crucifixion of the Son of God took place in the presence of tens of thousands of witnesses who came from every part of the known world; *God's providence ordered it so.* The facts of the life, ministry, and death of Jesus Christ could not be denied: "For the king knoweth of these things, before whom also I speak freely: *for I am persuaded that none of these things are hidden from him; FOR THIS THING WAS NOT DONE IN A CORNER"* (Acts 26:26).

The Nobleman's Son Healed

Verse 46: *"So Jesus came again into Cana of Galilee, where He made the water wine. And there was a certain nobleman, whose son was sick at Capernaum."*

This is the second time Jesus visited Cana. We remember that Nathanael lived in Cana, and it is believed that Mary had relatives there, as previously mentioned when Jesus *"made the water wine"* at a wedding.

"And there was a certain nobleman . . . ." This nobleman was no doubt attached to Herod's court and would be called "a royal person" (the literal meaning of *nobleman*).

It has been suggested that he might have been Chuza, Herod's personal steward, whose wife Joanna became one of our Lord's disciples: "And Joanna the wife of Chuza Herod's steward, and Susanna, and many others, which ministered unto Him of their substance" (Luke 8:3). Others suggest that this nobleman might have been Manaea, "which had been brought up with Herod the tetrarch, and Saul" (Acts 13:1).

If the Lord had wanted us to know this man's name I am sure He would have given it to us. The important thing here is not the name of the man, but the fact that a *nobleman,* a person connected with the king's court, would under *any* circumstance visit the Lord Jesus Christ. When the officers were sent to arrest Jesus and returned without Him, the Pharisees and chief priests asked, "Why have ye not brought Him?" The officers replied, "Never man spake like this Man." Then the Pharisees asked, *"Are YE also deceived? HAVE ANY OF THE RULERS OR OF THE PHARISEES BELIEVED ON HIM?"* (John 7:45–48).

The fact that this nobleman *did* come to Jesus proves that the Word of God attracts men of all ranks—from the highest to the lowest. In the first chapter of this salvation Gospel, *fishermen* were converted. In the third chapter, Nicodemus, a ruler of the Jews, was converted, and in the first part of our present chapter the Samaritan harlot was saved. In *this* verse, a nobleman, a royal person from the king's court, visited Jesus, and *his whole household* was saved as a *result* of that visit.

This nobleman's son *"was sick at Capernaum."* In the days of our Lord Capernaum was quite a city. It was located on the shore of the sea of Galilee, but so completely has the woe spoken by our Lord against this city been fulfilled (Matt. 11:23) that the very site of the city is a matter of dispute today. Jesus performed a number of outstanding miracles there. He healed the centurion's servant (Matt. 8:5–10); He restored life to Jairus' daughter (Mark 5:21–43 in part); and in our present study He healed the nobleman's son—three outstanding miracles, each performed upon members of the families of three distinctly leading classes of people. No doubt, as a result of these outstanding miracles, the Gospel was made known to every family in Capernaum, and it is sad indeed that Jesus was forced to say of that city, "And thou, Capernaum, which art exalted unto heaven, shalt be brought down to hell: for if the mighty works, which have been done in thee, had been done in Sodom, it would have remained until this day. But I say unto you, That it shall be more tolerable for the land of Sodom in the day of judgment, than for thee" (Matt. 11: 23,24). Capernaum had opportunity to become one of the greatest Christian centers of all times, but the people of that city rejected the Lord Jesus, and God had no alternative but to pronounce divine judgment upon them.

Verses 47—49: *"When he heard that Jesus was come out of Judaea into Galilee, he went unto Him, and besought Him that He would come down, and heal his son: for he was at the point of death. Then said Jesus unto him, Except ye see signs and wonders, ye will not believe. The nobleman saith unto Him, Sir, come down ere my child die."*

Sometimes God works through our children to bring us to Christ. The dire need of a loved one will often drive a hard-hearted man to his knees and bring him to the Lord. So it was with the nobleman: his concern for his son caused him to seek Jesus, for he had heard of the great miracles being wrought wherever He went.

Jesus knew the heart of this man, as He knows the hearts of all men; but in order to draw out from him the real *desire* of his heart He said to him, "You will not believe unless you see me do some outstanding miracle. You do not have the faith to believe that I can speak a word and your son will be healed. *Except ye see signs and wonders, ye will not believe."*

To this the nobleman replied, *"Sir, COME DOWN ERE*

MY CHILD DIE!" In other words, he said to Jesus, "You are *the only hope* of my child. He is as good as dead unless you heal him." Such faith always brings results with God. "Without faith it is impossible to please Him: for he that cometh to God must believe that He is, and that He is a rewarder of them that diligently seek Him" (Heb. 11:6).

Verse 50: *"Jesus saith unto him, Go thy way; thy son liveth. And the man believed the word that Jesus had spoken unto him, and he went his way."*

We find a similar incident in Matthew 15:21—28, when the Syrophenician woman came to Jesus on behalf of her daughter who was "grievously vexed with a devil." Jesus said to her, *"I am not sent but unto the lost sheep of the house of Israel.* Then came she and worshipped Him, saying, Lord, help me. But He answered and said, It is not meet to take the children's bread, and cast it to dogs. And she said, Truth, Lord: yet the dogs eat of the crumbs which fall from their masters' table. Then Jesus answered and said unto her, *O woman, great is thy faith: be it unto thee even as thou wilt. AND HER DAUGHTER WAS MADE WHOLE FROM THAT VERY HOUR."*

To the nobleman Jesus said, *"Go thy way: THY SON LIVETH."* And you will notice that *"the man BELIEVED the word that Jesus had spoken unto him."* The nobleman *"went his way,"* but from the verses that follow, it is obvious that he did not go home. According to Jewish time, his conversation with Jesus took place about one o'clock in the afternoon ("the seventh hour"—v. 52), but he did not return to his home until the day after. It is improbable that the nobleman would have asked Jesus to come down and heal his son if the distance had been too great to make the journey in a day. If the son was at the point of death, and his life depended upon Jesus reaching him shortly, it would not have been practical for the nobleman to travel a great distance to *get to* Jesus and then have to travel the same great distance back to his son. This would indicate

that there was only a short distance between Cana and
Capernaum where this man lived, and certainly he could
easily have gone home that evening; but he did not return
home until the next day.

Why would a devoted father, with a son at the point of
death, stay away from home all night? The answer in this
case is simple: *The nobleman had unshakeable faith in
the words of Jesus.* "Go thy way: *thy son liveth*"—and the
nobleman believed those words.   Therefore, since his son
was well, there was no need for him to hurry home, and
he wanted to hear more from this great Teacher; so he remained to listen to the wonderful words of Jesus, possibly
spending the night at an inn and listening to Jesus again
the next morning.   Later in the day, he returned home.

We must not pass over this verse without closely ob-
serving the almighty power of Jesus. He spoke only three
words—"Thy son liveth"—and miles away the boy was
healed.   Jesus spoke the words and it was done, proving
the mighty power of His word. And notice the unhesitating
confidence and faith of the nobleman, his faith in the power
of Jesus.   After Jesus said, "Go thy way, thy son liveth,"
the nobleman did not ask another question, he spoke no
further words.   Trusting completely in what Jesus said, he
went his way—not to his home, but to hear more of the
Master's teaching.   The faith of one who sincerely comes to
Jesus may be *weak* faith, but if it is *true* faith it will bring
results. If we do not ask correctly, Jesus corrects our prayers—and though He may not give us exactly what we ask
for, He will give us *better* than we ask.   He doeth all things
well!

Verses 51—53: *"And as he was now going down, his
servants met him, and told him, saying, Thy son liveth.
Then enquired he of them the hour when he began to
amend. And they said unto him, Yesterday at the seventh
hour the fever left him.   So the father knew that it was at
the same hour, in the which Jesus said unto him, Thy son
liveth: and himself believed, and his whole house."*

"As he was going down" simply means that the noble-man traveled down from Cana to Capernaum which, as previously stated, was near the seashore, while Cana was located in the hill country. Thus, one traveled "down" from Cana to Capernaum.

As the nobleman approached his home, his servants met him and told him, *"Thy son liveth."* You will notice that the nobleman did not call out, "How is my son?" By faith he already knew that the boy was well, and instead of asking his servants HOW his son was healed, he asked at what *hour* he began to amend. But the servants did not tell him at what hour the boy "began to amend"; instead, they answered, "Yesterday at the seventh hour *the fever LEFT him.*" This was not an abatement of the fever, a gradual lessening. The fever did not gradually subside: *it left him suddenly,* instantaneously. That is the way the Lord does business. "So the father knew that it was at the same hour, in the which Jesus said unto him, Thy son liveth."

The last part of this verse tells us that the nobleman *"himself believed, and his whole house."* If this man had not had *some* faith in Jesus he would not have traveled from Capernaum to Cana to make his request known. He had a degree of faith; he at least believed that Jesus was an extraordinary person. When Jesus said, "Thy son liveth," his faith was increased; he believed as far as it was possible for him to believe in proportion to the light he had. But the more we hear the Word of God and the more we feed upon the Word, the stronger our faith becomes. This is illustrated in the contrast between Lydia, who had studied the Old Testament Scriptures and walked in all the light she had, and the fortuneteller who was in total spiritual ignorance. Lydia was saved after one short Bible class; the fortuneteller followed Paul and Silas and listened "many days" before she was saved (Acts 16:14—18).

The nobleman exercised all the faith he had when he *went* to Jesus, and then when he heard Jesus speak, his faith was increased. When he returned home and the serv-

ants told him that his son was made well immediately the
very hour Jesus said, "Thy son liveth," his faith was perfected and he and his whole house trusted Jesus as Saviour.
(The "whole house" of course included his wife, his entire
family, and all the servants of his household.)

Christianity promises household salvation. In I Corinthians 1:16 we read that Paul baptized the household of
Stephanas. In Acts 16:15 the household of Lydia was baptized. In Acts 16:31—34, after Paul and Silas instructed
the Philippian jailer and his household in the Word of God,
they all believed and were baptized. If the father and mother in the home are truly born again, if they love the Lord
as they should and serve Him as He directs, they have a
perfect right, *on Bible grounds,* to claim their children for
Jesus. God pity the parents who do not live a Christian
life, a life which will demand the respect of their children!

Verse 54: *"This is again the second miracle that Jesus
did, when He was come out of Judaea into Galilee."*

"The second miracle that Jesus did" simply means that
He had worked only one other miracle in Galilee, and that
was at the marriage feast in Cana. Most of His early miracles were wrought in Jerusalem and Judaea, a fact that
throws light on the ignorance, blindness, and wickedness
of the Jews at Jerusalem. It was there, where the greater
part of His miracles were wrought, that they demanded
His death and condemned Him to be crucified.

It is interesting to note that in this salvation Gospel we
find the account of the miracles of Jesus in groups of threes:
Three miracles in Galilee—the first at the marriage feast in
Cana (ch. 2); the second when He healed the nobleman's
son; the third when He fed the five thousand (ch. 6). John
also gives the record of three miracles in Judaea—the first
at the pool of Bethesda (ch. 5); the second, the healing of
the blind man just after the feast of tabernacles (ch. 9);
the third when He raised Lazarus from the dead (ch. 11).
John also notes three appearings of our Lord to His dis-

ciples: "This is now the *third* time that Jesus shewed Himself to His disciples, after that He was risen from the dead" (John 21:14). See also John 20:19,26.

I love the account of Jesus healing the nobleman's son, because it teaches me that His Word is as good as His presence. This gives value to every promise of His mercy, His grace, His peace, and His keeping power; it gives value to every word that fell from His lips. The person who has believed on Jesus by faith and has laid hold on His Word has his feet fixed on the solid rock. What Christ has promised, He is able to do—yea, exceeding and abundantly above anything we think or ask. What He has undertaken, He will make good. He promises, "Him that cometh to me I will in no wise cast out." If you have come to Him, then you can rest assured that your name is written in the Lamb's book of life. Because HE lives, we live; because HE will never die, we will never die.

Believer, let us fill our hearts and minds with the words of Jesus, for they are the words of God, they are spirit and they are life (John 6:63).

CHAPTER V

1. After this there was a feast of the Jews; and Jesus went up to Jerusalem.

2. Now there is at Jerusalem by the sheep market a pool, which is called in the Hebrew tongue Bethesda, having five porches.

3. In these lay a great multitude of impotent folk, of blind, halt, withered, waiting for the moving of the water.

4. For an angel went down at a certain season into the pool, and troubled the water: whosoever then first after the troubling of the water stepped in was made whole of whatsoever disease he had.

5. And a certain man was there, which had an infirmity thirty and eight years.

6. When Jesus saw him lie, and knew that he had been now a long time in that case, he saith unto him, Wilt thou be made whole?

7. The impotent man answered him, Sir, I have no man, when the water is troubled, to put me into the pool: but while I am coming, another steppeth down before me.

8. Jesus saith unto him, Rise, take up thy bed, and walk.

9. And immediately the man was made whole, and took up his bed, and walked: and on the same day was the sabbath.

10. The Jews therefore said unto him that was cured, It is the sabbath day: it is not lawful for thee to carry thy bed.

11. He answered them, He that made me whole, the same said unto me, Take up thy bed, and walk.

12. Then asked they him, What man is that which said unto thee, Take up thy bed, and walk?

13. And he that was healed wist not who it was: for Jesus had conveyed himself away, a multitude being in that place.

14. Afterward Jesus findeth him in the temple, and said unto him, Behold, thou art made whole: sin no more, lest a worse thing come unto thee.

15. The man departed, and told the Jews that it was Jesus, which had made him whole.

16. And therefore did the Jews persecute Jesus, and sought to slay him, because he had done these things on the sabbath day.

17. But Jesus answered them, My Father worketh hitherto, and I work.

18. Therefore the Jews sought the more to kill him, because he not only had broken the sabbath, but said also that God was his Father, making himself equal with God.

19. Then answered Jesus and said unto them, Verily, verily, I say unto you, The Son can do nothing of himself, but what he seeth the Father do: for what things soever he doeth, these also doeth the Son likewise.

20. For the Father loveth the Son, and sheweth him all things that himself doeth: and he will shew him greater works than these, that ye may marvel.

21. For as the Father raiseth up the dead, and quickeneth them; even so the Son quickeneth whom he will.

22. For the Father judgeth no man, but hath committed all judgment unto the Son:

23. That all men should honour the Son, even as they honour the Father. He that honoureth not the Son honoureth not the Father which hath sent him.

24. Verily, verily, I say unto you, He that heareth my word, and believeth on him that sent me, hath everlasting life, and shall not come into condemnation; but is passed from death unto life.

25. Verily, verily, I say unto you, The hour is coming, and now is, when the dead shall hear the voice of the Son of God: and they that hear shall live.

26. For as the Father hath life in himself; so hath he given to the Son to have life in himself;

27. And hath given him authority to execute judgment also, because he is the Son of man.

28. Marvel not at this: for the hour is coming, in the which all that are in the graves shall hear his voice,

29. And shall come forth; they that have done good, unto the resurrection of life; and they that have done evil, unto the resurrection of damnation.

30. I can of mine own self do nothing: as I hear, I judge: and my judgment is just; because I seek not mine own will, but the will of the Father which hath sent me.

31. If I bear witness of myself, my witness is not true.

32. There is another that beareth witness of me; and I know that the witness which he witnesseth of me is true.

33. Ye sent unto John, and he bare witness unto the truth.

34. But I receive not testimony from man: but these things I say, that ye might be saved.

35. He was a burning and a shining light: and ye were willing for a season to rejoice in his light.

36. But I have greater witness than that of John: for the works

which the Father hath given me to finish, the same works that I do, bear witness of me, that the Father hath sent me.

37. And the Father himself, which hath sent me, hath borne witness of me. Ye have neither heard his voice at any time, nor seen his shape.

38. And ye have not his word abiding in you: for whom he hath sent, him ye believe not.

39. Search the scriptures; for in them ye think ye have eternal life: and they are they which testify of me.

40. And ye will not come to me, that ye might have life.

41. I receive not honour from men.

42. But I know you, that ye have not the love of God in you.

43. I am come in my Father's name, and ye receive me not: if another shall come in his own name, him ye will receive.

44. How can ye believe, which receive honour one of another, and seek not the honour that cometh from God only?

45. Do not think that I will accuse you to the Father: there is one that accuseth you, even Moses, in whom ye trust.

46. For had ye believed Moses, ye would have believed me: for he wrote of me.

47. But if ye believe not his writings, how shall ye believe my words?

As we follow Jesus in the Word of God we find that every step He took was a step of mercy and grace, from the day He entered His public ministry until He said, "It is finished. Father, into thy hands I commend my spirit." The beautiful and outstanding characteristic of His healing and of His helping hand is that He made no distinction among those whom He healed and helped. Regardless of nationality, color, or standing in life, He healed and helped *all* who came to Him in faith believing.

The predominant feature of His miracles and of the parables He gave is the spiritual significance they convey—i. e., when He healed the body, He pointed to the healing of the soul; He never healed a body simply to make someone well physically. None of the miracles of Jesus convey a more beautiful, more complete picture of the need of a sinner (and of God's plan of salvation FOR the sinner) than the one recorded in the first part of this chapter.

In the ministry of our Lord, the healing of the body was always subservient to the healing of lost souls. Jesus came into the world to seek and to save that which was lost, and as He healed the sick and opened the eyes of the blind, the miracle opened the way for Him to lead people into the door of salvation.

Verse 1: *"After this there was a feast of the Jews; and Jesus went up to Jerusalem."*

"After this" (or "after these things"), after the saving of the Samaritan woman, the revival among the Samaritans, and the healing of the nobleman's son, Jesus traveled from Galilee up into Jerusalem, the city of the temple, the city of worship, to attend *"a feast of the Jews"*; but Bible scholars do not agree as to which feast this was. Dr. Scofield suggests that it could have been the feast of Pentecost; other commentators believe that it was the Passover. If this *was* a Passover feast, then there were four Passovers during our Lord's ministry. This would make it certain that His ministry lasted three full years. At any rate, it *began* with a Passover and *ended* with a Passover, for John mentions three other Passover feasts by name (John 2:23; 6:4; and 12:1). Most Bible scholars agree that the Lord's ministry was at least three years, perhaps a bit more.

The expression *"feast of the Jews"* here is another of the many evidences that John's Gospel is for Gentile converts, and therefore he thought it needful and helpful to explain these Jewish feasts and ordinances, of which there were many.

The fact that Jesus made a special trip into Jerusalem to attend this particular feast shows that He respected the Mosaic ordinances and economy. The Mosaic system was appointed by God, and as long as that system continued, Jesus honored its ordinances, feasts, and ceremonies. He said, "Think not that I am come to destroy the law, or the prophets: *I am not come to destroy, but to fulfil"* (Matt. 5:17).

In this Dispensation of Grace we have the ordinances of baptism and of the Lord's Supper, neither of which should be neglected. Christians *should* be baptized and should observe the Lord's Supper scripturally. It is a sin for believers not to respect the ordinances of the New Testament Church.

Verses 2 and 3: *"Now there is at Jerusalem by the sheep market a pool, which is called in the Hebrew tongue Bethesda, having five porches. In these lay a great multitude of impotent folk, of blind, halt, withered, waiting for the moving of the water."*

Notice that John said, "There IS at Jerusalem by the sheep market a pool," for the pool was still there at the time of John's writing. Although after centuries of changes it is impossible to make a positive identification of such geographical places, when I visited the Holy Land some years ago I was shown a pool and the excavation of five porches which could easily have been this pool of which John wrote. I was greatly moved to realize that Jesus once walked beside that pool and stopped to heal a precious soul who for nearly forty years had sought healing for his withered, paralyzed body.

The *"sheep market"* was just inside the sheep gate in the Jerusalem wall. In Nehemiah 3:1 we read, "Then Eliashib the high priest rose up with his brethren the priests, and they builded the sheep gate; they sanctified it, and set up the doors of it . . . ." This was a gate through which the lambs were brought to be offered as sacrifices by worshippers in the temple. Those who traveled to Jerusalem from other cities at Passover time could not bring their own sacrificial animals, and it was customary for them to buy a lamb at the sheep market. Thus thousands of worshippers passed by this pool every feast day and saw the great multitude of sick folk who lay in the porches around the pool.

In the Hebrew tongue this pool was called "Bethesda," meaning "house of pity or mercy." It is not mentioned anywhere else in Scripture. This explanation of a Hebrew word shows again that John was writing not so much for the Jews as for the Gentiles.

"Around which were five porches." In the Scriptures the number "five" stands for *grace.* Jesus was *grace, mercy, and truth* as He stood before the sick, helpless people there.

These porches were undoubtedly covered—open on one side for air and sunshine, but protected on the other side and overhead to keep out the hot sun and inclement weather. Palestine is extremely hot at certain seasons of the year, and it would have been an absolute necessity to have a roof over these sick people.

In these porches lay *"a great multitude of impotent folk."* The Scripture does not tell us exactly how many people made up the "great multitude"—there could have been scores of them, for the five porches must have covered an area that could easily accommodate a goodly number; but we *are* told what was wrong with the people: they were *"blind, halt, withered."*

This speaks of physical blindness, of course, but it presents a picture of lost souls blinded by the devil and crippled by sin. Every sinner is spiritually blind. Paul tells us in II Corinthians 4:3,4, "If our Gospel be hid, it is hid to them that are lost: *in whom the god of this world hath blinded the minds of them which believe not,* lest the light of the glorious Gospel of Christ, who is the image of God, should shine unto them." Around us today we can see a multitude of sick people—not *physically* sick, but sick of soul, spiritually sick. We who have the Gospel message should be alert to see them, love them, and in the name of Jesus extend a helping hand, pointing them to Him who is able to save to the uttermost all who come unto God by Him.

These sick people were *"waiting for the moving of the water"* in the pool. This moving of the water was from heaven, not from earth, and there was no healing virtue in the water until that certain time.

Verse 4: *"For an angel went down at a certain season into the pool, and troubled the water: whosoever then first after the troubling of the water stepped in was made whole of whatsoever disease he had."*

A miracle was wrought at some "certain season," a miracle appointed by God and wrought by His power. As I have pointed out so many times, God's miracles do not come about simply to bring physical comfort; they always teach a deep spiritual truth. This miracle at the pool happened, no doubt, at the season when the most Jews were present in Jerusalem, and God allowed the miracle in order to remind the Jewish people that their God had not changed.

The Scripture does not tell us when the miracle began or when it ceased to be, or whether the angel was seen or invisible when he came down to trouble the waters; but this is not important, for if the Holy Spirit had wanted us to know these details they would have been made plain in the Word.

The Jewish people had strong faith in the ministry of angels, and during the four hundred silent years between Malachi and Matthew it could be that God chose to work through angels to keep the Jewish people reminded of the unseen things He is able to do. We know that during the transition period angels ministered in miraculous ways. This is clear from many accounts in the Gospels, and also in Acts.

In Luke 1:11−22 we read of Zacharias' experience in the temple, when the birth of John Baptist was promised:

"And there appeared unto (Zacharias) an angel of the Lord standing on the right side of the altar of incense. And when Zacharias saw him, he was troubled, and fear fell upon him. But the angel said unto him, Fear not, Zacharias: for thy prayer is heard; and thy wife Elisabeth shall bear thee a son, and thou shalt call his name John. And thou shalt have joy and gladness; and many shall rejoice at his birth. For he shall be great in the sight of the Lord,

and shall drink neither wine nor strong drink; and he shall
be filled with the Holy Ghost, even from his mother's womb.
And many of the children of Israel shall he turn to the Lord
their God.   And he shall go before Him in the spirit and
power of Elias, to turn the hearts of the fathers to the children, and the disobedient to the wisdom of the just; to
make ready a people prepared for the Lord.

"And Zacharias said unto the angel, Whereby shall I
know this? for I am an old man, and my wife well stricken
in years.

"And the angel answering said unto him, I am Gabriel,
that stand in the presence of God; and am sent to speak
unto thee, and to shew thee these glad tidings.   And, behold, thou shalt be dumb, and not able to speak, until the
day that these things shall be performed, because thou believest not my words, which shall be fulfilled in their
season.

"And the people waited for Zacharias, and marvelled that
he tarried so long in the temple.   And when he came out,
he could not speak unto them: and they perceived that he
had seen a vision in the temple: for he beckoned unto them,
and remained speechless."

Angels ministered to *Jesus* after His temptation in the
wilderness: "Then the devil leaveth Him, and, behold,
angels came and ministered unto Him" (Matt. 4:11).

An angel released *Peter* from prison:

"Peter therefore was kept in prison: but prayer was
made without ceasing of the Church unto God for him.
And when Herod would have brought him forth, the same
night Peter was sleeping between two soldiers, bound with
two chains: and the keepers before the door kept the prison.

"And, behold, the angel of the Lord came upon him,
and a light shined in the prison: and he smote Peter on
the side, and raised him up, saying, Arise up quickly.   And
his chains fell off from his hands. And the angel said unto
him, Gird thyself, and bind on thy sandals.   And so he did.
And he saith unto him, Cast thy garment about thee, and

follow me. And he went out, and followed him; and wist not that it was true which was done by the angel; but thought he saw a vision.

"When they were past the first and the second ward, they came unto the iron gate that leadeth unto the city; which opened to them of his own accord: and they went out, and passed on through one street; and forthwith the angel departed from him. And when Peter was come to himself, he said, Now I know of a surety, that the Lord hath sent His angel, and hath delivered me out of the hand of Herod, and from all the expectation of the people of the Jews" (Acts 12:5—11).

From Hebrews 1:7 we know that God created the angels, and from Hebrews 1:14 we know that angels are "ministering spirits, sent forth to minister for them who shall be heirs of salvation."

When we realize the Bible truth concerning the existence of angels and their ministry on earth, we should have no trouble believing that God sent an angel to the pool of Bethesda at a certain season to trouble the water there. This is one of the passages in the Word of God that we must accept by faith. We cannot explain it; therefore we must read it, believe it, and be taught whatever lesson we can receive from it, and not worry about the part we do not understand. If we believe in the verbal inspiration of the Scriptures we do not fret over such passages. The miracle at the pool of Bethesda was literal beyond any doubt, even though some outstanding teachers deny that it is part of the Scripture. Between Malachi and Matthew there was no prophet like Isaiah, Zechariah, Jeremiah, and others, and there was much confusion among the Jewish people. God allowed this miracle, I believe, this miraculous healing, to show His chosen people that He had not entirely rejected them.

At an appointed season an angel came down from heaven and *"troubled* the water"—that is, the water was disturbed, or stirred up. We need not suppose that the angel was seen by human eye; the Scripture does not comment on this: but at a certain hour on a certain day there was a sudden stir, a sudden *moving* of the water in the pool, and immediately after this miraculous moving of the water, whosoever first stepped *into* the water *"was made whole of whatsoever disease he had."* (The Greek reads, "with whatsoever disease he was held.") It made no difference whether the person was blind, halt, or withered; it made no difference how long he had been bound by that disease: he was made perfectly whole when he stepped into the troubled waters.

It is interesting to note in this passage that *"WHOSOEVER"* (regardless of nationality or position, whether king or beggar, young or old) "first after the troubling of the water stepped in, *was made whole of WHATSOEVER disease he had"* (blindness, leprosy, lameness, it made no difference); whosoever first stepped in was made whole of whatsoever disease he had—*but not WHENSOEVER!* The healing was not at just any time, under any and all conditions. Mark it well: the pool was there three hundred and sixty-five days in the year, and the people were there, waiting; but they were not healed "whensoever." *They were healed at "A CERTAIN SEASON" when the heavenly visitor troubled the waters in the pool.*

One might think that this multitude of needy folk would have been in the temple, which was only a stone's throw from the pool; but the sad truth is that the Power had departed from the temple and it had become a place of dead ceremony. There was no healing virtue, no power, there. And the same is true today. Even the *fundamental* churches are not doing what the Church was put here to do! If the local churches where the true Gospel is preached had been faithful to the Word, if we as ministers and Christian workers had discharged our duty as God intended that we should, there would not be so many cults and false religions in the land today. When needy souls do not find their need supplied where it *should be* supplied, they will seek other sources—and that is what has happened in the local churches today.

Sinners are with us always, every day in the year. There are multitudes of unbelievers who, like the impotent folk around the pool at Bethesda, are waiting to be healed of the disease of sin. But—also like the people at the pool— the sinner cannot be saved at just any time or anywhere under all conditions. This is not limiting the power of God; it is simply pointing out that God has a plan, and He operates according to that plan. John 6:44 tells us that no man can come to Christ except the Father (through the Holy Spirit) draw him. A person does not become a Christian "whosoever" he gets ready; he calls upon the Lord for salvation and healing from sin when the Holy Spirit troubles and draws him.

The sinner is saved by faith, and faith cometh by the Word of God (Rom. 10:17). The Holy Spirit uses the Word to bring conviction to the heart of the unbeliever and draw him to Jesus Christ; then upon receiving Christ the sinner is saved—and remember, "WHOSOEVER" can be saved regardless of "WHATSOEVER" sin he may have committed; but he *cannot* be saved "WHENSOEVER" he gets ready! He must be saved by hearing the Gospel, and through the drawing of the Holy Spirit (John 5:24; 6:44).

Verse 5: *"And a certain man was there, which had an infirmity thirty and eight years."*

Those of us who have even a reasonable portion of health and strength have no idea how to appreciate this man's position! We do not know how old he was, but from this verse we know that he had been sick for *thirty-eight years* of his life. We do not know how long he had been by the pool of Bethesda—but the way in which he answered Jesus certainly indicates that he had been there a long time.

Verse 6: *"When Jesus saw him lie, and knew that he had been now a long time in that case, He saith unto him,*

Wilt thou be made whole?"

Jesus in His omniscience knew this man's medical history as well as his spiritual condition. What a comfort to believers to know that Jesus knows every sickness and understands every disease, and when the doctors cannot diagnose the trouble the Great Physician always knows what to do. He can heal if it is within His divine will and wisdom to do so. Sometimes God gets more honor and glory from our being sick than He does when we are well; some of us are better testimonies and better examples of grace when we are sick than when we are well and strong. God forbid that I should grieve the heart of a shut-in or suffering saint —but it is true that some of us refuse to look up until God lays us flat on our back!

The miracle Jesus performed for this man was unsolicited and wholly unexpected. As was characteristic of Him, Jesus Himself opened the conversation; He did not wait for this man to cry out for help. Jesus always takes the first step; the very desire to be saved is planted in the unbelieving heart through the Word of God and the convicting power of the Holy Spirit. No person would ever want to become a bondslave of Jesus Christ if the Holy Spirit did not use the Word of God to create within him a thirst and hunger for righteousness.

Jesus asked this man a simple question: *"Wilt thou be made whole?"* (The Greek here reads, *"Hast thou a will* to be made whole?") Did the man really *want* to be healed? Jesus knew the man's heart, He knew his will; but He asked the question to awaken the man's desire and prepare him for the blessing He was about to bestow upon him.

(In the spiritual sense, through the Gospel preached by men of God, Jesus is asking all who hear the Word, "Do YOU have a will to be made whole spiritually?" Through the Gospel of the marvelous grace of God He is continually asking, "Do you wish to be saved? Do you have a will to live the Christian life?" Man is created in the image of

God, and God highly respects the will of man whom He created.)

Verse 7: *"The impotent man answered Him, Sir, I have no man, when the water is troubled, to put me into the pool: but while I am coming, another steppeth down before me."*

(The Greek word translated "Sir" is the same word commonly rendered "Lord." The same word is translated "Sir" throughout the fourth chapter, in the account of the Samaritan woman.)

"Sir, I have no man, when the water is troubled, to put me into the pool." The man was still thinking in terms of the pool and its healing waters; he was thinking in terms of the natural. He did not yet realize that he was in the presence of One who did not need to put him into the pool in order to make him whole. He did not realize that this One could speak a word and he would be completely healed.

Surely this impotent man considered human nature as heartless and unkind. Thousands of worshippers had passed him by; they had no time to stop and help him into the pool. Like so many religionists today, they were so busy with their religious activities that they had no time to help a poor, paralyzed man who had not walked a step in thirty-eight years!

Remember, beloved—this man was not lying in front of a bar on the street of forgotten men. He was not in a back alley. He was lying by the pool of Bethesda within a stone's throw of the sheepmarket where worshippers purchased animals for sacrifice in the religious ceremonies in the temple! and worshippers passed him as they entered and departed. Proverbs 14:20,21 tells us "The poor is hated even of his own neighbour: but the rich hath many friends. He that despiseth his neighbour sinneth: *but he that hath mercy on the poor, happy is he."*

Many church members today simply do not have time to win souls. They are so taken up with church activities

and so busy with church meetings and committees that they
do not have time to lend a helping hand to poor sinners
who have been paralyzed by sin.

I think this man's statement is among the saddest in the
Word of God—"I have no man to help me!" Christian, did
YOU find salvation entirely by yourself, without help from
anyone? Was there not someone who prayed for you, someone who visited you and talked with you about spiritual
things? Perhaps it was your mother—or it could have been
a neighbor, or your pastor, your Sunday school teacher, or
an evangelist. Maybe someone handed you a little Gospel
tract as he passed you on the street. How many people
played a definite part in bringing YOU to Jesus? *And what
have YOU done to help others find Him?* No man can help
God save you, but God uses human instruments to bring
you to the knowledge of salvation. The Word clearly teaches this: "Let him know, that he which converteth the sinner from the error of his way shall save a soul from death,
and shall hide a multitude of sins" (James 5:20). We cannot save sinners, but we can certainly present them with
the Gospel of the saving grace of our Lord and Saviour,
Jesus Christ. Do you know someone who might be saying,
"I have no man to help me find the true Gospel, the way
of salvation"? God forbid that any man point his finger in
my face at the judgment and declare that if I had helped
him he might have been saved! Jesus said to His disciples,
"Ye shall receive power, after that the Holy Ghost is come
upon you: and ye shall be witnesses unto me both in Jerusalem, and in all Judaea, and in Samaria, and *unto the
uttermost part of the earth*" (Acts 1:8). It is not only a
grand and glorious privilege to witness for Jesus, it is a
command!

Verses 8 and 9: *"Jesus saith unto him, Rise, take up thy
bed, and walk. And immediately the man was made whole,
and took up his bed, and walked: and on the same day was
the Sabbath."*

All Jesus needed to do was speak a word—and a miracle

happened. In this case He simply gave a command: *"Rise, take up thy bed, and walk."* He did not perform a miracle for the man to *see* and believe; He simply spoke, the man *heard,* and believed, *and obeyed.* If ever a man had a right to question or ask, "How?" this man had that right. But he did not question. He simply obeyed the Lord's command, he stood up, took up his bed, and *walked!* The same is true of the lepers in Luke 17:14. They could have said, "Why should we go and show ourselves to the priest? We are still covered with leprosy." But they did as Jesus bade them do, "and it came to pass, that, *as they went,* they were cleansed." The man to whom Jesus said, "Stretch forth thine hand" could have said, "My hand is paralyzed. I *cannot* stretch it forth." But he said no such thing. He simply stretched forth his hand, "and it was restored whole, like as the other" (Matt. 12:13). The man who was blind from birth did not ask, "Why should I wash in the pool of Siloam? Why not the river Jordan?" He went as Jesus commanded him, he "washed, *and came seeing!"* (John 9:7). In each of these miraculous healings, *the act of obedience* brought the blessing; *the power of healing* was in the Person—*Christ.*

When we believe His Word, all things are possible—and that is all He asks of us, that we believe His Word and abide by it. In the words of the Apostle Paul, "Yea, let God be true, but every man a liar . . ." (Rom. 3:4).

"Immediately the man was made whole, and took up his bed, and walked." Not only did this man *believe* the words of Jesus, he gave testimony to his faith: by taking up his bed he testified that he no longer needed it because he was healed. By walking he testified that his healing was not simply in his mind, but that he had actually been made physically whole, and legs that had not taken a step in so many years were now walking! His obedience proved his faith, and a great miracle was wrought in his life.

You will notice that this happened *"immediately."* It does not take Jesus all day to perform a miracle; He speaks the word and the miracle is accomplished. God created man; Jesus was God in flesh, and it was just as easy for Him to cause this man to stand and walk as it was for God to create muscle, bone, and sinew from the dust of the earth the day He made Adam. If we truly *believe GOD*, then it is not difficult to believe anything with which God has to do, for our God is still a God of miracles.

"And on the same day was the Sabbath." The beds used in the days of our Lord were not heavy wooden beds like we use today; they were nothing more than a mattress, or sometimes a thick cloth, and therefore the man's bed was not burdensome or hard to carry—but Jesus wrought this miracle on the Sabbath day, and the Jews were watching, always alert in their efforts to find something for which to criticize and condemn the Lord Jesus.

Verse 10: *"The Jews therefore said unto him that was cured, It is the Sabbath day: it is not lawful for thee to carry thy bed."*

"The Jews" refers to the Jews in Jerusalem—elders, chief priests, scribes, Pharisees. It does not mean the Jewish people as a whole. These Jews were strict religionists, sticklers for the law of Moses; and in their rebuke of this man they were not thinking only of the fourth commandment, "Remember the Sabbath day to keep it holy"—they were also thinking of a special law in Nehemiah and Jeremiah about bearing burdens on the Sabbath day:

"And it came to pass, that when the gates of Jerusalem began to be dark before the sabbath, I commanded that the gates should be shut, and charged that they should not be opened till after the sabbath: and some of my servants set I at the gates, that there should no burden be brought in on the sabbath day" (Neh. 13:19).

"Thus saith the Lord: Take heed to yourselves, and bear no burden on the sabbath day, nor bring it in by the gates of Jerusalem; neither carry forth a burden out of your houses on the sabbath day, neither do ye any work, but hallow ye the sabbath day, as I commanded your fathers" (Jer. 17: 21,22).

In this particular instance they were straining a point, for a man carrying merchandise on the Sabbath was quite different from a sick man carrying his bed after being miraculously delivered from paralysis that had held him bedfast for many years. According to the Law of Moses it was unlawful to carry a burden on the Sabbath; but to object to this dear man carrying his mattress on the Sabbath was nothing less than a demonstration of cruelty and was altogether contrary to the spirit of the Law of Moses. At the time God gave the law to the Israelites He made it unnecessary for them to carry burdens and merchandise on the Sabbath, but this certainly did not apply to the man who was walking for the first time in nearly forty years, carrying his bed because his Healer had commanded him to do so. The critics in this instance were people of whom Jesus said, "Ye blind guides, which strain at a gnat, and swallow a camel" (Matt. 23:24). We still have people like that today, always looking for something by which they can criticize those who are true servants of God.

Verse 11: *"He answered them, He that made me whole, the same said unto me, Take up thy bed, and walk."*

These are simple words; there was nothing spectacular about them, but they set forth a principle that we should not overlook. This man considered that the One who healed him was worthy of his obedience. No other man had ever offered to help him, and certainly no other man *could* have done for him what Jesus did. The same is true of the believer. Since Jesus is the only One who can save our souls, we should obey His words and follow His commands for our life.

Verse 12: *"Then asked they him, What man is that which said unto thee, Take up thy bed, and walk?"*

These religious leaders had seen this poor man lying in

the porch beside the pool of Bethesda; no doubt they had passed him by many times on their way to worship. It seems unbelievable that they had no pity in their hearts for him and for the multitude of impotent folk who lay in the porches by the pool. Now one of those poor people had been gloriously healed, he was every whit whole—standing, walking, carrying his bed; but instead of rejoicing with him, instead of asking him, *"WHO made thee whole?"* they asked, *"Who told thee to carry thy BED?"* They were not interested in the Man who possessed such great healing power; they wanted to know who would dare command someone to break their Sabbath!

Verse 13: *"And he that was healed wist not who it was: for Jesus had conveyed Himself away, a multitude being in that place."*

It is possible that the paralytic had heard of Jesus and the miracles He wrought, but he saw Him for the first time that day—and even then he did not know who He was. He simply knew that He was the most unusual Person he had ever met—kind, sympathetic, compassionate, with something in His voice that this poor cripple had never heard in any other voice. When Jesus asked, "Wilt thou be made whole?" the words gripped his heart and renewed his hope. Then this kind, sympathetic Person had said, "Rise, take up thy bed, and walk"—and suddenly disappeared. (The Scripture tells us that He *"conveyed Himself away."* The Greek says that He *"withdrew Himself secretly"* from the crowd that was in that place.)

Certainly it would not be impossible for Jesus to disappear from sight of the critical, unbelieving crowd. We find a similar incident in Luke 4:28—30, where "all they in the synagogue, when they heard these things, were filled with wrath, and rose up, and thrust (Jesus) out of the city, and led Him unto the brow of the hill whereon their city was built, that they might cast Him down headlong. BUT HE PASSING THROUGH THE MIDST OF THEM WENT

HIS WAY." John 10:39 tells us that "they sought again to take Him: BUT HE ESCAPED OUT OF THEIR HAND."

You see, it was foreordained before the foundation of the world that Jesus would die on the cross, and it was therefore not possible for human hands to take Him and destroy Him until the fulness of time had come, that He be nailed to the cross and lifted between heaven and earth. Until the time came for Him to be arrested, condemned, and crucified, the mob could not take Him; but when that moment arrived, He humbly yielded to them when He could have resisted through divine power. When Peter smote the high priest's servant and cut off his ear with the sword when the officers and men came to arrest Jesus in Gethsemane, He said to Peter, "Put up again thy sword into his place. . . Thinkest thou that I cannot now pray to my Father, and He shall presently give me more than twelve legions of angels? But how then shall the Scriptures be fulfilled, that thus it must be?" (Matt. 26:52—54). He had not come into the world to fight with the sword; He came to die for the sins of mankind.

Verse 14: *"Afterward Jesus findeth him in the temple, and said unto him, Behold, thou art made whole: sin no more, lest a worse thing come unto thee."*

Although the Scriptures do not tell us how long a time elapsed between the healing of the paralytic and the Lord's instruction to him in the temple, we conclude that it was only a *short* time—and it is interesting to note that the first place he went was to the temple, the place of worship, thus denoting that in his heart he knew that God had healed him.

The third chapter of Acts records the first Apostolic miracle—a man who was born lame was healed. Peter said to him, "In the name of Jesus Christ of Nazareth rise up and walk. And he took him by the right hand, and lifted him up: *and immediately his feet and ankle bones received strength"* (Acts 3:6,7). The man then went with Peter and

John into the temple, "walking, and leaping, and praising God." It is natural for those who are blessed of the Lord to want to go into the house of God. Those who have no desire to attend services in the house of God also bear no fruit of real conversion. Born again people do not need to be begged, coaxed, or tricked into going to church, nor do they need to be fed in the *social hall* of the church. A person who is truly born again will be led by the Holy Spirit into the sanctuary to be fed with the bread from heaven, the Word of God.

In the temple, Jesus found the man who had been healed, and said to him, *"Behold, thou art made whole: sin no more, lest a worse thing come unto thee."*

We must pray for spiritual insight and compare Scripture with Scripture in order to understand the meaning of this statement. When Jesus said, "Sin no more," did He mean that this man was to live the rest of his natural life wholly above sin? Was he to live a sinless-perfect life from that moment until he died, or a worse thing would come upon him?

We know from careful study of the Scriptures that Jesus did not mean this. Since He was omniscient He knew the history of this man from the moment he was born until the time He said to him, "Arise, take up thy bed, and walk." Undoubtedly He knew something in the man's life that had been the primary cause of his paralyzed condition.

Not all sick people are sick because of sin committed by themselves or any member of their family. Sickness and disease are not always the result of personal sin. The sickness and death of Lazarus was to the glory of God (John 11:4,40). Paul confessed that he prayed three times for God to remove the "thorn" from his flesh. God did not remove the thorn, but said, *"My grace is sufficient for thee"* (II Cor. 12:9).

We know that sin *is* responsible sometimes for illness among believers. Paul made this plain when he rebuked the Corinthians for disorder at the Lord's table, and said to them, "For this cause many are weak and sickly among you, and many sleep (are dead)" (I Cor. 11:30).

I believe God also speaks to *sinners* through sickness. Many times He calls parents through the illness of their children—and He is not cruel in doing this. It is a sad, sorrowful thing to see someone sick, or paralyzed, or the victim of tragedy; but it is *much more* sorrowful for them to spend eternity in hell. If God can speak through the illness—or even the death—of a loved one and bring the unsaved unto Himself, then the sickness is profitable and to His glory. God in His mercy and grace does all that a loving God *can* do to keep a person from spending eternity in hell before He finally says to the Holy Spirit, "Ephraim is joined to idols; let him alone!" (Please study the first chapter of Romans—all of it.)

Verse 15: *"The man departed, and told the Jews that it was Jesus, which had made him whole."*

Notice how this man answered the Jews: They had asked him who had told him to carry his bed on the Sabbath; but when he answered them, he told them that it was Jesus *"which had made him WHOLE."* The fact that he had carried his bed on the Sabbath did not enter his mind. He rejoiced because Jesus had made him whole, he was healed, and he entered the temple to give praise and worship to God. But the rulers could not see the glorious miracle that had been wrought; they only saw a man carrying a mattress on the Sabbath day. This man also was a Jew, and I am sure he had no idea that the rulers would attempt to kill Jesus for healing on the Sabbath. He was simply being obedient to and showing reverence for the leaders in the synagogue when he answered them.

Jesus Is Lord of the Sabbath

Verse 16: *"And therefore did the Jews persecute Jesus, and sought to slay Him, because He had done these things on the sabbath day."*

Verse 16 begins one of the most solemn and important passages in the four Gospels—a passage in which the Lord Jesus declares His divine nature, His unity with the heavenly Father, the high dignity of the office given to Him *by the Father* before the foundation of the world. No other place in the Gospels does Jesus dwell so completely and fully on these subjects as in this chapter. There is much that even the most spiritually minded person cannot comprehend in our Lord's account of Himself; such knowledge is too wonderful for the finite mind of man. We cry out with the Psalmist, "Such knowledge is too wonderful for me; it is high, I cannot attain unto it" (Psalm 139:6).

Greek scholars tell us that the verbs in this verse are all in the imperfect tense, meaning that the Jews at that very moment began to persecute Jesus, and from then until He was nailed to the cross they sought to slay Him.

In John 7:22,23 Jesus said to them, "Moses therefore gave unto you circumcision . . . and ye on the sabbath day circumcise a man. If a man on the sabbath day receive circumcision, that the law of Moses should not be broken; *are ye angry at me, because I have made a man every whit whole on the sabbath day?"*

The Jews knew that the Healer was much greater in this man's eyes than was the law of the Sabbath, and this angered them, in spite of the fact that this same Jesus testified of Himself, *"The Son of man is LORD even of the Sabbath day"* (Matt. 12:8). This was a direct repudiation of their strict observances of their traditional exactitudes having to do with the observance of the *letter* of the law over and above obedience to the *spirit* of the law. They proved their spirit when they asked the man—not who had *made him well,* but who had told him to break their Sabbath! "The kings of the earth set themselves, and the rulers take counsel together, against the Lord, and against His Anointed, saying, Let us break their bands asunder, and cast away their cords from us" (Psalm 2:2,3).

Verse 17: *"But Jesus answered them, My Father worketh hitherto, and I work."*

The Greek word here translated *"hitherto"* literally means "until now." In other words, *"Until now* my Father and I have been working together *since the beginning."* This declares His deity, and since He and the heavenly Father had worked together in perfect unity and harmony, He had not broken God's law when He healed the man on the Sabbath. Jesus did not come to break the law nor destroy it, but to fulfill it (Matt. 5:17).

"My Father worketh hitherto." It is God who sustains and preserves all life—not only *six* days in the week, but *seven.* God does not cease to work works of mercy and kindness on the seventh day; He supplies the needs of His creatures on that day as well as on the other six days. It is true that He rested from the work of *creation* on the seventh day, but He did not rest from works of mercy and grace.

"And I work." Since Jesus was God's Son and Lord of the Sabbath, He had a perfect right to work the works of God, even *on* the Sabbath. The fourth commandment was given to be honored, but God did not intend that there should be a cessation of the works of mercy on the Sabbath. Consider that the sun rises, the rain falls, the grass grows, the crops produce—even on the Sabbath. Think what would happen if God should cease to work for just one day! What Jesus meant was that God cares for and holds together all that has been created—the rising and setting of the sun, the fountains, the rivers, the rain, the seasons; God never ceases to work. ". . . He maketh His sun to rise on the evil and on the good, and sendeth rain on the just and on the unjust. . . Wherefore, if God so clothe the grass of the field, which to day is, and to morrow is cast into the oven, shall He not much more clothe you, O ye of little faith?" (Matt. 5:45; 6:30).

In Matthew 12:3—5 Jesus reminded the Jews of David's eating the shewbread in the temple, and gave the example of the priest working in the temple on the Sabbath:

"Have ye not read what David did, when he was an hungred, and they that were with him; how he entered into the house of God, and did eat the shewbread, which was not lawful for him to eat, neither for them which were with him, but only for the priests? Or have ye not read in the law, how that on the sabbath days the priests in the temple profane the sabbath, and are blameless?"

In Luke 14:5 He asked them, "Which of you shall have an ass or an ox fallen into a pit, and will not straightway pull him out on the sabbath day?"

Here in our present verse He used a much higher example—that of the heavenly Father working from the beginning. Since Jesus was the Son of God, one with the Father in dignity, honor, authority, and essence, *whatever the Father did* it was right for HIM to do. God gave the Sabbath for man's comfort and advantage; He never intended that the works of mercy should cease on the Sabbath. Such works are necessary to man's livelihood as well as to the livelihood of the animal kingdom. The Jews understood what Jesus meant when He declared Himself one with the Father. This is plainly shown in the next verse.

Verse 18: *"Therefore the Jews sought the more to kill Him, because He not only had broken the sabbath, but said also that God was His Father, making Himself equal with God."*

Now they had *two* reasons to destroy Him: first He had broken the Sabbath, and now He claimed to be the very Son of God! Since He had made Himself equal with God, according to their law He ought to die.

The statement Jesus made that day struck the Jews with much more force than it strikes us. They understood Him to say that God was *"His own particular Father,"* that He was not just a son through grace, but *the only BEGOTTEN Son* of God. We find the same rendering in Romans 8:32: "He that spared not His own Son, but delivered Him up for us all, how shall He not with Him also freely give us all things?"

Believers *are* sons of God, but we are *not* His own *particular Son:* "For as many as are led by the Spirit of God, they are the sons of God" (Rom. 8:14). The Jews clearly understood that Jesus was declaring Himself not just an ordinary son of God, but THE Son of God, equal *with* God. Jesus accepted their accusation; He did not modify His statement one iota.

The Oneness of the Father and the Son

The action of the Jews as described in verse 18 opened the way for the most comprehensive public discourse ever given by the Lord Jesus Christ concerning Himself and His relationship to Jehovah God, and also the dealings of Himself and God with man, now and in the hereafter.

First He discussed His relationship to the Father in unity of counsel and action (vv. 19,20).

He discussed His dealings with individuals—as Judge and as the only source of eternal life (vv. 21—27).

In verses 28 and 29 He discussed His position and power in the resurrection of the dead—at the Rapture and first resurrection, and in the second resurrection at the Great White Throne (the resurrection judgment).

He again declared His total dependence on God the Father involving the righteousness of His judgment, and declared that He was not bearing witness from Himself (vv. 30,31).

Verses 32 through 39 give a clear declaration of the witness borne to Him—a witness that is fourfold: (1) John the Baptist; (2) the miracles of Jesus; (3) God the Father; (4) the Scriptures.

In closing this powerful discourse Jesus reminded the Jews that their own unbelief was the reason they were not saved. They would not come to Him that they might have life (vv. 40—47).

Verses 19 and 20: *"Then answered Jesus and said unto them, Verily, verily, I say unto you, The Son can do nothing of Himself, but what He seeth the Father do: for what things soever He doeth, these also doeth the Son likewise. For the Father loveth the Son, and sheweth Him all things that Himself doeth: and He will shew Him greater works than these, that ye may marvel."*

"Verily, verily, I say unto you . . . ." The "double verily" here introduces another solemn truth that demands our careful consideration: *". . . the Son can do nothing of Himself."* Jesus here declares the impossibility of His acting or working independently of God the Father; because Father and Son are so completely one. This does not mean, however, that Jesus did not have the *power* to do anything. It is a mark of omnipotence not to be able to die or be annihilated; nothing can destroy omnipotence. In like manner, *to be unable to do anything of Himself* is not a mark of weakness or inability, but rather a mark of the highest power, nothing less than having power identical with the power of God the heavenly Father. Thus, God the Father can do nothing apart from the Son and God the Son can do nothing apart from the Father. Nothing can be done by *one* which is not equally done by the *other* since Father, Son, and Holy Ghost are one in essence, yet they are three distinct members of the Godhead.

This is omnipotence, and the mind of man cannot analyze it, it cannot be carried into a laboratory and broken down, nor can it be adequately described in man's language. We simply accept it as divine truth because Jesus has declared it.

"What things soever (the Father) doeth, these also doeth the Son likewise." Here is clearly declared the intimacy and unbroken communion between Jesus and God the Father from the beginning. Whatever the Father is doing, the Son is doing; and whatever the Son is doing, the Father is doing. They cannot be separated in their works.

Jesus then declares the reason for this unity, this complete cooperation and communion between the Father and Son: *"For the Father LOVETH THE SON." "For"* (the connecting word) is here to point out the preceding truths as the underlying cause of the Father's deep love for the Son; and *because* of that love, the Father *"sheweth Him all things that Himself doeth."* The Son does nothing apart from the Father, and the Father keeps no secret from the Son. This divine fact, along with the earlier statement of pre-existent cooperation—("My Father worketh hitherto, and I work")—establishes the eternal pre-existence of the relationship between God the Father and God the Son.

"And He will shew Him greater works than these, that ye may marvel." Here Jesus challenged His enemies. They had already seen miracles that would astonish any ordinary person; but He announced that God the Father would show the Son even greater things, mightier works, and they would marvel even more. The *"greater works"* mentioned here are the works described in the verses to follow—the resurrection and the judging. Also, if you will study the book of Acts you will see that the Jews *did* marvel and were confounded at the works performed by the apostles during the first days of the Church era—and they will be even *more* astonished when Jesus comes the second time as King of kings and Lord of lords, to judge the heathen, to make His enemies His footstool, to restore Jerusalem and to gather Israel back into the land God gave to Abraham. At that time He will convince the Jews of their sin of unbelief, and there will be a new heaven, a new earth, and the Pearly White City. The Millennium will be an astonishing fact when Jesus returns the second time.

Language breaks down when we attempt to fully describe things having to do with the Godhead, things divine and eternal. Paul said, "Thanks be unto God for His unspeakable gift" (II Cor. 9:15). Peter tells us that in Christ we have "joy *unspeakable* and full of glory" (I Pet. 1:8). The expressions in verses 19 and 20—"seeth the Father do . . . loveth the Son . . . sheweth Him all things . . . will shew

Him greater works"—are given to us by verbal inspiration to explain to the finite mind of man as far as it is possible for these things to BE explained to man. It is impossible to fully express the perfect unity between God the Father and God the Son—two divine Persons, yet one in essence, one in mind and will, but *two* in manifestation. As touching the Godhead, Father and Son are equal in every way, but Jesus the Son is inferior to the Father as touching His manhood, His earthly body. It is impossible for God to die; but He took a body like unto man's body, and in that body the sin-debt was paid. As touching Deity and the Incarnation, Jesus was always—from the beginning up to this present moment and throughout all eternity ahead— equal with the Father. These are divine truths which we accept by faith.

Think on these things: It is an exceedingly far greater work for God, through the shed blood of His only begotten Son, to repair a ruined man created in the *image* of God, than it was to *make* man in the first place. It is an exceedingly far greater work to *re-create* the spirit of man who has sinned than it was to create that spirit in the beginning. It cost God infinitely more to repair the sinful heart and re-create the fallen spirit of man than it did to create Adam from the dust of the earth and breathe into his nostrils the breath of life at the beginning of the human race.

Resurrection: Spiritual and Physical

Verse 21: *"For as the Father raiseth up the dead, and quickeneth them; even so the Son quickeneth whom He will."*

Here is declared the miracle of all miracles—the resurrection, both spiritual and physical. For God to raise men spiritually (in the new birth) and then raise them physically (in the first resurrection) is far greater work than Jesus had just wrought on the man who had been paralyzed for thirty-eight years!

The Jews had criticized Him for claiming to be equal with God; and here He declared that He was not only *equal* with God, but that He had the same power *God* had to give life and raise the dead. The Jews believed in the resurrection in the last day, as Martha said to Jesus concerning Lazarus (John 11:24); but only to GOD would they give credit for having power to raise the dead. *"The Son quickeneth whom He will"* distinctly declares that Jesus has authority to give life at will, either bodily or spiritually. He has the same power as God the Father in this respect. He possesses the greatest and highest of all gifts, and all He need do is to will and bestow.

The word translated *"quickeneth"* is a very strong word in the Greek, and means "makes alive." Jesus had power to make the dead live, whether that life be physical or spiritual. To the Ephesians Paul said, "And you hath He quickened (made alive) who were dead in trespasses and sins" (Eph. 2:1). *God* has power to give life; *Jesus* has power to give life. Our present verse declares His divine nature, His divine authority, and His absolute equality with God the Father.

Verses 22 and 23: *"For the Father judgeth no man, but hath committed all judgment unto the Son: That all men should honour the Son, even as they honour the Father. He that honoureth not the Son honoureth not the Father which hath sent Him."*

The truth declared here is that *in redemption* God honored the Son by committing to Him the authority to judge the world. This does not mean that His judgment is entirely apart from God the Father, for what *Jesus* does, the *Father* does. It means that judgment is work that God the Father has completely given over TO the Son, and therefore He will *judge* as the Son and not as the Father. It was Jesus the Son who *died* for sinners and it is Jesus the Son who will *judge* sinners: "Because He hath appointed a day, in the which He will judge the world in righteousness by that Man whom He hath ordained; whereof He hath given assurance unto all men, in that He hath raised Him from the dead" (Acts 17:31). In II Timothy 4:1 Paul speaks of "the Lord Jesus Christ, who shall judge the quick (the living) and the dead at His appearing and His kingdom." God the Father and God the Son are *one* in judgment; yet because Jesus paid the sin-debt willingly and purchased redemption for us, the Father has given to Him the work of judging the world.

The declaration that *"all judgment has been committed to the Son"* includes more than judging sinners and rewarding saints. In the Old Testament, judgment was used in the sense of ruling—i. e., "to judge" meant to *rule.* Therefore God the Father has given to Christ Jesus the Son the office of King and Judge, and He will rule as King of kings in the divine government of which there shall be no end (Isaiah 9:6,7).

"As the Father *raiseth up the dead and quickeneth them* . . . ." So we see that the work of giving life to spirits that are dead in sin is the ministry and work of all three Persons in the Godhead—Father, Son, and Holy Ghost. *God the Father* so loved us that He gave Jesus the Son to die for us. *Jesus the Son* willingly laid His life down for us, and no man can come to Jesus unless God draws him by and through *the Holy Spirit.* Study John 3:5,16; 6:44; 10:17,18; 16:7—9; II Cor. 3:6.

"All men should honour the Son, even as they honour the Father." The only way to please God the Father is to honor Jesus the Son—yes, even as we honor God the Father. The Son is to be worshipped as we worship the Father, for there is no inferiority in the Son; He is equal with the Father in dignity and in authority. Those who refuse to honor the Son thereby dishonor God the Father who sent Him into the world. There are literally thousands who declare that Jesus was no more than a great teacher; but He was God in flesh, and the Father is highly pleased when believers honor Christ and worship Him wholeheart-

edly.

In this day of liberalism, modernism, and the rise of many cults, the unity of the three Persons in the Godhead is a subject that needs to be preached more than ever before, and true believers need to give more attention to this subject than in times past. There are some well-meaning church people who, in ignorance, speak of God the Father as feeling one way toward sinners, God the Son as feeling in another manner toward sinners. They speak as though *God hates* man and the Son *loves* man. They speak as though Jesus the Son brought the love of God down to man, when on the contrary *God's love* allowed Jesus to come into the world that He might die for sinners! For believers, such ignorance is inexcusable when we have the Word of God before us and the Holy Spirit within us. If we would study the Trinity in the Word of God and let the Scriptures speak, keeping church doctrine and denominationalism out of it, God would reveal the fact that we worship ONE GOD manifest in *three Persons.*

It is impossible to understand the Word of God if we reject the truth of one God manifest in three Persons: the *Father* is eternal, the *Son* is eternal, the *Holy Ghost* is eternal. The Father is God, the Son is God, the Holy Ghost is God—three, yet *one;* one, yet *three.* There was never a time in all eternity behind us, there will never be a time in all eternity ahead of us, when any one of the three Persons of the Godhead did not (and will not) exist. Ministers preach this divine truth because the Word of God teaches it, and believers accept it by faith. Those who profess to worship God and yet deny the Son, do not know the Father. No one can believe in the God of the Bible and deny the doctrine of the Trinity. Hear what John the Beloved said about this in the second epistle that bears his name:

"For many deceivers are entered into the world, who confess not that Jesus Christ is come in the flesh. This is a deceiver and an antichrist. Look to yourselves, that we lose not those things which we have wrought, but that we receive a full reward. *Whosoever transgresseth, and abideth not in the doctrine of Christ, hath not God. He that abideth in the doctrine of Christ, he hath both the Father AND the Son.* If there come any unto you, and bring not this doctrine, receive him not into your house, neither bid him God speed: For he that biddeth him God speed is partaker of his evil deeds" (II John 7—11).

How We Obtain Life Eternal

Verse 24: *"Verily, verily, I say unto you, He that heareth my word, and believeth on Him that sent me, hath everlasting life, and shall not come into condemnation; but is passed from death unto life."*

Here we find another "double verily" prefacing an extremely important truth: *"He that heareth my Word . . . ."* Is Jesus speaking only of physical ears? No, He is not. He is speaking of hearing with the heart, *believing* with the heart, hearing with faith, hearing that is followed by obedience. He who hears the Word of Christ with the heart has life eternal:

"For by grace are ye saved through faith; and that not of yourselves: it is the gift of God: not of works, lest any man should boast" (Eph. 2:8,9).

GRACE saves us, and saving grace comes through faith— but how do we *get* the faith? Romans 10:17 answers: "So then faith cometh by hearing, and hearing *by the Word of God."*

We hear the Word of God, hearing the Word brings faith, and faith exercised in the finished work of Jesus brings life eternal. "Whosoever shall call upon the name of the Lord shall be saved" (Rom. 10:13). That is true—but no one can call in faith without first hearing and believing. No one can believe without hearing, and the hearing comes as the minister preaches the Word of God. Please study Romans 10:13—17.

There IS no salvation apart from hearing the Word of God. No wonder Satan has tried everything in his diabolical power to *discredit* the Word. If the devil could destroy the Word of God he could undermine Christianity.

"He that heareth my Word and BELIEVETH ON HIM THAT SENT ME . . . ." This part of the verse means to believe on God as the one *true* God, He who sent Jesus into the world to save sinners. It means to believe that the one true God is the *Father* of Christ Jesus who saves us. It means to believe what Peter teaches in I Peter 1:18—23 —that God the Father, God the Son, and God the Holy Ghost settled the sin question before the foundation of the world, and it was foreordained that Jesus would come into the world and pay the sin-debt. It means to believe that God so loved the world that He gave the most precious Jewel heaven held—His only Son—that HE might take the sinner's place in order that a holy God could be just and yet justify the ungodly.

We see again that the Father and the Son are one in salvation: the Father is just as much the object of saving faith as the Son is the object of saving faith. If we believe in God, we also believe in the Son; and when we believe in God the Son, we also believe in God the Father.

God is the *origin* of grace: "We see Jesus, who was made a little lower than the angels for the suffering of death, crowned with glory and honour; that He *by the grace of God* should taste death for every man" (Heb. 2:9).

In the same manner, God is the ultimate *object* of all faith: Christ was "foreordained before the foundation of the world, but was manifest in these last times for you. Who by Him do believe in God, that raised Him up from the dead, and gave Him glory; *that your faith and hope might be in GOD"* (I Pet. 1:20,21).

The faith that saves embraces the Word of God—not as something thought up by Jesus alone or spoken by Jesus alone; but as decreed in the secret council of God the Father, God the Son, and God the Holy Ghost in the beginning before the foundation of the world.

"He that heareth my Word, and believeth on Him that sent me, *HATH everlasting life.*" Whosoever hears the words of Jesus and believes on God the Father *has* (NOW, this very moment) *everlasting life.* The born again believer is reckoned justified, forgiven, pardoned, an heir to heaven while here on earth, joint-heir with Christ (Rom. 8:17). We are not to be *"at last* saved in heaven"; we are saved NOW. Eternal life is not something we will come into possession of when we die, or when we reach heaven, or at the resurrection; we possess eternal life the very second we believe. NOW, yes, *even now,* we sit together in heavenly places in Christ Jesus (Eph. 2:6). The born again believer is *justified*—which means that he will stand before God just as though he had never sinned. We are justified by faith in the finished work of Jesus Christ: "And by HIM all that believe are justified from all things, from which ye could not be justified by the law of Moses" (Acts 13:39). Being justified, we have peace with God: "Therefore being justified by faith, we have peace with God through our Lord Jesus Christ" (Rom. 5:1).

The believer possesses eternal life *"and shall NOT come into condemnation."* (The Greek language reads, "DOES not come into condemnation.") There IS no condemnation "to them which are in Christ Jesus . . ." (Rom. 8:1). The wrath of God does not abide on the believer because his guilt has been removed. The true believer has nothing to fear because "perfect love casteth out fear" (I John 4:18) and when we possess Christ we possess perfect love.

Christ is our sufficiency—in time, in judgment, in eternity. The true believer *"IS* (present tense) *passed from death unto life,"* he has *already* passed from spiritual deadness into a state of spiritual life. He has become a new creation in Christ Jesus: "Therefore if any man be in Christ, he is a new creature: old things are passed away; behold, all things are become new" (II Cor. 5:17).

There is much misunderstanding concerning what it means

to believe on Jesus Christ unto salvation. James 2:19 tells us that *demons* "believe and tremble"—but demons are not saved. There are tens of thousands of church members the world over who have *intellectual* belief—i. e., they believe that Jesus was a man, that He lived on earth and died on the cross; but they have never put their faith in His shed blood and finished work. It is easy to unite with a church and be baptized, pray three times a day, say grace at meals, give a tithe of all income; but *true believing* is not possible for the natural man in His own mind and strength. Faith to trust God for salvation in Christ is a *gift* that comes only by hearing God's Word. Thus this extraordinary verse opens, "He that *heareth my Word* . . . ." It is impossible to believe until we hear the Word—not only with the ear, but also with the *heart.*

This is an age when religions of "works" are growing by leaps and bounds. People are willing to work, willing to give, willing to *abstain from* certain things; but when the Jews asked Jesus what they should do that they might work the works of God He replied, *"THIS is the work of God: that ye BELIEVE on Him whom He hath sent"* (John 6:29).

Have YOU believed on Jesus—or do you simply believe *about* Him? Is your faith from the heart—or is it an *intellectual* belief? Do you believe in Jesus because of His Word, or because your parents have always been "religiously inclined"? Did you join the church because you reached a certain age, or because you considered it the right thing to do—or did you join the church and follow Christ in baptism because you heard the Word, believed on Jesus, and received Him as your Saviour? Think it over! Give diligence to make your calling and election sure; leave no stone unturned to know positively that your name is in the Lamb's book of life. "For what is a man profited, if he shall gain the whole world, and lose his own soul? or what shall a man give in exchange for his soul?" (Matt. 16:26).

Verse 25: *"Verily, verily, I say unto you, The hour is*

*coming, and now is, when the dead shall hear the voice
of the Son of God: and they that hear shall live."*

This "double verily" precedes a prophecy that points to
the wonderful works that were yet to be worked by the Son
of God. If the Jews wanted proof of His divine power and
authority, He would *give* them such proof if they would
listen to the account of the things He would do in the
future:

"The hour is coming, and now is" (a time was coming
and had already begun) *"when the dead shall hear the
voice of the Son of God . . . and live."* Jesus was speaking here of the *spiritually* dead. All sinners are dead in
trespasses and sins (Eph. 2:1), and the only possible way
for them to be made alive is to hear the Word.

To *"hear the voice of the Son of God"* means to hear
with the heart—to hear in faith believing. In the days to
follow, there would be many dead sinners raised to life by
hearing His wonderful words of life: ". . . the words that
I speak unto you, they are spirit, and they are life" (John
6:63).

"The hour is coming and now is" was partially fulfilled
in the days of Jesus; it was fulfilled more fully on the Day
of Pentecost and in the days following Pentecost, as the
apostles preached the marvelous grace of God: "And without controversy great is the mystery of godliness: God was
manifest in the flesh, justified in the Spirit, seen of angels,
preached unto the Gentiles, believed on in the world, received up into glory" (I Tim. 3:16).

The *"hour"* spoken of in this verse has already lasted
almost two thousand years, and will last until the bride of
Christ is complete and the Church is caught up to meet
the Lord in the clouds in the air (I Thess. 4:13—18).

Verses 26 and 27: *"For as the Father hath life in Himself; so hath He given to the Son to have life in Himself;
and hath given Him authority to execute judgment also,
because He is the Son of man."*

God is the author and source of life; Jesus is the author of *eternal* life: "And being made perfect, He became the author of eternal salvation unto all them that obey Him" (Heb. 5:9). In the eternal ages behind us, before the world was, before anything was created, it was foreordained of God in His everlasting councils that Jesus, the only begotten Son, would be the sole dispenser and giver of eternal life to those who hear His Word and believe from the heart: "And this is the record, that God hath given to us eternal life, and this life is in His Son" (I John 5:11).

The "giving" does not suggest that Jesus was inferior to the Father concerning His divine essence. The things mentioned in these two verses as being given to Him were given when He assumed His office as Mediator between God and men.

God has given to Jesus "authority to execute judgment also, *because He is the Son of man*"—and upon this fact is based the authority of Christ Jesus the Lord to act as the Righteous Judge of all men. His "judgment" here has to do with His humanity—as Son of man He will judge all men because He fully understands men. He experienced everything *we* experience, sin apart. He was tempted in all points as we are, therefore experimentally He has a full understanding of human conditions. He was very man, though *unimpeachable* man; there was no guile or sin in Him.

It is true that the Word of God tells us that God is the Judge of all (Heb. 12:23); but it is also true that it is God the Son, second Person of the Trinity, who will execute all judgment and sit on the *throne* of judgment in that final day.

Concerning the unsaved, Revelation 6:15—17 tells us that "the kings of the earth, and the great men, and the rich men, and the chief captains, and the mighty men, and every bondman, and every free man, hid themselves in the dens and in the rocks of the mountains; and said to the mountains and rocks, *Fall on us, and hide us from the face of*

Him that sitteth on the throne, and from the wrath of the Lamb: For the great day of His wrath is come; and who shall be able to stand?'' (Certainly "the Lamb" is none other than the Lord Jesus Christ.)

Again referring to unbelievers, we read, "And I saw a great white throne, and Him that sat on it, from whose face the earth and the heaven fled away; and there was found no place for them. And I saw the dead, small and great, stand before God; and the books were opened: and another book was opened, which is the book of life: and the dead were judged out of those things which were written in the books, according to their works. And the sea gave up the dead which were in it; and death and hell delivered up the dead which were in them: and they were judged every man according to their works. And death and hell were cast into the lake of fire. This is the second death. *And whosoever was not found written in the book of life was cast into the lake of fire*'' (Rev. 20:11–15). It is Christ who will judge the living and the dead at His appearing and kingdom. Believers will be judged and rewarded for their stewardship; some will receive a reward, some will suffer loss when their works are burned:

"For other foundation can no man lay than that is laid, which is Jesus Christ. Now if any man build upon this foundation gold, silver, precious stones, wood, hay, stubble; every man's work shall be made manifest: for the day shall declare it, because it shall be revealed by fire; and the fire shall try every man's work of what sort it is. If any man's work abide which he hath built thereupon, he shall receive a reward. If any man's work shall be burned, he shall suffer loss: but he himself shall be saved; yet so as by fire'' (I Cor. 3:11–15).

Believers will be judged for their stewardship—not as to whether they are saved or lost, for that question is settled in this life; but all Christians must give an account to God for their service and stewardship: "For we must all appear before the judgment seat of Christ; that every one may receive the things done in his body, according to that he hath done, whether it be good or bad" (II Cor. 5:10).

The Two Resurrections

Verses 28 and 29: *"Marvel not at this: for the hour is coming, in the which all that are in the graves shall hear His voice, and shall come forth; they that have done good, unto the resurrection of life; and they that have done evil, unto the resurrection of damnation."*

Those who listened to Jesus were astonished by what He said. They marvelled at the statement of His divine authority and commission to quicken those who were dead in sin, to give life to those who heard His Word and believed on Him, and to judge all things. But He said to them, "Marvel not, because there are more and greater things to come."

"The hour is coming, and now is . . . ." To use the present tense of a day so distant is proof that when God is speaking of something that *will* happen, it is as good as done. This is the same principle as is seen in Isaiah 9:6, where we read, *"Unto us a child IS born,"* instead of "a child *will be* born." Jesus was not born for many years after that prophecy was written, but when God said it, it was as good as done.

"All that are in the graves shall hear His voice." This is the same truth declared in Daniel 12:2: "Many of them that sleep in the dust of the earth shall awake, some to everlasting life, and some to shame and everlasting contempt." Here is set forth the eternal, scriptural truth of the resurrection of the dead—both good and bad. There is no such thing as soul annihilation; the body returns to dust, the born again spirit goes back to God, and the wicked spirit is consigned to hell. Notice, "ALL that are in the graves shall come forth"—not just the righteous, not just the wicked, not just a certain class, but ALL shall come forth—but *not all at the same time,* as we will learn in further study of this Scripture. The Word of God teaches

no such thing as a "general resurrection" or a "general judgment." One thousand years separate the two resurrections; the *righteous* dead will be raised at the Rapture in the first resurrection, the *wicked* dead will be raised one thousand years later:

"And I saw thrones, and they sat upon them, and judgment was given unto them: and I saw the souls of them that were beheaded for the witness of Jesus, and for the Word of God, and which had not worshipped the beast, neither his image, neither had received his mark upon their foreheads, or in their hands; and they lived and reigned with Christ a thousand years. *But the rest of the dead lived not again until the thousand years were finished. This is the first resurrection.* Blessed and holy is he that hath part in the first resurrection: on such the second death hath no power, but they shall be priests of God and of Christ, and shall reign with Him a thousand years" (Rev. 20:4—6).

If there is but one resurrection, why does the Bible say, "This is the FIRST resurrection. Blessed and holy is he that hath part in the FIRST resurrection"? Why does the Word speak of the FIRST resurrection if there is not a *second?*

Who are "the *rest* of the dead" who live not until a thousand years after the first resurrection? The answer is found in Paul's letter to the believers in Thessalonica: "The Lord Himself shall descend from heaven with a shout, with the voice of the archangel, and with the trump of God: *and the dead in Christ shall rise FIRST*" (I Thess. 4:16). Only the righteous dead will be raised in the first resurrection. Not one wicked person will be raised at that time. All of the wicked dead will be raised one thousand years later at the Great White Throne judgment.

Two classes of people will be raised, but they will be raised one thousand years apart—one group will be raised to happiness, glory, and eternal bliss (this is the "resurrection of life"); the other group will be raised a thousand years later in "the resurrection of destruction (or damnation)."

Those in the *"resurrection of life"* will be those who have *"done good"*—those who have worked the works of God by believing on His Son Jesus Christ. Those in the *"resurrection of damnation"* will be those who have "done evil"— they have refused to believe on Jesus, thereby calling God a liar (I John 5:10).

Will YOU be in the "resurrection of life"? or will you be in the "resurrection of damnation"? Your answer will depend on whether you believe on Jesus or *refuse* to believe on Him. Believing on Him brings life; refusing to believe on Him will automatically classify you for the resurrection of damnation: "He that believeth on Him is not condemned: but he that believeth not is condemned already, because he hath not believed in the name of the only begotten Son of God" (John 3:18).

Life does not end; verses 28 and 29 prove this. There will be *resurrection*—either to life eternal, or to eternal death. These verses also deny the doctrine that a loving God would not permit a soul to be tormented in hell. God is love, but He is also a consuming fire (Heb. 12:29). The Word of God clearly teaches that the wicked will be raised just as surely as saints will be raised (Acts 24:15; I Cor. 15:51—57).

Verse 28 tells us that at the first resurrection the dead shall *"hear His voice."* I Corinthians 15:52 tells us that the resurrection will be preceded by "the last trump." In I Thessalonians 4:16 we read of "a shout . . . the voice of the archangel . . . the trump of God." We do not know just how the voices or the trumpet will sound, but the dead will hear and come forth—the righteous dead at the Rapture, the wicked dead at the Great White Throne—and in each resurrection it is *bodies* that will be raised. The spirit of the righteous goes to Paradise at death, and the spirit of the wicked goes to hell. The Scripture is clear on this point: Paul said, "To me to live is Christ, and to die is gain. But if I live in the flesh, this is the fruit of my labour: yet what I shall choose I wot not.   For I am in a strait betwixt two, *having a desire to depart, and to be with Christ; which is far better"* (Phil. 1:21−23).

In II Corinthians 5:6−8 we read, "Therefore we are always confident, knowing that, *whilst we are at home in the body, we are absent from the Lord*: (for we walk by faith, not by sight:) we are confident, I say, and willing rather *to be absent from the body, and to be present with the Lord!"*

In Luke 23:43, Jesus said to the penitent thief on the cross, "To day shalt thou be with me in Paradise."

Concerning the spirits of the wicked at death, we need only one passage—Luke 16:19−31.   There was a rich man, there was a beggar.   The beggar died "and was carried by the angels into Abraham's bosom" (the place of peace and rest, *Paradise*).   The rich man also died, was buried, "and in hell he lift up his eyes, being in torments."   People do not open their eyes in the grave, so we know that hell is not the grave.   The rich man could see Abraham, with Lazarus on his bosom, and he cried out to Abraham, "Have mercy on me, and send Lazarus, that he may dip the tip of his finger in water, and cool my tongue; for I am tormented in this flame!   But Abraham said, Son, remember that thou in thy lifetime receivedst thy good things, and likewise Lazarus evil things: but NOW he is comforted, and (NOW) thou art tormented.   And beside all this, between us and you there is a great gulf fixed: so that they which would pass from hence to you cannot; neither can they pass to us, that would come from thence."

This passage alone is enough to repudiate the doctrine of "soul sleep."   Any person who will read the Word of God with an open mind and an open heart, not trying to prove a religious point but allowing the Holy Spirit to speak through the Word, can clearly see that the split second one departs this life he opens his eyes—either in Paradise, or in hell!   Thus saith the Lord—and I say with Paul, *"Let God be true,"* though every man on earth be proved a liar.   (See

Romans 3:4.)

The Witness Given to Jesus by the Father

Verse 30: *"I can of mine own self do nothing: as I hear, I judge: and my judgment is just; because I seek not mine own will, but the will of the Father which hath sent me."*

In verse 27 Jesus declared His authority to execute judgment upon all men, and in this verse He repudiates any idea that this judgment is a matter of His own will or of His own doing: "As I *hear,* I judge." Here again is declared the essential unity of Father and Son. The fact that Jesus was entirely willing to be in subjection to the Father's will is a divine guarantee of the infallible equity of His judgment: *"My judgment is just (righteous) because I seek not mine own will, but the will of the Father which hath sent me."* There was complete, unbroken harmony between the will of Jesus the Son and the will of God the Father. This is not suggestive of weakness, but rather a divine statement as to God's unutterable power. When Jesus said, "I can of my own self do nothing," He meant that He could not do anything contrary to the will of His heavenly Father. This was in accordance with His divine nature: as God the Son, His will was *one* with God the Father, and it was not possible for Him to seek His own will independently and apart from the Father's will.

This is set forth in Isaiah 11:2,3: "The Spirit of the Lord shall rest upon Him, the Spirit of wisdom and understanding, the Spirit of counsel and might, the Spirit of knowledge and of the fear of the Lord; and shall make Him of quick understanding in the fear of the Lord: and He shall not judge after the sight of His eyes, neither reprove after the hearing of his ears."

Jesus was the Son of God as to Deity, the Son of man as to the flesh; and *AS the Son of man* His will was human as well as divine. In the Garden of Gethsemane as He prayed, His perspiration became as great drops of blood. In Mark's description of the Lord's prayer in Gethsemane, he tells us that Jesus saw something that *amazed* Him (the Greek reads, "something of which He was terrified"). Read the account in Mark 14:32—42. If we study the Psalms that prophesy the horrible death the Lamb of God would die, we will understand more fully what He saw in the Garden that amazed or terrified Him. He could see through human eyes untainted by sin; He saw the horrors of sin, the terrible *wages* of sin, and prayed, "O my Father, if it be possible, let this cup pass from me: nevertheless not as I will, but as thou wilt" (Matt. 26:39). But Jesus was God, and therefore He could also see through divine eyes. The truth concerning the Trinity—Father, Son, and Holy Ghost, one God manifested in three Persons—must always be a deep subject to man. It is hard to conceive, and much, much *harder* to write about or describe in words.

Verse 31:   *"If I bear witness of myself, my witness is not true."*

Jesus recognized the fact that He was definitely on trial, defending His divine claims before Jews who refused to believe that He was the Son of God, very God in flesh. He was willing to accept and abide by the Bible rule of evidence under the law—the testimony of two or more witnesses:

"Whoso killeth any person, the murderer shall be put to death by the mouth of witnesses: but one witness shall not testify against any person to cause him to die" (Num. 35:30).

"At the mouth of two witnesses, or three witnesses, shall he that is worthy of death be put to death; but at the mouth of one witness he shall not be put to death" (Deut. 17:6). See also John 8:15—18.

The Jews before whom Jesus testified knew the law, and Jesus knew that they would declare His testimony untrue if He testified *alone* in His behalf; but there were other witnesses, as evidenced in the verses that follow.

The Witness of God the Father

Verse 32: *"There is another that beareth witness of me: and I know that the witness which He witnesseth of me is true."*

Jesus was speaking here of God His Father. The statement is in the present tense—*"beareth* witness . . . *witnesseth* of me."* The testimony of John the Baptist would be past tense, for it was over.

"And I KNOW that the witness which He witnesseth of me is true." Jesus was with God in the beginning and knew from the beginning that His testimony was perfect truth, because God IS truth and it is impossible for Him to lie (Heb. 6:18; Tit. 1:2).

The Witness of John Baptist

Verse 33: *"Ye sent unto John, and he bare witness unto the truth."*

Jesus referred here to the delegation sent by the Sanhedrin to question John, as recorded in chapter 1, verses 19—27. John plainly announced that he was *not* the Messiah, he was only the messenger announcing the *coming* of the Messiah. Then one day he said to them, *"Behold the Lamb of God!"*

This group of people accepted John the Baptist as a prophet, they rejoiced in him and followed him for a season, they heard the words of truth spoken by him concerning the coming of the Lamb of God. They *heard*—but they did not receive his testimony.

Verse 34: *"But I receive not testimony from man: but these things I say, that ye might be saved."*

It is true that John the Baptist was ordained of God to bear witness to the Messiah and to announce the coming

of the King; but Jesus did not depend altogether on the
testimony of John or of any other man. His testimony of
John the Baptist reminded the Jews of their inconsistency.
They believed that John the Baptist was a prophet, they
believed that he was sent from God, they even wondered
if he might be their expected Messiah—but they refused to
believe the Messiah whom John had announced. If the
scribes, elders, and chief priests believed John, if they truly
believed that he was a prophet, then to be consistent they
certainly should have believed the One whom he announced
as their Messiah and coming King. Please study Matthew
21:23—27.

Verse 35: *"He was a burning and a shining light: and
ye were willing for a season to rejoice in his light."*

Jesus paid high tribute to John in this testimony. Many
people today like to *"shine,"* but John was "a *burning* and
a shining light." Many religious leaders like to be in the
limelight but they do not like to *burn*. The more we burn
for Jesus, the brighter we shine before our fellowman. John
confessed that he was not THE Light, that he was only a
voice *announcing* the Light, but Jesus testified that John
was a light sent from above, "a burning and a shining
light." (Most Bible scholars agree that at this time John
was either dead or in prison. He gave forth the light God
sent him to give, and then his ministry was brought to a
close.)

Jesus reminded the Jews that they *"were willing to rejoice"* in John's light. Matthew 3:5 tells us, "Then went
out to him Jerusalem, and all Judaea, and all the region
round about Jordan." Even the Sadducees and Pharisees
came to his baptism (Matt. 3:7). The masses flocked to
John in the same way they flock to outstanding religious
leaders today; but they came to him in ignorance and followed him for the excitement of the crowds. Since they
expected the Messiah to be a great military leader who
would conquer the Romans and deliver Israel from the rule

of Rome, it is entirely possible that they followed John in hopes of receiving political favors when the Messiah *came.* They were willing to rejoice in John's light, they took great pleasure in going out to hear him speak, they even sub-mitted to his baptism—but they rejected his Christ!

"For a season" was used here to show these people how unstable they were. John's ministry stirred and moved them—but only for a little while. John did not change; his ministry remained the same; but the crowds who had followed him changed shortly.

The Witness of the Works of Jesus

Verse 36: *"But I have greater witness than that of John: for the works which the Father hath given me to finish, the same works that I do, bear witness of me, that the Father hath sent me."*

The miracles of Jesus were a far greater witness than the words of John the Baptist, even though John was cer-tainly sent by God the Father to announce the coming of Messiah. John worked no miracles, yet the people followed him in great multitudes; but when the true Messiah came working mighty miracles, the people paid no attention. They rejected Him and demanded His death.

There are three other times in the Gospel of John where Jesus appealed to the people to see His works and believe that He was sent from God, declaring that the miracles He performed were proof of His messiahship and of His deity:

John 3:2: "(Nicodemus) came to Jesus by night, and said unto Him, Rabbi, we know that thou art a teacher come from God: for no man can do these miracles that thou doest, except God be with him." The fact that Jesus did not deny what Nicodemus said is within itself a declaration of His deity.

John 10:25: "Jesus answered them, I told you, and ye believed not: the works that I do in my Father's name they bear witness of me."

John 15:24: "If I had not done among them the works which none other man did, they had not had sin: but now have they both seen and hated both me and my Father."

It is interesting to note that while liberals and modernists today deny the miracles of Jesus, the Jews never once questioned His statement concerning His miracles. They declared that He worked miracles by the power of *Satan,* but they did not deny the *fact* of the miracles.

Jesus worked many outstanding miracles, miracles that stepped over the laws of medicine and even over the laws of nature. He touched the leper—and the leprosy was cleansed. He spoke a word—and the stormy sea became calm. He commanded—and the dead came forth from the tomb. He walked on the sea—not in secret, but before witnesses. He performed His miracles in public, He did not do them in a corner; and all of His miracles were beneficial to man, not just an exhibition of power for the sake of drawing a crowd.

He speaks of His miracles as "the works which the Father hath given me to finish," thus declaring that what He was doing was not done of His independent will, but by the will of His heavenly Father. Everything He did, every step He took, every word He spoke, and every miracle He performed was testimony that God the Father sent Him into the world and that the Father was in Him as He tabernacled among men. Father and Son were ONE in works and in word.

The Witness of God Through the Scriptures

Verses 37 and 38: *"And the Father Himself, which hath sent me, hath borne witness of me. Ye have neither heard His voice at any time, nor seen His shape. And ye have not His Word abiding in you: for whom He hath sent, Him ye believe not."*

Jesus reminded the Jews that they had neither seen the

form of God the Father, nor heard His voice—pointing back
to God's words concerning Moses in Exodus 33:18—23: "And
he said, I beseech thee, shew me thy glory. And He said,
I will make all my goodness pass before thee, and I will
proclaim the name of the Lord before thee; and will be
gracious to whom I will be gracious, and will shew mercy
on whom I will shew mercy. And He said, Thou canst not
see my face: for there shall no man see me, and live. And
the Lord said, Behold, there is a place by me, and thou
shalt stand upon a rock: And it shall come to pass, while
my glory passeth by, that I will put thee in a clift of the
rock, and will cover thee with my hand while I pass by:
And I will take away mine hand, and thou shalt see my
back parts: but my face shall not be seen."

The Israelites had not understood or obeyed the voice
of God to their nation, neither had they obeyed the voice
of Moses, the one upon whom they had set their hope, as
attested in verse 45 of this chapter: "Do not think that I
will accuse you to the Father: there is one that accuseth
you, even Moses, in whom ye trust." NOW they refused
to hear the Father, who at that time was speaking to them
"by His Son, whom He hath appointed heir of all things,
by whom also He made the worlds" (Heb. 1:1,2). They
refused to see or hear the Son of God who was speaking
to them at that time, and yet Jesus Himself was the manifestation of the Father in visible form, the Father's repre-
sentation here on earth. To Philip He said, *"He that hath
seen me hath seen the Father"* (John 14:9). But the Jews
who had refused to hear the words of Moses in obedience,
now refused to hear the Word of God spoken by God Himself in flesh!

"Ye have not heard His voice at any time . . . ." Some
Bible teachers suggest that this refers to the time when God
spoke at the baptism of Jesus in Matthew 3, and also on
the Mount of Transfiguration in Matthew 17; but I do not
believe this to be the meaning. Jesus plainly declared here
that they had NOT heard God's voice nor seen His shape.

What Jesus said to them here was, "I am not speaking of an *audible* voice when I tell you that the Father hath given witness to me.   I am speaking of a very different kind of testimony—the eternal Word of God.   The Word was not only being *spoken* to them, the Word actually was standing in their presence—Jesus, the Word Incarnate.

"Ye have neither . . . seen His shape." Certainly this teaches that God the Father has form, that He is a Personality even though He is an eternal Spirit, as Jesus declared to the Samaritan woman.   God the Father has never been seen by mortal man, for no man could look upon God and live.   The Person who appeared to *Abraham* was God the Son, second Person of the Godhead.   It was HE who appeared to various prophets and people on various occasions in the Old Testament.   In I Timothy 6:15,16 Paul speaks of God the Father as *"the light which no man can approach unto;* whom no man hath seen, nor can see: to whom be honour and power everlasting.   Amen."

"Ye have not His Word abiding in you." These people were familiar with the Old Testament Scriptures, but those Scriptures did not abide in their hearts; their knowledge was only of the mind.   They proved their ignorance and spiritual darkness by refusing to receive God's Messiah, by refusing to believe God's Word as to who Jesus was.   If they had known the Word as it was recorded in the Old Testament, they would have *known* their Messiah, they would have believed on Jesus, they would have believed His words.

Verse 39:   *"Search the Scriptures; for in them ye think ye have eternal life: and they are they which testify of me."*

"Search the Scriptures" no doubt has a twofold meaning here: Greek scholars have agreed that the meaning could be "Ye DO search the Scriptures."   Others believe that Jesus meant "Go and search your own Scriptures," inviting the Jews to re-read and study the books of Moses, Isaiah, Zechariah.   "Examine your Scriptures—the Word given to

you by Jehovah through holy men of old. Become acquainted with the *prophecies* in your Scriptures, and you will
discover that they clearly testify of me and point me out as
your Messiah. If you really want to know what the God
of your fathers has to say about me, you will find His testimony of me in your Scriptures." As we follow the leaders
of the Jewish synagogue in their condemnation of Jesus, we
realize that they had studied the books of Moses, because
when Jesus did anything against the tradition of the Israelite fathers they immediately rebuked Him *according to the
LAW.*

You will notice that Jesus did not say, "READ the Scriptures," but "SEARCH the Scriptures, *for in them ye think
ye have eternal life."* *Think* as used here does not suggest
doubt or a matter of opinion. The Jews were really convinced that all they needed was to read the Scriptures religiously and practice the letter of the law diligently; but it
is not enough to *search* the Scriptures, nor even to study
them diligently. Jesus made it plain that we are to *hear*
the Word and believe on God, who sent Jesus: "He that
heareth my Word, and believeth on Him that sent me, hath
everlasting life, and shall not come into condemnation; but
is passed from death unto life" (John 5:24). We hear the
Word, we appropriate the Word; and unless we DO appropriate the Word and receive it into our heart, we do not
have eternal life (John 6:53—56).

Scripture alone cannot make one fit for heaven; *preaching*
cannot make one fit for heaven. He who hears the Word
through the preaching of the Word must allow the Holy
Spirit to appropriate the Word and make it part of him.
The eternal Word of the living God supplies the testimony
and gives the witness; but only the Holy Ghost can open
the heart and unite us to the body of Christ (I Cor. 12:12,
13). The Word of God is the life-giving seed, but it must
fall on good ground—a willing, open, receptive heart—or
it will not bring forth the new birth.

"Search the Scriptures . . . *they are they which testify*

of me." From Luke 24:27 we know that the books of Moses did prophesy concerning Jesus. In His conversation
with the disciples on the road to Emmaus we read, "Beginning at *Moses and all the prophets,* (Jesus) expounded
unto them in all the Scriptures the things concerning Himself." And yet, the unbelieving Jews failed to recognize
their Messiah, He whom the Old Testament Scriptures so
plainly set forth.

Jesus is the center, soul, heartbeat and bloodstream of
the entire Bible. If He were *taken out* of the Bible, it
would be an empty, meaningless book. His declaration
here is extremely weighty and important, placing the correct
value on the Old Testament Scriptures. There are those
today who would discredit the Old Testament, saying that
God is finished with it; but this is a doctrine of Satan. The
Old Testament is just as much the Word of God today as
it was when the Holy Ghost gave the Scriptures to holy
men and they penned them down. The Scriptures to which
Jesus referred in this verse were certainly from the Old Testament, for the New Testament had not been written at
the time He made these statements. The Old Testament
books testify (witness) of Jesus in specific and direct prophecies, in typical persons, in feasts, ceremonies, and promises. He was the complete fulfillment of the Old Testament Scriptures. He fulfilled every jot and tittle of the law,
He dotted every "i" and crossed every "t" (Matt. 5:17,18).
The Old Testament Scriptures were the voice of God, the
voice of the Word not yet in flesh. The sacrificial lamb, the
brazen serpent, the sacrifices and ordinances under the law—
all these were witnesses of Christ and pointed to Him.

Since Jesus commanded the Jews to diligently search the
books of the Old Testament, how much more should WE
search the entire Bible—the Old Testament as well as the
New. We should study to show ourselves approved unto
God, we should learn to rightly divide the word of truth,
because from Genesis to Revelation the Scriptures *still* testify of Jesus! One of the saddest things in the lives of be-

lievers today is the neglect of Bible study, and this is the secret of the gross ignorance that prevails in the average church concerning the fundamentals of the faith and the tremendous doctrines on the second coming of Jesus. We should hear the testimony concerning the Bereans: "These were more noble than those in Thessalonica, in that *they received the Word with all readiness of mind, and searched the Scriptures daily, whether those things were so"* (Acts 17:11).

Verse 40: *"And ye will not come to me, that ye might have life."*

This is one of the saddest statements Jesus ever made. It is sad because of the people to whom it was made—His own people, the Jews. The Old Testament declares that Judah was the apple of God's eye (Zech. 2:8), and therefore we know it was concerning His own beloved people that He said this.

Why did Jesus make this statement? The answer is in the chapter we are now studying: In verse 10 the man who was healed was rebuked by the Jews for carrying his bed on the Sabbath. They had just witnessed his amazing and miraculous healing, they had been exposed to a miracle that *only GOD* could perform; and yet they sought to slay Jesus for making the man whole and commanding him to carry his bed on the Sabbath.

John the Baptist had testified to them concerning Jesus, but they rejected his testimony although they followed him for a little season.

God the Father witnessed concerning His Son, and *the miracles of Jesus* bore testimony to His deity; but the Jews refused to receive such witness. The Jews were strict tithers, they washed their hands before meals, they refrained from certain meats, they kept holy days—but they would not come to Jesus.

Also, this is one of the saddest statements Jesus ever made because of the meaning contained IN the statement. This verse gives the reason why every poor soul in hell today is *there,* and why all who are so unfortunate as to spend eternity in hell will do so—*because they refused to come to Jesus.* UNBELIEF is the damning sin of the age. Thousands today will join the church, be baptized, prescribe to one religious formula or another: but they refuse to come to Jesus confessing their sins and believing in His finished work for salvation.

"Ye WILL NOT come to me" means, "Ye do not *will* to come to me, *ye have no heart, no desire or inclination,* to come to me that ye might have life." When Noah had completed the ark, God said to him, "Come thou and all thy house into the ark . . ." (Gen. 7:1). God's invitation to Noah was simple—*"Come."* That meant that God was already in the ark, and He invited Noah and his family to come in. God was *in Christ* (the Ark of this Dispensation of Grace). He said to the Jews (and to you and me), *"Come"*—but the Jews would not come to Him and there are *still* many who will not heed His invitation, they *will not* come to Him that they might have life. Some say, "Salvation just could not be that simple." But it IS! The sin-debt has been paid, salvation has been brought down to man, and today Jesus is saying, *"They that come to me I will in no wise cast out."*

We are saved by God's grace; God's grace becomes ours by faith; faith becomes ours by hearing; hearing becomes ours by the Word of God. God's preacher preaches the Word, we hear, believe, and receive the Word, and saving faith is the result. Faith exercised in Jesus Christ brings salvation by God's grace:

"And the Spirit and the bride say, Come. And let him that heareth say, Come. And let him that is athirst come. And whosoever will, let him take the water of life freely" (Rev. 22:17).

The Jews were not the last to refuse to come to Jesus that they might have life. Tens of thousands today have heard the invitation and refused to accept it. *All have sinned;* therefore by nature all are *dead* in trespasses and sins. Spiritual life is only in Christ, the fountain of ALL life—but in order for sinners to benefit from Christ, they must come TO Him by faith and believe on Him as Saviour. He who sincerely *believes* will come to Jesus and receive Him. The real reason unbelievers do not come to Jesus is that they have no desire to come to Him. Consequently they die in their sins and spend eternity in hell. The reason men are lost must be attributed to man's own will, not God's will. It is God's will to save all who will come to Him by Jesus Christ, but men love darkness rather than light because their deeds are evil. They do not come to God because *they have no will* to come to Him. Men spend eternity in hell—not because of the limitation of the shed blood, not because of Christ's lack of desire to redeem them, not for lack of a full invitation to all men—but because *their own stubborn will* sends them to hell. Man's ruin is entirely of himself because of his unwillingness to come to Jesus that he might have life.

Verse 41: *"I receive not honour from men."*

Had Jesus been seeking the praise of men He would not have made the preceding statements to the Jews. He was not *complaining* because the Jews refused to come to Him; He had not come to seek a great following or the praise of men. It was for their own sakes that He pointed out their unbelief. He was trying to show them the sad, darkened, ignorant state of their hearts spiritually. Jesus was not seeking followers from the standpoint of numbers. He could have called down twelve legions of angels to surround Him; He left heaven with its myriads of angels and the Old Testament saints in Paradise. He was not covetous of man's favor or praise. His glory came from God alone (v. 44).

Verse 42: *"But I know you, that ye have not the love of God in you."*

Here Jesus again declares His divinity by telling the Jews that He knew their hearts. The truth of the matter is, He had known them from the beginning—because He, with Jehovah, had borne with many generations of Israel. He knew they *professed* to worship the one true God, but by their conduct they proved the hypocrisy of their profession. They did not have the love of God abiding in them.

Verse 43: *"I am come in my Father's name, and ye receive me not: if another shall come in his own name, him ye will receive."*

The Jews refused to receive the Christ who came in the Father's name. If they had really loved God the Father they would have loved and honored God the Son.

"If another shall come in his own name, him ye will receive." This is a prophetic statement pointing to the coming of Antichrist who, when he does come, will be received as Messiah. He will be the *false* messiah, as set forth in the following Scriptures:

"Let no man deceive you by any means: for that day shall not come, except there come a falling away first, and that man of sin be revealed, the son of perdition; who opposeth and exalteth himself above all that is called God, or that is worshipped; so that he as God sitteth in the temple of God, shewing himself that he is God. Remember ye not, that, when I was yet with you, I told you these things? And now ye know what withholdeth that he might be revealed in his time. For the mystery of iniquity doth already work: only He who now letteth will let, until He be taken out of the way. And then shall that Wicked be revealed, whom the Lord shall consume with the spirit of His mouth, and shall destroy with the brightness of His coming: Even him, whose coming is after the working of Satan with all power and signs and lying wonders, and with all deceivableness of unrighteousness in them that perish; because they received not the love of the truth, that they might be saved" (II Thess. 2:3—10).

"I considered the horns, and, behold, there came up among them another little horn, before whom there were three of the first horns plucked up by the roots: and, behold, in this horn were eyes like the eyes of man, and a mouth speaking great things" (Dan. 7:8).

"And the beast was taken, and with him the false prophet that wrought miracles before him, with which he deceived them that had received the mark of the beast, and them that worshipped his image. These both were cast alive into a lake of fire burning with brimstone" (Rev. 19:20).

In our present verse, Jesus pointed to the future national reception of Antichrist, the Man of Sin. The *principle* of Antichrist was working in their hearts even at that very moment. They were forerunners of the nation's complete apostasy which will display itself immediately after the Rapture of the Church when the miracle-working Antichrist presents himself to the world and announces that he is God. He will sit in the temple professing to BE God—*and the nation Israel will receive him!* There will be, however, a remnant of 144,000 of the children of Israel who will be sealed to present the message of the Gospel of the kingdom during the time of great tribulation—a period of approximately seven years, the "time of Jacob's trouble."

"Anti" means *opposite*. Jesus came to declare God to man; He came to do the *will* of God. Antichrist will come in his own name, he will demand honor unto himself, he will seek worldly praise and glory. He will be exactly opposite to the Christ whom the Jews rejected.

With God there is no neutrality: men must either *receive* Christ—or *reject* Him and suffer the blinding delusions of the powers of the underworld, the powers of darkness. Men are either *with* Christ, or against Him; they are on His side or on the side of *Satan.* Jesus made this very clear to the Pharisees when they accused Him of casting out demons by the power of Beelzebub, prince of devils. The account is found in Matthew 12:22–32. In verse 30 of that passage Jesus said, *"He that is not with me is against me; and he that gathereth not with me scattereth abroad."*

The Antichrist will be Satan in flesh, just as Jesus was *God* in flesh. Satan is a self-made personality; pride caused him to become the deceiver, the murderer, the liar that he is. (Read Isaiah 14 and Ezekiel 28.) Antichrist will be revealed immediately after the Rapture of the Church. He will demand worship, and the Jews will worship and honor him as true Messiah. Jesus declared that Satan is the prince of this world; the Word of God proclaims him as the prince of the power of the air, the god of this age. Antichrist will possess all the power the devil himself possesses; he will work mighty miracles, even calling down fire from heaven. We read much concerning this personality in the book of Daniel, and also in The Revelation. He will not be revealed to the Church, however, for before the Antichrist is revealed Jesus will come the second time to receive His bride. There are many antichrists today—the correct classification for all who oppose the pure doctrine of Jesus Christ, His virgin birth, His atonement (His death, burial, and resurrection), His coming again; but there will be a personal Antichrist, the Man of Sin, the last world dictator. He will deceive all who do not have the seal of God in their forehead.

Verse 44:   *"How can ye believe, which receive honour one of another, and seek not the honour that cometh from God only?"*

There has never been a more religious people than the Jews, nor a more zealous people; but in spite of their professed zeal and religious demonstrations, they cared more for the praise of men than they cared about pleasing God. They sought honor and praise from one another. Jesus described them as doing all their works "to be seen of men: they make broad their phylacteries, and enlarge the borders of their garments, and love the uppermost rooms at feasts, and the chief seats in the synagogues, and greetings in the markets, and to be called of men, Rabbi, Rabbi" (Matt. 23:5—7). They were so occupied with praising each other, it was not possible for them to believe on Jesus until they stopped their earthly-mindedness and with sincere, honest heart sought God's praise rather than the praise of men.

The divine and eternal principle Jesus laid down here is simply the difference between true faith and counterfeit faith, the connection between the state of man's heart and his possessing the gift of faith. True faith is not in the head, it does not satisfy the intellect, and it is not simply being convinced intellectually; it has to do with the state of the heart. Insincerity of heart is a barrier to true believing. The person who is not completely honest of heart in his desire to know the truth will never find peace and satisfaction. Isaiah 26:3 says, "Thou wilt keep him in perfect peace, whose mind is stayed on thee: because he trusteth in thee." There can be no idols in the heart if we are to have perfect peace. Jesus must be in full control of soul, spirit, and body. The *good ground* are *"they which in an honest and good heart, having heard the Word, keep it, and bring forth fruit with patience"* (Luke 8:15).

Verses 45 and 46: *"Do not think that I will accuse you to the Father: there is one that accuseth you, even Moses, in whom ye trust. For had ye believed Moses, ye would have believed me: for he wrote of me."*

The Jews claimed to believe Moses, they clung to the *Law* of Moses and professed to hold him in respect and reverence; but the fact that they rejected Jesus was proof that they *did not* believe Moses—and Moses himself *accused* them of unbelief through the Scriptures God had given him. They read the books of Moses in the synagogues daily, and the words they read from his writings witnessed against them and declared their unbelief. Moses predicted this unbelief in Deuteronomy 31:25—27: "Moses commanded the Levites, which bare the ark of the covenant of the Lord, saying, *Take this book of the law, and put it in the side of the ark of the covenant of the Lord your God, THAT IT MAY BE THERE FOR A WITNESS AGAINST THEE.*

*For I know thy rebellion, and thy stiff neck: behold, while
I am yet alive with you this day, ye have been rebellious
against the Lord; and how much more after my death?"*

In verse 46 Jesus amplified what He had said in verse
45. Christ is so pre-eminent in the writings of Moses, the
witness of Moses was so clear concerning the coming of
the Messiah, that if the Jews had really *believed* Moses they
would have recognized their Christ and believed on Him
also. All five of the books of Moses prophesy concerning
Christ—in type, in typical persons, in ceremonies, feasts,
and offerings.

The liberals and modernists deny much of the Scripture
God has given to us through Moses—but you will notice
that Jesus spoke of him as a real person, a prophet, a man
of history who lived, and served, and wrote with authority.
Moses was inspired of God, he was God's faithful servant
and prophet, to him God gave the law—and surely God
honored Moses as no other man was ever honored, for He
came down from heaven and personally supervised his fun-
eral: "So Moses the servant of the Lord died there in the
land of Moab, according to the word of the Lord. And
(God) buried him in a valley in the land of Moab, over
against Beth-peor: *but no man knoweth of his sepulchre
unto this day"* (Deut. 34:5,6).

Verse 47: *"But if ye believe not his writings, how shall
ye believe my words?"*

Those who reject the books of Moses, *reject Christ.* Those
who reject Christ reject the books of Moses. To believe in
one is to believe in the other. To deny one is to deny
the other.

Notice the contrast between *"writings"* and *"words."*
Jesus was reminding the Jews that *writings* are accepted
and relied upon more than "sayings." If they did not believe the writings of Moses (and they did not), was it likely
that they would believe what Jesus said? The Greek word
here for "writings" is generally translated *letters,* as in

Luke 23:38. In II Timothy 3:15 it is rendered *Scriptures*. To me, this would be strong indirect evidence of the verbal inspiration of the Bible—God-breathed, dictated to holy men who penned down the message of the Holy Ghost.

As we come to the close of this great chapter, let us notice the charges Jesus brought against the Jews in this last section:

"Ye have not His Word abiding in you" (v. 38).

"Ye will not come to me, that ye might have life" (v. 40).

"Ye have not the love of God in you" (v. 42).

"I am come in my Father's name, and ye receive me not" (v. 43).

"Ye...seek not the honour that cometh from God only" (v. 44).

"Ye will not believe me because you do not believe Moses (vv. 46,47).

The basic charge, however, lies in verse 38. This explains all the other charges Jesus brought against the Jews. *If they had received the WORD,* then the other charges would not have been made against them. We are saved by hearing and receiving God's Word and trusting in the shed blood of Jesus as revealed to us by the Scriptures.

As we read the Scriptures and look into the mirror of God's Word, the perfect law of liberty that is able to make known God's plan of salvation, may we pray without ceasing that God will plant within us a deep love for the Word of God, and open our spiritual eyes that we may see the Saviour. He is there, on every page, in every verse; and if we would please God we must honor, cherish, reverence, and worship His only begotten Son, the Lord Jesus Christ, our Saviour!

CHAPTER VI

1. After these things Jesus went over the sea of Galilee, which is the sea of Tiberias.

2. And a great multitude followed him, because they saw his miracles which he did on them that were diseased.

3. And Jesus went up into a mountain, and there he sat with his disciples.

4. And the passover, a feast of the Jews, was nigh.

5. When Jesus then lifted up his eyes, and saw a great company come unto him, he saith unto Philip, Whence shall we buy bread, that these may eat?

6. And this he said to prove him: for he himself knew what he would do.

7. Philip answered him, Two hundred pennyworth of bread is not sufficient for them, that every one of them may take a little.

8. One of his disciples, Andrew, Simon Peter's brother, saith unto him,

9. There is a lad here, which hath five barley loaves, and two small fishes: but what are they among so many?

10. And Jesus said, Make the men sit down. Now there was much grass in the place. So the men sat down, in number about five thousand.

11. And Jesus took the loaves; and when he had given thanks, he distributed to the disciples, and the disciples to them that were set down; and likewise of the fishes as much as they would.

12. When they were filled, he said unto his disciples, Gather up the fragments that remain, that nothing be lost.

13. Therefore they gathered them together, and filled twelve baskets with the fragments of the five barley loaves, which remained over and above unto them that had eaten.

14. Then those men, when they had seen the miracle that Jesus did, said, This is of a truth that prophet that should come into the world.

15. When Jesus therefore perceived that they would come and take him by force, to make him a king, he departed again into a mountain himself alone.

16. And when even was now come, his disciples went down unto the sea,

17. And entered into a ship, and went over the sea toward Capernaum. And it was now dark, and Jesus was not come to them.

18. And the sea arose by reason of a great wind that blew.

19. So when they had rowed about five and twenty or thirty furlongs, they see Jesus walking on the sea, and drawing nigh unto the ship: and they were afraid.

20. But he saith unto them, It is I; be not afraid.

21. Then they willingly received him into the ship: and immediately the ship was at the land whither they went.

22. The day following, when the people which stood on the other side of the sea saw that there was none other boat there, save that one whereinto his disciples were entered, and that Jesus went not with his disciples into the boat, but that his disciples were gone away alone;

23. (Howbeit there came other boats from Tiberias nigh unto the place where they did eat bread, after that the Lord had given thanks:)

24. When the people therefore saw that Jesus was not there, neither his disciples, they also took shipping, and came to Capernaum, seeking for Jesus.

25. And when they had found him on the other side of the sea, they said unto him, Rabbi, when camest thou hither?

26. Jesus answered them and said, Verily, verily, I say unto you, Ye seek me, not because ye saw the miracles, but because ye did eat of the loaves, and were filled.

27. Labour not for the meat which perisheth, but for that meat which endureth unto everlasting life, which the Son of man shall give unto you: for him hath God the Father sealed.

28. Then said they unto him, What shall we do, that we might work the works of God?

29. Jesus answered and said unto them, This is the work of God, that ye believe on him whom he hath sent.

30. They said therefore unto him, What sign shewest thou then, that we may see, and believe thee? what dost thou work?

31. Our fathers did eat manna in the desert; as it is written, He gave them bread from heaven to eat.

32. Then Jesus said unto them, Verily, verily, I say unto you, Moses gave you not that bread from heaven; but my Father giveth you the true bread from heaven.

33. For the bread of God is he which cometh down from heaven, and giveth life unto the world.

34. Then said they unto him, Lord, evermore give us this bread.

35. And Jesus said unto them, I am the bread of life: he that cometh to me shall never hunger; and he that believeth on me shall never thirst.

36. But I said unto you, That ye also have seen me, and believe not.

37. All that the Father giveth me shall come to me; and him that cometh to me I will in no wise cast out.

38. For I came down from heaven, not to do mine own will, but the will of him that sent me.

39. And this is the Father's will which hath sent me, that of all which he hath given me I should lose nothing, but should raise it up again at the last day.

40. And this is the will of him that sent me, that every one which seeth the Son, and believeth on him, may have everlasting life: and I will raise him up at the last day.

41. The Jews then murmured at him, because he said, I am the bread which came down from heaven.

42. And they said, Is not this Jesus, the son of Joseph, whose father and mother we know? how is it then that he saith, I came down from heaven?

43. Jesus therefore answered and said unto them, Murmur not among yourselves.

44. No man can come to me, except the Father which hath sent me draw him: and I will raise him up at the last day.

45. It is written in the prophets, And they shall be all taught of God. Every man therefore that hath heard, and hath learned of the Father, cometh unto me.

46. Not that any man hath seen the Father, save he which is of God, he hath seen the Father.

47. Verily, verily, I say unto you, He that believeth on me hath everlasting life.

48. I am that bread of life.

49. Your fathers did eat manna in the wilderness, and are dead.

50. This is the bread which cometh down from heaven, that a man may eat thereof, and not die.

51. I am the living bread which came down from heaven: if any man eat of this bread, he shall live for ever: and the bread that I will give is my flesh, which I will give for the life of the world.

52. The Jews therefore strove among themselves, saying, How can this man give us his flesh to eat?

53. Then Jesus said unto them, Verily, verily, I say unto you, Except ye eat the flesh of the Son of man, and drink his blood, ye have no life in you.

54. Whoso eateth my flesh, and drinketh my blood, hath eternal life; and I will raise him up at the last day.

55. For my flesh is meat indeed, and my blood is drink indeed.

56. He that eateth my flesh, and drinketh my blood, dwelleth in

me, and I in him.

57. As the living Father hath sent me, and I live by the Father: so he that eateth me, even he shall live by me.

58. This is that bread which came down from heaven: not as your fathers did eat manna, and are dead: he that eateth of this bread shall live for ever.

59. These things said he in the synagogue, as he taught in Capernaum.

60. Many therefore of his disciples, when they had heard this, said, This is an hard saying; who can hear it?

61. When Jesus knew in himself that his disciples murmured at it, he said unto them, Doth this offend you?

62. What and if ye shall see the Son of man ascend up where he was before?

63. It is the spirit that quickeneth; the flesh profiteth nothing: the words that I speak unto you, they are spirit, and they are life.

64. But there are some of you that believe not. For Jesus knew from the beginning who they were that believed not, and who should betray him.

65. And he said, Therefore said I unto you, that no man can come unto me, except it were given unto him of my Father.

66. From that time many of his disciples went back, and walked no more with him.

67. Then said Jesus unto the twelve, Will ye also go away?

68. Then Simon Peter answered him, Lord, to whom shall we go? thou hast the words of eternal life.

69. And we believe and are sure that thou art that Christ, the Son of the living God.

70. Jesus answered them, Have not I chosen you twelve, and one of you is a devil?

71. He spake of Judas Iscariot the son of Simon: for he it was that should betray him, being one of the twelve.

In this chapter we find the account of one of the most spiritually significant miracles performed by Jesus during His entire earthly ministry. He worked many great works, but no other miracle was performed before so many people as was the feeding of the five thousand.

Also significant is the fact that this is the only miracle recorded by all four of the Gospel writers—Matthew, Mark, Luke, and John. Surely it must be important! It sets forth the omnipotent power of Christ—but it does more than that: *It points to the giving of His body that WE might have life*, and sets forth His mighty power by which He could lay His life down and take it again, that we might have life through His death, burial, and resurrection.

Feeding the Five Thousand

Verse 1: *"After these things Jesus went over the sea of Galilee, which is the sea of Tiberias."*

"After these things . . . ." There was an interval of time between the end of chapter 5 and the opening of chapter 6. We do not know how *long* a time elapsed, but if the feast referred to in the beginning of chapter 5 was the Passover, then almost twelve months of the Lord's ministry went unnoticed and unrecorded by John the Beloved (see v. 4). Chapter 6 deals with the ministry of Jesus in Galilee, and with the exception of the miracle at Cana (chapter 2) and the healing of the nobleman's son (chapter 4) this is the only record in the Gospel of John concerning the Lord's Galilaean ministry.

The sea of Galilee is a fresh-water lake approximately thirteen miles long and seven miles wide. The Jordan river empties into it, continues through it, and flows out on the other side. It lies about six hundred feet below sea level, and often sudden and severe thunderstorms arise across its waters. When I was in the Holy Land we crossed this sea in a very small motorboat, and in the crossing we encountered such a storm—and although it was not violent, the fact that it came on so suddenly assured me that the night the disciples were engulfed in a storm on the sea of Galilee, the weather could have been perfect when they left the shore and stormy before they reached the other side.

This sea was also called *"the sea of Tiberias."* (John is the only one of the Gospel writers who mentions this, which suggests that John's Gospel was written at a later date than Matthew, Mark, and Luke—perhaps written after the fall of Jerusalem. It seems reasonable to suppose that John used the name "Tiberias" because it was better known by the

Gentile readers, to whom John's Gospel was written, primarily.

Tiberias, a town situated on the west side of the sea of Galilee, was built by Herod Antipas, tetrarch of Galilee, sometime near the date of the birth of Jesus. It was a modern place in that day, and according to Josephus, the city continued to flourish for about forty years after the Lord's crucifixion. The town itself was named after Tiberias Caesar. About forty years after the crucifixion of Jesus, the Romans completely destroyed this city just as they destroyed every other city in Galilee.

This first verse tells us that Jesus crossed over the sea of Galilee, and according to Mark 6:31 this was in order that He might withdraw from the public eye for a season— "for there were many coming and going, and they had no leisure so much as to eat." Persecution by Herod's men was increasing also. John the Baptist had just been beheaded, and this could be another reason why Jesus departed to the other side of the lake. Comparing John's account with Matthew, Mark, and Luke, it seems that Jesus left the *west* coast of the sea of Galilee and landed on the northeast side near the town of Bethsaida. In Luke's account we are told that Jesus took the apostles "and went aside privately into a desert place belonging to the city called Bethsaida" (Luke 9:10).

Verse 2: *"And a great multitude followed Him, because they saw His miracles which He did on them that were diseased."*

The multitude did not follow Jesus because they believed Him to be the Messiah, nor because they believed that He was able to save them from sin. They saw His miracles, and the majority of the people followed Him out of curiosity and for excitement, hoping to see Him perform other miracles. They followed Jesus, yes—but they followed Him with the wrong motive. Those who profess to love and follow Jesus simply for personal comfort or gain are not born of the Spirit.

Verse 3: *"And Jesus went up into a mountain, and there He sat with His disciples."*

(The Greek reads, He went up "into THE mountain.") Bethsaida was situated in a mountainous area and it could be that Jesus had a favorite spot in this hill country where He went to commune with His heavenly Father, or where He rested from the multitudes who followed Him because of the miracles He had wrought in their presence. While we were visiting that area in the Holy Land, a missionary pointed out to us a very smooth, grassy spot at the base of the mountain, an inviting, amphitheatre-type place where five thousand people could easily have been seated, and some Bible scholars believe that this was the spot where Jesus fed the five thousand.

The *"disciples"* here probably refers to more than just the twelve; there could have been a score or more people in the group.

Notice, Jesus *"sat"*—denoting His humanity. He became weary in body and He loved to sit on the ground and fellowship with His disciples, even as *we* enjoy sitting at a picnic or in some other outdoor place, talking about the Word of God and exchanging experiences with fellow believers.

No doubt some of those who sat with Jesus that day did not continue to follow Him to the end. Only a short while later they turned back "and walked no more with Him" (v. 66). We still have such folk with us today. Ministers— especially *pastors*—have learned that not everyone who professes to love the Lord wholeheartedly can be depended upon to live up to their profession. There are *some,* thank God, who are faithful to the end; but some of us have learned through bitter experiences that men do not always tell the truth when they profess to be true disciples of the Lord Jesus Christ, fellow helpers with the ministers of the Gospel. The multitude departed from Jesus, and they will depart from the true minister today.

Verse 4:   *"And the passover, a feast of the Jews, was nigh."*

Again we notice the explanatory reference to "a feast of the *Jews,*" another explanation of Jewish customs, given for the benefit of Gentile readers.

"The passover . . . was nigh." Notice that Jesus did not go to *Jerusalem* to observe the Passover, but rather remained in Galilee. Up to the time He laid His life down for the sins of the world He always observed the ordinances of the law of Moses in order that He might fulfill all righteousness. Persecution of the early Christians had become severe in Jerusalem, and this fact evidently kept Jesus from going there. He was God as well as man, and in His perfect wisdom He deemed it wise not to go to Jerusalem just then; so He observed the Passover in Galilee.

The fact that it was the time of the Passover was the reason for a great multitude of people gathering so quickly, for at that time of the year Jews came from all over the known world, and thousands in transit on their way to Jerusalem would account for the gathering of five thousand so quickly.

It was not by accident that Jesus wrought this specific miracle at this particular time. The Passover feast was a time when the minds of the Jewish people were centered on the flesh of the lamb they would be eating, and of the blood that would be sprinkled. Jesus was always alert to every opportunity to present Himself to them as their own sacrificial Lamb, and He used this occasion to speak of the flesh and the blood which must be appropriated by those who wish to escape the damnation of hell.

Verses 5 and 6:   *"When Jesus then lifted up His eyes, and saw a great company come unto Him, He saith unto Philip, Whence shall we buy bread, that these may eat? And this He said to prove him: for He Himself knew what*

He would do."

John always emphasized the humanity as well as the divinity of Jesus, and the fact that He *"lifted up His eyes" and SAW the great crowd of people* does not mean that He did not know they would be there until He saw them with physical eyes.

Mark 6:34 tells us that when Jesus saw the people He "was moved with compassion toward them, because they were as sheep not having a shepherd: and He began to teach them many things."

Yes, Jesus had the heart of God—but He also had the heart of man and He knew that their bodies as well as their souls needed food. He was "moved with compassion toward them."   It encourages my heart and refreshes my soul to know that the same Jesus who looked out over five thousand hungry people (not counting women and children) and had compassion because of their need, also looks down today upon a crowded world and His great heart is touched with compassion for the poor, hungry multitudes of earth. He is still concerned about bread for the body, and "no good thing will He withhold from them that walk uprightly"; but many times God's hands are tied and the compassion of Jesus is hindered because men love sin and Satan more than they love God. When men love darkness rather than light, God has no alternative: under such conditions He *cannot* bestow His blessings upon whom He would.

Seeing the multitudes, Jesus asked Philip, *"Whence shall we buy bread, that these may eat?"* Philip was the logical one to ask where bread could be bought, because he was a native of Bethsaida, and if anyone knew where bread could be had in large quantities in that area, Philip certainly should know. But Jesus had another motive in asking the question: He knew what Philip would do, but He asked the question to prove him.

Five thousand hungry men, plus women and children, comprised a crowd of some magnitude; and since bread in that day was made by hand and baked in small ovens, there would not have been enough bread in the entire area to feed so great a crowd.   But Jesus knew exactly what would happen.   He knew the lad was there with his few loaves and fishes, He knew how the multitude would be fed; but He was dealing with men of slow hearts, and He therefore dealt with them as *man* would deal with man up to the point of the miracle of multiplying the loaves and fishes.

This was no accident; it did not just "happen"—it was foreordained of God before the world was.   Jesus came to work the works the Father had given Him to finish (John 5:36), and the feeding of the multitude at Passover time was one of those works, foreordained of God for that particular time to set the stage for the wonderful lesson on the bread of life.   Jesus *was* the bread that came down from the heavenly Father, that men might eat and never die spiritually.

Verse 7:   *"Philip answered Him, Two hundred pennyworth of bread is not sufficient for them, that every one of them may take a little."*

We do not know exactly what amount "two hundred pennyworth" would be in our money today, but it would certainly be much more than two dollars.   Some scholars have suggested that it would be six or seven pounds in English money, the equivalent of about twenty dollars in American currency.   But the point here is *not* how much bread two hundred pennies would have bought; the primary thought in this verse is that Philip, instead of thinking of *buying* the bread, should have said, "Master, you are equal to any occasion.   YOU feed them!"

Like Nicodemus, Philip was thinking in the realm of the natural.   He had not yet realized that this One whom he followed was God in flesh, the God who could supply bread for *five thousand* as easily as He could supply it for *five*.

Undoubtedly this two hundred pennies was the money in the common purse of the disciple band, and *Judas* carried the bag (John 12:6), so we do not know how Philip knew how much money it contained. But when Jesus asked him, "Whence shall we buy bread that these may eat?" Philip answered by giving Him a report on the state of the treasury.

This same sad situation is true today among many religionists. They value the results of their efforts by dollars and cents, not by souls won for Christ. Religion is becoming "big business" in America and around the world today, and if a certain undertaking is not a multi-million-dollar project, people look down on it and consider it unworthy of their time and effort, not realizing that God owns the cattle on a thousand hills, the silver and gold of the world are His, and we are but stewards in His service. Jesus asked the question of Philip in order to test his faith and to eventually prove to him that the Lord was Himself sufficient for any and all needs, able for any occasion.

Verses 8 and 9: *"One of His disciples, Andrew, Simon Peter's brother, saith unto Him, There is a lad here, which hath five barley loaves, and two small fishes: but what are they among so many?"*

While Philip and Judas were counting the pennies, Andrew was searching for bread—and he found it. Plenty of folk today are ready and willing to count the money, but not many are willing to go out in the highways and hedges and search for souls to give them the living bread. True, money matters must be taken care of, but money is secondary when compared to the souls of men. Andrew made his way through the crowd, and in that vast throng of people he found one little lad who had brought his lunch—five barley loaves and two small fishes.

These were not such loaves as we buy in the supermarket today. They were tiny loaves, more like our biscuits or buns, and it stands to reason that the fishes also were small; but it does not take much to accomplish big things when what little we have is surrendered to Jesus. He can take our *very little* and make it very *much*, as He did with the five loaves and two small fishes. He is still doing just that when we allow Him to take what we have and bless and multiply it. The tragedy today is that so few are willing for Jesus to have *them* along with what they possess!

Andrew had been with Jesus since the beginning of the Lord's ministry and had witnessed His miracles—even the changing of water into wine at the marriage in Cana. I am convinced that he knew Jesus could and would do the impossible. If he did not believe this, why did he search for even a small portion of food and persuade the lad to surrender his lunch into the Lord's hands? Even though he asked, "What are these among so many?" it seems evident to me that Andrew expected a miracle that would be adequate to the occasion.

Verse 10: *"And Jesus said, Make the men sit down. Now there was much grass in the place. So the men sat down, in number about five thousand."*

What a majestic contrast is presented here! Andrew had asked, "What are these among so many?" and Jesus answered very simply, "Make the men sit down." There was no excitement, no fretting, no irritation on His part because of the seeming lack of faith among His disciples; simply the instruction to seat the people. Mark 6:40 tells us, "They sat down in ranks, by hundreds, and by fifties." There was no confusion, no disorder. Jesus did nothing hurriedly or in a haphazard way. The Word of God clearly tells us, "Let all things be done decently and in order" (I Cor. 14:40).

"There was much grass in the place." This was in the springtime, just before the Passover—and in the Holy Land spring is the most beautiful time of the year. Cold weather has passed, the hot, burning heat of summer has not yet begun. The fields are green, and the poppies are blooming by tens of thousands. Against such a background, what a beautiful sight it must have been to see five thousand men and their families seated in orderly groups!

"So the men sat down, in number about five thousand."
John mentions only the men, but Matthew tells us that
there were "about five thousand men, *beside women and
children*" (Matt. 14:21). There is no contradiction here,
however, for the Greek word translated "men" in the first
part of our present verse is the word used for "people,"
and the word rendered "men" in the last part of the verse
is masculine, meaning "men only." So there were about
five thousand males, not counting wives and children. What
a sight, what an experience that must have been!

Verse 11: *"And Jesus took the loaves; and when He had
given thanks, He distributed to the disciples, and the disciples to them that were set down; and likewise of the
fishes as much as they would."*

Jesus did not make a big show by creating a heap or
mound of loaves and fishes. He did not come into the
world to be spectacular, but to offer men the bread of life.
It is a singular mark of His divinity that this is true, for
certainly *man* would have wanted to make a great show of
power in such a miracle as this! The Word tells us that
Jesus simply *"took the loaves—and when He had given
thanks"* He passed the food on to the disciples, who in
turn distributed it to the people where they were seated
on the ground.

The Greek word used here for *"thanks"* is the same word
used by Matthew, Mark, Luke, and Paul in speaking of the
Lord's Supper, where Jesus "gave thanks" when He took
the bread and the cup and passed them to His disciples.

As Jesus broke the bread and gave it to His disciples,
the miraculous multiplication of the bread took place; there
was a continual creation of bread, the loaf was constantly
replenished. The same thing happened as He broke the
fishes. He could have multiplied the loaves without breaking them, but in His breaking of the bread He was showing
the necessity for His broken body. His manner of distri-
bution of the loaves also shows us that the bread from heav-

en is sufficient for all—when one poor, hungry sinner receives the bread of life there is no less bread than before. God's grace abounds for all, and when one sinner is saved, that does not lessen the grace of God; there is still as much grace as before.   Jesus is the bread of life; His body was broken and His blood was shed for us.   We are saved by receiving His Word, and His precious blood washes away all sin for the believer.

Verse 12:   *"When they were filled, He said unto His disciples, Gather up the fragments that remain, that nothing be lost."*

"When they were filled" gives proof positive that the miracle was *real.*   Jesus served actual bread and fish; it was not a sensation, something the people simply imagined. They ate real food until they were filled and satisfied.   Further proof of this is the fact that Jesus instructed the disciples to *"gather up the fragments"*—a quantity of leftovers sufficient to fill twelve baskets!

Here is set forth a Christian principle: *we are not to be wasteful.*   Jesus instructed the disciples to gather up the remnants of the food "that nothing be lost."   It is a sin to waste the good things God affords for us, whether it be money, time, health, or opportunity.

Verse 13:   *"Therefore they gathered them together, and filled twelve baskets with the fragments of the five barley loaves, which remained over and above unto them that had eaten."*

Certainly none could deny that a mighty miracle had been wrought, for the entire multitude witnessed it. Some Bible scholars declare that this was the greatest miracle of our Lord's earthly ministry, and no doubt from many aspects they judge truly; but I think at best we are poor judges of such divine things, and little able to make comparisons. This miracle did manifest His creative power more than any of His other miracles—but since "without Him was not anything made that was made" it was not difficult for Him to take the loaves and fishes and multiply them to feed five thousand people. If we believe *"in the beginning, GOD,"* then we should have no trouble believing that God in flesh could take five loaves and two fishes, bless them, break them, and feed the multitudes! He could have fed five *million* people as easily and as sufficiently as He fed five thousand.

Verse 14: *"Then those men, when they had seen the miracle that Jesus did, said, This is of a truth that prophet that should come into the world."*

"Those men" here refers to the entire multitude of people who had just been fed. The Jews believed that any man sent from God or anointed by God was capable of working miracles, signs, and wonders, as evidenced by Nicodemus in chapter 3, verse 2, when he said, "Rabbi, we know that thou art a teacher come from God: for no man can do these miracles that thou doest, except God be with him."

This multitude had just witnessed a tremendous miracle— and since signs and wonders were expected to accompany any prophet or messenger of God, they confessed, "This is of a truth that Prophet that should come into the world." They thought Jesus was "that Prophet like unto Moses." They were familiar with the books of the law and knew that an outstanding Prophet would appear. John the Baptist had strengthened that belief when he announced the coming of One greater than himself, and after the fact of so great a miracle they said, "Truly, this IS that Prophet whom we have been expecting!" It is tragic that they were willing to accept Jesus as a great man, a great prophet, but they were not willing to accept Him as God in flesh, their expected Messiah. Men today are willing to accept Him as a great teacher, a great person, but liberals and modernists deny that He was virgin-born, God Incarnate.

Verse 15: *"When Jesus therefore perceived that they*

*would come and take Him by force, to make Him a king,
He departed again into a mountain Himself alone."*

This declares Christ's deity, His divine knowledge of the
secret intent of the hearts of the people: He knew they
were about to take Him by force and make Him king. The
Jews were looking for a political leader, and it is easy to
see why they thought that one who could work such a miracle as they had just witnessed could certainly lead them
out of Roman bondage. They were much more concerned
about their slavery under Roman rule than they were about
the slavery of sin that bound them. They were looking for
a political deliverer, not a Messiah to save them from sin.

Jesus withdrew from them and *"departed again into a
mountain Himself alone."*   (Again the Greek reads "THE
mountain.")   Matthew 14:23 and Mark 6:46 tell us that
Jesus sent the multitude away and went into the mountain to pray.

Verses 16 and 17:   *"And when even was now come, His
disciples went down unto the sea, and entered into a ship,
and went over the sea toward Capernaum. And it was now
dark, and Jesus was not come to them."*

Matthew and Mark both tell us that the Lord Jesus "con-
strained" the disciples to get into the ship and travel to
the other side. (The Greek reads, "He *obliged* or *compelled*
them.") They were still ignorant of the spiritual nature of
Christ's kingdom and were no doubt ready to go along with
the mob, put Him on the throne, and proclaim Him king.
Probably that is why He asked them,"Whom say the people
that I am?" (Luke 9:18). If the disciples were thinking along
with the masses, Jesus *knew* their thoughts and how contrary they were to the purpose for which He had come into
the world.   He had not come to be enthroned by force at
the demand of a mob. He knew that He *would be* King
of kings and Lord of lords, but the crown of thorns must
precede the kingly crown.   He came the first time to pay

the sin-debt; He will come the second time to reign in right-eousness, and the Church will reign with Him.

The disciples *"went down unto the sea, and entered into a ship, and went over the sea toward Capernaum."* We are not told who the ship belonged to, but very probably it belonged to Peter or one of the other fishermen. They had left their nets to follow Jesus, but that does not necessarily mean that they had disposed of all of their equipment. The last chapter in this Gospel tells us that after the crucifixion, yes, even after Jesus had appeared to the disciples after the resurrection, Peter chose to return to his nets. He said to the other disciples, "I go a fishing." They answered, "We also go with thee." Evidently they entered into their own fishing vessel which they kept on the sea of Galilee and had used many times in their ministry with Jesus.

"And it was now dark, and Jesus was not come to them." These words also have a tremendous spiritual truth. The Greek word here translated "dark" means *darkness.* Without Jesus on board, all was darkness. The disciples were in the midst of the sea of Galilee, a treacherous body of water where disastrous storms came quickly. Four of these men were fishermen; they had sailed that sea since boyhood, and they well knew the danger of being on its waters in the middle of the night. They sensed their need for the Saviour's presence, they experienced the discomfort and disappointment of His absence. We, too, need the company of Jesus every moment of every hour of our lives. Without Him, life becomes dark, stormy, and dangerous.

Verse 18: *"And the sea arose by reason of a great wind that blew."*

The Greek here reads, "The sea was being raised, stirred." The waves were beginning to lash against the sides of the little ship. Typically speaking, the disciples experienced what believers still experience today. They had just enjoyed a mountain-top experience—they had witnessed the miracle of the feeding of the five thousand. This experience was followed by darkness at the midnight hour, tempest-tossed, in the midst of the stormy sea of Galilee. So Christians today enjoy the miracle of the new birth and become possessors of the Holy Spirit, being made new in Christ. We enjoy our first love, and then suddenly the storm clouds lower, temptations begin to beat upon us, trials beset us; but thank God, "we are more than conquerors through Him that loved us."

Jesus had become the object of the disciples' faith in the matter of material provision as they witnessed the miracle of the loaves and fishes. Now He makes Himself the object of their faith as having to do with fear and danger. He who had given thanks as He broke the bread and literally created food for thousands, was also Creator—and Commander—of the wind and waters. The purpose of the storm was in the plan and program of God, to lead the disciples into a deeper faith and more complete trust in Him. As we grow in grace we increase in faith.

Verses 19—21: *"So when they had rowed about five and twenty or thirty furlongs, they see Jesus walking on the sea, and drawing nigh unto the ship: and they were afraid. But He saith unto them, It is I; be not afraid. Then they willingly received Him into the ship: and immediately the ship was at the land whither they went."*

Notice that the disciples were rowing, they were not using sails. Matthew and Mark both tell us that the wind was "contrary," and from this we gather that the wind was against them, which would account for their "rowing" instead of using sails. They had rowed twenty-five or thirty furlongs before Jesus came to them walking on the sea.

Some might ask, "Why did not the Scriptures say *exactly* what the distance was?" Let it be remembered that the disciples were in a boat, tossed about on a stormy sea on a very dark night, and they could not be expected to give an exact measure of their distance from shore. The *Holy Spirit* knew to the hair's breadth, and could have told John the precise number of furlongs; but it so pleased Him to let John use the popular mode of expression—*"about* twenty-five or thirty furlongs." (Webster's dictionary defines a "furlong" as approximately one-eighth of a mile. So we are safe in saying that the disciples were in the middle of the sea, two or three miles from land in either direction.)

In the midst of the sea they saw Jesus *"walking on the sea, and drawing nigh unto the ship: and they were afraid."* Here was suspension of all the laws of nature—Jesus walking across the stormy sea as you or I would walk along a concrete sidewalk. It was as easy for Him to *walk* on the waters as it was for Him to *create* them in the first place. Again we see the divinity of Jesus. The entire miracle was of the supernatural, and there is nothing that can unnerve and alarm human nature quite as much as being brought suddenly face to face with power (or beings) connected with another world. The disciples were only men; they did not have the New Testament as we do today, and while they accepted Jesus as their Messiah they had known Him personally but a short while.

Matthew gives an interesting account of this experience. In Matthew 14:24—33 we read:

"The ship was now in the midst of the sea, tossed with waves: for the wind was contrary. And in the fourth watch of the night Jesus went unto them, walking on the sea. And when the disciples saw Him walking on the sea, they were troubled, saying, It is a spirit; and they cried out for fear. But straightway Jesus spake unto them, saying, Be of good cheer; it is I; be not afraid.

"And Peter answered Him and said, Lord, if it be thou, bid me come unto thee on the water. And He said, Come. And when Peter was come down out of the ship, he walked on the water, to go to Jesus. But when he saw the wind boisterous, he was afraid; and beginning to sink, he cried, saying, Lord, save me. And immediately Jesus stretched forth His hand, and caught him, and said unto him, O thou of little faith, wherefore didst thou doubt? And when they

were come into the ship, the wind ceased. Then they that
were in the ship came and worshipped Him, saying, Of a
truth thou art the Son of God!"

Peter was spokesman for the group at this time, and I
believe it was because the rest of the disciples were fright-
ened beyond speech; but Peter cried out to the Lord. Not
only did *Jesus* walk on the water, but He gave *Peter* power
to do the same (and of course, Peter walked on the WORD).
When Peter said, "Lord, IF it be thou, bid me come unto
thee on the water," Jesus did not say, "Peter, it IS I."
No, He simply invited, *"Come!"* and on that Word Peter
walked. As long as he kept his eyes on Jesus all was well;
but the moment he turned his gaze to the angry waves
around him, he began to sink. You will notice that when
Peter began to sink, he did not dress up his prayer, he did
not put any fancy, Sunday-morning "frills" on it such as
"most holy, righteous, omniscient, omnipotent, omnipresent,
almighty, sovereign God." No, if he had taken time to do
that, the fish would have been nibbling his toes before he
finished the high-sounding, great, swelling, noble words of
the introduction to his prayer. There was no time for arti-
ficiality or hypocrisy. Peter simply prayed from his heart,
"LORD, SAVE ME!" Three little words—but Jesus stretched
out His hand and caught him, lifted him up, reprimanded
him for his lack of faith, and *"when they were come into
the ship, the wind ceased."*

It is right to recognize the sovereignty of Almighty God;
but we do not need to "dress up" our prayers in order to
be heard. God knows the heart, and if our prayers are
from the heart God understands. Even when we are under
such burdens that we cannot pray, words will not come,
"the Spirit Himself maketh intercession for us with groan-
ings which cannot be uttered" (Rom. 8:26).

When Jesus entered the little ship it immediately arrived
at its destination—further evidence to the disciples that He
was truly the Christ and not a spirit. When He stepped
onto the little ship, distance was nullified; His presence

brought protection and deliverance. He does the same to-day, spiritually speaking, for all who will believe on Him and trust Him. All believers are in a stormy world. Jesus said, "In the world ye shall have tribulation: but be of good cheer; I have overcome the world" (John 16:33).

The Church, too, is in a stormy world; but when Jesus comes for His Church we will instantaneously be taken out of the storm and be at our eternal destination—with Jesus. Thus the disciples here are a type of the Church in the world—and praise God, Jesus is coming soon, with the voice of the archangel and the trump of God, when the dead in Christ will be raised and living saints will be caught up to meet Jesus in the clouds in the air!

Without a doubt these two miracles (the feeding of the five thousand and Jesus' walking on the water) were given to prepare the hearts and minds of the disciples to receive the tremendous truths which were to be immediately declared in the Lord's discourse on the bread of life. They were on the other side of Calvary; they did not have the New Testament as we do, and their witnessing the miracle, receiving the broken bread and fishes, would help them to understand when Jesus announced Himself as the bread of life. When He said, "My flesh is meat indeed and my blood is drink indeed," they would immediately remember the miracle of the loaves and fishes. Thus they would understand and would exercise faith in Jesus—not only as Messiah, but as the bread of life. The breaking of the bread and the Lord's walking on the water strengthened their spiritual comprehension and helped them to have more faith in Jesus as Messiah, Son of God, and yet receive Him as man.

The Next Day

Verses 22—24: *"The day following, when the people which stood on the other side of the sea saw that there was none other boat there, save that one whereinto His disciples were entered, and that Jesus went not with His*

disciples into the boat, but that His disciples were gone
away alone; (howbeit there came other boats from Tiberias
nigh unto the place where they did eat bread, after that
the Lord had given thanks:) When the people therefore
saw that Jesus was not there, neither His disciples, they
also took shipping, and came to Capernaum, seeking for
Jesus."

The multitude had observed that Jesus did not accompany
His disciples when they entered into the ship, but when
they searched for Him the next morning they could not
find Him. No wonder they were amazed when they found
Him at Capernaum! They knew He had not sailed with
the disciples; they knew He could not have walked around
the shore and reached the other side so quickly. They never once thought of His having crossed the sea *miraculously,*
walking on the water.

Verse 23 is parenthetical; it means that there were other
boats from the city of Tiberias, not too far from where Jesus
had wrought the miracle, though there were no boats at
the exact spot from which the disciples embarked, except
the little ship on which they sailed. The Holy Spirit carefully placed this parenthetical statement here in order to
show how the multitude followed the Lord to Capernaum.
If this verse of explanation were not here, the liberals and
modernists would ask, "How did the crowds get to the
other side of the sea if there were no other boats?"

"The people" in verse 24 does not necessarily refer to
the entire five thousand. When Jesus sent them away (Matt.
14:23) undoubtedly the greater part of them went to their
homes, or continued traveling toward Jerusalem to attend
the Passover. Evidently the people who *"also took shipping
and came to Capernaum"* were that portion of the five
thousand who did not return home or journey on into Jerusalem.

Those who followed the Lord to Capernaum probably included many who had followed Him from place to place
without any spiritual desire (vv. 26,36). Wherever He went,

they were there to witness His miracles. They sought after Him—but for the wrong purpose. Their following was carnal. They loved the excitement and glamor, with the ultimate hope of getting something out of it.

Verse 25: *"And when they had found Him on the other side of the sea, they said unto Him, Rabbi, when camest thou hither?"*

The Scripture does not tell us exactly where the crowd found Jesus. Verse 59 tells us that He taught in the synagogue at Capernaum, but it is unlikely that the people disembarked and went immediately from the ship to the synagogue. It could be that they found Jesus on the shore of the sea of Galilee, and He spoke to them concerning the bread of life as recorded in verses 26 through 40; and then as they "murmured at Him" (v. 41) they could have traveled on to the synagogue as He continued the discourse.

"When camest thou hither?" They were surprised to find Jesus on the opposite side of the sea of Galilee. When they had last seen Him He was going into the mountain to pray, and they could not understand how He could possibly have reached Capernaum since He did not sail in the ship with the disciples.

It is interesting to note that Jesus did not answer their question. We could suggest many reasons *why* He did not, but I personally believe it was because if He had *told* them how He arrived on the other side, they would not have believed Him. Furthermore, if He had told them that He had *walked across the water* they would probably have taken up stones to stone Him, as they did in other instances. He knew their minds, their thoughts, their hearts; and He wasted no words in answering their question. Instead, He replied by exposing their actual motive for following Him.

Christ's Discourse on the Bread of Life

The discourse on the bread of life is divided into two

parts: (1) In verses 26 to 40 the Lord discusses the error
made by the multitude in applying the miracle of the loaves
and fishes only to physical need, rather than to deeper
spiritual needs.   Instead of answering their spoken question
He answered the state of their hearts.   (2) In verses 43 to
59 He replies to the murmuring Jews, His own people.   In
each of those divisions, however, we find the same two tremendous truths: "First, *Christ is the bread from heaven,
the bread of life;* and second, Christ came from God, sent
OF God, for a singular purpose: *that all who eat of this
bread shall live forever.*

Two "double verilies" occur in each of the two divisions.
In the first part the "double verilies" introduce denials by
Jesus concerning the suppositions of His hearers (vv. 26,32),
and in the second part of the discourse they introduce conditions for the possession of life eternal (vv. 47,53).   Also in
each of these divisions Christ speaks of the provision God
the Father made for life for the world (vv. 33,51).   Each of
the two parts of this great discourse contains a twofold
declaration concerning the unbeliever's coming to Christ
(vv. 37,44).

Each of the two divisions contains a reference to the
manna which God provided in the wilderness (vv. 32,58).
Also in each of the two parts we find divine assurance that
Christ Jesus the Lord will raise all true believers from the
dead (vv. 40,54).

Verse 26:   *"Jesus answered them and said, Verily, verily,
I say unto you, Ye seek me, not because ye saw the miracles, but because ye did eat of the loaves, and were filled."*

We find this same situation today.   Certainly to feed the
hungry and clothe the naked is a Christian act, but unless
we use wisdom provided by the Lord in such matters we
can do more harm than good.   Ministers in the church must
use keen discrimination in giving relief to the poor and
destitute.   When the church continually furnishes food and
money for the poor, those who are helped sometimes make

false professions of faith in order to assure the food and
money continuing to come in.   There are those who will
join a church and attend services simply for what they can
get in temporal things—food, clothing, money to pay bills.
To follow Christ for such things is nothing short of hypocrisy.   There are times when most of us truly do need help
from other believers; but an honest, sincere, able-bodied
person needs such help only temporarily.   When the valleys
are passed and the hard places are overcome, he whose
heart is right with God will provide for his own family
(I Tim. 5:8).

Verse 27:   *"Labour not for the meat which perisheth, but
for that meat which endureth unto everlasting life, which
the Son of man shall give unto you: for Him hath God
the Father sealed."*

Here is something *forbidden.*   We are *not* to labor only
for the things that satisfy the body.   It is honorable to work
for food and clothing, but we are to look beyond physical
needs and put spirit and soul first.   *"Labour not"* is negative, but there is a positive side here, too: we are instructed to labor for spiritual food—*"that meat which endureth unto everlasting life."*

This does not pertain to redemption (only the blood of
Jesus Christ redeems).   It means that we are to be laborers
together with Christ, good soldiers, faithful stewards.   If we
obey the negative part of the command and "labour not"
exclusively for things that perish, and then obey the positive
part of the command and strive earnestly for things that
satisfy the spirit and soul, we have a divine promise: *Jesus
will provide that which satisfies,* spiritual food that endures
forever and brings everlasting life.

"For Him hath the Father sealed."   Here is divine declaration that Jesus Christ is the *only* one appointed by God
to give this spiritual food.   He is the sole dispenser of spiritual bread, spiritual meat, spiritual milk and spiritual drink.
Actually, the reference is to the custom of setting apart a

person for a specific ministry or mission. In the Old Testament we read, "Write ye also for the Jews, as it liketh you, in the king's name, and seal it with the king's ring: *for the writing which is written in the king's name, and sealed with the king's ring, may no man reverse*" (Esther 8:8).

The statement here in verse 27 signifies that in the eternal ages behind us, before the world was, in the eternal councils of God the Father, God the Son, and God the Holy Ghost, the Father appointed, commissioned, and *sealed* the Son, the Word Incarnate, to be the sole giver of everlasting life. The office Jesus occupies was set apart for Him by God the Father, and He is the only one who can fill that office. He is seated at the right hand of the Majesty; He earned that position because He finished the work the Father gave Him to do. He fulfilled the law and the prophets, and satisfied the righteousness and holiness of God.

The miracle of the loaves and fishes had prepared the way and set the stage for Jesus to announce Himself as the bread of life, and He began that announcement by telling the Jews not to labor for things that perish, but for the things of the Spirit, things that lead to everlasting life.

Verse 28: *"Then said they unto Him, What shall we do, that we might work the works of God?"*

The Jews seemed to understand that the words of Jesus in the preceding verse had a moral implication in contrast with their materialistic ideas, and they wanted to know how they could do works that would please God and thus bring them into possession of this imperishable, spiritual bread of which He had been speaking. These were dedicated religionists—but their religion was one of "do's" and "dont's," of feasts and ceremonies; and the reply Jesus gave them struck at their idea that the receipt of favor, mercy, and grace from God depended upon human merit, self-effort, and good works. Man's fallen condition should in itself be enough to remove such ideas from the mind, and yet religions that *major* on works are growing by leaps and bounds. Men fail to recognize their wholly depraved condition—helpless, hopeless, hellbound. Man has corrupted anything and everything he has ever touched, so God ruled man out of it so far as redemption is concerned. We are not redeemed with corruptible things, but with the precious blood of Jesus. God alone meets the need of man in his lost condition, for what God demands, only God could provide. The LAW could not provide redemption because of the weakness of the flesh (Rom. 8:1—3). Only God could meet man's need for redemption, and He met that need in the Person of His Son, the Lord Jesus Christ.

Verse 29: *"Jesus answered and said unto them, This is the work of God, that ye believe on Him whom God hath sent."*

This is the doctrine set forth in Romans and Galatians through the inspired pen of the Apostle Paul—*justification by faith* in contrast with the futility and emptiness of good works. *Grace* says, "Trust." The *law* says, "Do." Because of the weakness of the flesh, man could not do what the law demanded; but *Jesus IN flesh FULFILLED the law* and therefore became "the *end* of the law for righteousness to everyone that believeth" (Rom. 10:4). We work the works of God when we believe on Jesus. We are saved by trusting *Jesus*—not by "works" of righteousness, but *by faith IN the Righteous One.* The Jews, however, were not willing to *accept* redemption by faith. They wanted something tangible, some outward evidence that they could see, feel, or experience. To them, "seeing" was *believing.* They said to Jesus, *"Come down from the cross* and we will believe on you!" but HE said, *"Believe* on me, and I will give you everlasting life."

Man wants to "do" something, "perform" something, "live" something. The rich young ruler in Matthew 19:16— 22 came running to Jesus, fell down before Him and asked, "Good Master, what good thing shall I DO, that I may have eternal life?" Yet because of unbelief he refused to do what Jesus told him to do. He believed that Jesus was a good man, a great teacher; but he did NOT believe that He was the Son of God, God in flesh—and Jesus knew this.

Saul of Tarsus asked, "Lord, what wilt thou have me to DO?" (Acts 9:6). On the Damascus road, blinded by the heavenly light, prostrate on the ground, he heard and obeyed the words of Jesus. He was saved—and subsequently became the greatest preacher the world has ever known, apart from the Lord Himself.

The Philippian jailer asked Paul and Silas, "What must I DO to be saved?" (Acts 16:30). They replied, "Believe on the Lord Jesus Christ, and thou shalt be saved, and thy house. And they spake unto him *the Word of the Lord,* and to all that were in his house." The Word brings faith, and faith exercised in the finished work of Jesus brings salvation.

There was nothing wrong with the question, *"What shall we DO?"* What was wrong was that Jesus instructed the Jews—and they refused to do as He instructed. That is the sad case *today*—when God's minister tells the people (from God's Word) what they must do to be saved, the masses refuse to obey. Only a small minority are willing to simply believe on Jesus, trust in His shed blood and finished work, and not try to save themselves by works of righteousness or by joining a church, or by baptism, or by any of the many other things that can be counted as "good works." After all, according to Isaiah 64:6, *"We are all as an unclean thing, and all our righteousnesses are as filthy rags;* and we all do fade as a leaf; and our iniquities, like the wind, have taken us away."

CHRIST is our righteousness (I Cor. 1:30), Christ "whom God hath set forth to be a propitiation through faith in His blood, to declare His righteousness for the remission of sins that are past, through the forbearance of God; to declare, I say, at this time His righteousness: that He might be just, and the justifier of him which believeth in Jesus. . . Therefore we conclude that a man is justified by faith without the deeds of the law" (Rom. 3:25—28). Also, "To him that worketh not, but believeth on Him that justifieth the ungodly, his faith is counted for righteousness" (Rom. 4:5).

It is true that "faith without works is dead" (James 2:26), but *faith PRECEDES works.* Works without faith are dead works, but after one exercises true faith in Jesus Christ, he works because he is a child of God. Faith in the finished work and shed blood of Jesus is so immeasurably the first thing in Christianity, that we can safely say it is, in a sense, the *great* work of ALL works.

Verse 30: *"They said therefore unto Him, What sign shewest thou then, that we may see, and believe thee? What dost thou work?"*

Here the Jews began to demonstrate their unbelief still more fully. If you want to know what is in the heart of a man, exhort him to simply *believe on Jesus* for salvation! Men are willing to work, give their money, join the church— but when we exhort them to simply *believe,* they are offended. Man wants to *work* his way to heaven or *live* his way to heaven; but the divine truth is that we are saved *by grace* through *faith,* and "the *just* shall *live* by faith." We are *rewarded* for *works* of faith, and whatsoever is NOT of faith is sin; but we are saved entirely of grace!

"What sign shewest thou then?" The Greek language here shows a definite sneer (sarcasm) in the question. These men were not sincere; they were asking Jesus, "Who are YOU to speak in such a manner? What *evidence* can you give that you are the Messiah—evidence that we can SEE? What *proof* can you give that you are what you *say* you are?" Faith cries out, "Believe and SEE!" Unbelief challenges, "Let us SEE, and we will *believe.*" But these people would *not* have believed. If what they had already seen and heard of the works and words of Jesus had not convinced them of His identity, they would not have believed even if He had come down from the cross! The rich man in hell pleaded with Abraham, "I pray thee, therefore . . .

that thou wouldest send (Lazarus) to my father's house: for I have five brethren; that he may testify unto them, lest they also come into this place of torment." Abraham replied, "They have Moses and the prophets; let them hear *them. . .* If they hear not Moses and the prophets, *neither will they be persuaded, though one rose from the dead!"* (Luke 16:27—31). So it was with the unbelieving Jews who challenged Jesus for signs of His messiahship.

Verse 31: *"Our fathers did eat manna in the desert; as it is written, He gave them bread from heaven to eat."*

Here the Jews make a comparison—Jesus' feeding of the five thousand, compared to Moses and the manna when God fed Israel on the wilderness journey from Egypt to Canaan.   His feeding of the five thousand was not proof enough that He was Messiah.   In their eyes He had done nothing greater than what happened in the days when the Israelite fathers were fed with manna.   In other words, they said, "What proof do you have that you are a greater prophet than Moses was?"

There are many people like that today.   To the unbeliever, dead teachers seem to speak with more authority than living ones.   Moses was dead and long buried—but he had led the Israelite fathers when God had fed them with manna from heaven.   Jesus had taken five loaves and two small fishes and fed thousands—but to the unbelieving Jews that was no greater feat than the miracle of the manna.   How many people today are always referring to *"the good old days"* when this-or-that was true!   Jesus said to the Pharisees, "Woe unto you! *for ye build the sepulchres of the prophets, AND YOUR FATHERS KILLED THEM!"* (Luke 11:47).   These Jews were not ignorant of the Scriptures. They quoted here from Psalm 78:24—29, and from the words of Jesus in the next verse we conclude that they actually *gave Moses credit* for giving their fathers manna from heaven!

Verse 32: *"Then Jesus said unto them, Verily, verily, I*

*say unto you, Moses gave you not that bread from heaven;
but my Father giveth you the true bread from heaven."*

Evidently the Jews believed that the miracle of the manna
was even greater than the miracle of the loaves and fishes,
and that it was Moses who had *performed* that miracle—
which made him a greater prophet than Jesus; but it was
God, not Moses, who sent the manna down from heaven,
and Jesus plainly declares to the Jews that not only did
Moses *not* give manna to the fathers, but that the manna
was not even *the true bread*, bread that brings everlasting
life. The manna was bread that satisfied only the body,
whereas the *true* bread (which they could receive if they
would believe on Him) would satisfy the *inner* man.

"My Father giveth you the true bread from heaven."
Notice the present tense of the verb here. Jesus did not
say, "My Father WILL give you the true bread," or "My
Father HAS GIVEN you the true bread." In the Greek,
"giveth you" actually means "is offering you." God, in
Christ, was at that very moment offering the living bread
to these unbelieving Jews, bread that could and would satisfy spirit and soul if they would only believe.

The *"true bread"* refers to the Lord Jesus Christ, who is
the fulfillment of the type. The manna was *real*, it was
food for the body; but it was only a *type* of a far better
food—*Christ*, the spiritual food. The same Greek word is
used in other Scriptures—i. e., in John 1:9 Jesus is the "true
Light"; in John 15:1 He is the "true vine"; in Hebrews 8:2
He is the "true tabernacle"; in Hebrews 9:24 He is the fulfillment of ALL types and figures under the Mosaic system.

Verses 33 and 34: *"For the bread of God is He which
cometh down from heaven, and giveth life unto the world.
Then said they unto Him, Lord, evermore give us this
bread."*

When we first read this passage, the meaning seems to
be that Jesus was revealing to them that He, the Son of

God, was the true bread of God, the divine food for man's soul; but Greek scholars tell us that the verse would be more correctly rendered, "The *bread of God* is that bread which cometh down from heaven," for the Jews did not seem to understand here that our Lord was speaking of Himself—or that He was speaking of a *person,* for that matter. If they understood that He was speaking of a person, why did they not murmur against Him, as they did in other instances when He referred to Himself as being one with God, or being *from* God, and why did they say, *"Lord, give us this bread?"*

If we carefully analyze the lessons Jesus taught, we will see that He *gently* unfolded tremendous truths to the people, knowing that they were slow to believe. This was true as He led them into the great truth concerning the bread of life: First of all He spoke of the bread in general. Then He declared, "I AM the bread." Then, "The bread is my flesh," and finally the bold declaration, "Except ye *eat* my flesh and drink my blood, *you have no life in you!"*

However, the truth of this verse is not destroyed if we read, "The bread of God is Christ," or "The bread of God is that bread which cometh down from heaven." Either reading is sound doctrine. Christ IS the true bread, the bread of God, and *"cometh down from heaven"* points to the divine origin of the bread.

Notice, Jesus said that the "true bread . . . *giveth life unto the WORLD."* This is in sharp contrast with the manna which God gave to the children of Israel, the twelve tribes which numbered about 600,000 men and their families. The *true* bread, the bread of God, is sufficient for *the whole world!*

"Lord, evermore give us this bread." The fact that the Jews referred to Jesus as "Lord" points to the sincerity of their request—they believed in His power (they had witnessed His miracles), but they refused to believe in His *mission.* They refused to believe that He had come into the world to save sinners.

Verse 35: *"And Jesus said unto them, I am the bread of life: he that cometh to me shall never hunger; and he that believeth on me shall never thirst."*

This authoritative declaration could have but one of two effects upon those who heard it. To *receive* Christ meant life abundant and eternal. To *reject* Him meant eternal death, eternal separation from God. The hearers were forced to make a choice. Jesus had presented Himself to them as the bread of life, and they must either receive Him as such or reject Him as such.

When Jesus told the Samaritan woman about the living water she said, "Sir, *give me this water,* that I thirst not, neither come hither to draw." When He told the Jews about the bread of life, they said, *"Evermore give us this bread"*—but there the similarity ends. The Samaritan woman meant what she said, and when Jesus revealed to her that He was speaking of Himself, she received Him, she was saved, she left her waterpot and ran into the city with an artesian well of living water bubbling in her soul. By contrast, the Jews rejected the bread of life and went away hungry. The desire for the bread was brought forth by listening to the words of Jesus—but whereas the Samaritan woman heard His words and believed, the *Jews* heard His words and refused to believe.

We satisfy our natural hunger by eating bread and meat, assimilating the food to the use of our bodies. We satisfy natural thirst by drinking water. *Christ* is the bread that satisfies the inner man, He is the living water that satisfies the soul; but we must receive Him, appropriate Him, make Him ours by faith. He alone can satisfy the heart of man. No man has yet been satisfied until he has come into the right relationship with Christ by faith in His finished work.

Bread is the staff of life, physically speaking. Bread gives nourishment, strength, and sustenance to the physical body. Spiritually, Christ becomes to the believer what natural bread becomes to the body; He communicates His life to us, He becomes a part of us, He dwells in our hearts, He is the life and strength of our soul, the complete and adequate supply of every spiritual need. Man cannot live without bread (physical food), but Jesus said to Satan, "Man shall not live *by bread alone,* but by every word that proceedeth out of the mouth of God." Just as we cannot live physically without bread, we cannot live spiritually without Christ, who saves and sustains us. Paul said, "I can do all things through Christ, which strengtheneth me" (Phil. 4:13).

In our present verse, Jesus began speaking *directly:* "I AM the bread of life." The personal pronouns "I" and "me" are used thirty-five times in this discourse on the bread of life. The Jews found themselves without excuse, for Jesus led them to the very door of salvation. The invitation is simple: *"He that cometh to me shall never hunger; and he that believeth on me shall never thirst."* All who come to Jesus with a hungry heart find their hunger *satisfied;* all who come to Him thirsting after righteousness *are filled.* This does not mean that the believer will never long for spiritual food or drink, or that he will never feel an emptiness of spirit, or a deficiency. Paul cried out, "O wretched man that I am! who shall deliver me from the body of this death?" (Rom. 7:24). Matthew 5:6 tells us that if we hunger and thirst after righteousness we shall be filled. Jesus simply meant that He is able and willing to supply the need of man's soul and spirit. He gives "peace that passeth understanding," grace sufficient for any and all occasions, and He has promised never to leave us nor forsake us. We have heaven's bread and drink at our disposal whenever we hunger or thirst.

It is most interesting to study the sermons of Jesus and see how simple are His words and illustrations. For instance, what little child does not understand what *bread* is? Jesus spoke in terms that even little children could understand. He said, "If you are hungry, come to me and eat. If you are thirsty, come to me and drink. I will satisfy your hungry spirit and your thirsty soul until we reach the Pearly White City."

Men without Christ are forever seeking something to satisfy the emptiness within them, but Jesus is the only one who *can* satisfy that emptiness. The terms of salvation are simple and easily understood. Just come to Jesus, believe on Him, trust Him, receive Him—and regardless of how sinful you may have been or how hard your heart may be, He will save you. The words of this verse are powerful, precious words. Take them into your heart and soul, rest on them. Jesus will satisfy your inner man, and you will neither hunger nor thirst again.

Verse 36: *"But I said unto you, That ye also have seen me, and believe not."*

These were not stupid, ignorant men to whom Jesus was speaking. They were the chief priests, the scribes and elders —students of the Old Testament Scriptures. They had seen Jesus in action; they had watched Him as He took the pitifully few loaves and fishes and fed five thousand hungry men and their families. Some of them had followed His ministry with keen interest. Yet, while they had seen with their eyes, they had refused to believe with their hearts. They lacked appreciation of the real character of His Person, His acts, or His ways.

There are many today who hear Him—but go no further than these Jews did. The masses of mankind still refuse to believe on Him. Oh yes—they believe that He WAS, they believe that He lived as a historical person, they believe that He was an outstanding leader and a great teacher; but they refuse to believe that He was very God—*life,* and the Author of life. They believe intellectually and historically, but they refuse to believe unto salvation. Tragic, but true!

Divine Election and the Free Will of Man

Verse 37: *"All that the Father giveth me shall come to*

me; and him that cometh to me I will in no wise cast out.''

Jesus foresaw the unbelief of the Jews, but their unbelief did not thwart God's plan and purpose in sending Jesus into the world. The Jews rejected Him and demanded His death—but their rejection of Him does not frustrate the program of a sovereign God who knew the end in the beginning. All of this was taken into consideration when the Godhead blueprinted and perfected God's plan of the ages. Therefore, Jesus could say to the Jews, "All that the Father giveth me shall come to me. Everything He *planned,* everything He designed to give to me, will come to me; all things will happen exactly as the Father planned them, *in due time.''*

God has plenty of time to work out His program, and all things will climax on schedule exactly as He planned them in the beginning. In Genesis 3:15 He promised the Saviour, and Galatians 4:4,5 tells us that *"when the fulness of the time was come,* God sent forth His Son,'' exactly as He had planned and promised. Jesus knew the Jews would not accept Him. It is true that He wept over them—but He wept in sorrow, not in anxiety.

The language in the English is very weak here. *"All that the Father giveth''* is expressed in neuter singular and means "Everything, the whole thing, that the Father giveth me shall come to me.'' This speaks of the Church as a body. God gives Christ the Church, the entire body. Christ is the head and the foundation of the Church, but it is up to the *individual* to choose to be IN that body. The entire mystical body, the entire company of believers, shall come to Christ—every single part, every member. *Not one* will be missing at the completion of the Church!

Notice: *"ALL that the Father giveth me''* is expressed in neuter gender (singular) and points to the *entire body* of believers. *"HIM that cometh to me''* is in the masculine gender (singular) and means *each individual* who exercises faith in Jesus Christ and accepts His offer of salvation by faith. No individual who comes to Christ will be turned away.

There is also a change in the verbs rendered "shall come" and "cometh." The Greek verb translated "shall come" stresses the arrival, and the one who has arrived being *present*—that is, the New Testament Church is just as sure to be completed and be with Jesus as if it were already there. The Greek verb translated "cometh" denotes the act of approaching, and marks the voluntary decision of the person who approaches. The individual comes to Jesus voluntarily; he is not forced or compelled to come. Jesus invites, "Come unto me, and I will in no wise cast you out."

The New Testament Church, the body of Christ, will be saved in its entirety and presented to Him without spot or wrinkle. Not one member of the true Church will be lost; that is the reason we read in Romans 8:28, "We know that all things work together for good to them that love God, to them who are the called according to His purpose." Not each little individual thing, but *ALL things working together*, are for the good of the believer. The reason is declared in Romans 8:29: "For whom (God) did foreknow, He also did predestinate to be conformed to the image of His Son, that He might be the firstborn among many brethren." Each blood-washed believer is predestined to be conformed to the image of God's dear Son, and whatever is necessary to mold us into that image, God allows it to happen. (Study Hebrews chapter 12.) God chastens every child of His. We are molded through chastening; we are to be conformed to the image of God's Son, and those who are conformed to that image will be glorified: "Whom He did *predestinate*, them He also *called:* and whom He called, them He also *justified:* and whom He justified, them He also *glorified*" (Rom. 8:30).

The *body* of Christ is elected, but individuals become members of that body through personal choice. Not all will *accept* the invitation even though the invitation is *given* to all; but those who do come to Jesus will be received, even as many as believe on His name. From eternity behind us

God the Father has given Jesus a people to be His own
precious, peculiar possession; and this people is the New
Testament Church, purchased with God's own blood (Acts
20:28).

Verse 38:   *"For I came down from heaven, not to do
mine own will, but the will of Him that sent me."*

The opening word in this verse connects it with the preceding verse, and its significance lies in the fact that Jesus
came from heaven to carry out—not His *own* will, but the
will of God the Father in the eternal salvation of those who
come to Him.   Since it is the will of God the Father to
save all who come to Him by Jesus Christ, it is impossible
for any one of them that come to be cast out.   Jesus came
into the world for the very purpose of receiving all who
come to Him in faith believing.

Verse 39:   *"And this is the Father's will which hath sent
me, that of all which He hath given me I should lose nothing, but should raise it up again at the last day."*

Again the neuter gender is used—*"ALL which He hath
given me,"* pointing to the complete body made up of all
born again, blood-washed believers.   Here is the guarantee
of His keeping power, His guarding care for His own:
"While I was with them in the world, I kept them in thy
name: those that thou gavest me I have kept, and none of
them is lost, but the son of perdition; that the Scripture
might be fulfilled. . . As thou hast sent me into the world,
even so have I also sent them into the world.   And for their
sakes I sanctify myself, that they also might be sanctified
through the truth" (John 17:12,18,19).   The fact that He
will lose not even *one* is directly followed by the declaration that He will resurrect the entire body, He will *"raise
it up again at the last day."*

Verse 40:   *"And this is the will of Him that sent me,
that every one which seeth the Son, and believeth on Him,
may have everlasting life: and I will raise him up at the*

last day.''

Here Jesus repeats the statement of the resurrection. In the first part of the verse He gives assurance that He will lose no part of the whole, no part of the body. The entire body is the gift of the Father to the Son. In the last part of the verse, *each individual* has eternal life because that individual put his faith in the Son. These are deep, tremendous truths, and the more study we give them the more appreciation we have for them and the stronger our faith becomes.

The verb translated "seeth" would be better rendered *"beholdeth.''* It is a very strong word and indicates careful beholding, close contemplation—not seeing Jesus with the physical eye, but beholding Him with the *inner eye,* with the heart. Everyone who beholds Jesus with the heart and receives Him is saved and will be raised up at the last day. (It is the *body* that will be raised, not the spirit.)

Verse 41: *"The Jews then murmured at Him, because He said, I am the bread which came down from heaven.''*

The Greek verb here is in the imperfect tense and means "they were *beginning* to murmur.'' It has already been suggested (v. 25) that when the crowd found Jesus and asked, "When camest thou hither?'' it was probably on the seashore. It is highly improbable that immediately following their landing they would have rushed into the synagogue with the question, "When camest thou hither?'' By verse 59, however, we know that He was later in the synagogue.

Evidently there was a break, a pause, in His teaching. He began teaching the crowd before He entered the synagogue, and I suggest the break is here between verses 40 and 41. *"The Jews''* would not necessarily be the crowd who followed Jesus, but more than likely would be the leaders and outstanding persons in the synagogue in Capernaum.

The Jews were noted for "murmuring.'' They murmured in the wilderness, and they were still murmuring when Jesus offered them the living bread which would have given them

everlasting life. However, Jesus did not say those exact
words ("I am the bread which came down from heaven").
They probably constructed the saying by putting three state-
ments together. Jesus first said, "I am the bread of life."
Then He said, "I came down from heaven." Then He said,
"The bread of God is He which cometh down from heaven."

Verse 42: *"And they said, Is not this Jesus, the son of
Joseph, whose father and mother we know? How is it then
that He saith, I came down from heaven?"*

Our English language does not fully convey the meaning
of the word *"this."* The *Greek* word used here suggests
contempt. In other words, "Is not this that fellow who
was born to Joseph and Mary?"—implying of course that
Jesus was conceived out of wedlock, an illegitimate. They
believed Him to be the natural son of Joseph and Mary.

"Whose father and mother we know" indicates that Joseph was still living at that time, and also shows that Joseph and Mary were well known in the city of Capernaum
where Jesus gave this discourse on the bread of life.

*"How is it then that He saith, I came down from heav-
en?"* The humility of Jesus was a tremendous stumblingblock for the Jews. He was not the glamorous, military
personality they had expected in their Messiah, and they
despised Him. They wanted a leader who would wear a
crown, who would lead an army and deliver Jewry from the
Romans, a man of power, wealth, and social standing. This
Christ, poverty-stricken, followed by poor peasants, fishermen, and tax collectors, this Christ who claimed that He
had come to suffer and die for the people, was offensive to
them; and the fact that He claimed to have come down
from heaven made them even more angry. They said, "Away
with Him!" They slandered Him, scorned Him, they would
even have stoned Him except that they feared the common
people.

Verses 43 and 44: *"Jesus therefore answered and said
unto them, Murmur not among yourselves. No man can*

come to me, except the Father which hath sent me draw him: and I will raise him up at the last day."

What is Jesus really saying to the Jews in these verses? They were murmuring because He said that He came down from heaven; they would not believe on Him because (so they said) He was an impostor; they claimed to know His parents, Joseph and Mary. But Jesus knew their hearts, and He knew that was not the *real* reason they did not believe on Him. These people boasted that they were descendants of Abraham, had never been in bondage to any man, and did not need to be set free. They were completely blind to their need of a Saviour, they were in total ignorance concerning spiritual things. Religious? Yes! They followed the law to the letter—and to their own satisfaction; but they were lost and without God. Going about to establish their own righteousness, they refused to submit to the righteousness of God, the Lord Jesus Christ.

Human nature has not changed. These Jews considered that they were *born* righteous, being of the seed of Abraham, and that they did not need a Saviour. Man likes to think that he can save himself, that salvation lies within his own power. People are willing to "join . . . work . . . do . . . give . . . live"—but they are not willing to humble themselves and confess to God that they are hopeless, helpless, totally depraved, hell-bound sinners, and then literally fling themselves at the feet of Jesus and cry out for mercy through His shed blood and finished work! The natural man is *so corrupt* that even when he is exposed to the preaching of the Gospel, unless the Holy Spirit bears the message home to his heart he resists the message and refuses to receive it. That is one reason so few people are being saved today—they attend church, they hear the Word, but they hear with the physical ear only. Or if they *are* brought under conviction by the message, they refuse to return to hear *more*. The Holy Spirit disturbs them and they run away, lest they be disturbed to the place where they will really *want* to be saved!

The natural man loves darkness, loves the world and things of the world. It is unnatural for sons of Adam to seek God; therefore God sent His Son to pay the sin-debt and make salvation free for all who would accept it. After Jesus ascended back to heaven, the Holy Ghost came into world and has been here since Pentecost, reproving, rebuking, drawing men to Jesus—if they will hear the Word and allow Him to draw them.

The divine truth declared in verse 44 is a startling truth, a humbling, disturbing truth, one which in every age has drawn hatred and opposition from mankind. Men think they can *live* as they please, do *what* they please, repent *when* they please, *believe* when they please, and *be saved* when they please. The average person thinks he can "sow wild oats" and then when he is ready to settle down and be saved he will go to church and *get* saved. He thinks that he can have salvation whenever he so desires; but this is *man's* idea, not God's, and is contradictory to the words of Jesus recorded here.

My dear friend, if you are not saved now, do not count on being saved when you "get ready," or when you "make up your mind" to be saved. You will be saved when the Holy Spirit convicts and draws you; and if the Holy Spirit never again convicts you, if you are never again drawn by the Spirit, you are just as sure to spend eternity in hell as the sun is sure to rise in the east. Have you been called by the Holy Spirit? Have you felt that you should give your heart and life to Jesus but have not yet done so? *Now,* this very moment if the Holy Spirit is dealing with you, lay this commentary down, get on your knees and ask God to save you in the name of Jesus and for Jesus' sake—and He will do it!

Salvation is entirely of the Lord (Jonah 2:9). The natural man has neither knowledge, desire, faith, nor inclination toward the Lord Jesus Christ until he hears the Gospel and the Word penetrates his heart. No man will *ever* come to

God until he is exposed to the WORD of God. Jesus said, "No man can come to me except the Father which hath sent me draw him." He did not mean that it is a physical impossibility for man to come to God; He was speaking of *moral* inability. Man's will is not tuned to the will of God. It is the nature of man to ignore God and, like Adam, attempt to hide from Him and make excuses for lack of faith and service. Mark 7:21−23 paints a sordid word-picture of the human heart: *"For from within, out of the heart of men, proceed evil thoughts, adulteries, fornications, murders, thefts, covetousness, wickedness, deceit, lasciviousness, an evil eye, blasphemy, pride, foolishness: all these evil things come from within, and defile the man."*

The truth is that man cannot come to God because he does not have a WILL to come. We read in Genesis 37:4 that the brothers of Joseph "hated him and could not speak peaceably unto him." They could not speak peaceably unto him because they *would* not. They hated him without a cause, and they had no *will* to say anything peaceable to him or about him.

In John chapter 1 we learned that Jesus was in the world and the world knew Him not. He came unto His own (the Jews) and His own *received* Him not. "But *as many* as received Him (Jews or Gentiles), to them gave He power to become the sons of God, even to them that believe on His name: WHICH WERE BORN, not of blood (man's blood, heredity), NOR OF THE WILL OF THE FLESH (no flesh has ever been willing to submit to God and follow Him until a new heart is placed in the body of flesh), NOR OF THE WILL OF MAN (Adan: was not willing to be subject to God; no man has ever been willing until God gave him a new spirit), BUT OF GOD" (John 1:10−13). God gives the power, God does the "borning" when we do the *receiving*—but *how do we do the receiving?* How do we come to the place where we *desire* to receive Jesus? We find the answer in the words of Romans 10:13−17, words inspired of the Holy Ghost and penned by the Apostle Paul:

"For whosoever shall call upon the name of the Lord shall be saved. How then shall they call on Him in whom they have not believed? and how shall they believe in Him of whom they have not heard? and how shall they hear without a preacher? and how shall they preach, except they be sent? As it is written, How beautiful are the feet of them that preach the Gospel of peace, and bring glad tidings of good things! . . . So then faith cometh by hearing, and hearing by the Word of God."

Now let us look at this passage in reverse: Faith comes by hearing, and hearing by the Word. The preacher is called of God, sent by God to preach the Gospel. He preaches the Word, the unbeliever hears the Word, and the Word brings faith to his heart. He exercises that faith and calls on the name of the Lord—and is saved. Therefore, no man can come to Jesus until he is drawn through hearing the Word and the power of the Holy Spirit.

Jesus said to His disciples, "Nevertheless I tell you the truth: It is expedient for you that I go away: for if I go not away, the Comforter will not come unto you; but if I depart, I will send Him unto you. And when He is come, He will reprove the world of sin, and of righteousness, and of judgment: Of sin, because they believe not on me; of righteousness, because I go to my Father, and ye see me no more; of judgment, because the prince of this world is judged" (John 16:7—11).

We might express it this way: A person may not be hungry, but if he comes into a room where a table is laden with delicious food, seeing the food and smelling the aroma can—and often does—create an appetite. In the same manner, a sinner may not be hungry for the things of God when he attends a service; but as the minister puts the living bread (the Word) before him, through the Word the Holy Spirit creates an appetite for the things of God in the unbelieving heart, the sinner is convicted of his sinfulness and convinced that the Gospel is good. He is therefore drawn to the table of living bread, he eats, and lives forever!

The truth of this verse does not lessen the responsibility of the individual, however. We must not suppose that the doctrine here takes away man's responsibility to God for his soul. This passage does not teach limited atonement. If man is lost, it will be because he chose not to accept salvation, not because God *willed* him to be lost. God is "not willing that any should perish, but that ALL should come to repentance" (II Pet. 3:9).

In the last part of this verse we read, *"And I will raise him up at the last day."* For the third time in these verses Jesus stresses the importance of the resurrection and declares that at the last day He will raise up all who come to Him in faith believing. Divine attraction is the *beginning* of salvation, and divine attraction comes through the Word of God. Resurrection is the *completion* of salvation. We are *saved by His GRACE*; we will be *raised by His mighty POWER.* He is the author and finisher of our faith, the author and finisher of our salvation. He is the Alpha and the Omega—the beginning and the end (and all that we need in between). "For in Him dwelleth all the fulness of the Godhead bodily. And ye are complete in Him, which is the head of all principality and power" (Col. 2:9,10).

Verse 45: *"It is written in the prophets, And they shall be all taught of God. Every man therefore that hath heard, and hath learned of the Father, cometh unto me."*

Here Jesus reminds the Jews that He has taught them nothing but that which was taught in their own Scriptures. By reference to the Old Testament prophets, He confirms the necessity for man to be taught of God. For instance, in Isaiah 54:13 we read, "All thy children shall be *taught of the Lord;* and great shall be the peace of thy children." But Jesus did not mean that in this dispensation all mankind—nor even all church members—will be "taught of God." He meant that all who are *God's children by faith* are taught of God.

"Every man therefore that hath heard, and hath learned

of the Father, cometh unto me." These words shed light
on the preceding verse. The meaning is that every man
who comes to Christ does so because he first heard the
Word and learned of God. The only possible way for men
to know that God so loved us that He gave Jesus to save
us, is to hear the WORD of God. From the Word we learn
that *God IS, God LOVES, God GAVE,* and *God saves*
"for Christ's sake" (Eph. 4:32). Every man who has heard
the Word has heard the account of God's love, and of the
death, burial, and resurrection of Jesus "according to the
Scriptures." Therefore every man who has heard Christ
through the Word has heard of the love, mercy, and provision of God. If he *receives* the Word, the Word brings
faith, faith (by God's grace) brings salvation. So we link
the two verses: "No man can come to me except my Father which hath sent me draw him. . . Every man therefore
that hath heard, and hath learned of the Father, cometh
unto me!"

Jesus here shows that God draws men by teaching the
Word, not by legal statutes, not by signs and wonders, not
by emotion or physical attraction, *but by gracious instruction,* teaching through the Gospel of grace; and that teaching has Christ as its center and its object.

The fact that Jesus quoted from Isaiah 54:13 does not
imply that the Scripture provided Him with His doctrine.
He simply confirmed His doctrine by quoting Old Testament
Scripture. The Old Testament is the New Testament *in-
folded,* and the New Testament is the Old Testament *unfolded.*

Verse 46:   *"Not that any man hath seen the Father,
save He which is of God, He hath seen the Father."*

Jesus wanted His listeners to clearly understand that
when He spoke of the Father He was speaking of the eternal God whom no man has ever seen, God the eternal
Spirit.

"He which is OF God, HE hath seen the Father." Here

Jesus speaks of Himself. John 1:18 told us, "No man hath seen God at any time; the only begotten Son, which is in the bosom of the Father, He hath declared Him." Jesus was trying to impress upon the hearts and minds of the Jews that the appearances of God as recorded in the Old Testament were not made by the Eternal Spirit who is from everlasting to everlasting, but by the second Person of the Trinity. He appeared in various forms—sometimes as the Angel of the Lord, sometimes as a Man. (Read Joshua 5:13—15.) There are many places in the Old Testament where Deity appeared—but it was always the Son, never God the Eternal Spirit. No mortal man could look upon God and live. It is true that we will see God, but it will be when we have become like Him (I John 3:1—3).

The Living Bread

Verse 47: *"Verily, verily, I say unto you, He that believeth on me hath everlasting life."*

Jesus repeats here what He said in verse 35—"I am the bread of life: he that cometh to me shall never hunger; and he that believeth on me shall never thirst." The Jews of course reminded Him that their fathers had eaten manna in the wilderness, and He then presented the subject from the point of view of gifts from the heavenly Father—both the manna that the fathers ate, and Himself, the *true* bread that the Father had given to the world. NOW He shows the contrast between those who received the manna, and those who receive the *living bread.* The fathers had eaten manna in the wilderness—and they died. Those who partake of the living bread will be partakers of *eternal life.*

Verses 48—51: *"I am that bread of life. Your fathers did eat manna in the wilderness, and are dead. This is the bread which cometh down from heaven, that a man may eat thereof, and not die. I am the living bread which came down from heaven: if any man eat of this bread, he shall*

*live for ever: and the bread that I will give is my flesh,
which I will give for the life of the world.''*

Even though the manna was miracle bread given by God,
it did not maintain physical life in perpetuity; the people
died. Jesus, the antitype, the bread of life, came down from
heaven—and whosoever will eat of that bread shall *not* die.
God's divine purpose in *giving* the bread was to provide
life eternal.

Notice the change of tense here.   In verse 50 we read
"cometh down,'' and in verse 51 we read *"came* down.''
"Cometh down'' indicates the inherent characteristic of the
true bread (it is eternal), and in this is defined that which
is essential to its nature (it is continually life-giving), and to
the circumstances indicated concerning the coming of the
true bread.   There is always bread; it is never scarce.   "He
that believeth on (Jesus) shall never hunger.''   The past
tense—"came down''—points out the historic fact of the
coming of the bread, the act by which Jesus became incarnate.   "For the bread of God is He which cometh down
from heaven, and giveth life unto the world'' (v. 33).

Jesus speaks of the fact that God the Father sent Him—
but at the same time He makes it clear that He came voluntarily, of His own will.   There was perfect harmony and
agreement between the Father and the Son, between the
Father's *sending* the Son into the world, and the Son's
coming into the world of His own accord.

I confess that we are now in deep water.   There are
some who see no difference between "I am the bread of
life'' (v. 35), and "I am the living bread'' (v. 51); but there
IS a difference.   When Jesus said, "I am the bread of life,''
He stressed the impartation of life through Himself—i. e.,
because of who He was, because of His nature and power,
*He was the bread that would impart life to all who would
eat or appropriate.*   When He said, "I am the living bread''
He was emphasizing the essential *principle and quality* of
life which was IN HIMSELF: *"For as the FATHER hath
life in Himself; so hath He given to the SON to have life*

in Himself" (ch. 5, v. 26). Jesus as "the living bread" *did not BEGIN to live—He WAS in the beginning, LIVING;* but when He said, "I am the bread of life," He had brought down to man bread that would give life to all who would eat. The manna that the fathers ate in the wilderness sustained life *for a DAY,* but all who exercise faith in Christ and receive the *living* bread will live FOREVER.

As Jesus neared the close of His great discourse on the bread of life, His hearers were astounded when He said, *"The bread that I will give is my flesh, which I will give for the life of the world."* This was completely beyond their understanding!

Hebrews 10:1—10 sheds light on this: "For the law having a shadow ,of good things to come, and not the very image of the things, can never with those sacrifices which they offered year by year continually make the comers thereunto perfect. For then would they not have ceased to be offered? because that the worshippers once purged should have had no more conscience of sins. But in those sacrifices there is a remembrance again made of sins every year. For it is not possible that the blood of bulls and of goats should take away sins. Wherefore when He cometh into the world, He saith, Sacrifice and offering thou wouldest not, but a body hast thou prepared me: In burnt-offerings and sacrifices for sin thou hast had no pleasure. Then said I, Lo, I come (in the volume of the book it is written of me,) to do thy will, O God. Above when He said, Sacrifice and offering and burnt-offerings and offering for sin thou wouldest not, neither hadst pleasure therein; which are offered by the law; Then said He, Lo, I come to do thy will, O God. He taketh away the first, that He may establish the second. By the which will we are sanctified *through the offering of the BODY OF JESUS CHRIST once for all."*

Jesus took a body of flesh in order that He might suffer death, and by the grace of God taste death for *every man:*

"We see Jesus, who was made a little lower than the angels for the suffering of death, crowned with glory and honour; that He by the grace of God should taste death for every man. . . Forasmuch then as the children are partakers of flesh and blood, He also Himself likewise took part of the same; that through death He might destroy him that had the power of death, that is, the devil; and deliver them who through fear of death were all their lifetime subject to bondage. For verily He took not on Him the nature of angels; but He took on Him the seed of Abraham. Wherefore in all things it behoved Him to be made like unto His brethren, that He might be a merciful and faithful High Priest in things pertaining to God, to make reconciliation for the sins of the people. For in that He Himself hath suffered being tempted, He is able to succour them that are tempted" (Heb. 2:9,14−18).

Yes, Jesus was God in a body of flesh, reconciling the world unto Himself. Since God thundered out, "The soul that sinneth, it shall die" (Ezek. 18:4) and since "the wages of sin is death" (Rom. 6:23), it was a divine imperative that someone die to pay the sin-debt−and that "someone" had to be sinless. What God demanded in payment of the sin-debt, only God could provide, and He *did* provide redemption in Jesus: ". . . God was in Christ, reconciling the world unto Himself, not imputing their trespasses unto them; and hath committed unto us the word of reconciliation. Now then we are ambassadors for Christ, as though God did beseech you by us: we pray you in Christ's stead, be ye reconciled to God. For He hath made Him to be sin for us, who knew no sin; that we might be made the righteousness of God in Him" (II Cor. 5:19−21).

Jesus laid His life down and shed His blood *"for the life of the world."* His body was offered in sacrifice as an atonement for sin for all mankind. The invitation is, "If *any* man−or ALL men−eat of this bread . . . ." ALL are invited to come to the table of living bread and be filled, and "if any man eat of this bread he shall live forever."

Verses 52−54: *"The Jews therefore strove among them-*

*selves, saying, How can this Man give us His flesh to eat?
Then Jesus said unto them, Verily, verily, I say unto you,
Except ye eat the flesh of the Son of man, and drink His
blood, ye have no life in you. Whoso eateth my flesh, and
drinketh my blood, hath eternal life; and I will raise him
up at the last day."*

Few verses in all the Word of God have been so per-
verted by teachers, preachers, and religious leaders as this
passage. The Jews were not the only people to strive about
the meaning of these verses. Men have declared them to
mean what God never intended the meaning to be. Unbelievers *cannot* interpret the Bible; the *natural man* cannot
receive the things of the Spirit of God. When man makes
the Scripture mean what he *wants* it to mean, he turns
bread into poison. When unsaved people interpret the Bible,
that which was written for our admonition becomes a stumbling block. We are to study and rightly divide the Word
as we are led by the Spirit, because HE is the only one
who can rightly interpret the Word of God.

Eating and drinking here is not *literally* eating the flesh
and drinking the blood of Jesus Christ; these words have
nothing to do with the sacrament of the Lord's Supper.
(We should *observe* the Lord's Supper by eating the un-
leavened bread and drinking the fruit of the vine; but these
elements are certainly not the body and blood of Jesus
Christ. *Transubstantiation* is not taught in the Bible; it is
a dogma of man.)

Unbelievers struggle long and laboriously to make religion a thing of ceremonies, forms, feasts, sacraments, ordinances, "doings" and "not-doings." The unbeliever re-
coils at the truth of Christianity—salvation by grace through
faith in the shed blood—*plus nothing.* Men are anxious to
do, but slow to *believe.* The "flesh and blood of the Son
of man" simply means the sacrifice of His body, the shed-
ding of His blood on the cross when He died for the sins
of the world. The atonement Jesus made through His death;
the satisfaction He gave through His sufferings as our per-

fect, sinless substitute; the redemption He purchased through His blood by willingly enduring the penalty for our sins, is the true meaning of the flesh and the blood of the Son of man.

When Jesus announced that He had come down from heaven, the Jews "murmured" at Him; but when He made the announcement concerning His flesh and blood they became increasingly angry and *"strove among themselves."* The same Greek word is used in James 4:2 where it is translated "fight." In other words, when Jesus said, "Except you eat my flesh and drink my blood, you have no life in you" the Jews became "fighting mad"! They were indeed ready to destroy Him.

The Scriptures do not tell us just *how* the Jews "strove among themselves." I can imagine that they began to discuss the matter very angrily and violently, in great excitement. "How can this Man give us His flesh to eat?" Their expression was one of scorn, sarcasm. "Who does this fellow think He is? How can He give us His flesh to eat and His blood to drink?" Like millions today, the Jews were determined to keep their religion in the natural realm. They refused to think in the realm of the supernatural. Such is the mind of man. The unregenerate refuses to receive the supernatural by faith; he must SEE—and then *believe.* But true faith causes us to know and be assured *without* seeing.

In answer to their question as to how this could be, Jesus made one of the most important declarations of His earthly ministry. Up to this point He had led the Jews step by step, but here He clearly declared to them the paramount doctrine of the Gospel of the grace of God, a most startling doctrine: *"EXCEPT ye eat the flesh of the Son of man, and drink His blood, YE HAVE NO LIFE IN YOU!"*

This was the Passover season. Many of those who heard the Lord at this time were on their way to the city of Jerusalem to attend the Passover, and in passing through the Capernaum area they heard Jesus speaking of the bread of life. Their minds no doubt were on the Passover, and how

suitable then for Jesus, through this discourse, to direct
their minds to Himself, their *true* Passover, their true sacrifice for sin. (In connection with this please study the
entire tenth chapter of Hebrews.)

The Jews were all familiar with the first Passover—that
night in Egypt when the death angel passed through, and
the firstborn in every house was slain throughout the land
except where the blood had been applied. That night the
flesh and blood of the lamb slain were the means of life
to the Israelites, the means of safety and deliverance. They
obeyed God concerning the lamb, they followed His command in every minute detail, and as a result they were delivered and set free. In like manner, Jesus wanted the Jews
to understand that HIS flesh and HIS blood were to be the
means of safety and life for them, the means of deliverance
from the wrath of God which abides upon all who do not
believe. His statement should not have startled them to
such great degree, for such reference was not entirely new
to them. They had read the books of Moses, they knew
how God had dealt with the fathers to bring about their
deliverance from Egypt. What they could not understand
(and therefore refused to receive) was the statement that
the flesh and blood of Jesus would give them *eternal* life,
life for their souls in the same way that the blood of the
Passover lamb slain in Egypt had brought *physical* deliverance. Jesus had come to give His flesh and His blood that
they might have life for the soul—*eternal* life.

Eating and drinking here is with the heart, with soul
and spirit, *by faith*, not physically. The flesh and blood
of Jesus means the vicarious sacrifice of His body on the
cross. All who are saved *MUST by faith* lay hold on the
cardinal truth of salvation—the death of Jesus on the cross;
and *except* we by faith lay hold on His sacrifice (His body
and His blood) there is no hope of salvation, for there can
be no eternal life apart from His broken body and His shed
blood.

According to the doctrine of Jesus, we are *saved* by eat-

ing the flesh and drinking the blood, and we *live* by eating
the flesh and drinking the blood. So, if we can discover
in the Word of God *how* the believer lives, we will have
the meaning of eating His flesh and drinking His blood:

In Romans 1:16,17 we read, "For I am not ashamed of
the Gospel of Christ: for it is the power of God unto salvation to every one that believeth; to the Jew first, and
also to the Greek. For therein is the righteousness of God
revealed from faith to faith: as it is written, *The just shall
LIVE by faith."*

The *justified* man, he who possesses eternal life, *lives*
that life by faith—and where does he *obtain* that faith? "So
then *faith cometh by hearing, and hearing by the Word of
God"* (Rom. 10:17).

NOW: "In the beginning was the WORD, and the Word
was with God, and the Word WAS God. . . And the Word
was made flesh, and dwelt among us, (and we beheld His
glory, the glory as of the only begotten of the Father,) full
of grace and truth" (John 1:1,14).

Therefore, to eat the flesh and drink the blood of the
Son of God is to appropriate His Word. Receiving the
Word brings saving faith, and when we are saved by faith
we "desire the sincere milk of the Word, that (we) may
grow thereby" (I Pet. 2:2). We grow by feeding on the
milk, meat, and bread of the Word. Thus, to eat the flesh
and drink the blood of the Son of God is to receive and
appropriate His Word into our very heart and life—the en-
grafted Word that saves the soul, the incorruptible seed that
brings eternal life.

Under the Old Testament economy with which the Jews
were very familiar, the body of the sin-offering was essen-
tially a part of the sacrifice just as much as the blood.
Please study Leviticus 4:1—12; 16:27; Exodus 29:14; and
Hebrews 13:10—13. The body of the *Passover lamb* had to
be *eaten* as well as the blood sprinkled on either side of
the doorposts and across the lintel. The flesh and blood
of Jesus are mentioned together here because He had the

cross in view, the offering of Himself as the sin-offering. He tried to make it plain that He was speaking of the *death* of His body, through which He would give life to man's soul. The Christ Incarnate (His sinless life) could not have saved us. His crucifixion was a divine imperative if the atonement were to be made possible, if the sin-offering were to satisfy the heavenly Father.

Verse 55: *"For my flesh is meat indeed, and my blood is drink indeed."*

The Greek word translated *"meat"* is the word used for our English word "food." It means any edible food, not flesh alone. The meaning here is that the flesh of Jesus is truly food, and the blood of Jesus is truly drink—food and drink for the spirit, the inner man. This is the same truth set forth in verse 35. We appropriate this living food and drink by faith, and all who have believed on Jesus know by personal experience that His broken body and shed blood bring life eternal, as well as peace to the inner man.

Verse 56: *"He that eateth my flesh, and drinketh my blood, dwelleth in me, and I in him.*

Notice that *all* are invited; not one is excluded. "He that eateth . . . he that drinketh"—the invitation is to all; but *the individual* must eat; one person cannot receive Christ for another person. Each individual must receive Him into the heart by faith.

Notice, too, the close, intimate relationship between Christ and the Christian—*"He . . . dwelleth in me, and I in him."* This intimate union between Christ and the believer is borne out in the following Scriptures:

Romans 8:1: "There is therefore now no condemnation to them which are *in Christ Jesus,* who walk not after the flesh, but after the Spirit."

Colossians 1:27: "To whom God would make known what is the riches of the glory of this mystery among the Gentiles; which is *Christ in you,* the hope of glory."

Colossians 3:3: "For ye are dead, and your life is hid *with Christ in God.*"

Already believers "sit together in heavenly places *in Christ Jesus*" (Eph. 2:6).

We know that food and drink keep the physical body alive and cause it to grow, and our food and drink become part of the body. The same is true in the spiritual sense: When we receive the Word of God, the living Word, we are appropriating Christ and He becomes part of us, the new creation (II Cor. 5:17).

Verse 57: *"As the living Father hath sent me, and I live by the Father: so he that eateth me, even he shall live by me."*

Here is made known the intimate union between the be-liever and Christ in a higher, more noble way, by a more mysterious figure than that of food as related to the body. The illustration here concerns the first and second Persons of the Trinity—God the Father and God the Son. In other words, Jesus said, "The Father sent me into the world to be born of the Virgin Mary, to become the God-man—God in flesh. You see me in a body just like your body, yet I am God. I am in the Father, the Father is in me. In the same way, when you receive my finished work, and put your faith in me as your Saviour, WE live in the same union and communion as the Father and I enjoy now."

The same relationship exists between the believer and Jesus as existed between Jesus and the Father when Jesus tabernacled among men.   Every born again child of God possesses divine nature NOW, but that divine nature abides in a tabernacle of flesh. We are just as human after we are born again as we were *before* the new birth, but *the inner man* is changed. We possess the Holy Spirit (Rom. 8:9,14, 16); we possess divine nature (II Pet. 1:4).

When Jesus lived on earth, Son of God and Son of man, He was equal with the Father as touching His deity, and He lived through and by the Father. The Son was never without the Father, nor the Father without the Son. In the same manner, the believer lives through and by Christ. We receive our spiritual strength from Him: "I am crucified with Christ: nevertheless I live; yet not I, but Christ liveth in me: *and the life which I now live in the flesh I live by the faith of the Son of God, who loved me, and gave Himself for me*" (Gal. 2:20).

In our present verse we see something beautiful indeed, precious beyond human description: We see God the Father, eternal Jehovah God, the living Father; and Jesus the Son who lived BY the Father—that is, God the Father communicated life to the Son by eternal generation. The Son was in the beginning *with* the Father, the Father was in the beginning with the Son; *each is eternal. Because* the living Father became the living Son, took a body like unto our body and IN that body conquered the world, the flesh, and the devil, fulfilled the law and the prophets and satisfied every demand of God's holiness and righteousness, *believers* are alive! We are sons of God, and because HE lives, WE live. Jesus has life which is communicated by *eternal generation;* believers have eternal life by *RE-generation,* and by that regeneration we are living sons of God NOW, partakers of divine nature NOW.

Verse 58: *"This is the bread which came down from heaven: not as your fathers did eat manna, and are dead: he that eateth of this bread shall live for ever."*

This verse is simply a summary of the discourse on the bread of life. The Jews had boasted that their fathers ate manna in the wilderness. Jesus here points back to that statement, and repeats the truth He had previously declared—*i. e.,* that HE was the true bread which God had sent down from heaven to feed the world through the sacrifice of Himself, His broken body and His shed blood. He reminds the Jews that the manna their fathers ate in the wilderness did nothing for the soul, the fathers received no spiritual benefit from the manna; but whosoever ate of the

true bread would live forever; the living bread would give
and sustain everlasting life.

Verse 59:   *"These things said He in the synagogue, as
He taught in Capernaum."*

The discourse on the bread of life more than likely began
at the seashore.   Whether Jesus walked slowly from the sea-
side to the synagogue, or whether He gave part of the discourse by the seashore and some time elapsed between that
part of His teaching and the last part, we do not know; but
we do know that the last part of His discourse was given
in the *synagogue* at Capernaum.   As has already been said,
the break in the discussion seems to be at verse 41 where
we are told that the Jews then "murmured at Him, because He said, I am the bread which came down from. heav-
en."   Possibly Jesus gave them the message recorded in
verses 26 through 40, and then as He traveled from the seashore up to the synagogue they murmured about what He
had said.   He then continued the discourse with verse 43,
and the message from there on through the rest of the discussion was delivered in the synagogue.

Who Can Hear the Truth?

Verse 60:   *"Many therefore of His disciples, when they
had heard this, said, This is an hard saying; who can hear
it?"*

The many who turned and walked away from Jesus were
not true believers.   They turned from Him because they
would not hear the truth.   They had followed Him for the
loaves and fishes, for the excitement of the crowd and the
miracles He performed; but they were never truly born again.
"This is an hard saying."   The English word "hard"
is a little misleading here.   What Jesus said about eating
His flesh and drinking His blood does not mean "hard" in
the sense of being *"difficult to understand."*   The Greek indicates that this did not have so much to do with under-

standing or comprehending as with the fact that it was "hard to the feelings"—it *shocked* them. They could not understand why Jesus used such terms. This same word is used in Matthew 25:24: "Thou art an hard man," and in Jude 15, the "hard speeches which ungodly sinners have spoken against Him."

Not only did they consider the Lord as having given them "an hard saying," but they asked, *"Who can HEAR it?"* What sensible person would believe such statements, or follow the Person who *made* such statements? They considered Jesus a religious fanatic and refused to believe Him. We remember that in John 5:24 He said, "He that heareth my word, and believeth on Him that sent me, hath everlasting life, and shall not come into condemnation; but is passed from death unto life," and in John 12:48 we read, "He that rejecteth me, and receiveth not my words, hath one that judgeth him: the Word that I have spoken, the same shall judge him in the last day."

Verse 61: *"When Jesus knew in Himself that His disciples murmured at it, He said unto them, Doth this offend you?"*

The omniscience of Christ is again set forth here. He knew their thoughts, He knew what was in their hearts— and He spoke at the very instant of their murmuring! He immediately asked them, "Doth this offend you?" Or, "Does what I have just said put a stumbling block before you?"

Verse 62: *"What and if ye shall see the Son of man ascend up where He was before?"*

When Nicodemus asked, "How can these things be?" Jesus replied, "If I have told you *earthly* things and ye believe not, how shall ye believe, if I tell you *heavenly* things?" Now to the Jews He is saying, "If you refuse to see the doctrine I have already given you concerning my flesh and my blood, if you refuse to receive my sacrifice, what will you think soon when you see my body actually

taken up into the clouds and I disappear from your sight?''
And after His death, burial, and resurrection, the disciples
witnessed *exactly that:*

"When they therefore were come together, they asked of
Him, saying, Lord, wilt thou at this time restore again the
kingdom to Israel?   And He said unto them, It is not for
you to know the times or the seasons, which the Father
hath put in His own power.   But ye shall receive power,
after that the Holy Ghost is come upon you: and ye shall
be witnesses unto me both in Jerusalem, and in all Judaea,
and in Samaria, and unto the uttermost part of the earth.
And when He had spoken these things, while they beheld,
He was taken up; and a cloud received Him out of their
sight.   And while they looked stedfastly toward heaven as
He went up, behold, two men stood by them in white ap-
parel; which also said, Ye men of Galilee, why stand ye
gazing up into heaven?   This same Jesus, which is taken
up from you into heaven, shall so come in like manner as
ye have seen Him go into heaven" (Acts 1:6—11).

Jesus had told the Jews that He came down from heaven,
but each time He spoke of His human body and claimed to
be the Son of God, they became more and more angry with
Him.   They looked upon Him in a human body and could
not accept His statement that He came down from heaven
and would give them His flesh to eat.   What were they to
think when they saw His body ascending up *into* heaven!
If they would not believe that He came *from* heaven, if
they would not believe His doctrine as He stood in their
presence, they certainly would not believe it after they witnessed His ascension.

"Where He was before" again declares the pre-existence
of Christ, His existence with the Father in the beginning,
which was made clear in the very first chapter of John's
Gospel.

Verse 63:   *"It is the Spirit that quickeneth; the flesh*
profiteth nothing: the words that I speak unto you, they
are spirit, and they are life."

Bible scholars do not fully agree on the meaning of this verse—but again, if we hope to understand what Jesus said here we must compare spiritual things with spiritual and leave our own ideas out of it. Paul said, "Now we have received, not the spirit of the world, but the Spirit which is of God; that we might know the things that are freely given to us of God. Which things also we speak, not in the words which man's wisdom teacheth, but which the Holy Ghost teacheth; comparing spiritual things with spiritual" (I Cor. 2:12,13).

"It is the Spirit that quickeneth." To quicken means *to make alive.* The Spirit brings life. Paul said to the Ephesians, "You hath He *quickened,* who were dead in trespasses and sins." The first part of this verse then, means that the Holy Spirit quickens the unbeliever when faith is exercised in the finished work of the Lord Jesus Christ: "Verily, verily, I say unto thee, Except a man be born of water and of the Spirit, he cannot enter into the kingdom of God. That which is born of the flesh is flesh; and that which is born of the Spirit is spirit" (John 3:5,6). So it is the spirit (the inner man) that is born of God, and it is God who does the "borning" (John 1:12,13).

"The flesh profiteth nothing." Regardless of what we may do in the flesh, how we may live or sacrifice in the flesh, or how pure we may *keep* the flesh, our self-righteousness is as filthy rags in the sight of God (Isa. 64:6). The sinless life of Jesus could never have saved us; salvation demanded His death. Had He never died, we could never have been saved through His sinless flesh. The sinlessness of Jesus only showed the exceeding sinfulness of man. The broken body and shed blood of Jesus made salvation possible. Jesus was the Word in flesh; therefore "faith cometh by hearing, and hearing by the Word of God" (Rom. 10:17). We receive eternal life when we receive the Word of God.

"The words that I speak unto you, they are spirit, and they are life." Jesus had just said, "Except you eat my flesh and drink my blood, you have no life in you." Here

He declares that His WORDS are spirit and life. Therefore, what He is actually saying is that eating His flesh
and drinking His blood is receiving His Word into the heart.
The words of Jesus bring life, with the Holy Spirit as the
attending Physician at the new birth. It is the *Word* that
brings saving faith, and the Holy Spirit is the power that
opens the heart and draws men to God. When the heart
receives the Word, life eternal is the result.

Verse 64: *"But there are some of you that believe not.
For Jesus knew from the beginning who they were that believed not, and who should betray Him."*

Jesus was well aware of those who did not truly believe
that He was the Messiah. They followed Him *professing*
to be His disciples, but they followed Him for material
reasons—for the loaves and fishes, for the excitement of the
crowds; they did not believe in Him as Saviour and Lord.
If they had, they would not have been offended by His
doctrine.

Notice the declaration of His omniscience: He *"knew
from the beginning"* who would not believe. Jesus was
never deceived by the crowds that followed Him. He knew
their hearts all the way, all the time. He knew *"who
should betray Him."* This points to Judas Iscariot. Jesus
knew when He chose Judas as one of the twelve that it
was he who would betray Him; He knew Judas was a devil,
as evidenced by the last two verses in this chapter.

Verse 65: *"And He said, Therefore said I unto you, that
no man can come unto me, except it were given unto him
of my Father."*

In verse 45 Jesus declared that those who heard Him in
faith (with the heart) and who learned of the Father, would
come to Him as Saviour. God so loved the world that He
gave Jesus to die for sinners, and those who hear that message, in faith believing, will come to Jesus. Thus He is
saying here, to those who have rejected His discourse on

the bread of life, that the fact of their rejection of Him as Messiah was proof that they did not know God the Father. If they did not believe in Him as the Son of God, they could not be drawn by the Holy Spirit.

Verse 66: *"From that time many of His disciples went back, and walked no more with Him."*

At this point many of those who had followed Jesus up to that time turned their backs on Him and *"walked no more with Him."* No doubt they had thought that He would soon be crowned King and would deliver them from the Romans; but at the close of His discourse on the bread of life they gave up all hope and rejected Him. These people were never born again; they were simply following Jesus for what they could get out of it, hoping that eventually He would become king and they would profit by having been associated with Him.

Jesus and the Twelve — Peter's Confession of Faith

Verse 67: *"Then said Jesus unto the twelve, Will ye also go away?"*

Jesus did not ask this question in order to find out what the twelve would do. He knew the minds of these twelve men just as He knows the minds and hearts of *all* men; but He asked the question to prove their faith and draw from them the confession made by Peter in the very next verse.

The Greek here translated *"Will* ye go away?" actually means "Do you *wish* to go away? Have you a *will* to go away?"

Verse 68: *"Then Simon Peter answered Him, Lord, to whom shall we go? Thou hast the words of eternal life."*

It was only the night before that Peter was spokesman for the disciples and said, "Lord, if it be thou, bid me come unto thee on the water" (Matt. 14:28). Now he is again spokesman for the group. He answers not only concerning his *own* faith, but for the other disciples as well: *"Lord, TO WHOM shall we go?"* Peter was convinced that there was none other to take the place of Jesus—no other teacher, no other master, none to whom they could go. It is true that Christians are often tried—"Yea, and all that will live godly in Christ Jesus shall suffer persecution" (II Tim. 3:12). Christianity has its cross, but today we can still ask, *"To whom shall we go?"* Where else could we turn to find what Christianity offers? No other religion *has* what Christianity offers. All religions can be catalogued under one of two headings: (1) fear; (2) love. Christianity is the only religion that can be classified under "love." We serve Jesus because we love Him, not because we fear Him, not because we are afraid of what He will *do* to us. Believers will escape the damnation of hell—but that is not why we serve the Lord. We surrender our all to Him because we love Him—and we love Him because *He first loved us.* Neither the world nor other religions can offer what Christianity offers to all who will come to Christ in true faith believing.

"Thou hast the WORDS of eternal life." Peter had been paying close attention; he listened closely the day Jesus said, "He that heareth my WORD, and believeth on Him that sent me, hath everlasting life, and shall not come into condemnation; but is passed from death unto life" (John 5:24). It is most interesting that later in Peter's ministry, after Jesus had returned to heaven, God sent His angel to the house of Cornelius and told him to send for Peter, *who would tell him WORDS* whereby he and all his house would be saved (Acts 11:13,14). It is the *Word of God* that makes known the way of eternal life. It is the *Word of God* that gives power to become new creations in Christ Jesus: "As many as received Him, to them gave He power to become the sons of God, even to them that believe on His name: which were born, not of blood, nor of the will of the flesh, nor of the will of man, but of God" (John 1:12,13).

Jesus did have the words of eternal life—*He was THE WORD in flesh,* and Peter understood this. He understood the discourse on the bread of life; he knew Jesus was speaking of the WORD, and that eating the flesh and drinking the blood of the Son of man meant simply hearing, receiving, and appropriating the Word. Thank God for Peter's confession of faith: "To whom shall we go? *THOU hast the Words of eternal life.*" In John 17:8 Jesus said, "I have given unto them the words which thou gavest me; and they have received them, and have known surely that I came out from thee, and they have believed that thou didst send me."

Verse 69: *"And we believe and are sure that thou art that Christ, the Son of the living God."*

The Greek language here is very strong, very emphatic. In other words, Peter said, "It does not matter what *others* do; they may all walk away. But WE have known all along, we have *believed* all along, that you are the true Messiah. *You alone* can give eternal life, and the reason you *have* the words of eternal life is because *thou art THE Christ, the Son of the living God!*" It is the same confession Peter made in Matthew 16:16 when he said, "Thou art the Christ, the Son of the living God."

Peter confessed all that he understood about Jesus as the Christ, the Son of God. From Matthew 16:22,23 we know that he did not understand the death Jesus was to die, the sacrifice He was to make. He did not understand that it was through the shed blood that salvation and redemption from sin would be made possible. As yet, he had no idea that Jesus would be arrested, cruelly treated, and finally nailed to a cross. Jesus told the disciples of these things at the appointed time, but they did not believe in His resurrection until after He was raised and appeared to them.

Judas a Devil

Verses 70 and 71: *"Jesus answered them, Have not I*

*chosen you twelve, and one of you is a devil? He spake
of Judas Iscariot the son of Simon: for he it was that
should betray Him, being one of the twelve."*

The Greek word translated "chosen" simply means to
select one for an office. The fact that Judas Iscariot was
chosen to be an apostle does not mean that he was born
again, saved by grace and washed in the blood. We read
in Luke 6, verses 13—16, "And when it was day, He called
unto Him His disciples: and of them *He chose twelve,*
whom also He named apostles; Simon, (whom He also
named Peter,) and Andrew his brother, James and John,
Philip and Bartholomew, Matthew and Thomas, James the
son of Alphaeus, and Simon called Zelotes, and Judas the
brother of James, and Judas Iscariot, which also was the
traitor."

In Acts 6:5 we read that among the first deacons "they
chose Stephen, a man full of faith and of the Holy Ghost
. . . ." In Acts 15:22 we read, "Then pleased it the apostles and elders with the whole church, to send *chosen* men
of their own company to Antioch with Paul and Barnabas
. . . ." In each of these references, the Greek word translated "chosen" is the same word used in our present passage. Judas was *chosen* for the office of apostleship, but
he was never saved.

In John 13:18 Jesus said, "I speak not of you all: I
know whom I have chosen: but that the Scripture may be
fulfilled, He that eateth bread with me hath lifted up his
heel against me." In this verse Jesus distinctly pointed out
that He was not speaking of the entire twelve, because He
knew Judas from the beginning.

The fact that a person fills an office in the church, even
though he may fill it well, does not mean that he is born
again. Read the solemn words of Jesus in Matthew 7:21—23:

"Not every one that saith unto me, Lord, Lord, shall
enter into the kingdom of heaven; but he that doeth the
will of my Father which is in heaven. Many will say to
me in that day, Lord, Lord, have we not prophesied in thy

name? and in thy name have cast out devils? and in thy name done many wonderful works? *And then will I profess unto them, I never knew you: depart from me, ye that work iniquity!"* It is possible for a person to accomplish tremendous things in the name of religion—even in the name of Christ—and yet not be a born again Christian.

Judas was never saved; this is clear from many Scriptures. Christ Himself points this out in our present passage. He again makes this plain in John 13:10,11 when He washed the disciples' feet: "Jesus saith to him, He that is washed needeth not save to wash his feet, but is clean every whit: and ye are clean, *but not ALL. For He knew who should betray Him; therefore said He, Ye are not all clean."*

Jesus knew that Judas was not saved; He called him a devil six months before Judas betrayed Him. "Why then," some will ask, "does the Bible say that *Judas by transgression fell?"* It is true that Judas "by transgression fell," but *from what did he fall?* He fell from the office of apostleship and ministry:

"And they appointed two, Joseph called Barsabas, who was surnamed Justus, and Matthias. And they prayed, and said, Thou, Lord, which knowest the hearts of all men, shew whether of these two thou hast chosen, that he may take part of this *MINISTRY AND APOSTLESHIP, from which Judas by transgression fell,* that he might go to his own place" (Acts 1:23—25).

One can be a minister of Satan even while professing to be a minister of Jesus Christ, for just as truly as Jesus has ordained ministers, so does *the devil* have ordained ministers: "For such are false apostles, deceitful workers, transforming themselves into the apostles of Christ. And no marvel; for Satan himself is transformed into an angel of light. Therefore it is no great thing if his ministers also be transformed as the ministers of righteousness; whose end shall be according to their works" (II Cor. 11:13—15).

You will notice in the passage just quoted from Acts, Judas "went to *his own place."* Certainly hell does not

belong to Judas, and we could not say that he went "to
his own place" if he simply dropped into hell as all other
unbelievers do at death.   There is no other place in the
Bible where this statement is made about *another* person—
in fact, there are several things said about Judas in the
Scriptures that are not said of any other person. For instance, no other person is called a "devil," and no other
person is called "the son of perdition."

Now in answer to the question, "*Why* did Jesus choose
a devil to fill the office of apostleship, *why* was Judas chosen as one of the twelve?" we will turn to John 17:12,
where Jesus answers that question Himself:

"While I was with them in the world, I kept them in
thy name: those that thou gavest me I have kept, *and none
of them is lost, but the son of perdition; THAT THE
SCRIPTURE MIGHT BE FULFILLED.*"

Before the world was, before anything was created, God
planned, perfected, and finished the blueprint of the ages
including the plan of salvation. He knew the end in the
beginning, and we accept these things by faith even though
we may not understand them.   Personally, I believe the
same spirit dwelt in Pharaoh as in Judas Iscariot, and I
further believe that Judas will return to this earth during
the tribulation period.   I believe he has an unfulfilled ministry, the record of which is found in II Thessalonians 2:
1—12:

"Now we beseech you, brethren, by the coming of our
Lord Jesus Christ, and by our gathering together unto Him,
that ye be not soon shaken in mind, or be troubled, neither
by spirit, nor by word, nor by letter as from us, as that
the day of Christ is at hand. Let no man deceive you by
any means: for that day shall not come, except there come
a falling away first, and *that man of sin* be revealed, *the
son of perdition;* who opposeth and exalteth himself above
all that is called God, or that is worshipped; so that he as
God sitteth in the temple of God, shewing himself that
he is God.

"Remember ye not, that, when I was yet with you, I told you these things? And now ye know what withholdeth that he might be revealed in his time. For the mystery of iniquity doth already work: only He who now letteth will let, until He be taken out of the way. And then shall that Wicked be revealed, whom the Lord shall consume with the spirit of His mouth, and shall destroy with the brightness of His coming: Even him, whose coming is after the working of Satan with all power and signs and lying wonders, and with all deceivableness of unrighteousness in them that perish; because they received not the love of the truth, that they might be saved. And for this cause God shall send them strong delusion, that they should believe a lie: that they all might be damned who believed not the truth, but had pleasure in unrighteousness."

Notice in verse 3 of this passage, the monstrosity who will appear after the Rapture of the Church is called "that MAN OF SIN, THE SON OF PERDITION." According to the words of Jesus, He lost only one of the twelve—JUDAS, whom He called the son of perdition, and He lost him that the Scriptures might be fulfilled. I believe Judas still has a work to do in the person of the Man of Sin, the Antichrist, who will appear on earth immediately after the Rapture of the Church.

We must not question Christ's wisdom in choosing Judas as one of the twelve apostles, any more than we question why God raised up Pharaoh that He might drown him in the Red Sea: "For the Scripture saith unto Pharaoh, Even for this same purpose have I raised thee up, that I might shew my power in thee, and that my name might be declared throughout all the earth" (Rom. 9:17).

Judas never went the way of the Lord. In Luke 22:4 we read, "And *he went his way,* and communed with the chief priests and captains, how he might betray (Jesus) unto them." The man who goes "HIS way" and not the way of the Lord, not led by the Spirit, is certain to fall!

CHAPTER VII

1. After these things Jesus walked in Galilee: for he would not walk in Jewry, because the Jews sought to kill him.

2. Now the Jews' feast of tabernacles was at hand.

3. His brethren therefore said unto him, Depart hence, and go into Judaea, that thy disciples also may see the works that thou doest.

4. For there is no man that doeth any thing in secret, and he himself seeketh to be known openly. If thou do these things, shew thyself to the world.

5. For neither did his brethren believe in him.

6. Then Jesus said unto them, My time is not yet come: but your time is alway ready.

7. The world cannot hate you; but me it hateth, because I testify of it, that the works thereof are evil.

8. Go ye up unto this feast: I go not up yet unto this feast; for my time is not yet full come.

9. When he had said these words unto them, he abode still in Galilee.

10. But when his brethren were gone up, then went he also up unto the feast, not openly, but as it were in secret.

11. Then the Jews sought him at the feast, and said, Where is he?

12. And there was much murmuring among the people concerning him: for some said, He is a good man: others said, Nay; but he deceiveth the people.

13. Howbeit no man spake openly of him for fear of the Jews.

14. Now about the midst of the feast Jesus went up into the temple, and taught.

15. And the Jews marvelled, saying, How knoweth this man letters, having never learned?

16. Jesus answered them, and said, My doctrine is not mine, but his that sent me.

17. If any man will do his will, he shall know of the doctrine, whether it be of God, or whether I speak of myself.

18. He that speaketh of himself seeketh his own glory: but he that seeketh his glory that sent him, the same is true, and no unrighteousness is in him.

19. Did not Moses give you the law, and yet none of you keepeth

the law? Why go ye about to kill me?

20. The people answered and said, Thou hast a devil: who goeth about to kill thee?

21. Jesus answered and said unto them, I have done one work, and ye all marvel.

22. Moses therefore gave unto you circumcision; (not because it is of Moses, but of the fathers;) and ye on the sabbath day circumcise a man.

23. If a man on the sabbath day receive circumcision, that the law of Moses should not be broken; are ye angry at me, because I have made a man every whit whole on the sabbath day?

24. Judge not according to the appearance, but judge righteous judgment.

25. Then said some of them of Jerusalem, Is not this he, whom they seek to kill?

26. But, lo, he speaketh boldly, and they say nothing unto him. Do the rulers know indeed that this is the very Christ?

27. Howbeit we know this man whence he is: but when Christ cometh, no man knoweth whence he is.

28. Then cried Jesus in the temple as he taught, saying, Ye both know me, and ye know whence I am: and I am not come of myself, but he that sent me is true, whom ye know not.

29. But I know him: for I am from him, and he hath sent me.

30. Then they sought to take him: but no man laid hands on him, because his hour was not yet come.

31. And many of the people believed on him, and said, When Christ cometh, will he do more miracles than these which this man hath done?

32. The Pharisees heard that the people murmured such things concerning him; and the Pharisees and the chief priests sent officers to take him.

33. Then said Jesus unto them, Yet a little while am I with you, and then I go unto him that sent me.

34. Ye shall seek me, and shall not find me: and where I am, thither ye cannot come.

35. Then said the Jews among themselves, Whither will he go, that we shall not find him? will he go unto the dispersed among the Gentiles, and teach the Gentiles?

36. What manner of saying is this that he said, Ye shall seek me, and shall not find me: and where I am, thither ye cannot come?

37. In the last day, that great day of the feast, Jesus stood and cried, saying, If any man thirst, let him come unto me, and drink.

38. He that believeth on me, as the scripture hath said, out of his belly shall flow rivers of living water.

39. (But this spake he of the Spirit, which they that believe on him should receive: for the Holy Ghost was not yet given; because that Jesus was not yet glorified.)

40. Many of the people therefore, when they heard this saying, said, Of a truth this is the Prophet.

41. Others said, This is the Christ.   But some said, Shall Christ come out of Galilee?

42. Hath not the scripture said, That Christ cometh of the seed of David, and out of the town of Bethlehem, where David was?

43. So there was a division among the people because of him.

44. And some of them would have taken him; but no man laid hands on him.

45. Then came the officers to the chief priests and Pharisees; and they said unto them, Why have ye not brought him?

46. The officers answered, Never man spake like this man.

47. Then answered them the Pharisees, Are ye also deceived?

48. Have any of the rulers or of the Pharisees believed on him?

49. But this people who knoweth not the law are cursed.

50. Nicodemus saith unto them, (he that came to Jesus by night, being one of them,)

51. Doth our law judge any man, before it hear him, and know what he doeth?

52. They answered and said unto him, Art thou also of Galilee? Search, and look: for out of Galilee ariseth no prophet.

53. And every man went unto his own house.

In this chapter the controversy between Christ and the Jews grows in intensity, and the scene moves from Galilee to Jerusalem.   The circumstances are now connected with another feast of the Jews—the feast of tabernacles.   (John recorded the Jewish feasts in chronological order.)

Since great multitudes of Jews always attended these feasts, Jesus' "brethren" invited Him to go into Judaea and display His mighty miracles and works.   They wanted Him to manifest Himself to the world in hopes that He would be made King and would restore Israel to her former national glory.   They did not believe in Him as Messiah (v. 5), but they believed in His power and hoped that He would use that power to achieve fame and popularity.

He told them, however, that this was not the purpose for which He had come into the world, and instructed them

to go on up to the feast, leaving Him to come later.   After
they had gone, He *did* go up to the feast—but He went
alone, "not openly, but as it were in secret" (v. 10). Through
His omniscience He knew the people, He knew the trend
the renewed controversy would take.   Therefore He moved
and ministered in view of His coming crucifixion.   Everything He did and said was to the end that He might do
the will of God, and it was God's will that His Son be
lifted up on the cross and pay the sin-debt in full, thereby
opening the door of salvation for sinners.   Jesus knew the
Jews would seek Him at the feast, and therefore He moved
among them in secret.

The events recorded in chapter 6 took place about the
time of the Passover feast, which was in the springtime.
Events in chapter 7 took place in early fall, the time the
feast of tabernacles was held.

Verse 1:   *"After these things Jesus walked in Galilee:
for He would not walk in Jewry, because the Jews sought
to kill Him."*

Whatever Jesus did in Galilee during the months between
the events recorded in chapter 6 and the opening of chapter
7, John passes over in silence. Almost all of John's Gospel
has to do with the ministry of Jesus in or near Jerusalem.
We find exceptions only in chapters 1, 2, 4, and 6.   Bible
scholars agree that at this period in the ministry of the
Lord, He was absent from Jerusalem for about eighteen
months.

The statement *"Jesus walked in Galilee"* must be taken
figuratively and does not mean that He was continually
walking, but that He dwelt in Galilee as He went about
His ministry there.

"He would not walk in Jewry" means that He did not
walk in Judaea.   (The same Greek word here translated
"Jewry" is rendered "Judaea" in verse 3.)   He did not
choose to walk in Judaea because He knew that one group
there wanted to destroy Him while another group wanted

to make Him king. It was not in divine plans that He should be made king at this time, nor had He come into the world to be destroyed at the hands of men. Therefore during that particular period of His ministry He did not minister in Judaea.

"The Jews sought to kill Him." This does not mean that *all* of the Jews wanted to kill Jesus. It was the rulers of the Jewish nation—members of the Sanhedrin, chief priests, scribes and elders—who wanted to kill Him. Mark 12:37 tells us that "the common people heard Him gladly." It seems that down through the ages it has been "the common people" who love and appreciate the Gospel of the marvelous grace of God. True, there are some outstanding people who embrace Christianity—great men of science, great educators, great politicians and statesmen have become Christians—but they are few in number; and in I Corinthians 1:26—31 Paul tells us why this is true: "For ye see your calling, brethren, how that not many wise men after the flesh, not many mighty, not many noble, are called: But God hath chosen the foolish things of the world to confound the wise; and God hath chosen the weak things of the world to confound the things which are mighty; and base things of the world, and things which are despised, hath God chosen, yea, and things which are not, to bring to nought things that are: that no flesh should glory in His presence. But of Him are ye in Christ Jesus, who of God is made unto us wisdom, and righteousness, and sanctification, and redemption: That, according as it is written, He that glorieth, let him glory in the Lord."

The day Jesus healed the paralytic by the pool of Bethesda was the day the Jews made up their minds to destroy Him (John 5:16—18). But they could not destroy Him, they could not silence Him, nor could they keep the masses from listening to Him. However, their own minds were made up to put Him to death, and from that day forward they sought means by which they could accuse Him.

There is a definite lesson here for believers: According

to the example Jesus gave in this passage, we are not to
deliberately expose ourselves to danger. We are not to
tempt the Lord (Matt. 4:7). If we come upon danger un-
aware, or if danger overtakes us, God is able to deliver us;
but we are not to deliberately court danger or death. It
takes much more "nerve" and grace to live a dedicated
Christian life than it does to die a martyr's death.

Verse 2:   *"Now the Jews' feast of tabernacles was at
hand."*

There were three outstanding feasts in the Jewish year—
the Passover (representing what we know as Easter), the
feast of Pentecost, and the feast of tabernacles, which was
held in autumn after the harvest in the seventh month of
the Jewish year:

"Thou shalt observe the feast of tabernacles seven days,
after that thou hast gathered in thy corn and thy wine: and
thou shalt rejoice in thy feast, thou, and thy son, and thy
daughter, and thy manservant, and thy maidservant, and
the Levite, the stranger, and the fatherless, and the widow,
that are within thy gates. Seven days shalt thou keep a
solemn feast unto the Lord thy God in the place which the
Lord shall choose: because the Lord thy God shall bless
thee in all thine increase, and in all the works of thine
hands, therefore thou shalt surely rejoice" (Deut. 16:13−15).

The seventh month was outstanding in the Jewish year
because during that month the Jews observed quite a number of ordinances according to the Law of Moses. On the
first day of the seventh month they observed the feast of
trumpets. The tenth day was the Day of Atonement, and
on the fifteenth day the feast of tabernacles began.

There are several peculiarly interesting things about this
feast. First of all, it was an occasion of rejoicing for the
Jews. For seven days they lived in little booths (little
houses made of branches) in remembrance of the temporary
dwellings in which they lived when they came out of Egypt:

"Also in the fifteenth day of the seventh month, when

ye have gathered in the fruit of the land, ye shall keep a feast unto the Lord seven days: on the first day shall be a sabbath, and on the eighth day shall be a sabbath. And ye shall take you on the first day the boughs of goodly trees, branches of palm trees, and the boughs of thick trees, and willows of the brook; and ye shall rejoice before the Lord your God seven days. And ye shall keep it a feast unto the Lord seven days in the year. It shall be a statute for ever in your generations: ye shall celebrate it in the seventh month. Ye shall dwell in booths seven days; all that are Israelites born shall dwell in booths: that your generations may know that I made the children of Israel to dwell in booths, when I brought them out of the land of Egypt: I am the Lord your God" (Lev. 23:39—43).

In the second place, more sacrifices were offered at the feast of tabernacles than at any other of the Jewish feasts:

"On the fifteenth day of the seventh month ye shall have an holy convocation; ye shall do no servile work, and ye shall keep a feast unto the Lord seven days: And ye shall offer a burnt-offering, a sacrifice made by fire, of a sweet savour unto the Lord; thirteen young bullocks, two rams, and fourteen lambs of the first year; they shall be without blemish: and their meat-offerings shall be of flour mingled with oil, three tenth deals unto every bullock of the thirteen bullocks, two tenth deals to each ram of the two rams, and a several tenth deal to each lamb of the fourteen lambs: and one kid of the goats for a sin-offering; beside the continual burnt-offering, his meat-offering, and his drink-offering.

"And on the second day ye shall offer twelve young bullocks, two rams, fourteen lambs of the first year without spot: and their meat-offering and their drink-offerings for the bullocks, for the rams, and for the lambs, shall be according to their number, after the manner: and one kid of the goats for a sin-offering; beside the continual burnt-offering, and the meat-offering thereof, and their drink-offerings.

"And on the third day eleven bullocks, two rams, four-teen lambs of the first year without blemish; and their meat-offering and their drink-offerings for the bullocks, for the rams, and for the lambs, shall be according to their number, after the manner: and one goat for a sin-offering; beside the continual burnt-offering, and his meat-offering, and his drink-offering.

"And on the fourth day ten bullocks, two rams, and fourteen lambs of the first year without blemish: Their meat-offering and their drink-offerings for the bullocks, for the rams, and for the lambs, shall be according to their number, after the manner: and one kid of the goats for a sin-offering; beside the continual burnt-offering, his meat-offering, and his drink-offering.

"And on the fifth day nine bullocks, two rams, and four-teen lambs of the first year without spot: and their meat-offering and their drink-offerings for the bullocks, for the rams, and for the lambs, shall be according to their number, after the manner: and one goat for a sin-offering; beside the continual burnt-offering, and his meat-offering, and his drink-offering.

"And on the sixth day eight bullocks, two rams, and fourteen lambs of the first year without blemish: and their meat-offering and their drink-offerings for the bullocks, for the rams, and for the lambs, shall be according to their number, after the manner: and one goat for a sin-offering; beside the continual burnt-offering, his meat-offering, and his drink-offering.

"And on the seventh day seven bullocks, two rams, and fourteen lambs of the first year without blemish: and their meat-offering and their drink-offerings for the bullocks, for the rams, and for the lambs, shall be according to their number, after the manner: and one goat for a sin-offering; beside the continual burnt-offering, his meat-offering, and his drink-offering.

"On the eighth day ye shall have a solemn assembly: ye shall do no servile work therein: But ye shall offer a burnt-offering, a sacrifice made by fire, of a sweet savour unto the Lord: one bullock, one ram, seven lambs of the first year without blemish: Their meat-offering and their drink-offerings for the bullock, for the ram, and for the lambs, shall be according to their number, after the manner: and one goat for a sin-offering; beside the continual burnt-offering, and his meat-offering, and his drink-offering" (Num. 29:12—38).

In the third place, once every seven years at the feast of tabernacles the Law of Moses was publicly read to all the people:

"And Moses commanded them, saying, At the end of every seven years, in the solemnity of the year of release, in the feast of tabernacles, when all Israel is come to appear before the Lord thy God in the place which He shall choose, thou shalt read this law before all Israel in their hearing. Gather the people together, men, and women, and children, and thy stranger that is within thy gates, that they may hear, and that they may learn, and fear the Lord your God, and observe to do all the words of this law: and that their children, which have not known any thing, may hear, and learn to fear the Lord your God, as long as ye live in the land whither ye go over Jordan to possess it" (Deut. 31:10—13).

In the fourth place, during the feast of tabernacles water was taken from the pool of Siloam every day, and with great reverence was poured upon the altar; and while the water was being poured upon the altar, all the people sang the twelfth chapter of Isaiah:

"And in that day thou shalt say, O Lord, I will praise thee: though thou wast angry with me, thine anger is turned away, and thou comfortedst me. Behold, God is my salvation; I will trust, and not be afraid: for the Lord JEHOVAH is my strength and my song; He also is become my salvation. Therefore with joy shall ye draw water out of the wells of salvation. And in that day shall ye say, Praise the Lord, call upon His name, declare His doings among the people, make mention that His name is exalted. Sing unto the Lord; for He hath done excellent things: this is known in all the earth. Cry out and shout, thou inhabitant of Zion: for great is the Holy One of Israel in the midst of thee" (Isa. 12:1—6).

In the fifth place, the feast of tabernacles began only five days after the great Day of Atonement, and the minds of the people were fresh and alert concerning the ordinances of the scapegoat and the high priest's going into the holy of holies once a year to offer blood on the mercyseat. There was much rejoicing during the feast of tabernacles. Some of our outstanding Bible scholars have called it the holiest and greatest of the Jewish feasts. It was truly "a time of jubilee." It was the last in the order of Jewish feasts; it finished the feasts and festivities of the Jewish religious year. The people had labored untiringly, they had gathered their grain and their food; and when the year's work was finished, when the fruits of their labors were gathered and stored, they observed the feast of tabernacles. Thus it was an occasion of unusual and special rejoicing as the people remembered the days in Egypt and the time when God delivered the Israelite fathers from Egyptian bondage.

Every *fiftieth* year the feast of tabernacles followed after the great jubilee and the proclamation declaring liberty to all. The feast of tabernacles is that unusual and special feast which will be kept by the Jews after they are restored to Jerusalem after that city is rebuilt in the Millennium, the future kingdom of the Lord Jesus Christ: "And it shall come to pass, that every one that is left of all the nations which came against Jerusalem shall even go up from year to year to worship the King, the Lord of hosts, and to keep the feast of tabernacles" (Zech. 14:16).

To me, the feast of the *Passover* was definitely a type of the crucifixion of the Lord Jesus Christ. The feast of *Pentecost* was a type of the coming of the Holy Spirit; and the *feast of tabernacles* was a type of the second coming of the Lord to gather His people into their own land, the land promised to Abraham. It points to the day when Christ will come as King of kings and Lord of lords, to sit on the throne of His father David and gather His people into one glorious nation to reap the harvest of the earth and bring this dispensation to a climax; the time when He will come forth to bless His people, to destroy the enemies of God and the righteous, the time when He will proclaim jubilee throughout the earth. It is then that men will beat their swords into plowshares and their spears into pruning hooks. There will then be peace on earth, good will toward men.

Verse 3: *"His brethren therefore said unto Him, Depart hence, and go into Judaea, that thy disciples also may see the works that thou doest."*

"His brethren" here were no doubt relatives of Joseph and Mary. They might have lived in Nazareth or in Capernaum. Naturally they observed the ministry of Jesus with much curiosity and interest, but at that time they did not believe on Him as very God or as Messiah.

I personally believe that other children were born to Mary and Joseph after the birth of Jesus. He was the firstborn— but I believe the Scripture teaches that other children were born of the union of Mary and *Joseph,* and these were probably included in the "brethren" mentioned here. They would have been half-brothers to Jesus *according to the flesh.* The Scripture is very clear and the Holy Spirit is extremely cautious to assure us that Joseph was the husband of *Mary,* the mother of Jesus:

"Now the birth of Jesus Christ was on this wise: When as *His mother Mary* was espoused to Joseph, *before they came together, she was found with child of the Holy Ghost.* Then Joseph her husband, being a just man, and not willing to make her a publick example, was minded to put her away privily. But while he thought on these things, behold, the angel of the Lord appeared unto him in a dream, saying, Joseph, thou son of David, fear not to take unto thee Mary thy wife: *for that which is conceived in her is of the*

Holy Ghost. And she shall bring forth a Son, and thou shalt call His name JESUS: for He shall save His people from their sins. Now all this was done, that it might be fulfilled which was spoken of the Lord by the prophet, saying, Behold, a virgin shall be with child, and shall bring forth a Son, and they shall call His name Emmanuel, which being interpreted is, God with us. Then Joseph being raised from sleep did as the angel of the Lord had bidden him, and took unto him his wife: *and knew her not till* she had brought forth her firstborn Son: and he called His name JESUS" (Matt. 1:18−25).

In Luke 2:33 we read, "And Joseph and His mother (the mother of Jesus) marvelled at those things which were spoken of Him."

Whoever these "brethren" were, they thought that Jesus should go into Judaea, that the disciples there might see the works, the mighty miracles, He was doing. The *"disciples"* referred to are undoubtedly those who believed on Him as mentioned in chapter 2, verse 23: "Now when He was in Jerusalem at the passover, in the feast day, *many believed in His name,* when they saw the miracles which He did." The statement of "His brethren" definitely indicated that Jesus had disciples in Judaea and at Jerusalem.

Verse 4: *"For there is no man that doeth any thing in secret, and he himself seeketh to be known openly. If thou do these things, shew thyself to the world."*

In other words, the "brethren" said to Jesus, "If a man wants to be known, he must do what he is doing in the open, not in secret. If you really are the Messiah as you claim to be, if you want to establish a great following, then go up to Jerusalem to the feast and demonstrate your power openly where you can be seen by the multitudes."

This statement proves that the "brethren" mentioned here were not born again. All truly born again people know that Christianity does not seek the praise of men, nor does it long for a crowd of well-wishers. Christianity serves to the glory of God, not to gain the favor of the masses or publicity from the world. Jesus worked mighty miracles, yes—He fed the hungry, healed the sick, clothed the naked, opened the eyes of the blind, cleansed the lepers, and raised the dead—but this part of His ministry was only a sideline. His primary purpose was to die on the cross that we might have life through Him. He came primarily to save souls, not to bless bodies.

Verse 5: *"For neither did His brethren believe in Him."*

This verse is clear: these "brethren" did not have faith in Jesus as Messiah or Saviour, they did not believe that He was God's Christ; therefore they were not saved by grace. Being "brethren" did not save them. There are people to-day who think that because they were born into a Christian home and reared by Christian parents or grandparents, they themselves are saved. They think that the righteousness of their relatives is enough for them also. This is sad, because they will certainly learn differently when they stand before God. Mark 3:35 tells us who is a brother or a sister to Jesus: "For whosoever shall do the will of God, the same is my brother, and my sister, and mother."

Verse 6: *"Then Jesus said unto them, My time is not yet come: but your time is alway ready."*

This is proof positive that the earthly ministry of Jesus was blueprinted in every detail from the beginning. He lived and ministered according to a pre-ordained plan, and everything He said or did fitted into that plan perfectly. But no one understood the divine depth of meaning in His answer. They thought He was speaking only of the time when He should go up to the feast.

"Your time is alway ready." This could be said only to unbelievers. In the life of the *believer* "all things work together for good . . . the steps of a good man are ordered by the Lord." But for these unconverted "brethren," it made no difference *when* they went up to the feast because

they were of the world and were *like* the world; therefore
their presence would cause no excitement, nor would they
face persecution or death.

Verse 7: *"The world cannot hate you; but me it hateth,
because I testify of it, that the works thereof are evil."*

In John 15:19 Jesus said to His disciples, "If ye were of
the world, the world would love his own: but because ye
are not of the world, but I have chosen you OUT of the
world, therefore the world hateth you." Since He said here
to these brethren, "The world cannot hate you," we know
that they were unbelievers.

*"Me it hateth, because I testify of it, that the works
thereof are evil."* Here is the true cause of the Jews' hatred
of the Lord Jesus Christ. It was not only because He
claimed to be Messiah; they hated Him because of His
doctrine—He preached against their wicked lives. They
were covetous, they were guilty of hypocrisy, adultery, and
many other gross sins. Jesus cried out against their sins,
and they hated Him for it. Unconverted men still hate
preachers who name sin and preach against ungodliness.

Unregenerate man is capable of any and all ungodliness:
"For from within, out of the heart of men, proceed evil
thoughts, adulteries, fornications, murders, thefts, covetousness, wickedness, deceit, lasciviousness, an evil eye, blasphemy, pride, foolishness: *all these evil things come from
within, and defile the man"* (Mark 7:21—23).

It is unnatural for the unconverted person to love righteousness, purity, and holiness. These he loves only after
God has put a new heart in his bosom and given him a
new spirit through the miracle of the new birth. Jesus was
truth, love, purity, holiness—and yet they hated Him.

To His disciples Jesus said, "These things I have spoken
unto you, that *in me* ye might have peace. In the world
ye shall have tribulation: but be of good cheer; I have
overcome the world" (John 16:33). In I John 3:13 we read,
"Marvel not, my brethren, if the world hate you." The

more dedicated and consecrated a Christian is, the more he will be despised by the world. The world hated Jesus, and those who attempt to *live* like Jesus will be hated today. A minister who preaches the Word of God without fear, favor, or compromise will be hated—not by all, but by many. The Christian who lives a separated life will be hated by the majority of unbelievers. The only person well spoken of by all is a compromiser: "Woe unto you, when all men shall speak well of you: for so did their fathers to the false prophets" (Luke 6:26).

Verse 8: *"Go ye up unto this feast: I go not up yet unto this feast; for my time is not yet full come."*

This was not a command; the Greek language speaks in this tone: "If you want to go to Jerusalem at this time, go. Do not wait for me."

"For my time is not yet full come." Jesus did not say that He would not attend the feast at all; He simply said that it was not yet time for Him to go. Our Lord did nothing before the appointed time, He made no move by accident.

Verse 9: *"When He had said these words unto them, He abode still in Galilee."*

The "brethren" started on their journey to Jerusalem; Jesus stayed on in Galilee until it was time for Him to go up to the feast. *Where* He abode in Galilee we are not told.

Verse 10: *"But when His brethren were gone up, then went He also up unto the feast, not openly, but as it were in secret."*

We do not know how long a time elapsed after the "brethren" departed before Jesus left Galilee to go up to the feast at Jerusalem, but He probably left very shortly after they did. He knew His brethren wanted to make a public show of Him, hoping to see Him perform miracles and startle the crowds. Their desires were carnal, not spiritual, and Jesus would not oblige them. Also, He had not forgotten that there was a group in Galilee who wanted to take Him by force and make Him king (John 6:15); therefore, when He finally went up to Jerusalem to attend the feast He went alone, *"not openly, but as it were in secret."*

Jesus never sought publicity, He never tried to be spectacular. The only time He deliberately put Himself in the public eye was at the last Passover, just before His crucifixion when, in accordance with the plan of God the Father, He rode into Jerusalem on a little donkey as prophesied by Zechariah: "Rejoice greatly, O daughter of Zion; shout, O daughter of Jerusalem: behold, thy King cometh unto thee: He is just, and having salvation; lowly, and riding upon an ass, and upon a colt the foal of an ass" (Zech. 9:9). In connection with this, please read Matthew 21:1−11; Mark 11:1−11; Luke 19:28−40; John 12:12−19.

Verse 11: *"Then the Jews sought Him at the feast, and said, Where is He?"*

"The Jews" referred to here were the rulers of the nation—the Pharisees, scribes, chief priests, members of the Sanhedrin. They sought Jesus, but not because they wanted to learn of Him. They wanted to be rid of Him, they were plotting to put Him to death; and they knew that He would attend the feast, because that was the custom of all dedicated Jews.

"Where is He?" In the Greek, the word rendered *"He"* suggests contempt and hatred, as if they asked, "Where is that fellow who claims so much? We know there is nothing to His claims." (In connection with this please read Matthew 27:62−66.)

Verse 12: *"And there was much murmuring among the people concerning Him: for some said, He is a good man: others said, Nay; but He deceiveth the people."*

The *"much murmuring among the people"* suggests that groups would gather and talk in low voices, muttering and murmuring against Jesus. These people were the multitudes of Jews who had gathered from far and near for the feast of tabernacles. The rulers of the Jews had stirred these crowds by their false reports and accusations of Jesus, hoping to cause the multitudes to hate Him as they themselves hated Him; but in spite of their efforts, there were still many among the crowds who respected Him as a prophet even though they did not acknowledge Him as Messiah or the Son of God.

"Some said, He is a good man: others said, Nay; but He deceiveth the people." Some of the people agreed with Nicodemus; they knew that no man could do what Jesus was doing except God be with him. The opposing crowd said, "He *deceiveth* the people!" Jesus was the greatest *divider of men* who ever lived—and He is just the same today. He divided every group to whom He spoke or ministered. Some loved Him, some hated Him; some wanted to crown Him king, others wanted to put Him to death. To some He was "the savour of life," to others He was "the savour of death" (II Cor. 2:16). There is no middle ground with Jesus; He draws out our true character. In Matthew 12:30 He said, *"He that is not with me is against me; and he that gathereth not with me scattereth abroad."*

Of His first advent Jesus said, "Think not that I am come to send peace on earth: I came not to send peace, but a sword. For I am come to set a man at variance against his father, and the daughter against her mother, and the daughter in law against her mother in law. And a man's foes shall be they of his own household!" (Matt. 10:34—36). Strife and *conflict of opinion* always occur when the Gospel is preached in all of its purity and power. There is nothing wrong with the Gospel—the trouble is with *human nature.* When a person boasts that there has been no conflict or strife in his church for many years, he is simply saying, "The full Gospel is not preached in my church." Where there is no conflict among church members, the Gospel has NOT been preached in its entirety. God's preacher is instructed to "preach the WORD; be instant in season, out of season; reprove, rebuke, exhort with all longsuffering and doctrine" (II Tim. 4:2); and when a minister begins to reprove and rebuke people of sin, they will declare *war* on that preacher, just as they did when *Jesus* preached the truth.   It is well to consider that quietness, stillness, is not life; *it is stagnation and death!*

Verse 13:   *"Howbeit no man spake openly of Him for fear of the Jews."*

Those who *hated* Jesus were not afraid to publicly announce their opposition to Him, but those who respected Him and believed that He was sent from God were afraid to openly declare their belief because they would then be persecuted by the rulers and would be put out of the synagogue.   They knew how dangerous it would be to openly favor Jesus, or to display interest in Him or respect for Him.

Even today *the fear of MAN* is a powerful tool of the devil.   There are preachers who *know* the whole truth, but they will not preach it because they fear the reaction of their parishioners.   God pity such a minister!   We are to fear GOD, not man!   The fourth chapter of Acts records the inspiring account of the disciples' fearless preaching of the Gospel.   Though threatened and imprisoned, Peter and John said, "Whether it be right in the sight of God to hearken unto YOU more than unto GOD, *judge ye.*   For we cannot but speak the things which we have seen and heard."   When they were released from custody, they *immediately* "went to their own company, and reported all that the chief priests and elders had said unto them."   In verses 29 and 31 of that chapter we read their prayer: *"Lord, behold their threatenings: and grant unto thy servants, that with all BOLDNESS they may speak thy Word . . . AND WHEN THEY HAD PRAYED, THE PLACE WAS SHAKEN WHERE THEY WERE ASSEMBLED TOGETHER; AND THEY WERE ALL FILLED WITH THE HOLY*

*GHOST, AND THEY SPAKE THE WORD OF GOD WITH
BOLDNESS!"* What a testimony!

Jesus at the Feast of Tabernacles

Verse 14: *"Now about the midst of the feast Jesus went
up into the temple, and taught."*

Since the feast of tabernacles lasted seven days, if Jesus
arrived in *"the midst of the feast"* He arrived about noon
of the *fourth day,* and *"went up into the temple, and
taught."* The outer court of the temple was sheltered to
protect the people against the heat in summer and the cold
in winter. It was here that the pious Jews assembled to
hear the doctors of the law discuss religious subjects, ex-
pound the law, and instruct in the tradition of the fathers.
(See Luke 2:46,47.) It was in this outer court that Jesus
taught on this occasion. We are not told *what* He taught
that day, but there can be no doubt that He gave the people simple Gospel messages and plain spiritual truths, as
was His custom *wherever* He taught. Whatever He said,
wherever He said it, was the Word of God and was given
with authority.

Verse 15: *"And the Jews marvelled, saying, How knoweth this Man letters, having never learned?"*

They marveled at the Lord's knowledge of the Scriptures
and the wisdom with which He spoke. He had never attended their theological schools, He had never been taught
by the scribes and Pharisees, He had no formal education
such as Paul spoke of when he said, "I am verily a man
which am a Jew, born in Tarsus, a city in Cilicia, *yet
brought up in this city at the feet of Gamaliel, and taught
according to the perfect manner of the law of the fathers
. . ."* (Acts 22:3).

"How knoweth this Man letters, having never learned?"
Insofar as the Jews knew, Jesus had never attended school—
and yet He had perfect knowledge of the Scriptures and

spoke with such words of wisdom as to cause them to marvel—not only at His *words,* but at His manner and ability
in public speaking.

It is interesting to note that the Greek word here translated *"letters"* is rendered "learning" in Acts 26:24. In
John 5:47 the same word is translated "writings," and in
II Timothy 3:15 it is rendered "Scriptures." The meaning
is actually "a written character, a letter in the alphabet."
So in reality the Jews were saying that Jesus had never
learned His A B C's, therefore they could not understand
how He could preach and teach with such wisdom and
understanding.

The Jews were proud people, filled with conceit and self-
esteem, and they classified as "ignorant" anyone who had
not been formally trained in their institutions—especially as
having to do with religion.   The same is true in a large
measure today—i. e., some of the big denominations will
not ordain a minister unless he has completed certain scho-
lastic requirements in their denominational schools. I believe in Christian education, but I also believe that a man
called of God to preach *will preach* whether or not man
puts *his* stamp of approval on his preaching.

Verse 16: *"Jesus answered them, and said, My doctrine
is not mine, but His that sent me."*

This is the same thought given in John 5:30, 8:28, and
12:49: "I can of mine own self do nothing: as I hear, I
judge: and my judgment is just; because I seek not mine
own will, but the will of the Father which hath sent me. . .
I do nothing of myself; but as my Father hath taught me, I
speak these things. . . For I have not spoken of myself; but
the Father which sent me, He gave me a commandment,
what I should say, and what I should speak."   Jesus wanted
His audience to understand that what He was saying was
not something He had thought up, the product of His own
mind; what He proclaimed was the Word and doctrine of
Jehovah God.   Here again is shown His inseparable union

with God the Father. He did not speak as a rabbi nor as one of the apostles; He spoke the Word of the living God; He WAS the Word, tabernacling in flesh.

Verse 17: *"If any man will do His will, he shall know of the doctrine, whether it be of God, or whether I speak of myself."*

This applies to the exercise of the individual human will, the *definite intention* to DO God's will. In other words, if these people were willing to *do* the will of God, they would *know* whether or not the words of Jesus were the doctrine of God, or something He had made up Himself. To do God's will is not just a matter of faith, but a matter of the heart being in harmony with God in all things, being wholly surrendered to Him. If the Jews had believed that the message Jesus gave was from God, they would have understood that His voice was the voice of God speaking to men—and such learning was not obtainable in the theological schools of the rabbis.

If an individual has a heart and mind to do God's will, then God will make His will *known* to that individual in all truth. Notice I John 2:27: "But the anointing which ye have received of Him abideth in you, and ye need not that any man teach you: but as the same anointing teacheth you of all things, and is truth, and is no lie, and even as it hath taught you, ye shall abide in Him."

Are you seeking the will of God for YOUR life? If so, then in simple, child-like faith and with an honest heart, yield completely to Jesus with all the understanding you possess. Walk with God according to the measure of light you have, and God will give you *further* light, with wisdom, knowledge, and understanding. As you walk day by day in the light, He will give you more light until you are walking fully in His will.

Verse 18: *"He that speaketh of himself seeketh his own glory: but He that seeketh His glory that sent Him, the same is true, and no unrighteousness is in Him."*

(A more literal translation would be, "He that speaketh FROM Himself"—that is, the message he delivers is his *own* message, not the message of God.) The man who is called, commissioned, and ordained of God to preach the Gospel is interested, first and foremost, in bringing glory to the Lord Jesus Christ and to the heavenly Father. The person who exalts *self* is speaking *from* himself, not from God, and this will be true of the minister who undertakes to prepare and deliver a message on his own ability without being sent of God and filled with the Spirit. Such a man will magnify his own wisdom and understanding, he will want honor bestowed upon himself and not upon God. The person who is not called of God and led by the Spirit speaks *from* himself, *for* himself, and *exalts* himself. True believers can recognize this immediately. Those who are born of God will know whether or not a minister is speaking *from God* or from his own understanding and ability. A man who has a reasonable education can prepare and deliver a sermon, perhaps delivering it *well;* but that is not necessarily preaching the Gospel.

The last part of this verse is true of the Lord Jesus Christ only: *"He that seeketh His glory that sent Him, the same is true, AND NO UNRIGHTEOUSNESS IS IN HIM!"*

Verse 19:   *"Did not Moses give you the law, and yet none of you keepeth the law? Why go ye about to kill me?"*

Jesus here refers to the great respect and reverance the Jews had for Moses and the law. It may be that He more specifically had in mind the very Scripture that had been read to them that day, because once every seven years at the feast of tabernacles, the law was read publicly (Deut. 31:10,11), which law contained the command "Thou shalt not kill" (Deut. 5:17). They were now about to break that commandment literally. (They had already broken it in their hearts, because they would have killed Jesus if they had not feared the common people.) Thus Jesus said to them, "You *profess* to honor Moses, you *profess* to keep his law; yet you go about to kill me even though the Law of Moses declares 'Thou shalt *not* kill.' "

Verse 20: *"The people answered and said, Thou hast a devil: who goeth about to kill thee?"*

It seems that this statement came from the common people who had gathered in Jerusalem at that time; it does not stand to reason that the rulers would have made such a statement, because they knew they *were* "going about" to kill Him!

"Thou hast a devil" was probably a statement they had heard from the rulers concerning Jesus, for in Matthew 12: 22—24 we read, "Then was brought unto (Jesus) one possessed with a devil, blind, and dumb: and He healed him, insomuch that the blind and dumb both spake and saw. And all the people were amazed, and said, Is not this the son of David? *But when the Pharisees heard it, they said, This fellow doth not cast out devils, BUT BY BEELZEBUB THE PRINCE OF THE DEVILS!"*

In John 8:48 we read, "Then answered the Jews, and said unto Him, Say we not well that thou art a Samaritan, *and hast a devil?"*

Also in John 10:20, "many of them said, *He hath a devil, and is mad; why hear ye Him?"* So we see that the Jews many times made the statement that Jesus was possessed of a devil. The crowds therefore simply repeated what they had heard the rulers say about Him. This is borne out by the question they asked Him: *"WHO goeth about to kill thee?"* The common people and those who had come from outside Jerusalem did not know of the diabolical scheme to kill Jesus. Most of them knew nothing of the intentions of the rulers, and they considered the Lord to be insane for making the statement that they were going about to kill Him.

Verse 21: *"Jesus answered and said unto them, I have done one work, and ye all marvel."*

The miracle to which Jesus referred was the healing of
the paralytic at the pool of Bethesda as related in chapter
5, which was the only outstanding miracle He had publicly
wrought in Jerusalem—yet the people were still amazed,
still wondering, *concerning* that miracle: *"Ye all marvel,"*
not only because of the miracle, but because it was performed on the Sabbath.   In spite of the glorious healing of
a pitiful human being, they would not forgive Him for
breaking their Sabbath.

Verses 22,23: *"Moses therefore gave unto you circumcision; (not because it is of Moses, but of the fathers;) and
ye on the sabbath day circumcise a man. If a man on the
sabbath day receive circumcision, that the law of Moses
should not be broken; are ye angry at me, because I have
made a man every whit whole on the sabbath day?"*

Circumcision was first given to Abraham (Gen. 17:10).
It was not an ordinance first communicated to Moses, as
was the Levitical system, but Moses added it to the law
because it was an ordinance that had been handed down
from Abraham to Isaac, and from Isaac to Jacob.   Jesus
pointed out to the Jews that in *obedience* to this ordinance
handed down from the fathers, circumcision was administered on the eighth day after a child was born, and if the
eighth day fell on the Sabbath, then circumcision was *administered* on the Sabbath.   In other words, they laid the
law of the Sabbath aside—and justly so—in order to keep
the law of circumcision, a rite that was the sign and seal
of a covenant with God; and by so doing they gave testimony that a work of righteousness might be done on the
Sabbath, even though the Law of Moses declared, "Remember the Sabbath day to keep it holy."   Yet they were angry
with Jesus for following the same principle and *healing* on
the Sabbath.

Verse 24: *"Judge not according to the appearance, but
judge righteous judgment."*

If the Sabbath should be broken to keep a *ceremonial*

ordinance such as circumcision, how much *more* should a deed of *mercy* be allowed on the Sabbath day! We should never judge by appearance only. We should weigh a matter very carefully from every aspect and judge *justly,* not simply by what we see, remembering that "the Lord seeth not as man seeth; for man looketh on the outward appearance, but the Lord looketh on the heart" (I Sam. 16:7).

Verse 25: *"Then said some of them of Jerusalem, Is not this He, whom they seek to kill?"*

The people who asked this question were not of the group who asked, "WHO goeth about to kill thee?" These people had undoubtedly lived in Jerusalem and had followed the ministry and movements of Jesus, and thus they knew the plan of the chief priests and scribes to put Him to death.

Verse 26: *"But, lo, He speaketh boldly, and they say nothing unto Him. Do the rulers know indeed that this is the very Christ?"*

What Jesus had to say, He said openly, publicly—and yet the chief priests made no effort to arrest Him and stop His teaching. The common people were impressed by this, and they asked, "Could it be that our rulers have changed their minds about this Prophet? Were they convinced by the mighty miracles and bold speech of this Man that He truly IS the Messiah?" But it was *the restraining power of Almighty God* that held back the enemies of Jesus, for *His hour "was not yet come."*

Verse 27: *"Howbeit we know this Man whence He is: but when Christ cometh, no man knoweth whence He is."*

"We know this Man from whence He is." The majority of the people thought Jesus was a Nazarene. Even in His triumphal entry into Jerusalem they cried, "This is Jesus the prophet of Nazareth of Galilee" (Matt. 21:11). When He taught in the synagogue in Nazareth they asked, "Is not

this the carpenter's son? Is not His mother called Mary? and His brethren, James, and Joses, and Simon, and Judas? And His sisters, are they not all with us?" (Matt. 13:55,56). In Luke 4:22 they asked, "Is not this Joseph's son?"

But Jesus was not born in Nazareth; He was born in Bethlehem as prophesied in Micah 5:2: "But thou, Bethlehem Ephratah, though thou be little among the thousands of Judah, yet out of thee shall He come forth unto me that is to be ruler in Israel; whose goings forth have been from of old, from everlasting."

There was no excuse for the scribes and Pharisees not knowing this prophecy concerning the city where their Messiah was to be born, and in the thirty years that had elapsed since His birth they could have learned *every detail* of His birth, as prophesied throughout the Old Testament. Their ignorance was inexcusable.

"When Christ cometh, no man knoweth whence He is." This statement was probably made because of Isaiah 53:8, which says in part, ". . . Who shall declare His generation?" or because of Malachi 3:1: ". . . The Lord, whom ye seek, shall suddenly come to His temple . . . ." They were expecting Messiah to appear suddenly and mysteriously, and they simply could not believe that this Man was the one for whom they waited. We need to realize that it is never profitable to take part of a verse to prove a point, nor should we take Scripture out of context. The Jews had read, "the Lord shall suddenly come to His temple"—but they had not rightly divided the Word of truth. He came the first time as a *Lamb;* He will come the *second* time as the Lion of the tribe of Judah. He came the first time a babe in the manger; when He comes the second time, every eye shall see Him and all the kindreds of the earth shall wail because of Him. It is dangerous to take only a *portion* of a verse to prove a point, and that is exactly what these Jews did. They were very poor scholars of their books of prophecy.

Verses 28 and 29:   *"Then cried Jesus in the temple as*

*He taught, saying, Ye both know me, and ye know whence
I am: and I am not come of myself, but He that sent me
is true, whom ye know not. But I know Him: for I am
from Him, and He hath sent me."*

Here is an unusual statement which implies deep emotion on the part of Christ. Jesus *"cried"* out, or raised His
voice to a high pitch, which was not His custom. Our
Lord is only said to have "cried" or lifted up His voice in
four other places in the Scriptures: Matthew 27:50 when
He yielded up the ghost; Mark 15:37 (the same occasion),
John 7:37 as He offered the living water, and again in John
12:44. In Matthew 12:19 we read a quotation from Isaiah
42:2: "He shall not strive, nor cry; neither shall any man
hear His voice in the streets." We must remember that
when He cried out on this occasion He was addressing a
large crowd, which condition might have necessitated a
louder voice in order to be heard.

In our present verse, what Jesus said to the Jews was,
"You see me with the physical eye—but you do not see
me for what I really am. You see me as another prophet
or person, but you do not know me as God in flesh, your
Messiah." And again He clearly points out to them that
He did not come into the world at His own bidding, He
did not come of Himself, and if they had really known the
true God as they claimed to know Him they would have
known His only begotten Son when He came.

The knowledge spoken of by Jesus in verse 29 is far beyond man's ability to comprehend. It has to do with His
unity in the Godhead. Jesus knows the Father, and the
Father knows the Son, in a sense that no one else can know
either the Father OR the Son: "As the Father knoweth me,
even so know I the Father . . ." (John 10:15).

Matthew 11:27 also enlightens us here: "All things are
delivered unto me of my Father: and no man knoweth the
Son, but the Father; neither knoweth any man the Father,
save the Son, and he to whomsoever the Son will reveal

Him."

"*I am from Him.*" God the Father had no beginning; life was not imparted to Him, for He IS life. The same is true of the Son—Jesus is from eternal generations, *one* with God, *equal* with God from all eternity, yet *a distinct Person*, the second Person of the Godhead. He came *from* God.

"*And He hath sent me.*" Jesus did not mean that God had sent Him as *Moses* and other prophets were commissioned and sent; He meant that He was "the sent One," the One promised from all eternity; He was the seed of the woman that should bruise the serpent's head (Gen. 3:15).

Verse 30: "*Then they sought to take Him: but no man laid hands on Him, because His hour was not yet come.*"

Incensed with anger at His declarations, these people wanted to kill Him! They knew full well what He was saying, they understood that He was openly declaring Himself to be the Son of God, their Messiah. But they could not take Him because all that Jesus did and said from start to finish of His earthly ministry was in accordance with God's plan and God's will from all eternity, and it was NOT God's plan or intention that this angry mob should destroy His beloved Son before the appointed time. Therefore the enemies of Jesus were restrained by direct, divine power. (See also John 8:20 and 18:6.) They could not touch Him without God's permission. We must remember that Jesus did not die a martyr's death; when His hour finally came, He willingly laid His life down (John 10:17,18; Luke 23:46).

Beloved, nothing "just *happened*" in the life of Jesus, and the same is true of the born again believer. The Christian cannot be destroyed by Satan nor by the enemies of the Gospel, and whatever comes his way must come with God's permission. Some are called upon to die a martyr's death (as in the case of Stephen); but others are called upon to present themselves a *living* sacrifice (Rom. 12:1). In this dispensation, God is not calling men to *die* for Him, but to *live* for Him!

Verse 31: *"And many of the people believed on Him, and said, When Christ cometh, will He do more miracles than these which this Man hath done?"*

The *"many"* who believed on Jesus were not the scribes, Pharisees, rulers of the Jews, but *the common people* — and it seems that they believed in faith, with all of the understanding they had. They believed that Jesus was Messiah, they believed He was "that Prophet," but it is not clear whether they were actually born again at this point. At least they became learners, and most of them were truly saved after the crucifixion when Peter preached on the Day of Pentecost and three thousand souls were saved.

"When Christ cometh, will He do more miracles than these which this Man hath done?" The Greek word used here not only means "more" in *number*, but also great in *character*. What these people really asked was, "Do we need greater evidence than this Man has given? When Christ comes, will He be able to do greater things than we have seen here?" Some of these folk had followed Jesus and witnessed His miracles for some time now, and their question was both reasonable and intelligent. They recognized Him as more than just another prophet sent from God.

Verse 32: *"The Pharisees heard that the people murmured such things concerning Him; and the Pharisees and the chief priests sent officers to take Him."*

We do not know whether the chief priests and rulers of the synagogue moved among the crowds and overheard what the people said as they "murmured," or whether these things were reported to them; but at any rate, they decided it was time to silence this Man and put an end to His preaching, lest the multitudes turn to Him and they find themselves out of office. So they *"sent officers to take Him"* — but the power of Almighty God restrained the officers and they could not take Him because His "hour" was not yet come.

In Matthew 23:13 Jesus speaks of these rulers of the synagogue, who would neither receive Him nor allow others to do so. He said, *"Woe unto you, scribes and Pharisees, hypocrites! For ye shut up the kingdom of heaven against men: FOR YE NEITHER GO IN YOURSELVES, NEITHER SUFFER YE THEM THAT ARE ENTERING TO GO IN!"*

Verse 33: *"Then said Jesus unto them, Yet a little while am I with you, and then I go unto Him that sent me."*

Here Jesus directs His attention to the officers who had been sent to arrest Him. He knew why they were there, and so, in effect, He explained to them, "You have come to arrest me, but if you will just be patient a little longer you will have no *need* for the handcuffs. When my hour is come I will willingly leave this world and return to my heavenly Father who sent me—but *until that time* you cannot lay hands on me!" No wonder these men returned to the Sanhedrin and said in amazement, *"Never man spake like this Man!"* (v. 46). They had never before been sent to arrest anyone like the Lord Jesus Christ.

Verse 34: *"Ye shall seek me, and shall not find me: and where I am, thither ye cannot come."*

This verse contains a message to the officers, to the people in general, and to all unbelievers. There can come a day when it is eternally too late for a person to seek the Lord; that day came for many of the Jews, for in 70 A. D., Titus the Roman *completely destroyed Jerusalem,* and tens of thousands of Jews were slaughtered in the streets of that city! No doubt some of these same officers and the very people who listened to the words of Jesus that day were among the number slain in that terrible deluge of blood. God is longsuffering, He is of tender mercy, it is not His will that any should perish, and He has no pleasure in the death of the wicked; but His Word plainly declares,

"Behold, *now* is the accepted time; behold, *now* is the day of salvation" (II Cor. 6:2b). Proverbs 27:1 warns, "Boast not thyself of to morrow; for thou knowest not what a day may bring forth." And Isaiah 55:6 says, "Seek ye the Lord while He may be found, call ye upon Him while He is near."

It would also be well to consider the warning of Proverbs 1:22−33:

"How long, ye simple ones, will ye love simplicity? and the scorners delight in their scorning, and fools hate knowledge? Turn you at my reproof: behold, I will pour out my spirit unto you, I will make known my words unto you. Because I have called, and ye refused; I have stretched out my hand, and no man regarded; but ye have set at nought all my counsel, and would none of my reproof: I also will laugh at your calamity; I will mock when your fear cometh; when your fear cometh as desolation, and your destruction cometh as a whirlwind; when distress and anguish cometh upon you.

"Then shall they call upon me, but I will not answer; they shall seek me early, but they shall not find me: for that they hated knowledge, and did not choose the fear of the Lord: They would none of my counsel: they despised all my reproof.

"Therefore shall they eat of the fruit of their own way, and be filled with their own devices. For the turning away of the simple shall slay them, and the prosperity of fools shall destroy them. But whoso hearkeneth unto me shall dwell safely, and shall be quiet from fear of evil."

God is love−but He is also a consuming fire, and there is a limit to His mercy. Please read Job 27:9; Isaiah 1:15; Jeremiah 11:11; 16:12,13; Ezekiel 8:18; Hosea 5:6; Micah 3:4; Zechariah 7:13; Matthew 25:11,12; Revelation 6:12−17; 9:1−12; and 16:1−11.

When Jesus declared, *"Where I am, thither ye cannot come"* He was speaking of heaven and His return to the Father. Jesus could say, "Where I *am*" because as God

He never *ceased* to be in heaven, even though He was on earth in a body of flesh. In John 3:13 He called Himself "the Son of man *which is in heaven,*" even though at that time He was speaking to Nicodemus and was plainly present on earth.

"Thither ye cannot come." They could not because they would not. Unbelievers cannot go where Jesus is; one must be born again in order to enter that celestial city. The only way for a person to hear God say, "Well done!" is to believe on the Lord Jesus Christ, trust Him, and confess Him as Saviour: "If thou shalt confess with thy mouth the Lord Jesus, and shalt believe in thine heart that God hath raised Him from the dead, thou shalt be saved. For with the heart man believeth unto righteousness; and with the mouth confession is made unto salvation" (Rom. 10:9,10).

The wicked cannot enter heaven; this is made very plain in God's Word. "And there shall in no wise enter into it any thing that defileth, neither whatsoever worketh abomination, or maketh a lie: but they which are written in the Lamb's book of life" (Rev. 21:27).

Verse 35: *"Then said the Jews among themselves, Whither will He go, that we shall not find Him? Will He go unto the dispersed among the Gentiles, and teach the Gentiles?"*

"The Jews" here undoubtedly means more than just the rulers, scribes, and elders. This reference included those who had traveled from surrounding territory into Jerusalem for the feast. Most certainly it would refer to those who heard our Lord say the words in the preceding verses. When they asked, *"Whither will He go?"* they thought He was going to leave the feast, leave Jerusalem, and go to another city; and they wondered where He would go that they could not follow if they chose to do so. They were completely ignorant of the spiritual meaning of the Lord's words.

They further asked, *"Will He go unto the dispersed among the Gentiles, and teach the Gentiles?"* (In other words, "Has He finally become so provoked with the Jews that He will leave here and go over into Gentile territory to teach the *Gentiles?*") It could be that they thought He meant that since the *majority* of the Jews had rejected His teachings, He would go to those whom James mentions as "the twelve tribes which are scattered abroad" (James 1:1), and *beginning with them* would proceed to teach the Gentiles. This is a singular example of the way in which a prophecy can be unconsciously uttered by a foe, for this is precisely what Paul and his companions did not too many years later.

Verse 36: *"What manner of saying is this that He said, Ye shall seek me, and shall not find me: and where I am, thither ye cannot come?"*

The rulers of the Jews hated Jesus with bitter hatred, and they intended to silence Him forever as soon as they could find opportunity to do so; yet His words disturbed them. The manner of their question shows that they recognized a hidden meaning in our Lord's words. They had expected the Messiah to deliver them from Roman rule, but *this* Man spoke strange words. They were vexed by their own inability to answer Him, but at the same time they *feared* Him because they were unable to stop His influence with the people. Yet, much as they feared and hated Him, they could not touch Him. He had divine protection until His "hour" should come.

The Great Prophecy
Concerning the Coming of the Holy Spirit
(Study Acts 2:2—4)

Verses 37—39: *"In the last day, that great day of the feast, Jesus stood and cried, saying, If any man thirst, let him come unto me, and drink. He that believeth on me, as the Scripture hath said, out of his belly shall flow rivers of living water. (But this spake He of the Spirit, which they that believe on Him should receive: for the Holy Ghost was not yet given; because that Jesus was not yet glorified.)*

There must have been an interval of about three days between the message in verse 36 and that beginning in verse 37, for in verse 14 we learned that Jesus went to the temple and taught about the *"midst"* of the feast. There is no record of what Jesus did during the three latter days of the feast. If He continued preaching (which seems likely) we can be certain that the power of God restrained His enemies and they could not interfere.

"In the last day, that great day of the feast . . . ." This was evidently the eighth day of the feast—and the eighth day, like the first, was observed as a special Sabbath (Lev. 23:39). On this eighth day, special sacrifices were offered unto Jehovah: "Ye shall offer a burnt-offering, a sacrifice made by fire, of a sweet savour unto the Lord: one bullock, one ram, seven lambs of the first year without blemish: Their meat-offering and their drink-offerings for the bullock, for the ram, and for the lambs, shall be according to their number, after the manner: and one goat for a sin-offering; beside the continual burnt-offering, and his meat-offering, and his drink-offering" (Num. 29:36—38).

On the day preceding "that great day of the feast" the pilgrims had left their booths and marched seven times around the city, and as they marched they shouted "Hosanna!" The crowds marched behind the priests and Levites, bearing golden vessels. At the brook of Siloam these vessels were filled with water and carried to the temple, where the water was poured into a silver vessel on the eastern side of the altar where the burnt-offering was sacrificed. As this took place, the people sang, "Ho, everyone that thirsteth, come ye to the waters! and with joy shall ye draw water out of the wells of salvation."

This custom of drawing water was a human institution and is nowhere mentioned in the Law of Moses; yet such a setting was ideal for Jesus to give His invitation to sinners who needed living water.   Therefore, clothed with divine authority, standing before that great crowd, He began, *"If any man thirst, let him come unto me, and drink."* Here is promised a twofold source of divine refreshment and satisfaction: Jesus, the living water, *satisfies the thirsty soul;* and when we come to Him and receive the living water, we are indwelt by the Holy Spirit, we possess *"rivers of living water,"* and by means of the rivers of living water, *others* are satisfied.

Verse 38 clearly teaches that when we drink of the living water, when a well of living water springs up within us, we are to be channels of blessing to others, channels through which the life-giving spiritual water flows, to quench the thirst of needy souls.   It has pleased God in this dispensation to work through His children.   He expects us to be channels of blessing.

Notice that Jesus uses the plural—not *river,* but *"RIVERS of living water."*   Only God knows what can and should be accomplished through a Spirit-filled life; the possibilities are unlimited!   We should be careful not to let anything clog the channel and prevent our being a blessing to those with whom we come in contact.   Ephesians 5:18 instructs us to be *"filled* with the Spirit," and we can be filled with the Spirit only as we are cleansed by the blood (I John 1:7), and by the renewing of our minds: "Be not conformed to this world: but be ye transformed by the renewing of your mind, that ye may prove what is that good, and acceptable, and perfect, will of God" (Rom. 12:2).   The divine and singular purpose of the Holy Spirit is to glorify Christ (John 16:14), and the Spirit accomplishes this ministry through born again believers who are willing to surrender soul, spirit, and body, presenting themselves "a living sacrifice, holy, acceptable unto God" (Rom. 12:1), yielding their members "as instruments of righteousness unto God" (Rom. 6:13).

The feast of tabernacles was the last feast of the year. Now the ceremonial activities of the feast were over, the

last offering had been made, the people were ready to return
to their homes, and Jesus took advantage of this opportunity to announce the coming of the Holy Spirit to dwell
in the believer and make him a channel of blessing. This
was an ideal time for Him to make known the ending of
the old dispensation and the beginning of the new. The
old sacrifices would be void *and the NEW sacrifice would
Himself FULFILL all previous sacrifices.*

"If ANY man thirst, let him come unto me, and drink."
It has been pointed out over and over again in these studies
that salvation is for ALL—Jew or Gentile, bond or free,
rich or poor, learned or unlearned—all are invited to drink
of the water of life; but notice that Jesus said, *"if any man
THIRST, let HIM come."* There must be a thirst, and the
individual must drink for himself!

In order to fully appreciate the setting here, we must
realize that in Jerusalem and surrounding areas at certain
seasons of the year, water was scarce and very precious.
With thousands coming into Jerusalem for the feast of tabernacles, the water supply was undoubtedly very low, and
water had been brought from the pool of Siloam for the
ceremony. This circumstance offered a perfect background
for the invitation Jesus gave, that whosoever thirsted should
come to Him and be filled. Whatsoever the need of a soul—
pardon, peace, grace, mercy, strength—that need can be met
in the Lord Jesus Christ, the fountain of life.

Please notice, verse 38 says he who believes on Jesus
"as the SCRIPTURE hath said"—not as man may *think,*
not as *denominational* doctrine may teach, but "according
to the *Scriptures"* (I Cor. 15:1—8). To believe on Jesus
"as the Scripture hath said" is to believe in His Incarnation, His sinless life, His atoning death, His burial, His
resurrection, and His bodily ascension—not according to
religion, not according to tradition, but according to "thus
saith the LORD." And he who believes on Jesus *according
to God's holy Word* will become a channel of blessing for
others. *"Out of his belly shall flow rivers of living water!"*

(In connection with this, please study these Scriptures in the Old Testament: Isaiah 12:3; 35:6,7; 41:18; 44:3; and Zechariah 14:8.)

"Thus spake (Jesus) of the Spirit." This very definitely eliminates the thought of any relationship between the "water" in this verse and water baptism, because it emphatically says that Jesus was speaking of the Holy Spirit, *"which they that believe on Him should receive."* Then, lest someone misunderstand the meaning of *"should* receive," the Word continues, *"for the Holy Ghost was not yet given; because that Jesus was not yet glorified."* These words were spoken before Pentecost, before Jesus ascended back to the Father, and therefore the Holy Ghost had not yet come into the world to take up His abode in the hearts of believers.

This does not mean that the Holy Spirit was not in the world at that time; *He was*—but not as He abides in this Dispensation of Grace. In the Old Testament era the Holy Spirit came upon men for a specific ministry and then departed from them; not until Jesus was glorified did He come to abide. The Holy Spirit was one with the Father and the Son, a distinct Person of equal authority, eternal as God the Father and God the Son are eternal; but He did not take up His abode here on earth until Pentecost. Certainly the Holy Ghost was in the Old Testament era (Gen. 6:3). David spake as the Holy Ghost moved him (Mark 12:36). Isaiah spoke of the "vexing" of the Holy Spirit (Isa. 63:10, 11). John the Baptist was filled with the Holy Ghost even before his birth (Luke 1:15), and Peter tells us that the very Word of God "came not in old time by the will of man: *but holy men of God spake as they were moved by the Holy Ghost"* (II Pet. 1:21).

The People Divided

Verses 40—42: *"Many of the people therefore, when they heard this saying, said, Of a truth this is the Prophet.*

*Others said, This is the Christ. But some said, Shall Christ
come out of Galilee? Hath not the Scripture said, That
Christ cometh of the seed of David, and out of the town
of Bethlehem, where David was?"*

"The people" here evidently indicates the multitude in
general, made up primarily of the common people, and not
the chief priests and Pharisees. The clear, bold invitation
Jesus had just given arrested the hearts of many. No person
had ever before *given* such an invitation, no *ordinary* person
would *dare* do so. Therefore the people confessed, "Of a
truth this is THE Prophet"—meaning "that Prophet that
was to come" as promised in Deuteronomy 18:15,18:

"The Lord thy God will raise up unto thee a Prophet
from the midst of thee, of thy brethren, like unto me; unto
Him ye shall hearken . . . I will raise them up a Prophet
from among their brethren, like unto thee, and will put my
words in His mouth; and He shall speak unto them all
that I shall command Him."

"Others said, This is the Christ," but still others were
skeptical, refusing to believe, and this group asked, *"Shall
Christ come out of Galilee?"* Such objection was based on
their impression that this Preacher, wonderful as He seemed
to be, *was* a Galilaean, a Nazarene, and therefore could
not be the Christ. They were totally ignorant concerning
the birthplace of our Lord.

From verse 42 we know that most of the Jews had some
knowledge of the Scriptures, and many of them were familiar
with the prophecies concerning the coming of Messiah.
Even the common people knew that He was to be of the
lineage of David and that He was to be born in Bethlehem,
the *birthplace* of David. The sad thing is that they knew
the Scriptures from the historical and geographical standpoint, as do many teachers today, but they do not know
the Christ whom the Scriptures offer.

Verse 43: *"So there was a division among the people
because of Him."*

The words Jesus spoke in Luke 12:51 are literally fulfilled here: "Suppose ye that I am come to give peace on earth? I tell you, Nay; but rather division." He is still dividing men: families—sometimes husband and wife—do not agree concerning Him; and as long as time goes on, as long as Satan is loose in this world, there will be divisions among people because of Jesus and the Word of God. It is true that the Word draws men to Jesus; but when the Word is rejected, those who reject it go *further from* Jesus. Any minister who preaches the pure, unadulterated Word of God will have unrest in his congregation. If *Jesus* could not please everyone, how can today's minister please all men and still preach the Gospel as it is laid down in the Word of God?

Verse 44: *"And some of them would have taken Him; but no man laid hands on Him."*

No doubt the general run of the people who lived in Jerusalem and knew how the religious leaders felt about Jesus would have arrested Him in order to make a good impression on the members of the Sanhedrin. Certainly the *leaders* of the Jews would have arrested and imprisoned Him if they could have done so.

"But no man laid hands on Him." Here again we see divine intervention. It was not the appointed time for the Lord's enemies to take Him; His hour was not yet come (see also Matt. 26:5; Mark 14:2; Luke 22:2), and the officers who had been sent to arrest Him returned to the Sanhedrin without Him.

Verse 45: *"Then came the officers to the chief priests and Pharisees; and they said unto them, Why have ye not brought Him?"*

We do not know how much time elapsed between verse 32 (where the officers were sent to arrest Jesus) and verse 45. These men were probably given orders to arrest Him at the first opportunity, but they were afraid of the crowds, afraid

lest they stir up the multitudes against the scribes and
Pharisees, who were certainly in the minority. Thus the
feast days ran their course, the feast came to a close, and
the officers returned, empty-handed, to face the chief priests
and Pharisees, who immediately asked, *"Why have ye not
brought Him?"*

Verse 46: *"The officers answered, Never man spake like
this Man."*

When the officers stood on the sidelines and listened to
the words of Jesus, they did not realize that those words
were "spirit and life." There is no doubt in my mind that
the power of His words arrested their hearts and minds.
The Sanhedrin had no doubt sent the most capable, most
efficient officers available—but be it king or peasant, the
Word of God is sharper than any twoedged sword and will
pierce the heart of any man who will *listen* to it!

Also, these officers were influenced by the attention and
attitude of the people. Never had they seen anyone exert
such influence on a crowd as this Man did. The majority
of the common people listened, spellbound, as Jesus spoke
His wonderful words of life. In Matthew 7:28,29, when
Jesus finished the Sermon on the Mount, "the people were
astonished at His doctrine: for He taught them as one
having authority, and not as the scribes."

On the night in Gethsemane when Judas led the officers
and men to arrest Jesus, we are told that "Jesus therefore,
knowing all things that should come upon Him, went forth,
and said unto them, *Whom seek ye?* They answered Him,
Jesus of Nazareth. Jesus saith unto them, *I AM HE. . .*
As soon as He had said unto them, I am He, *they went
backward, AND FELL TO THE GROUND!"* (John 18:4—6).
This was the same Jesus to whom the officers were listening. No wonder they said to the high priests and Pharisees, *"Never man spake like this Man."* They could not
arrest Jesus because His words arrested *them!*

Verses 47 and 48: *"Then answered them the Pharisees,*

Are ye also deceived? Have any of the rulers or of the Pharisees believed on Him?"

The word here translated *"deceived"* means "to lead astray." In other words, the Pharisees asked, "Are YOU being led astray by His teaching? Are YOU following His error?" The Greek language here implies ridicule, sarcasm, displeasure, anger—even *hatred.*

"Have any of the rulers or of the Pharisees believed on Him?" This question was intended as proof that it was an impossibility for Jesus to be the true Messiah, because if all of the *learned teachers* in Israel had refused to follow Him, if the religious leaders had rejected Him, then certainly He *could not* be the Messiah.

Verse 49: *"But this people who knoweth not the law are cursed."*

According to what the scribes and Pharisees say here, the crowds which were following Jesus were composed of ignorant, common people who had not attended ecclesiastical schools, they were not taught in the Scriptures; therefore they were *"cursed,"* and that was the reason they were following after this Nazarene.

The same is true today to a large degree. The religious leaders often fight with the weapons of the Pharisees in this verse. Those who do not agree with them are branded as ignorant, unlearned men—yet Paul says that God has chosen the simple things to confound the mighty and the wise (I Cor. 1:26—31). Down through the ages the great reformers and teachers such as John Wesley, Martin Luther, and others, have been mistakenly branded as ignorant, unlearned, and common.

Verses 50 and 51: *"Nicodemus saith unto them, (he that came to Jesus by night, being one of them,) Doth our law judge any man, before it hear him, and know what he doeth?"*

Wherever we find the name of Nicodemus we always

read that he came to Jesus *by night.* It could be that the
Holy Spirit is pointing out that Nicodemus was a spiritual
coward when he first came to the Lord, afraid to confess
Him openly because, since he was *himself* a Pharisee, he
knew there would be repercussions in the Sanhedrin if he
openly confessed his faith in Jesus. Later, while the disciples were hiding for fear of the Jews, Nicodemus came
with Joseph of Arimathea to claim the body of Jesus, and
helped to bury Him in Joseph's tomb (John 19:38—42).

"Nicodemus. . .(being one of them)" means that he was
one of the outstanding religious leaders of the day. He was
a ruler among the Jews, perhaps one of the greatest teachers in all Israel (see John 3:10). Since he held a position
in the Sanhedrin, he was present at their council, he heard
their deliberations concerning Jesus. Therefore he could
speak from a position of equality with the other members
of that governing body, and in verse 51 he was trying to
show them that even while they were pleading "the law,"
they were *breaking* that same law.

Notice how cautiously Nicodemus dealt with this problem: *"Doth our law judge ANY man before it hear him,
and know what he doeth?"* He did not mention Jesus by
name, nor did he specifically mention the case at hand.
He spoke in general, using universal application of the law.
Through this approach, he granted that they honored the
Law of Moses, but a great principle of that law was that
no man should be condemned without first being allowed
to testify in his own defense. (Read Deuteronomy 1:17;
19:15).

It took a great deal of courage for this man to speak out
in the Sanhedrin, even in such general terms. It could have
cost him his life! The other members could have turned
on him and cried out, "Crucify *Nicodemus!*" I cannot help
admiring him for his stand, timid though it was. Not all
Christians have the same amount of courage, not all have
the same degree of boldness.

Verse 52: *"They answered and said unto him, Art thou*

also of Galilee? Search, and look: for out of Galilee ariseth no prophet."

Words of bitter contempt, scorn, and hatred on the part of the rulers of the Jews! They were actually asking Nicodemus if HE with his education, ability, understanding of the law, and authority in their synagogue, was joining the crowds that followed this fanatical Galilaean. The suggestion was an insult—after which they said to him, in effect, "Go back and search the Scriptures, Nicodemus. Study the prophecies concerning our Messiah before you defend this impostor; because if you will study the books of Isaiah, Jeremiah, and Zechariah, you will learn that *out of Galilee ariseth no prophet."* (The Greek reads, "A prophet out of Galilee has not been raised.")

The members of the Sanhedrin were so angry, so violently enraged, that they were at the point of insanity to make such an absurd statement! Being familiar with the Old Testament prophecies, they undoubtedly knew that Elisha, Elijah, Amos, Jonah, and Nahum came out of Galilee; they were born in that area. In Matthew 4:12—16 we read, "Now when Jesus had heard that John was cast into prison, *He departed into Galilee;* and leaving Nazareth, He came and dwelt in Capernaum, which is upon the sea coast, in the borders of Zabulon and Nephthalim: *That it might be fulfilled which was spoken by Esaias the prophet,* saying, The land of Zabulon, and the land of Nephthalim, by the way of the sea, beyond Jordan, *Galilee of the Gentiles;* the people which sat in darkness saw great light; and to them which sat in the region and shadow of death light is sprung up." Certainly the statement of the Pharisees in this verse was not true.

Verse 53: *"And every man went unto his own house."*

The Sanhedrin by now had realized that they could not arrest Jesus at this time. They were afraid to take Him because of the common people. The officers they sent to arrest Him could not touch Him, and returned to the chief

priests with the report, "Never man spake like this Man."
The fact that they had failed in their attempt to silence
the hated Galilaean was a tremendous blow to the pride of
the members of the Sanhedrin. They had been so sure they
would do away with Him during the feast days; but on the
contrary, Jesus had attended the feast in humility and meek-
ness, He had made no attempt to be spectacular, yet He
had led the feast in glory and honor. The Sanhedrin therefore dispersed and went home in humiliation.

The rulers of the Jews were defeated for the moment, but
the devil never gives up easily and I have no doubt that
the Sanhedrin, under his control, simply desisted until some
other scheme could be worked out. We will see in the
next chapter another of the ingenious plans they worked
out in their efforts to trap Him.